G000271603

LORDSHIP AND LEARNING
STUDIES IN MEMORY OF TREVOR ASTON

The exercise of lordship in England is examined in relation to personal and tenurial dependence, estate management, and changing social and economic conditions. In addition the formation of kingdoms and national identities in early medieval Britain and Ireland and the relationship between lords and peasants in Byzantium are explored. In contributions on medieval education the institutions of late medieval Oxford are reassessed; the provisions made for their archives by medieval corporations and the practical importance of muniments are explained; and material from across western Europe is deployed to show how images were used to convey non-verbal messages to the non-literate.

Trevor Aston (1925–1985)

Lordship and Learning

Studies in memory of Trevor Aston

Edited by

Ralph Evans

THE BOYDELL PRESS

First published 2004
The Boydell Press, Woodbridge

ISBN 1 84383 079 5

The Boydell Press is an imprint of Boydell & Brewer Ltd
PO Box 9, Woodbridge, Suffolk IP12 3DF, UK
and of Boydell & Brewer Inc.
668 Mt Hope Avenue, Rochester, NY 14620, USA
website: www.boydellandbrewer.com

A catalogue record for this book is available
from the British Library

Library of Congress Cataloging-in-Publication Data
Lordship and learning : studies in memory of Trevor Aston / edited by
    Ralph Evans.
      p. cm.
    Includes bibliographical references and index.
    ISBN 1–84383–079–5 (acid-free paper)
    1. Great Britain – History – Anglo-Saxon period, 449–1066. 2. Great
Britain – History – Medieval period, 1066–1485. 3. Great Britain –
Intellectual life – 1066–1485. 4. Nobility – Great Britain – History –
To 1500. 5. Great Britain – Intellectual life – To 1066. I. Aston, T. H.
(Trevor Henry) II. Evans, Ralph (T. A. Ralph)
DA130.L67 2004
941.01 – dc22   2003027992

This publication is printed on acid-free paper

Printed in Great Britain by
The Cromwell Press Ltd., Trowbridge, Wiltshire

Contents

Illustrations

Preface

It was some ten years ago that James Howard-Johnston proposed a volume of essays to celebrate the contribution to historical scholarship of Trevor Aston. He found that Rosamond Faith was thinking on similar lines, and together they easily persuaded Thomas Charles-Edwards and Ralph Evans to join them in an informal group devoted to realizing this idea. It was thought that the volume should have a thematic coherence, and should be centred as far as possible on Trevor's own principal interests. First approaches to likely contributors received a very positive response, and a provisional list of contents was soon assembled. From an early stage the enterprise received wholehearted support from Trevor's wives, Margaret and Judith, and from his good friend and literary executor David Vaisey. The project took a great step forward when Boydell & Brewer agreed to publish the volume, and we are very pleased to acknowledge the extreme patience and goodwill towards the project of Caroline Palmer and Vanda Andrews. Crucial too at that stage was the generosity of the Past and Present Society, Corpus Christi College, Oxford and St John's College, Cambridge, who agreed to make donations towards the cost of publication. The editing of the volume was entrusted to Ralph Evans, once Trevor's apprentice in the craft of historical editing. Progress from outline plan to final text has been marked by more delays, detours and alarms than we would have liked, but the contents of the published volume are in fact remarkably close to the original proposal. For their forbearance in permitting us to achieve this we are much indebted to contributors who have accepted a long wait between the submission and publication of their papers. Phillip Judge is to be congratulated on making the admirably clear maps and plans that illustrate several of the contributions. And we have much appreciated the encouragement that many others, too numerous to name here, have offered since our scheme was launched. But most of all of course we are grateful to those of Trevor's pupils, friends and colleagues who have contributed studies to this volume in his memory.

Thomas Charles-Edwards   *Ralph Evans*
Rosamond Faith   *James Howard-Johnston*

Introduction

RALPH EVANS

Trevor Aston was a charismatic and inspiring historian, teacher and editor, and it is a mark of the deep affection and respect in which he was held by those who knew him well that nearly twenty years after his death in 1985 his friends and colleagues should wish to publish a collection of studies in his memory. Trevor Henry Aston was born in Fulham in 1925 but at an early age moved with his family to Woolbeding in Sussex. Brought up in the home for tubercular children where his mother was matron, he entered formal education at a late age but was nonetheless accepted at Midhurst grammar school. After unsettled early years in the school he went to live with its remarkable headmaster, the historian Norman Lucas, and his wife, who recognized his abilities and proved a truly formative influence. Under the guidance of the Lucases Trevor won an exhibition to St John's College, Oxford, which he entered in 1943 to read philosophy, politics and economics. After two terms at Oxford he joined the royal marines as a lieutenant and remained in that service for the remainder of the war, in home waters and without seeing action. On his return to Oxford in 1946 he transferred to the school of modern history; he was an extremely assiduous student and took first-class honours in 1949. As a graduate student in medieval history Trevor was in 1950 elected first a senior scholar of Wadham College and then a junior research fellow of Corpus Christi College. His research, under Reginald Lennard, took him to the Huntington Library in California to study the archives of Battle Abbey in his home county of Sussex. In 1952 he was elected a tutorial fellow of Corpus Christi College; his thesis on the Battle estates was still in preparation and was never to be completed.

In 1954 Trevor married Margaret Bridges, who had recently graduated from Lady Margaret Hall. Margaret Aston's distinguished career as an ecclesiastical historian was to follow interests by no means identical with Trevor's, yet her subtle investigations of popular religion and culture have intersected at some points with Trevor's concerns with education. These related not to intellectual history in the narrow sense but rather to the social, institutional and practical aspects of higher education. He knew that the extent and nature of literacy and of elementary schooling in medieval England were difficult but important subjects, and saw their implications both for universities and for estate administration. To this volume Margaret contributes a paper that widens the investigation of these questions by drawing on a range of material from pre-reformation Europe to analyse the ways in which non-verbal images were used to convey messages to the laity. Trevor would surely have appreciated this broad approach to medieval learning.

Trevor Aston was a dedicated undergraduate tutor, treating his subject, his teaching and his students with great seriousness. He is particularly remembered for his special subject on the manorial economy. And it was an achievement of some significance to continue the study of medieval agrarian history at Oxford. Manorial history has certainly had other distinguished practitioners and teachers in Oxford –

including Vinogradoff and Lennard before Trevor, and Eric Stone, Barbara Harvey and Richard Smith during and after his time – but despite its fundamental importance to the understanding of medieval England it has generally failed to engage the attention of Oxford's large and prestigious faculty of history, being more closely associated with, for example, Cambridge or Birmingham. Trevor's pupils later recalled his rigorous method of teaching directly from the documents and the respect he accorded their views. Some became professional historians in different if not entirely unrelated areas. They include the legal historian Paul Brand, who has done so much to describe and explain the growth of a legal profession in England in the thirteenth century. Paul's work has not been restricted to the Westminster-based serjeants and attorneys who formed the elite of the profession, and in this volume he shows how the worlds of the local lawyer and the estate administrator can profitably be examined side by side. Among Trevor's pupils who continued in agrarian history Rosamond Faith wrote, at Leicester under HPR Finberg, a pioneering thesis on the peasant land market; much later she returned to Oxford to work with Trevor first in the university archives and then on the history of the university. Her study of medieval peasantries has brought her back to the subject of much of Trevor's own research, lordship in Anglo-Saxon England, as in her paper on domesday Devon in this volume. Not all of Trevor's teaching was of undergraduates. The thesis of his pupil Neil Stacy on the estates of Glastonbury Abbey (which had previously received Lennard's attention) has long been highly regarded by specialists but its publication was sidelined by its author's successful career as an actor. There is now renewed interest in the economy of the twelfth century, and it is very appropriate that the publication of a volume in memory of Trevor Aston should make the results of Neil's work on the Glastonbury demesnes more widely available.

In his early years at Corpus Trevor's historical interests came to centre on domesday and its implications for pre-conquest society. On 11 May 1957 he delivered to the Royal Historical Society a paper on 'The origins of the manor in England' that was published in the society's transactions of the following year. It was a masterly tour de force that took issue with the idea that the manorial system was essentially a creation of a relatively short period just before and especially immediately after the Norman conquest. Trevor stressed the aristocratic and hierarchical nature of Anglo-Saxon society and pushed the dependent status of a significant portion of the peasantry back at least to the seventh century: there may never have been a largely free Old English peasantry and the development of manorial structure was a long process which had begun very early in the Anglo-Saxon period. Seldom can an article have succeeded so dramatically in reversing the historical orthodoxy. Yet this triumph had some unfortunate consequences. The brilliance of its presentation obscured the provisional and incomplete nature of the argument, which was accepted without much question.

One Anglo-Saxon scholar who continued to disagree with at least one aspect of Trevor's case was Eric John, who fully shared his relish for an argument. Despite their long-running disagreements, when the idea for this volume was originally floated Eric John was the first to offer a contribution. It was gratefully accepted, but Eric John himself died before the volume was complete, and its inclusion is in a sense a dual memorial. The article on the origins of the manor was reprinted several times, and when it was included in the festschrift for his friend Rodney Hilton in 1983 Trevor acknowledged the surprising ease with which his views had been adopted. Returning to an area in which he had long since ceased to be active, he there added a substantial 'postscript' in which he stood by his chronology of manorialization but related the process more closely to changes in population and settlement patterns. Only quite recently have the important issues surrounding the origins of the manor again been debated. Indeed estate structure and settlement patterns in late Anglo-Saxon England and in the century or so after the conquest are now at the heart of one of the most vigorous areas of medieval English history, in which comparisons with continental Europe in the same period and with England in the later middle ages play a prominent part. Peter Coss, who was one of Trevor's co-editors of the Hilton festschrift and who joined the editorial board of *Past and Present* in the final year of his editorship, has published a large body of work on the English gentry from the eleventh to the four-teenth century. For this volume Peter has written a provocative historiographical paper that takes issue with some of the assumptions embedded in discussion of the earlier period, and in particular with the use of the term gentry.

The spectacular success of Trevor's first major publication would have been hard to follow, and this probably engendered a longstanding reluctance to return to print. Not that the pace of his work slackened. His further investigation of the nature of lord-ship and dependence in late Anglo-Saxon England was the subject of a remarkable paper delivered in 1964, but printed for the first time only now. Had it been published immediately it might have given an invaluable lead in the elucidation of crucial aspects of pre-conquest society. Some of its suppositions have been modified by the scholarship of the last four decades, but it is included in this volume because even now it offers valuable insights into the nature of late Old English lordship.

Despite the originality of his own research and the quality of his teaching it was as an editor that Trevor Aston was to become best known in the historical world. The journal *Past and Present* was launched in 1952 by a group of predominantly Marxist historians; Trevor was one of several historians recruited to its board in 1958 in order to broaden its base. At first an assistant editor to the journal's founder, John Morris, he was himself editor effectively from 1960 (and formally from 1963) until his death. He succeeded in applying the highest scholarly standards to the journal without losing its wide-ranging approach; under his energetic direction *Past and Present* became one of the leading historical journals of the English-speaking world, committed to the examination of 'social, economic and cultural changes, and their causes and conse-quences'. While Trevor was very much the journal's controlling influence, it remained a genuinely cooperative venture with a very active editorial board. Crucial therefore was the excellent relationship between the editor and the chairman of the board, first John Morris and then Rodney Hilton, the outstanding medievalist of his generation, who always had the greatest respect for Trevor and complete confidence in his abilities. Trevor had an appetite for editorial and administrative minutiae and for strategic, even entrepreneurial, management. For years he read every article submitted to the journal, until sheer volume made this impossible; until 1972, when the first subeditor was employed, he read every article accepted, both in galley and page proof. Scripts received were routinely read by several members of the board before the editor decided on acceptance or rejection, and it became normal practice for the editor to compile a list of revisions that would be required before publication. The ideal of accessibility, that every article in *Past and Present* should be comprehen-sible to the serious amateur, long remained a real aspiration, though it was steadily eroded by the professionalization of historical writing. From time to time doubts arose as to whether the journal had been too successfully incorporated into the main-stream, losing its distinctiveness. This was a serious question that was earnestly debated, but in fact the geographical and chronological coverage of *Past and Present*, as well as the nature and the variety of the questions its authors addressed, remained most impressive. Besides his strictly editorial role Trevor was engaged in the financial management of the journal, dealt with its printers, and took great pleasure in orga- nizing its highly successful annual conferences. In addition he established the series of volumes, both anthologies and monographs, that became Past and Present Publica- tions. As the journal itself recorded shortly after his death, 'Trevor Aston's creative drive and the breadth of his historical interests and imagination have sustained and helped to shape *Past and Present* for almost a generation.' Most of the contributors to this volume had work published in the journal by Trevor, and Peter Coss is still a member of its editorial board.

Trevor Aston's energies were not fully absorbed by his teaching and management of *Past and Present*. Corpus Christi College was his home for more than thirty years, and he was devoted to it. He held a rather idealized notion of the college, drawn both from the founder's intentions and a more general concept of the republic of scholar- ship, and it was inevitable that he should sometimes be disappointed by the quotidian reality; his failure to conceal his disappointment did not necessarily promote harmony in the community he held so dear. His detailed concern for the fabric and furnishings of the college, on which he brought to bear both his regard for tradition and his enthu- siasm for modern design, could drive a bursar to distraction but has left a strong imprint on Corpus. He naturally maintained a deep interest in the history of the college, in its buildings and estates, and in its corporate identity. He was for example keeper of the college plate; he was an active supporter of the college's magazine, *The Pelican*; and he promoted the production of its biographical register, in which by a happy chance the very first entry was his own. And, most important, from 1956 to 1985 he was librarian and archivist; under his direction the library of Corpus became one of the strongest undergraduate collections in the university.

Among the historians who were his colleagues at Corpus Trevor found lifelong friends. Derek Hall, the medieval legal historian who was president of the college from 1969 until his untimely death in 1975, was a very good friend to Trevor. Thomas Charles-Edwards, a former pupil of Trevor's, was a tutorial fellow of Corpus from 1971 until his migration to Jesus College in 1997 as Jesus professor of Celtic and was one of Trevor's closest and most valued friends. Like Trevor he studied Anglo-Saxon England, but the main focus of his research has been on Welsh and Irish language, laws and institutions. In this volume he shows the value of looking at the adjacent and overlapping nations of Britain and Ireland together, and delineates the complex ways in which they defined themselves in the early middle ages. Trevor was one of those in Oxford's history faculty who pressed for a less anglocentric curriculum; such things change only slowly in Oxford, but the greater attention now given there to non- English British history is very much in accordance with his wishes. Trevor was also close to the Byzantinist James Howard-Johnston, likewise a fellow of Corpus since 1971, who shared with him an interest not only in history but also in politics and art. Trevor's historical outlook was by no means insular, and he liked to see the issues that preoccupied him in English history analysed in quite different contexts. It might be suggested that some of the fundamental questions about the relationship between lords and peasants that so exercised Trevor have been asked surprisingly infrequently by historians of Anglo-Saxon England, but that in part this simply reflects the nature of the sources. The same may well be true of Byzantine historiography. In this volume James shows that skilful interrogation of the sources can reveal more than at first seems likely about rural society and economy in the Byzantine empire. And Trevor continued to take note of the work of younger scholars. In 1985 Isobel Harvey was elected to a junior research fellowship at Corpus to continue her investigation of popular unrest in fifteenth-century England. Although she knew Trevor for only a short period before his death she was captivated by his conversation and was filled with admiration for him as scholar and man. To this volume she has contributed a paper that is in part a response to Trevor's observation in 1961, in relation to the Robin Hood ballads, that we need to know much more about medieval outlaws and crime and their social context: Isobel here presents a detailed study of poaching and its relationship to social and political discontent in the fifteenth century.

Trevor was also a significant figure in the faculty of history and in the university. It was typical that as chairman of the faculty from 1965 to 1968 he encouraged the broadening of the syllabus. And he attached great importance to library provision. He was chairman of the history faculty's library committee from 1965 to 1985, a curator of the Bodleian Library 1968–85, and a member of the Shackleton committee on university libraries in 1966, of the Kneale committee in 1967 and of the university libraries board 1980–3. In addition he was a member of the university's influential general board of faculties from 1963 to 1970. The issues he took up within the university included the fair treatment of university lecturers who were not fellows of colleges and the introduction of joint-honours degrees.

This dynamism was harnessed for new purposes in the late 1960s. It was largely at the instigation of Alan Bullock that a full-scale new history of the University of Oxford was undertaken, and it was he who identified Trevor Aston as the man to take charge of it, memorably describing him as the most powerful locomotive in the university without a train to pull. When the project for the new history was launched by the university in 1968 Trevor was appointed general editor and director of research; he resigned his tutorial duties and became senior research fellow of his college. In the following year he became keeper of the university archives in succession to WA Pantin, who had notably combined oversight of the archives with research into the university's history. These appointments were seen as complementary, and they united areas that were already close to Trevor's heart, for he was fascinated by the nature of Oxford and the relationship of the university to society at large, whether in his own day or earlier periods. At a time when the history of education was emerging as a distinct, indeed fashionable, discipline Trevor was concerned that the new history of Oxford, covering the long period from the origins of the university in the twelfth century to the decade in which the history itself was proposed, should be a work of serious and comparative scholarship. He was keen to determine its general character, and to ensure for example that the university was placed in its social context and that such questions as the origins and careers of graduates were fully treated in every period. The new history was a remarkably extensive cooperative venture, involving dozens of contributors in various countries, with a small central research staff in Oxford. The progress of an undertaking that depended on so many individual contributors, over whom the editors had no real control, was bound to be difficult. The passage of more than a decade without the publication of a volume threatened the survival of the project in more stringent times, but the appearance of volume one in 1984, with two substantial chapters by the general editor, ensured its survival. Seven of the history's eight volumes were to appear after Trevor's death, but by then he had determined its overall shape and character, though not the exact nature of each volume. His lack of intervention once a volume's editor or editors had been appointed evoked some surprise, and even criticism, but it was a strategy that recognized the realities of an academic and publishing venture of this kind. While the history certainly has an overall uniformity, each volume has a very distinctive character that reflects the preoccupations of its editor or editors and the current historiography of the period in question.

A similar mix of direct involvement and decisive delegation characterized Trevor's role as keeper of the university's archives. For the day-to-day running of the archives he relied first on a specially deputed member of the staff of the Bodleian Library and then – an innovation of his own time – on a professional archivist employed exclusively to manage the university's records. Trevor's confidence in his deputies was well founded, and here as elsewhere he was careful to avoid overly intrusive supervision. Yet he took a well informed and active role in the management of the archives and was acutely aware of his place in the succession of keepers, especially his two immediate predecessors Billy Pantin and Strickland Gibson (the much admired editor of the university's medieval statutes), and Bryan Twyne, who in the seventeenth century had charge of the archives both of the university and of Corpus Christi College, as did Trevor in the twentieth. Trevor followed easily in the tradition of the scholar-archivist, and continued almost too conscientiously the practice of Gibson and Pantin in annually offering the university committee responsible for the archives both ceremonial hospitality and a learned 'oration' on some aspect of the archives or a historical issue on which they shed light. That these lengthy disquisitions would have been better suited to a historical conference than to a formal university occasion is a measure of how seriously Trevor took his duties. Trevor had no professional training in archival management, but he was fully alert to the issues raised by modern record-keeping. He was certainly concerned to ensure that the documents in his care were preserved according to the best and most up-to-date practice, and the archives gave some scope for his fascination with technology. The second of Trevor's papers included in this volume exemplifies his approach to archives, for it examines the physical provision made for muniments in England, comparing many institutions over a long period, with an eye to the practicalities of archive-keeping, the function and significance of archives, and their institutional context. Similar themes in the relationship between an academic institution and its archives are carefully examined in this volume by Malcolm Underwood, an alumnus of Corpus Christi College who worked with Trevor on college and university archives in Oxford, and on the history of the university, before becoming archivist of St John's College in Cambridge.

In all these activities Trevor Aston showed a fine disdain of regular working hours and of administrative demarcation between his various enterprises. His assistant archivist might be called on to undertake research connected with the history of the university, whose researchers might in turn work on a project for the archives, or the college, or the faculty. Such behaviour might have defied the narrow norms of departmental accounting but it permitted a flexible and cooperative approach which made good use of the resources available. Rather surprisingly in a man with such a strong personality and pronounced views Trevor proved to be a very good collaborator and team leader. He expected his assistants to bring a high degree of initiative and independent judgement to their work and was skilful in bringing together and presenting the work of a group of researchers. One of his most notable research schemes was the analysis by computer of the wealth of data about the medieval universities contained, but in a sense buried, in AB Emden's biographical registers. This was an early and influential exemplar of the application – on a characteristically grand scale – of computing to research in the humanities.

And it was this cooperative research that overcame Trevor's reluctance to return to print. It was in collaboration with his assistants Gregor Duncan and Ralph Evans (a former subeditor of *Past and Present*) that he published several substantial articles on the medieval universities, while his chapter on university and college property and finances in the first volume of the history of the university was written jointly with Ros Faith and was based partly on research by Ruth Vyse, the university's assistant archivist. Much of Trevor's work on the medieval university concerned the academic hall at Oxford and its counterpart at Cambridge, the hostel; the central role of these societies had been recognized by Emden and Pantin but had continued to be overshadowed by an anachronistic concentration on the colleges. His estimation of the importance of the halls was shared by Jeremy Catto, co-editor with Evans of the two medieval volumes of the history. In this volume, building on Trevor's as well as his own earlier work, Jeremy presents a much needed systematic and coherent reassessment of the role of hall and college in late medieval and early Tudor Oxford.

Trevor's second chapter in the history of the university was on the estates of Merton College before the black death. If Trevor's failure to write a major monograph on agrarian history was undoubtedly a serious loss to medieval scholarship, his study of Merton's estates – too often overlooked by agrarian historians in this somewhat unlikely setting – revealed his profound understanding of medieval estate administration and the manorial economy. It drew of course on his own extensive research in the college's archives, but also on that of Graham Kent, the first subeditor of *Past and Present* and simultaneously Trevor's research assistant, and of Underwood, Evans and Faith. It also took advantage of the work by Paul Harvey on the college's manor of Cuxham, both his classic monograph and his exemplary edition of the manor's documents. No-one has done more than Paul Harvey to expand our understanding of the medieval manor and its records, and in this volume his reconsideration of early evidence about manorial reeves enables him to put forward a new model of estate management and the relationship between lords and rural communities in the eleventh and twelfth centuries. This would have been of the greatest interest to Trevor, as it will doubtless be to all students of rural England in this period. Also in this volume Evans appropriately returns to the records of Merton manors to reflect on the relationship between lord and tenant around 1300 as manifested in the manorial court.

Trevor's historical concerns were not confined to the middle ages. If he thought a subject important he would find it worthy of attention in any place or period. His annual orations as keeper of the university archives included several substantial papers on modern topics that went well beyond the narrow bounds of university history. His address of 1972 entitled 'Undergraduate lodgings in Oxford 1868–1914' was a substantial piece of urban social history that sadly remained unpublished. And in 1977 he drew on a very considerable amount of research in college and university archives to consider the effects of the agricultural depression of the late nineteenth century; this topic too was left to other scholars to discuss in print. Another historical enterprise in whose inception he took a leading role was a project to promote the serious historical study of the climate. Furthermore Trevor had a longstanding fascination with anthropology and was sympathetic to the application of anthropological concepts to historical analysis. This was clearly apparent in the support and encouragement he gave to his second wife, Judith, when she embarked on research on attitudes to death, a subject very much at the juncture of the two disciplines.

Trevor Aston was a man not only of wide intellectual curiosity but also of immense creative energy, and could sustain a remarkable intensity of concentration. His work, whether on original documents or scripts for publication, showed an unusual combination of speed and accuracy, and he could work to exacting scholarly standards without being overcome by a stifling perfectionism. Yet throughout his career there was an alternation of high creativity with paralysing doubt and despondency, a clinically recognized condition of manic depression that naturally had a profound influence on his personal and his professional life. He was thus by no means the easiest or least demanding of friends or colleagues. Tall, powerfully built and strikingly handsome, Trevor had an imposing physical presence to match his intellectual forcefulness. He possessed great charm and an engaging manner that revealed his genuine interest in other people, and real understanding of their difficulties, but on occasion he could also be brusque or overbearing, or in dark times worse. He seemed indeed an almost superhuman figure, with both strengths and weaknesses of epic proportions. For those who knew him best the former far outweighed the latter. They remember him as a uniquely inspiring teacher, stimulating colleague and irreplaceable friend. The studies published here together with two of his own papers demonstrate that there has been much important new research on the major historical issues with which Trevor grappled; they also show that his own work and the lead he gave remain very relevant to the concerns of historians today. As researcher and writer, as teacher, editor and archivist, and as the driving force behind a range of historical initiatives Trevor Aston made an enormous contribution to historical scholarship: this volume is offered as a memorial to his achievement.

Published works of TH Aston

Edited volumes

Crisis in Europe, 1560–1660: essays from Past and Present (Routledge & Kegan Paul 1965, 1969, 1970, paperback edition 1974)

Social relations and ideas: essays in honour of RH Hilton (Past and Present Publications, Cambridge University Press 1983), with PR Coss, CC Dyer, JI Thirsk

The English rising of 1381 (Past and Present Publications, Cambridge University Press 1984, paperback edition 1987), with RH Hilton

The History of the University of Oxford (8 vols Oxford University Press 1984–2000), general editor

The Brenner debate: agrarian class structure and economic development in pre-industrial Europe (Past and Present Publications, Cambridge University Press 1985), with CHE Philpin

Landlords, peasants and politics in medieval England (Past and Present Publications, Cambridge University Press 1987)

Articles

'The English manor', *Past and Present* 10 (November 1956), 6–14 (review article of EA Kosminsky, *Studies in the agrarian history of England in the thirteenth century*)

'The origins of the manor in England', *Transactions of the Royal Historical Society* 5th series viii (1958), 59–83; reprinted in WE Minchinton (ed), *Essays in agrarian history* i (David & Charles for British Agricultural History Society 1968), 9–35; reprinted in Aston, Coss, Dyer and Thirsk, *Social relations and ideas*, 1–25, with 'postscript', 26–43

'Robin Hood', *Past and Present* 20 (November 1961), reprinted in RH Hilton (ed), *Peasants, knights and heretics: studies in medieval social history* (Past and Present Publications, Cambridge University Press 1976), 270–2

'The dating of the rolls' in reprint of *Wellingborough manorial accounts* AD *1258–1323*, ed FM Page (Northamptonshire Record Society viii, first published 1936, reprinted 1965), xxxix–xlii

'The date of John Rous's list of the colleges and academical halls of Oxford', *Oxoniensia* xlii (1977), 226–36

'Oxford's medieval alumni', *Past and Present* 74 (February 1977), 3–40

'The medieval alumni of the University of Cambridge', *Past and Present* 86 (February 1980), 3–86, with TAR Evans and GD Duncan

'The college archives', *The Pelican* [Corpus Christi College, Oxford] 1981–2, 61–4

'The endowments of the university and colleges to *circa* 1348' in JI Catto and TAR Evans (eds), *The early Oxford schools* (History of the University of Oxford i Oxford University Press 1984), 265–309, with RJ Faith

'The external administration and resources of Merton College to *circa* 1348', ibid 311–68

1

The Making of Nations in Britain and Ireland in the Early Middle Ages

TM CHARLES-EDWARDS

Nationality in earlier centuries is a concept sometimes mishandled because we are inclined to think that if the word *nation* does not have a clearly defined and fixed meaning it is useless for the historian.* Much more plausible is the opposite view, namely that because nationality is a shifting and contentious idea, because what gives one nation its sense of identity may be unimportant for another nation, the whole issue of nationality is far more interesting than it would be otherwise.[1] The criteria of ethnicity not only shift between one nation and another but within a single nation from one period to another. Just as today what determines national identity in the former Yugoslavia is not what is crucial in Britain, so also Yugoslav identity is not what it was twenty-five years ago.

If nationality was and is variable, some issues are much more likely to arise in one period than another. In an era of mass electorates and mass media elites have both the need and the means to persuade the general population that all, elite and non-elite alike, have a common identity. Democratic states, in which legitimate government requires the consent of the people, need to define the people in question; and they cannot define it merely as those subject to the power of the particular state. Persons acknowledged to be alien may be among those who inhabit the territory although they do not belong to the people or nation.

These questions were not current in the same way in the middle ages. This has encouraged some to claim that, while *ethnicities* have existed since the dawn of history, *nations* are a characteristic phenomenon of modernity, created by nationalism.[2] Similarly, rapid modernization has often led to the incorporation of older and smaller-scale peoples into new and larger nations, as in modern Africa. Here too it is tempting to distinguish between ethnicity and nationality. The co-existence of larger and smaller identities within a single polity is, however, an ancient as well as a modern phenomenon, exemplified not just by modern Britain but by that model of

* An earlier version of this paper formed an O'Donnell lecture in the University of Edinburgh. I am very grateful for the hospitality shown to me on that occasion.

1 The variability of early medieval ethnicity is well shown by W Pohl, 'Telling the difference: signs of ethnic identity' in W Pohl and H Reimitz (eds), *Strategies of distinction: the construction of ethnic communities, 300–800* (1998).
2 For example EJ Hobsbawm, *Nations and nationalism since 1780* (1990), 9–10.

nationality, ancient Israel with its twelve tribes.[3] There are compelling objections to positing a universal distinction between ethnicity and nationality: first, if the distinction is between modern nation and pre-modern ethnicity, the powerful continuities between the identities of some nations in the pre-modern and modern periods must be unduly depreciated;[4] second, where there exists a polarity between larger and smaller-scale identity, the basis of the contrast varies so much from one case to another. If we assert a fundamental contrast between large nation and small ethnicity – perhaps between the French as a nation and the Bretons as an ethnicity – we are met with an uncomfortable fact: what constitutes an ethnicity in one case – perhaps language – will constitute a nation in another. In one case the smaller-scale identity will be the stronger and more conscious; in another it will be the larger. When there is a state including two or more peoples within its territory there has often been a contrast between one relatively powerful people and another or others which are weaker; and in such cases the state may be identified with the more powerful people. Here again one might be tempted to distinguish the more politically effective nation from the less effective ethnicity. Yet, such is the instability of power, any such conceptual diktat would mean that particular peoples would be at one point nations, at another ethnicities. It is better to accept that the one flexible concept, *nation*, must do for Bretons and Frenchmen, Hausa and Nigerians, Mercians and English, and that in the middle ages as in the contemporary world it is a habitually contentious notion.

Bede and the 'languages of nations'

I shall not, therefore, engage in any search after the essence of the nation, for no such essence is to be found. Instead I shall take as my starting point a statement on the nations of Britain made by Bede in the eighth century. He says that in his day there were, including Latin, *quinque gentium linguae*, 'five languages of nations', in Britain: those of the Britons, the Picts, the Irish and the English, and finally Latin.[5] But he also uses the Latin word *gens* for such smaller units as the Northumbrians, the Mercians, and the peoples of Leinster and Munster.[6] In general he denies the status of being a *gens* to the two principal constituent units of Northumbria, Deira and Bernicia; but he is not entirely consistent in this policy, was probably unusual in the extent to which he maintained the distinction between *gens* and *provincia*, and may not himself have maintained the distinction earlier in his career.[7]

---

[3] The importance of the old testament model of nationality is rightly stressed by A Hastings, *The construction of nationhood: ethnicity, religion and nationalism* (1997), 195–6.

[4] Hastings, 35–65 argues this case, especially in relation to England.

[5] Bede, *Historia ecclesiastica gentis Anglorum* (hereafter *HE*), ed and trans B Colgrave and RAB Mynors as *Bede's ecclesiastical history of the English people* (1969), 1.1, where the five are compared with the five books of the pentateuch; cf 3.6, where Latin is not included.

[6] For example Bede, *HE*, 3.9 (*gens Nordanhymbrorum, hoc est ea natio Anglorum, quae ad Aquilonalem Humbre fluminis plagam habitabat*), 3.3 (*gentes Scottorum, quae in australibus Hiberniae insulae partibus*).

[7] See J Campbell, 'Bede's *reges* and *principes*' in his *Essays in Anglo-Saxon history* (1986), 86–8 for general discussion of *gens* and *provincia*. There is one example of *gens* used for the Northumbrians in *HE*, 3.2 (*in tota Berniciorum gente*). Bede uses *gentes* for the Bernicians and the Deirans in *Chronica maiora*, §531. See also JM Wallace-Hadrill, *Bede's ecclesiastical history of the English people: a historical commentary* (1988), 87, 226–8 (on p 212, lines 5–6).

We shall be compelled to look further afield, for as the Germanic inhabitants of Britain made a distinction between themselves and the *Wealas*, the Welsh or, rather, Britons, so did the Franks in the sixth century distinguish themselves from the *Walas*, the Gallo-Romans.[8] The boundary between the *Walas* and the non-Walas thus crossed the English Channel and distinguished Germanic from non-Germanic peoples both in Britain and in Gaul. In considering the nationalities of Britain we need to keep one eye directed at Gallo-Romans, Franks, Frisians and Saxons. The prime target of investigation, then, is the *gens* of Bede in the larger sense – for example the Picts – and what distinguished such a unit from yet larger ones, such as *Walas*, and smaller ones, also called *gentes* by Bede, such as the Northumbrians.

The larger *gens* of Bede is a linguistic unit. We may compare it to the relationship in Old English between the word for a people or *gens*, *þeod*, the king of a people, *þeoden*, and their language, *geþeode*, which itself may be used as a term for a people. The same relationship is seen in Welsh, where the word for language, *iaith*, is also used as a word for a nation or people.[9] Yet among the Franks by the eighth century language was no longer a mark of nationality: some Franks spoke Frankish, a Germanic dialect, a *lingua teudisca*, as did Charlemagne, while some spoke Romance, *lingua romana*.[10] Moreover this term for their native Germanic language, *lingua teudisca*, 'the language of the people', modern *Deutsch* or Dutch, although it suggested a connection between language and nation (*theud-*, *theod-*: Old English *þeod*), was in fact applied to all west Germanic languages, including English, and not merely to the Frankish dialect.[11] Language came to cut across the Frankish people, linking some to Germanic speakers further east and north, some to Romance speakers further south. Furthermore, though Gregory of Tours in the sixth century might see the Franks as a unitary *gens*, some of the Franks themselves may still have thought that they were a federation of peoples (not just Salians but Amsivarii, Bructeri, Chamavi and Chattuarii).[12] Even after Clovis (*d.* 511) divisions endured: in the seventh century the appearance of a written *lex ribuaria* as opposed to *lex salica* indicated that in law, too, the Franks did not see themselves as homogeneous. The process of assimilating other peoples into the Franks was still going on: *lex salica* speaks of Franks or other *barbari* who live according to Salic law; small groups of non-Salian Franks but also Alamans, Saxons and even Sarmatians have left their names in modern France.[13] Salic law, therefore, was doubly inadequate as a mark of Frankishness: some non-Frankish barbarians lived by it and some Franks did not.

8   *Pactus legis salicae*, ed KA Eckhardt (Monumenta Germaniae Historica, leges 4.1 1962), title 41, trans TJ Rivers, *Laws of the Salian and Ripuarian Franks* (1986), 86–7. The best witness to the Malberg glosses, Eckhardt's *A2*, is defective for 41.8, but its exemplar may well have had *uualaleodi* as in 41.9–10. On the Frankish sense of nationality see E Ewig, 'Volkstum und Volksbewusstsein im Frankenreich des 7. Jahrhunderts' in his *Spätantikes und fränkisches Gallien* (2 vols 1976–9) i.232–6.

9   On the famous declaration of the old man of Pencader, linking *gens* and *lingua*, see RR Davies, 'The peoples of Britain and Ireland, 1100–1400: names, boundaries and regnal solidarities', *Transactions of the Royal Historical Society* 6.v (1995), 18.

10   Nithard, *Histoire des fils de Louis le pieux*, 3.5, ed P Lauer (1926), 102–8. Einhard, *Vita Karoli*, ch 29 refers to Charlemagne's *patria sermo* in a context which makes it clear that it was Germanic.

11   The report of the papal legates (1st edn 773, 2nd edn 839), printed in *English historical documents* i, 2nd edn, ed D Whitelock (1979), no 191, says that the decrees were read out before Offa and a joint lay and clerical assembly both in Latin and *theodisce*.

12   E Zöllner, *Geschichte der Franken bis zur Mitte des 6. Jahrhunderts* (1970), 2.

13   *Pactus legis salicae*, 41.1, ed Eckhardt; Ewig, 234–6.

The conquests of Clovis may not have strengthened the unity of the Franks as much as they stressed the contrast between Franks (and their other Germanic allies and recruits) and Gallo-Romans. In the early sixth century this contrast remained clear. The Malberg glosses show that for the Franks the Romans were *Walas*, 'foreigners', 'aliens': they stood to the Franks as the *Wealas* (the Britons) stood to the English. As in Wessex in the seventh century so in Gaul in the sixth there were two parallel social hierarchies, one for the Franks and another for the *Walas*, both meeting in the king.[14] At the top of the Frankish hierarchy were the *antrustiones*, members of the royal *trustis*; at the top of the hierarchy of the *Walas* were the *convivae regis*, men of such rank that they might be admitted to the table of the king. The wergilds, however, marked the superiority of the Franks. Moreover, the two peoples fulfilled partly different roles: the army was composed largely of Franks, the episcopate largely of Romans.[15] Their perception of their neighbours was also different: Gregory of Tours recounts with something akin to horror the summoning by Sigebert of the *gentes* from across the Rhine: the Gallo-Roman continued to think that the Rhine marked the limits of civilization.[16] In the shorter prologue to *lex salica*, however, the four wise men who were to re-establish the true Frankish law came from the east, from over the Rhine.[17]

As the secondary identification of *Francus* with 'freeman' suggests, the exemplars of ethnicity were not, in the early middle ages, to be found in the lower strata of society.[18] Slaves and half-freemen were not normally considered to be members of the *gens*.[19] In one form or another this had often been true in antiquity: the Athenians were the free natives of Attica as opposed to slaves and resident aliens. The same might have been said of the Franks in the eighth century. Since the core of a *gens* was its aristocracy, it is not surprising that characteristics of nationality coincided to a considerable extent with symptoms of nobility. The Northumbrian Imma was taken prisoner after the battle of the Trent in 679 by the followers of a Mercian *comes*.[20] In order to avoid being killed as a part of the feud between the kings and aristocracies of Northumbria and Mercia, Imma had to pretend that he was not one of the nobles (*ex nobilibus*) but a peasant (*rusticus*) and, what is more, poor, married and only present on the battlefield in order to bring up supplies for the fighting men. All quite untrue, but Imma was believed until it was perceived from his appearance, his dress and the way he talked that he was not a *rusticus* but a noble. Every item among these symptoms of noble status might have appeared in a list of symptoms of nationality.

For the Franks language largely ceased to be an effective criterion of Frankishness as soon as many of them began to speak Romance.[21] For the English, however, it

---

[14] *Pactus legis salicae*, 41, ed Eckhardt; Ine, chs 23.3, 24.2, 32, 46.1, 54.2, 70, *Die Gesetze der Angelsachsen*, ed F Liebermann (3 vols 1903–16) i.100–18.

[15] Gregory's great-uncle Duke Gundulf was the exception in a family studded with bishops: Gregory of Tours, *Decem libri historiarum* (hereafter *Hist*), 6.11. He was also the exception in that he bore a Germanic name, sharing the same first element with the king of the Burgundians, Gundobad, into whose kingdom he was born.

[16] Ibid 4.49.

[17] *Pactus legis salicae*, ed Eckhardt, 2–3.

[18] Zöllner, 115.

[19] Cf Lombardic *fulcfree*: *Edictus Rothari*, ed F Beyerle (1962), chs 216, 224, 225, 257.

[20] Bede, *HE*, 4.22 (20).

[21] Although, as the *polyptiques* show, the peasantry around Paris and Rheims had by the ninth century adopted Germanic names. For the contrast in the eighth century between Franks from the Loire north-

remained important. Yet linguistic identity was complex in similar ways for both the English and the Franks. Bede could distinguish between linguistic forms according to which *gens* used them: whereas the Northumbrians and the Kentishmen said 'Caelin', the West Saxons said 'Ceawlin'.[22] We would say that, while dialect distinguished one (smaller) English *gens* from another – West Saxon from Northumbrian – language distinguished the larger *gentes* of the British Isles – English from Pict. Bede however uses the one word, *lingua*, for what distinguished the West Saxons from the Northumbrians on the one hand, and the English from Picts, Britons and Irish on the other. Moreover it was possible for the papal legates in 786 to use *theodisce* ('in the [Germanic] vernacular') to refer to text being read out in English: at one level language united the English with their Germanic neighbours. In one way or another, therefore, language buttressed three levels of identity: that of the smaller *gens*, such as the West Saxons; that of the larger *gens*, such as the English; and, finally, that of speakers of one or other of the Germanic dialects, or at least the west Germanic dialects, all lumped together under the one heading of *lingua theudisca*, and regarded by Bede as *gentes* related by kinship.[23]

English national identity

The problem of English nationality in the early middle ages is not unlike that of Irish nationality: there was a concept of an English nation long before there was a united English kingdom, just as the national identity of the Irish sustained the claims put forward by the Uí Néill that their king ruled over all the Irish; Irish nationality was not the creation of a kingship of Ireland or of Tara. Moreover, there is a vital distinction between the Frankish conquests in Gaul and the English conquests in Britain. Although elements of other peoples might be involved, and although the Franks were themselves a federation of smaller peoples, nonetheless the conquests were essentially made by one people, the Franks. Indeed the Frankish sense of identity was closely tied to their military successes: the Franks were a people 'powerful in arms', conquerors of Roman territory.[24] In the fourth century the Bructeri were perhaps the most prominent people within the Frankish federation; yet, because they remained on the east side of the Rhine and also remained pagan until about 700, they appear to have ceased to be regarded as Franks.[25] Yet the conquests and settlements in Britain were made by elements of several peoples temporarily unified by the leaders of war-bands.[26] The incomers would have considered themselves as, say, Frisians or Jutes, not as English. Englishness was forged in Britain, not in Germany, whereas the

---

wards and Romans south of the Loire see the continuation of Fredegar, ch 25: *The fourth book of the chronicle of Fredegar with its continuations*, ed and trans JM Wallace-Hadrill [1960], 98–9. This is a good example to show that symptoms of nationality might be important for the peasant as well as for the noble. For the importance of dress as an indicator of Frankish nationality see Einhard, *Vita Karoli*, ch 23.

22 Bede, *HE*, 2.5.
23 Ibid 5.9 (*quarum in Germania plurimas nouerat esse nationes, a quibus Angli uel Saxones, qui nunc Brittaniam incolunt, genus et originem duxisse noscuntur*).
24 *Fortis in arma [armis]*, according to the longer (eighth-century) prologue to *lex salica*: *Lex salica*, ed KA Eckhardt (Monumenta Germaniae Historica, leges 4.2 1969), 2.
25 Gregory of Tours, *Hist*, 3.9 (in text quoted from the lost *Historia* of Sulpicius Alexander); Bede, *HE*, 5.11.
26 Bede, *HE*, 1.15; Wallace-Hadrill, *Commentary*, 22; S Bassett, 'In search of the origins of Anglo-Saxon kingdoms' in S Bassett (ed), *The origins of Anglo-Saxon kingdoms* (1989), 23–7.

Franks, although in origin a federation of distinct peoples, had acquired a unity before they ever settled west of the Rhine. It remains uncertain when a man who was a Frisian came to regard himself as more English than Frisian.

I accept entirely the arguments put forward by Patrick Wormald against the theory that the so-called *bretwaldas* fostered a sense of English nationality.[27] One does not have to deny the reality of the power wielded by the rulers named in Bede's list of seven great kings in book 2, chapter 5, for whether they wielded real power or not they did not rule, or aspire to rule, over the English as such.[28] It is clear that Bede divides them into two subclasses, those who claimed to rule over the southern English, namely the peoples south of the Humber, and those who claimed to rule over the island of Britain. None of them claimed to rule the English as such; and there was no English political entity, in the sense of an over-kingdom ruled by a *bretwalda*, which could have created the English nation. Yet there was undoubtedly a concept of an English nation, most notably in Bede's *Ecclesiastical history of the English people*.

Wormald has further argued that the source of this concept of an English people is ecclesiastical. The idea was born in Rome in the active mind of Pope Gregory the Great. From him it was transmitted to the see founded by his disciples at Canterbury, and so to Bede. The clue is that the English came to be known as the English, and not as the Saxons, their name both for continental writers, other than Gregory and his successors, and also for the Celtic peoples: for the Britons the English were the *Saeson*, for the Irish, the *Saxain*. But those who knew the English as Saxons did not thereby distinguish them from the Saxons of northern Germany. Similarly, Bede records that the Britons of his day used the corrupt form *Garmani* for the English, thus again tying together the English and the continental Germanic peoples.[29] There is no evidence in such terminology of any notion of the English as a separate people, rather than a collection of different elements of Germanic stock – *Garmani* – or as part of one larger entity, a Saxon people extending across the North Sea.

There were two preconditions to be satisfied before there could be a notion of English nationality: first, the English had to be distinguished from their neighbours in the British Isles, Britons, Irish and Picts; second, they had to be distinguished from the Germanic peoples of the continent. When the Britons of Bede's day described the English as *Garmani* they satisfied the first condition but not the second. According to Wormald, then, it was the Rome–Canterbury axis that sowed the seed of an English nation: the mission of Augustine (596/7) was conceived as a mission to convert a *gens*, the English people.[30] The converts may have known themselves as Jutes,

[27] P Wormald, 'Bede, the *bretwaldas* and the origins of the *gens Anglorum*' in P Wormald, DA Bullough and R Collins (eds), *Ideal and reality in Frankish and Anglo-Saxon society: essays presented to JM Wallace-Hadrill* (1983), 102. It is a corollary that there was a real change when Alfred assumed power over Mercia and employed the concept of an *Angelcynn* to include Mercians as well as West Saxons within his kingdom: S Foot, 'The making of *Angelcynn*: English identity before the Norman conquest', *Transactions of the Royal Historical Society* 6.vi (1996).

[28] For different views of the *bretwaldas* see S Keynes, 'Rædwald the bretwalda' in CB Kendall and PS Wells (eds), *Voyage to the other world: the legacy of Sutton Hoo* (1992); TM Charles-Edwards, 'The continuation of Bede, s.a. 750: high-kings, kings of Tara and "bretwaldas"' in AP Smyth (ed), *Senchas: studies in early and medieval Irish archaeology, history and literature in honour of Francis J Byrne* (1999).

[29] Bede, *HE*, 5.9.

[30] But cf ibid 2.4 (*ad praedicandum gentibus paganis*). The notion of *gens* as a partner to *ecclesia* is seen, applied to the Northumbrians and their church, ibid 3.20.

Saxons, Swabians, Frisians and Angles, and may have been surprised to find that, in the scheme of divine providence, they were all English.[31] Nevertheless, the influence of the metropolitan see of Canterbury, especially after the arrival of Theodore in 669, gradually accustomed them to this novel idea.

The general drift of this argument is very appealing. There are, however, difficulties which suggest that it is not the sole explanation. First, there is an implicit contrast between the scope of the political authority of the *bretwaldas*, whose claims from Edwin onward to rule the whole of Britain were too wide, and the claim of Canterbury to be the metropolitan see for the English. Edwin (*d*. 633), Oswald (*d*. 642) and Oswiu (*d*. 670) cannot have fostered a sense of English nationality because they wished to rule several peoples. Their rule over the men of Lindsey was probably not significantly different from their rule over the Picts to the north of the Forth; that the one people was English and the other Pictish was not always of great consequence.[32] The authority of Archbishop Theodore, however, was accepted by all the English peoples and not by the Britons, the Picts or the Irish of Britain.[33] So far the argument works well, but it should be noticed that the claim of the archbishops from Theodore's arrival up to the time of Bede's death in 735 was to authority not just over the English but over the whole of Britain.[34] As with the *bretwaldas*, the claim was too wide to have a national scope. True, the reality was that Theodore and his successor Berhtwald had effective authority only over the English, but the whole burden of Wormald's argument has encouraged us to pay much more attention to ideal and ambition, rather than humble reality, as active agents behind the creation of a sense of nationality.

A vital clue to the second difficulty in the way of Wormald's argument is that the English came to be called *Angli* and not *Saxones*, even though their neighbours knew them as Saxons. Gregory the Great's adoption of the term *Angli* thus appeared to be the starting point from which the English were to obtain their name. The first problem here is that this papal usage is supposed to be transmitted *via* Canterbury; yet there is important evidence that, in the long period from 669 to 731 during which Theodore and Berhtwald were archbishops, Canterbury knew the English as Saxons and their language as the Saxon language. Bede tells us that Berhtwald ordained Tobias as bishop of Rochester, a man of wide education in the learning and language of Greek, Latin and English, *saxonica lingua atque eruditione*.[35] It may reasonably be suggested that Bede used *saxonica lingua* rather than *lingua Anglorum* (his normal phrase) because his source spoke of 'the Saxon language'; but the source is likely to have been Canterbury.[36] Archbishop Theodore himself used the phrase *saxonico vocabulo* in the acts of the council of Hatfield: the name Haethfelth is a 'Saxon word'. He, however, was *archiepiscopus Brittaniae insulae* and he sat together with 'the

[31] Ibid 1.15, 5.9; for the Swabians of Swaffham see E Ekwall, *The concise dictionary of English place-names* (4th edn 1960), 455.

[32] Bede, *HE*, 4.26 (24) describes the *regnum Anglorum* as extending north of the Forth in the years before the battle of Nechtanesmere. Note the inconsistent attitude of Stephen, *Vita S Wilfridi*: the Picts are bestial (ch 19) but they are on friendly terms with Wilfrid (ch 21).

[33] Bede, *HE*, 4.2 (*isque primus erat in archiepiscopis cui omnis Anglorum ecclesia manus dare consentiret*).

[34] N Brooks, *The early history of the church of Canterbury* (1984), 71–2, 83.

[35] Bede, *HE*, 5.8.

[36] Wormald, 'Bede', 123 n105.

other bishops of the island of Britain'.[37] In this use of the adjective Saxon for the English language Bede was transmitting usage which conflicted with his own and was thus all the more telling as evidence. Secondly, there are examples in early Welsh texts of *Eingl*, *Angli*, being used for the English: the contrast between Gregory the Great and all other external usage is not absolute.[38]

Brooks, however, has argued that a sense of English nationality can be traced back to Kent, and more particularly Canterbury, in the time of Æthelberht's overlordship in southern England. He interprets the shift towards Roman patterns of dress, which spread generally though England in the first half of the seventh century, as shown by Helen Geake, as initiated by a Kent in which Augustine and his companions were setting about making Canterbury a new Rome of the English.[39] He also argues that the origin myth of the English, found in its fullest form in a British guise in the *Historia Brittonum*, derived from the Kent of Æthelberht.[40] As he recognizes, however, such symptoms as these attest the existence of a sense of English identity by the end of the sixth century; how and when it came into existence remains to be shown.

Not long after the council of Hatfield, Ine promulgated the first West Saxon laws to be written down.[41] They survive as an appendix to Alfred's laws but may be accepted as a substantially genuine late seventh-century text.[42] Ine proclaims himself king of the West Saxons, but in the course of his laws he makes provision for *Wealas* as well as his Germanic subjects. In contexts in which he is contrasting members of the two peoples he generally uses *Englisc* of the one group and *Wilisc* of the other.[43] By *Wilisc* he means not Welsh in our sense but British. The contrast between *Englisc* and *Wilisc* is, however, not just a matter of nationality, but also one of status. The status of the person who is *Wilisc* is always inferior to that of the person who is *Englisc* even if they are, for example, both slaves who have lost their freedom as a penalty for some offence.[44] There is, in other words, a British social hierarchy as well as an English

---

[37] Bede, *HE*, 4.17/15.

[38] N Brooks, *Bede and the English* (2000), 19; see also M Richter, 'Bede's *Angli*: Angles or English?', *Peritia* iii (1984). *Eingl* is found in the poems that Sir Ifor Williams judged to be genuine sixth-century compositions of the poet Taliesin: *The poems of Taliesin*, ed I Williams with English version by JEC Williams (1968), 3.20, 7.28. In both cases it is possible to translate *Eingl* by Angles rather than English, but against this is the fact that these particular poems do not use *Saeson* (Saxons, English).

[39] N Brooks, 'Canterbury, Rome and the construction of English identity' in JMH Smith (ed), *Early medieval Rome and the Christian west: essays in honour of Donald A Bullough* (2000), esp 244–6. H Geake, *The use of grave-goods in conversion-period England, c.600–c.850* (1997), summary of conclusions on 129–30. It may be important that Geake dates the change to *c*580 in Kent, *c*600 elsewhere; the change started in Kent before the arrival of Augustine.

[40] N Brooks, 'The English origin myth' in his *Anglo-Saxon myths: state and church* (2000).

[41] *Gesetze*, ed Liebermann i.88–123; for the date see ibid iii.65.

[42] This is shown by differences in syntax and in the organization of the text. See P Wormald, *The making of English law: King Alfred to the twelfth century* i *Legislation and its limits*, 103–5; P Wormald, '*Inter cetera bona . . . genti suae*: law-making and peace-keeping in the earliest English kingdoms', *Settimane di Studio sull'Alto Medioevo* xlii (1995), repr in his *Legal culture in the medieval west: law as text, image and experience* (1999). Wormald sees six separate sets of edicts within the existing text.

[43] Ine is king of the West Saxons, *Wesseaxna kyning*, in the prologue: *Gesetze*, ed Liebermann i.88. Cf Ine, chs 23.3–4 (*Wealh* v *Engliscmon*), 32 (*Wilisc mon*), 46.1 (*Englisc* v *Wilisc*), 54.2 (*Wylisc* v *Englisc*), 74 (*Wealh* v *Englisc*).

[44] See for example Ine, chs 23.3–24.2, 54.2. That Englishness is a status in late seventh-century Wessex is also suggested by a comparison with other elements in Ine's vocabulary. When he is considering someone as of free birth he refers to him as *cierlisc* (chs 18, 37, 54) but when the person is a freeman who is the head of a household he is a *ceorl* (chs 38, 57). The suffix *-isc* is typically used by Ine when the context is one of status, whether this is also a matter of ethnicity (*Wilisc*, *Englisc*) or not (*cierlisc*).

one. There are British nobles who are superior in status to English commoners but inferior to English nobles.[45] In these laws those who are West Saxons when considered in relation to their king and to other Germanic peoples are English when considered in relation to their British neighbours. The king is still king of the West Saxons, even though he rules over many Britons; the kingdom is the kingdom of the West Saxons because they are the dominant people, not because they constitute all the subjects of their king or all the inhabitants of the kingdom.

At a time, therefore, when Canterbury termed the English *Saxons*, Ine, though himself king of the West Saxons, used the term *English* to make the distinction between the English and the Britons. The context of the distinction was secular not ecclesiastical. Ine's usage suggests that the concept of English nationality may have had deeper roots than Wormald's argument would allow.

This combination of ethnicity and status suggests an explanation of the notorious fact that there are hardly any British loanwords in English whereas Welsh has never been especially impervious to English loans. Although English was impervious to British loans, it was much readier to admit Latin; British admitted both Latin and English.[46] In other words, the early Old English normative language did not reject loanwords *per se* but only ones identified as British. Again this suggests strong social attitudes underlying linguistic behaviour and, in particular, the perception of the British language as socially inferior. In early medieval Britain nationality came to be closely linked to language. As we saw earlier, the Welsh *iaith* (language) also means nation; the Old English *geþeode* (language) is what unites a *þeod*, a people. Bede distinguishes his four nations by language. Ultimately, as we know, the British population in what became England was to be assimilated to the dominant people.[47] In the process they necessarily abandoned their native language for that of the conquerors. The latter regarded the British language as the principal mark of a defeated and inferior people whose land they were proud to have taken and whose god they long rejected. For an English person to use a British word would have been to risk social disgrace. The fact that so few words passed from British into English can hardly be due to a lack of interaction between the two languages, for that would leave the considerable traffic the other way, from English into British, quite unexplained. In any case, a mass extermination of the British population is not the explanation, for even if that were plausible for parts of southern England it is not plausible for Northumbria;

---

45 Ine, ch 24.2 compared with ch 51. Note that 120 shillings corresponds to 'the 1200 man': cf VI Æthelstan 8.2, *Gesetze*, ed Liebermann 178 and *Wer*, ch 1, ed Liebermann, 392. B Yorke, *Wessex in the early middle ages* (1995), 72.

46 M Förster, 'Keltisches Wortgut im Englischen' in H Boehmer et al, *Texte und Forschungen zur englischen Kulturgeschichte: Festgabe für Felix Liebermann* (1921; also published separately 1921); the list has hardly changed in D Kastorsky, 'Semantics and vocabulary' in RM Hogg (ed), *The Cambridge history of the English language* i *The beginnings to 1066* (1992), 318–19; TH Parry-Williams, *The English element in Welsh: a study of English loan-words in Welsh* (Cymmrodorion record series x 1923), ch 2. The only reservation is that the chronology of the English loans in Welsh has not been properly worked out, so that it is uncertain how old many of them were. It is unfortunately very difficult to determine which Latin loanwords entered English after settlement in Britain and before the seventh century: HF Nielsen, *The continental backgrounds of English and its insular development until 1154* (1998), 150–4. A standard textbook, AC Baugh and T Cable, *A history of the English language* (5th edn 2002), 81–2, still operates on the false assumption that spoken Latin had died out in Britain too early to have any effect on the Anglo-Saxon settlers.

47 For some discussion as to how long this may have taken see M Gelling, *The west midlands in the early middle ages* (1992), ch 4, esp 70–1.

yet even in the north and west there appear to have been very few linguistic borrowings from British. It is difficult to escape the conclusion that the English attitude to language was a prime cause of the deep division between themselves and the Britons, and thus of the unity of the Germanic-speaking peoples of Britain. What it does not explain is the appearance of a clear distinction between the English and the Germanic peoples of the continent.

The first problem, then, is how the Germanic-speaking peoples of Britain – whatever the origins of their ancestors, whether they came from Jutland or from the Rhineland – came to distinguish themselves as English from the Germanic-speaking peoples of the continent. The evidence of Ine suggests that an ecclesiastical perception of the unity of the English cannot be a sufficient explanation. The likelihood is that, around 700, language was the principal dividing line between *Englisc* and *Wilisc*. But language as a mark of national identity is not unproblematic. It will be remembered that Bede could term the West Saxon variety of English a *lingua*, just as English itself was a *lingua*; and, moreover, the divide between *Wealas* or *Walas* and speakers of Germanic languages crossed the Channel. Aspects of language might unite the English to continental Germanic-speakers in a single *lingua theudisca* rather than dividing them.[48]

A further problem, but also a clue to an answer, is that none of the dialectal peculiarities within English, already evident to Bede, derived from the diverse origins of the English on the continent.[49] Mercian was not different from West Saxon because continental Anglian was different from continental Saxon. The problem is made worse by an apparent contradiction between the archaeological and the linguistic evidence. The latter suggested that Old English was closely linked with Frisian – more closely than with Old Saxon and the other languages of the North Sea littoral.[50] The implication of this is that there was already linguistic diversity in the area between Jutland and the Rhine in the fourth and fifth centuries; otherwise there would have been no reason why Old English should have been closer to Frisian from the start, since Frisian would not yet have been a separate variety of Germanic. And yet this diversity did not come through into Old English, even though the settlers in Britain came from more than one Germanic people. A simple reading of the linguistic evidence might suggest that a majority of the Anglo-Saxon settlers were Frisians. The archaeological and historical evidence indicates, however, that this cannot be true. The artefactual diversity of the settlers continued through the migration period to be reinforced and adapted in Britain. Thus an early mixture of Anglian and Saxon settlement in the midlands and East Anglia was subsequently overlain by strong links with Scandinavia, just as Kent was moving closer to the Franks.[51] At no period before about 600 does early Anglo-Saxon archaeology suggest a cultural uniformity such as

---

[48] Admittedly by the seventh century some Franks may have been monoglot Romance-speakers; this may explain why Cenwalh, king of Wessex, found the language spoken by Agilbert, his Frankish bishop, foreign (*barbara loquella*): Bede, *HE*, 3.7.

[49] A Campbell, *Old English grammar* (1959), 3–4, as opposed to K Brunner, *Altenglische Grammatik* (3rd edn 1965), 2–3; HF Nielsen, *Old English and the continental Germanic languages* (1981, 2nd edn 1985), 223–52; Nielsen, *Continental backgrounds*, 77; J Hines, 'Philology, archaeology and the *adventus Saxonum vel Anglorum*' in A Bammesberger and A Wollmann (eds), *Britain 400–600: language and history* (1990).

[50] Campbell, §3.

[51] J Hines, *The Scandinavian character of Anglian England in the pre-Viking period* (1984); J Hines, 'The Scandinavian character of Anglian England: an update' in M Carver (ed), *The age of Sutton Hoo*

might explain the uniformity of Old English; still less does it suggest that the Anglo-Saxons were really a colonial outpost of Frisia.[52] Moreover the ubiquity of the term *Saxones* for the English indicates a connection with Saxons rather than with Frisians.[53]

An argument proposed by John Hines arises from an interpretation of the linguistic diversity on the continent and its relationship to Old English.[54] When one has varieties of a language all in one geographical continuum, sound-changes will start in one area and spread along the continuum more or less far as the case may be. Sometimes one area will be the starting point of most linguistic change so that one can then talk of conservative versus progressive dialects. This, according to Hines, is the case among the Germanic dialects along the North Sea coast. Those towards the Scandinavian end of the continuum were relatively conservative; those towards the Rhineland end relatively progressive. So far, this is just what is called a wave model of language change: the wave advances to a certain point and then fades. What Hines then does is to introduce the notion of a language as a set of norms: actual speech performance varies around the norm, but the norm is a central determinant of language even if actual speech performance fails to accord perfectly with it (this is Saussure's distinction between *langue* and *parole*). Such a norm may, however, be invested with all sorts of cultural and social values, including ethnic identity and social status. Moreover, if a central aspect of the norm is distinctiveness, that is as a mark of being different from some other linguistic variety, one has a powerful agent of linguistic change. Such differentiation can be progressive.

Looked at simply in terms of the wave model of linguistic change, English was at the most progressive end of the continuum along the North Sea from Norway down to the Rhine, now extended over the straits of Dover into Britain. If there had been a sixth-century dialectologist he might have seen that the local varieties of Germanic changed more as he travelled on this clockwise journey along the coastlands from Scandinavia to Britain. The suggestion, therefore, is that instead of seeing Old English as an essentially mechanical development from an Anglo-Frisian mother tongue, with no allowance being made for cultural values expressed by linguistic variation, we should think of English arising from a new 'settler' norm, one which placed a high value on distinguishing its linguistic performance from that of the more conservative dialects in their North Sea homelands. It was simply fortuitous, in political terms, that Frisian happened to be the most progressive of the North Sea dialects. The point was not to resemble Frisian but to be different from the homelands as a whole.

It may be that this way of looking at the origins of English can be strengthened by bringing in the Britons. Among them the linguistic situation was complicated by the existence, as late as the sixth century, of two languages that were spoken by Britons.[55]

(1992); SC Hawkes, 'Anglo-Saxon Kent *c.*425–725' in PE Leach (ed), *Archaeology in Kent to AD 1500* (1982).

[52] Hines, 'Philology, archaeology and the *adventus*', 27–9.

[53] Saxons and Frisians are perceived as distinct peoples by Venantius Fortunatus: *Venanti Honori Clementiani Fortunati presbyteri italici opera poetica*, ed F Leo (Monumenta Germaniae Historica, auctores antiquissimi 4.1 1881), 9.1.

[54] J Hines, 'The becoming of the English: identity, material culture and language in early Anglo-Saxon England', *Anglo-Saxon Studies in Archaeology and History* vii (1994); J Hines, 'Focus and boundary in linguistic varieties in the north-west Germanic continuum' in VF Faltings, AGH Walker and O Wilts (eds), *Friesische Studien* ii (1995).

[55] KH Jackson, *Language and history in early Britain* (1953), 119–21.

Depending on who was speaking, either British or Latin might be, in Gildas's words, 'our language'. The few indications suggest that the core strength of Latin lay not just in towns as opposed to countryside or aristocrats as opposed to peasants, but also, by the fourth century, in the civilian as opposed to the military elite.[56] As late as the early sixth century language was relatively unimportant as a mark of ethnicity. Britons thought of themselves as the original inhabitants of Britain: the land was their land; all others were outsiders and interlopers. This perception is still there to be reported by Bede in the eighth century – and indeed it endured into the later middle ages. On the other hand there was the potential for a much higher value to be placed upon language as a mark of British identity. If the civilian elite – the elite educated by grammarians and rhetoricians – were to lose ground to a more military ordering of society, the way would be open for a British identity which was linguistic. By Bede's time this had happened. Bede has both the notion of the Britons as the autochthonous population of Britain – the non-settlers as opposed to the settlers – and the notion of the Britons as the speakers of British.[57] In what became Brittany – significantly conceived as a new Britain for the Britons beyond the sea – this linguistic identity may have emerged earlier than in the home island.

Yet if Britishness was becoming more linguistic during a period of military struggle with the English, it is also true that by Bede's time many of the descendants of fourth-century Britons were now speaking English. Behind the development of both Britishness and Englishness lie two things: not just a sizeable migration across the North Sea and the consequent development of a settler norm in Britain, but also a linguistic assimilation of Britons into this new settler community. From the point of view of the assimilated, Hines's settler norm of Old English will have been a new Germanic *koin*. By this I mean that, just as the numerous local dialects of ancient Greece were irrelevant to Syrians, Persians and Egyptians learning Greek in the wake of Alexander's conquests, so too a Briton learning English attempted to learn the settler norm and not, let us say, the Jutland variety. On the settler side the apparent uniformity of Old English may be explained by the development of a colonial standard in which progressive features were valued; on the British side it may be explained on the grounds that any surviving Jutish or Saxon or Anglian features would be irrelevant. They learnt what we may term the distinctively British form of Germanic, what became English.[58]

The process by which assimilation occurred can only partially be reconstructed. Possibilities are, however, suggested by Bede and by Ine's West Saxon laws. The first is the role of the royal household in forming an elite. The second is the association between language and English ethnicity.

The royal household's importance lay in the way in which it recruited adolescent nobles, both from its own kingdom and from others, and gave them an opportunity to

---

56 M Lapidge, 'Gildas's education and the Latin culture of sub-Roman Britain' in M Lapidge and D Dumville (eds), *Gildas: new approaches* (1984), esp 48–50; the British settlement in Armorica, probably led in the fifth century by British armies such as that commanded by Riothamus, established British as the dominant language in all but the eastern part of Brittany. On Gildas see further 25–6 below.

57 Both are in Bede, *HE*, 1.1.

58 For reasons for suspecting an influence of Celtic, and even specifically British Celtic, on North Sea Germanic see P Schrijver, 'The Celtic contribution to the development of the North Sea Germanic vowel system, with special reference to coastal Dutch', *North-Western European Language Evolution* xxxv (1999). It remains to be determined how far this influence was *via* Old English.

distinguish themselves militarily and to live a life considered appropriate to a noble.[59] If an adolescent was successful at this stage he established a reputation which might be rewarded by gifts of treasure from a foreign king and by a gift of land by his native king. These gifts gave the young adult the wherewithal to set himself up as a local landed noble, even if his father was still alive. In Ine's West Saxon kingdom at the end of the seventh century there were both English and British nobles. If we then assume that such British nobles were recruited into the royal household, they would be subject to exactly the same norms of behaviour as their English counterparts. They would seek to speak the language of the king's hall just as their English contemporaries might seek to forget those Jutish or Anglian or Saxon vowels they had picked up from their grandfathers. At this level, then, the same royal and aristocratic community will have prescribed the norms for the settler and for the assimilated native. It is important that the royal household was in much the strongest position to impose standards of aristocratic behaviour upon impressionable youth (*geoguð*). It is also important that the young aristocrats were able to take service in other kingdoms and thus other royal households than their own.[60] The mobility of the young noble is a recurrent theme in the early medieval Germanic world: one only has to think of the story about Alboin, that his father would not dream of allowing his son to sit at his table, however heroic his deeds upon the battlefield, until he had been given arms by another king.[61] This mobility of aristocratic youth will have helped to underpin a relative linguistic homogeneity. Yet it can only be an accessory cause, since it certainly did not prevent the emergence of dialects in Old English by the early eighth century.

For those of lesser rank the association between status, language and ethnicity may still have been a powerful lever even without a period of service in the royal household. In Ine's laws, although they are West Saxon, ethnic distinctions are, as we have seen, denoted by the opposition between *Wilisc* and *Englisc*, that is to say, the distinction was between the (British) foreigner and the English, not between Welsh and Saxon. When a West Saxon was contrasting himself with a Briton, he called himself English. The contrast was also, however, one of status: a British noble had half the wergild of an English noble and similarly down the social hierarchy. Other things being equal, a man could always better himself by adopting English in preference to British nationality.

The striking success of the English in spreading their language and their nationality far beyond the limits marked by their early cemeteries suggests that language rather than descent or burial customs became the overriding criterion of national identity.[62] In the sixth century a brooch might mark one out as Saxon rather than Anglian,

---

[59] The crucial references are: Bede, *Historia abbatum*, ch 1, where Bede, speaking of Benedict Biscop, *minister Oswiu regis*, says that when aged about twenty-five he was due to receive a grant of land *suo gradui competentem*; Bede, *HE*, 3.14, on Oswine's ability to attract young nobles from almost all the English kingdoms; and Stephen, *Vita S Wilfridi*, ch 2. See TM Charles-Edwards, 'The distinction between land and movable wealth in Anglo-Saxon England' in PH Sawyer (ed), *Medieval settlement* (1976), 182–3.

[60] Bede, *HE* 3.14.

[61] Paul the Deacon, *Historia Langobardorum*, 1.23, ed. L Bethmann and G Waitz (Monumenta Germaniae Historica, scriptores Langobardicarum et Italicarum saec. VI–IX, 1878), 61.

[62] This may have some influence on the phenomenon discussed by Geake, *Grave-goods*, 120–4, of a revival of Roman, including Romano-British, styles of artefact as opposed to the more Germanic styles of the migration period; these revived styles would perhaps have been just as readily accepted whether someone's ancestors were from the other side of the North Sea or from Britain.

but language marked one out as English rather than British. If persons of British descent had not been able to transfer themselves into an emerging English identity by changing language, English could never have become the dominant language of Britain.

The Britons

The Britons were for two reasons different from the start. First, unlike Franks, English and, later, Scots, they were not a conquering people except in Brittany. On the contrary they were very conscious of territorial contraction. Second, they began as direct heirs of the Roman empire, not as intruders into it, as were the Franks, nor yet living beyond its borders, as did the Irish both of Ireland and of Scotland. In this the Welsh resembled the *Romani* of Aquitaine more than they resembled the Franks or the Irish.

The first consequence of the Roman inheritance was the importance – already touched on – of the territory and the community inhabiting that territory. In the sixth century the Britons of Wales sometimes preserved the Roman sense of the *civitas*, the community of the *cives*, the fellow citizens. The preservation of the values is especially striking when the Latin is as bad (and as living) as it is in an inscription of the sixth century at Penmachno in Gwynedd:[63]

>   CANTIORI HIC IACIT VENEDOTIS CIVE FUIT
>   CONSOBRINO MAGLI MAGISTRATI

Another inscription, from Llantrisant in Anglesey and belonging to the same period, distinguishes *parentes* (kinsmen) and *cives* (fellow citizens). A man from another territory might distinguish himself as belonging to that other territory, as an inscription of the fifth or early sixth century in Carmarthenshire characterizes a man as *elmetiaco*, from Elmet in Yorkshire or from Elfed, also in Carmarthenshire.[64] These inscriptions, however, attest loyalties at a more local level than that of the nation. They raise, therefore, a problem. It is often said by scholars who feel like trumpeting a few absolute truths for a change that in the middle ages men were clearly conscious only of local associations, village, *pagus* or kindred. Only sublime and literate persons, a distrusted breed, made much of kingdom, nation or empire, *regnum*, *gens* or *imperium*. More specifically, and more plausibly, it has been argued that even men such as Gregory of Tours felt a strong attachment to *civitas* but an uncertain sense of *Romania* as a whole – that a consequence of the collapse of imperial authority in the west was a retreat into the *civitas*.[65] If one applies such a notion to the Britons one might expect that even sublime and literate persons would think far more often of Dyfed or Gwynedd than of the Britons. After all, it might be said, when the word *Cymry* emerges in the tenth century applied by the Britons of Wales to themselves and those of Cumbria to themselves, it asserts the primacy of the local district, *bro*. The Cymry are those who share the same *bro* (*Com-brog-*).[66] The unity of Wales, so one might

---

63 VE Nash-Williams, *Early Christian monuments of Wales* (1950), no 103. Note the characteristic features of spoken late Latin: confusion between *i* and *e* (IACIT, CIVE), confusion between *o* and *u* (CONSOBRINO), loss of final -*s* (CIVE).

64 Ibid nos 53 (Llantrisant), 87 (Carmarthenshire).

65 Ewig, 'Volksstum und Volksbewusstsein', 231–2. The same could not be said of his friend Venantius Fortunatus, but then he was an Italian by birth.

66 For a critique of this position see TM Charles-Edwards, 'Language and society among the insular Celts, 400–1000' in MJ Green (ed), *The Celtic world* (1995).

argue, has never been more than a fragile construction out of the powerful loyalties of the *bro*.

No doubt there is some truth in this argument, but it is nevertheless easy to show that the analogy with the Gaul of Gregory of Tours is misleading. For this we have the evidence of a man whose life may have overlapped that of Gregory: Gildas. Though difficulties have been raised, Gildas's *floruit* may be placed in the first half of the sixth century.[67] In relation to Gaul he lies between Sidonius Apollinaris (bishop of Clermont in the 470s) and Gregory of Tours. Yet his outlook on the relationship of his people to the Romans is different from those of both Sidonius and Gregory. Gregory, it will be remembered, used *gens* only of barbarian peoples, never of the Romans. Nor did he have a conception of a *gens Gallorum* as against the *gens Francorum*. For him the non-barbarian inhabitants of Gaul are just *Romani*, though it must also be said that he rarely talks of Romans, whereas he is always using such *civitas*-based terms as *Arverni* and *Turonenses*.[68] To all this Gildas is a complete contrast. For him the *Romani* are a *gens*, just like the *Britanni*; the Romans are ruled by *reges*; their state is not a *res publica* as in Gregory, but simply a *regnum*. The *Britanni* are, because they are *Britanni*, not Romans.[69] Though he contrasts *cives* and *barbari*, and *cives* can include Roman citizens outside Britain, it more often refers to the Britons.[70] If Gregory of Tours appears to have no sense at all of Gallic nationality, Gildas has a powerful sense of British nationality. Moreover both Gregory of Tours and his contemporary Venantius Fortunatus were quite clear that the Britons (no one distinguished Bretons from Britons at this period) were a different people from the Romans.[71] Gildas had some sense that the Britons were part of a wider community, fellow citizens, *cives*, of a fading Roman empire.[72] Other early British sources, from both sides of the Channel, make it clear that Britons were to be contrasted with the barbarians.[73] Gregory of Tours and Venantius Fortunatus, however, excluded them:

---

[67] C Stancliffe, 'The thirteen sermons attributed to Columbanus and the question of their authorship' in M Lapidge (ed), *Columbanus: studies on the Latin writings* (1997), 177–81, 185. DN Dumville, 'Gildas and Maelgwn: problems of dating' and 'The chronology of *De excidio Britanniae*, book I' in Lapidge and Dumville, *Gildas*.

[68] For examples of *Romani* see Gregory of Tours, *Hist*, 3.18, 33. For his lack of sympathy for Justinian's conquest of southern Spain, even though the Visigoths had, at that date, not yet abandoned Arianism, ibid 4.8 (Justinian's soldiers *male pervaserant* various *civitates*).

[69] Gildas, *De excidio Britanniae*, ed and trans M Winterbottom as *Gildas: the ruin of Britain* (1978), ch 25 (*Romani* and *Britanni*), ch 5 (*reges*), ch 6 (*regnum*), ch 17 (Britons seek help from the Romans). Cf Gregory of Tours, *Hist*, 5.19, 6.30, 10.2 (*res publica*).

[70] For *cives* not being confined to Britons see Gildas, *De excidio*, chs 4.1, 4; for *cives* referring only to Britons, ibid 10.2, 15.2, 3, 19.2, 3, 4, 20.3, 25.2, 26.1, 4 (the last is especially clear).

[71] Gregory of Tours, *Hist*, 3.18; *Fortunati opera poetica*, ed Leo, 3.5 (praising Felix, bishop of Nantes).

[72] Another inscription at Penmachno (Nash-Williams, no 104) may indicate that Gildas was not unique in feeling such links:] FILI AVITORI // IN TE(M)PO[RE] / IVSTI[NI] CON[SVLI]. This was found near the Eagles Hotel and was then moved to the church. Justinus was consul in AD 540. His name was used in the district of Lyons in Burgundy until the seventh century for dating purposes. The name of Basilius, consul in 541, was used in Vienne and its district for the same purpose. For a detailed discussion of the problems arising from this fragmentary inscription see JK Knight, 'Penmachno revisited: the consular inscription and its context', *Cambrian Medieval Celtic Studies* xxix (summer 1995).

[73] See the early Breton *Excerpta de libris Romanorum et Francorum*, ed and trans L Bieler as *Canones wallici* in his *Irish penitentials* (1963). According to the A version, ch 61 (pp 148/9): 'If any Catholic lets his hair grow in the fashion of the barbarians, he shall be held an alien from the church of God and from the table of every Christian until he makes amends for his offence'. Cf the synod of the grove of victory, ch 4, *Irish penitentials*, 68–9: 'They who afford guidance to the barbarians, thirteen years, provided there be no slaughter of Christians or effusion of blood or dire captivity.'

Venantius Fortunatus explicitly described the Britons as a barbarian people, while the way Gregory and the earlier council of Tours wrote about them implicitly carried the same message.[74] Finally Gildas strongly identified the people, *Britanni*, with the island, *Britannia*. The existence of the Picts, a separate *gens*, within *Britannia*, and the incursions of Irish and Saxons had not disturbed this identification at all. For Gildas the Picts, just as much as Irish and Saxons, were recent intruders into Britain.[75] To the people, *Britanni*, there corresponded a territory, *Britannia*; and *Britannia* was the inheritance of the Britons. This was what enabled Gildas to make so pervasive a use of an analogy between the Britons and *Britannia* on the one hand and the people and land of Israel on the other.

On one important issue Britain remained quite different from Gaul. One of Gildas's concessions to the unity of the old *populus romanus* is the assumption that Latin is *nostra lingua*.[76] Of course this does not mean of necessity that the Britons generally spoke Latin; it may mean only that Latin was used by many of them and was not used by the Saxons. The use of Latin thus distinguished the people of the Britons from that of the Saxons. Yet whatever the situation in Roman Britain, the Britons in the post-Roman period were gradually coming to use only British as a normal spoken language; the decline of Latin as a native spoken language may have been complete by the end of the seventh century.[77] This was quite different from Gaul. There Celtic may have survived up to the end of the empire in a few pockets, but there would have been no temptation for a Gregory of Tours to rest a sense of Gallic nationalism upon Gaulish.[78] Moreover in the seventh century, as we have seen, some Franks were coming to speak Romance, while Romans in the north were voting with their personal names for Frankishness. In post-Roman Gaul the significance of language for nationality was low; in post-Roman Britain it was very high. Not only had Celtic survived, but the Saxon invaders conspicuously failed to speak British. It looks as though language may have been important for them as a mark of status and nationality – to separate them from the *Wealas*. It is no surprise, therefore, that already in early vernacular Welsh poetry the word *iaith* (language) may be used to signify nation.[79] This nation remained that of the Britons rather than of the Welsh in the modern sense. Early Welsh literary tradition moves with ease from Cornwall up to Stirling; Welsh

---

[74] *Fortunati opera poetica*, ed Leo, appx 2 (to Justin II, 565–78, and the empress Sophia):
        Currit ad extremas fidei pia fabula gentes,
        Et trans Oceanum terra Britannica fauet . . .
        Illinc Romanus, hinc laudes barbarus ipse,
        Germanus, Batauus, Vasco, Britannus agit.
   (The happy tale of the faith runs to the furthest nations; and across the ocean, the British land approves . . . On one side the Roman offers praises, on the other even the barbarian – German, Batavian, Basque, Briton.) Cf council of Tours, AD 567, ch 9, *Concilia Galliae, a. 511 – a. 695*, ed C de Clercq (1963): *Adicimus etiam, ne quis Brittanum aut Romanum in Armorico sine metropolis aut comprouincialium uoluntate uel literis episcopum ordinare praesumat* (We also add that no-one should be so bold as to ordain a Briton or a Roman in Armoricum without the consent of the metropolitan or of the bishops of the same province or letters of authorization).

[75] N Wright, 'Gildas's geographical perspective: some problems' in Lapidge and Dumville, *Gildas*.

[76] Gildas, *De excidio*, ch 23.3.

[77] Jackson, *Language and history*, 123–4.

[78] PY Lambert, *La langue gauloise* (1995), 10–11.

[79] On the use of *iaith* see *Poems of Taliesin*, ed Williams, 9.15n; see too 13 above. On the change from Britons to Welsh see H Pryce, 'British or Welsh? national identity in twelfth-century Wales', *English Historical Review*, cxvi (2001).

hagiography demonstrates the continuance of links with Brittany. Their native saints were Britons, not merely Welsh, just as the saints of the English were much the same whether one was in Northumbria or in Wessex.[80]

A sense of deprivation is sometimes a powerful spur to national feeling. In the early middle ages British nationality was coming to be expressed in the language of deprivation. The theme is 'we was robbed'. In the best attested version this is put in a legal dress. The Britons have not just been deprived of their lands by the English: they have been unjustly, even fraudulently, deprived of their lands. The Britons have a legal claim which, even if it cannot be put before a human tribunal, can bring about the support of saints and their relics; and Celtic saints being what they were, this augured ill for the Saxons.

Though we should not think that a British cowherd in the tenth century spent a fair proportion of his waking hours thinking what an ass Vortigern was, there is enough of a consistency of view about the events of the fifth century and their implications for the Britons to imply a wide currency for the ideas I am going to describe. For this description I shall take as my centrepiece the tenth-century poem *Armes Prydein*, 'The prophecy of Britain'. This is indeed a prophecy, but it is also openly concerned with things present and past, with the tax-gatherers of the English over-king and the trickery of Hengest and Horsa. My interest in the text is in its view of the past and how an argument based upon the past is used to justify attitudes in the present.[81]

In Gildas, as we have seen, the island *Britannia* and the people *Britanni* are so closely linked that *Britannia* is regularly used for the people. A similar attitude stands behind *Armes Prydein*. Even though we are now in the tenth century, and there is no denying the power of the English king (who may be Æthelstan or his brother Edmund), power which he can make effective in Wales as well as in England, the English are still perceived as intruders upon the soil of Britain. The Cymry still include the other Britons, of Strathclyde and Cornwall.[82] And they are still the rightful owners of the land of Britain. The poet seems to envisage the ancient kings, Cadwaladr of Gwynedd and Cynan of Brittany, returning not just as warriors but as prosecutors and judges to convict the Saxons of land-grabbing:

> They will ask the Saxons, What had they been seeking?
> What is the extent of their right in the land they hold?
> Where are their acres, from whence did they set out?
> Where are their kindreds? From what land have they come?

The Saxons stand dumbfounded and tongue-tied at this judicial inquiry. They make no reply, and the poet therefore concludes:

> Since the time of Vortigern they have trampled upon us.
> By justice the shareland of our kinsmen will not be won.

---

[80] As observed by P Wormald, '*Engla lond*: the making of an allegiance', *Journal of Historical Sociology* vii (1994), repr in his *Legal culture*.

[81] *Armes Prydein*, ed I Williams, English trans by R Bromwich (1972). This has been dated to *c*930 by Williams, to *c*940 by DN Dumville, 'Brittany and *Armes Prydein vawr*', *Études Celtiques* xx (1983) and to 940 by A Breeze, '*Armes Prydein*, Hywel Dda, and the reign of Edmund of Wessex', ibid xxxiii (1997). It derives much of its understanding of history from the *Historia Brittonum* in the first place, and ultimately from the English origin myth probably composed in Kent *c*600, but this matter is put to a quite new use. Cf Brooks, 'English origin myth'.

[82] Charles-Edwards, 'Language and society', 712.

But, just in case there is any possibility of a counter-argument, the poet adds a further accusation and a judgement:

> Why have they trampled upon the status of our saints?
> Why have they broken down the rights of St David?
> When they come face to face, the Cymry will ensure
> That the foreigners shall not go from the place where they stand
> Until they repay sevenfold the value of what they have done,
> And certain death in return for their wrong.

All this is only the more generalized conclusion of an argument which begins by stating that it is the Britons whose possession is by right of descent, and that Hengest and Horsa bought Thanet by cunning from Vortigern. The implication seems to be that Thanet was purchased in return for faithful service against the Picts and the Irish, but the Saxons treacherously rebelled. The conditions of the sale were thus unfulfilled and the Saxon occupation thereby became illegal. 'Their acquisition was at our expense and not by descent.'[83]

In *Armes Prydein* the analogy between a dispute over land and the struggle for the mastery of the island of Britain is explicit. This was natural, given the close identification of the *Britanni* with *Britannia*. It was also useful to dress up the British case in the worthiest of legal robes, in order to rebut the obvious reply, used both by Bede and Wulfstan, that God had judged the Britons and found them wanting.[84] From his judgement seat there was no appeal.

The British sense of nationality in the early middle ages is unusually closely linked to language and to territory. The sense that Britain was the land of the Britons is enough to explain why Gildas saw the Picts as late intruders. To a certain extent he was correct: the Picts appear to have been a federation of smaller peoples created by conditions on the Roman *limes* (as were the Franks and the Alamans). In the first century BC there would probably have been no more significant a boundary between the Votadini (later the British Gododdin) and the Verturiones (later the Pictish sub-kingdom of Fortriu) than there was between the Votadini and their neighbours to the south, the Brigantes. While, therefore, there was sometimes continuity at the more local level (of Verturiones and Votadini), the larger-scale identities (Britons and Picts) were shaped by Rome. The Caledonii and Verturiones may well have been Britons in AD 43, but they were Picts by the fourth century.[85] Once they were Picts, but not before, the Pictish language diverged from the British: in this instance linguistic diversity was a consequence not a cause of national distinctiveness. Bede's situation, in which Britons and Picts were distinguishable by language, was a fairly recent development.[86]

---

83 *Armes Prydein*, lines 133–44; ibid line 33 (my translation). For suggestions as to the legal background of the argument presented in *Armes Prydein* see TM Charles-Edwards, *Early Irish and Welsh kinship* (1993), 296–7.

84 Bede, *HE*, 1.22; Wulfstan, *Sermo lupi ad Anglos*, ed D Whitelock (3rd edn 1963), lines 184–99.

85 Tacitus, *Agricola*, chs 29, 34–8; A Ritchie, *Perceptions of the Picts: from Eumenius to John Buchan* (1994).

86 KH Jackson, 'The Pictish language', appx 1, in F Wainwright (ed), *The problem of the Picts* (1955), 161–6. The distinct characteristics of Pictish are all consequences of phonological change in the late Roman and post-Roman periods; Jackson's appendix does not, therefore, bear out his suggestion (as summarized ibid. 152) that Pictish was a separate branch of Celtic introduced into the island before British. K Forsyth, *Language in Pictland: the case against non-Indo-European Pictish* (1997) argues

The national identity of the Britons was thus reshaped in opposition to newly formed nations within Britain: first the Picts and then the English. On the other side the creation of Old English is a matter of the greatest historical importance, since it was part and parcel of the creation of an English national identity. That was partly the emergence of Hines's settler norm, distinguishing the Germanic speakers of Britain from those on the continent, and partly the long process of assimilating Britons. The different attitudes to British and Latin loanwords suggest that this settler identity was established in contradistinction to the military elite of the native British kingdoms, namely to the core political strength of British as opposed to Latin speech. On the British side of the language divide a national identity centred on language as well as on territory emerged from the long military struggle against the English. If an English identity was created in the fifth and sixth centuries, the opposing British identity was transformed; and both changes occurred not just at the same time but as elements in one historical process. A British identity is older than its English counterpart, but it was the English who gave the Britons their abiding association of language, land and nation.

The Irish

Pre-Viking Ireland, so we are led to understand by most of the evidence, was ethnically homogeneous. While Britain might harbour, by the seventh century, four great languages, including Irish, Ireland had only one. Moreover it had a vernacular law that was explicitly associated with national identity, while the island's notable places were the subject of a single, slowly developing, narrative tradition (*dindshenchas*). Early Irish culture seems all-embracing, and, on its own territory, unchallengeable. Yet this cultural unity may not have been, as it was perhaps intended to appear, an organic and ancient tradition but rather a deliberate creation – not so much an inescapable bequest from remote antiquity as a political order created by a mixture of violence and cultural reinterpretation in the fairly recent past.[87]

From 637 until 1002 Ireland was dominated by a confederation of dynasties led by the Uí Néill. During this period of almost four centuries the Uí Néill monopolized the title of king of Tara, while their allies, the Éoganachta of Munster and the Connachta west of the Shannon, admitted the superiority of the king of Tara and largely preserved peace on their common borders.[88] Outside the bounds of this confederation of kingdoms, however, lay two entire provinces, those of Leinster and Ulster. Both had to endure the aggression of the Uí Néill and both remembered the days when their leaders too had entered Tara as kings. For them the Uí Néill were, in words put into the mouth of St Brigit, an 'offspring that sheds blood and will be an accursed stock and will hold sway for many years'.[89] The most urgent question about the early Irish sense

---

that the only language of the Picts was Brittonic, but she uses a label of Pritenic for the language of northern Britain (north, that is, of the Forth) before the major linguistic changes of the late Roman and post-Roman period. In my opinion this is unhelpful.

[87] The most important discussion is by D Ó Corráin, 'Nationality and kingship in pre-Norman Ireland' in TW Moody (ed), *Nationality and the pursuit of national independence* (1978).

[88] E Bhreathnach, 'Temoria: caput Scottorum?', *Ériu* xlvii (1996); TM Charles-Edwards, 'Irish warfare before 1100' in T Bartlett and K Jeffery (eds), *A military history of Ireland* (1996); TM Charles-Edwards, *Early Christian Ireland* (2000), 469–521, 569–85.

[89] *Vita prima S Brigitae* in *Triadis thaumaturgae . . . acta*, ed J Colgan (1647); also in *Acta sanctorum*, 1 February; and trans S Connolly in *Journal of the Royal Society of Antiquaries of Ireland* cxix (1989),

of nationality is therefore this: was that sense of nationality created or merely usurped by the Uí Néill and their allies?

Three central pillars of Irish nationality in the seventh and eighth centuries were language, law and the cults of the native saints. All three could be, and were, exported to Irish settlements in Britain.[90] The first clue to an answer to our question is, however, a simpler matter: the name *Féni*, and in particular the ambiguity of its meaning. Just as *Angli* might mean either Angles or English, so also the *Féni* were either those within the alliance led by the Uí Néill or else the Irish as a whole. In the narrower sense *Féni* excluded the provinces of Leinster and Ulster. The Leinstermen and Ulstermen, Laigin and Ulaid, were 'noble races' (*cenéla*, kindreds, here used for peoples perceived as communities recruited by descent) and as such might be placed alongside the *Féni*.[91] Yet in power both the Laigin and the Ulaid were subordinate to the Uí Néill – unwilling, even rebellious, distinguishable from but accepted as appendant to Leth Cuinn (Conn's half), that part of Ireland subject to the Uí Néill and the Connachta.[92] Neither the Laigin nor the Ulaid denied the pre-eminence of the king of Tara, since it was their boast that in the past their kings too had ruled in Tara.[93]

The duality of meaning possessed by the name *Féni* is seen in conceptions of the native law (native as contrasted with the law of the church). On the one hand it was the law of 'the men of Ireland', but on the other, although *Fénechas* usually seems to mean 'Irish law', it could also be used to exclude the Ulaid.[94] Yet even then it is made clear that the Ulaid have the same law as the *Féni*. When differences are mentioned, notably over the legal status of women, the view associated with the Ulstermen is shown to be erroneous, and no longer held even by them.[95] The Ulstermen, therefore, might have had their own distinctive rules in the past, but by the seventh century one law was common to the entire island. The pan-Irish status of Irish law was reinforced by the invocation of St Patrick's authority to confirm the validity of a single native law in a Christian Ireland.[96]

Rather different ambiguities emerge from the origin legends of the Irish.[97] What became the standard account, conveniently termed the Milesian legend, according to which the Irish were descended from Míl Espáine (Míl of Spain), was under active development from the late seventh century. The Milesian legend was a learned creation for a wider political purpose. The reality of its political tendency is revealed

---

§62. For a similar judgement in a Munster text see K Meyer, 'The Laud genealogies and tribal histories', *Zeitschrift für Celtische Philologie* viii (1910–12), 313, lines 19–23.

90 Scottish Gaelic is a daughter-language of Old Irish; for the law see WDH Sellar, 'Celtic law and Scots law: survival and integration', *Scottish Studies* xxix (1989); for saints see WJ Watson, *The history of the Celtic place-names of Scotland* (1926), ch 10.

91 'The saga of Fergus mac Léti', ed and trans DA Binchy, *Ériu* xvi (1952), 37, §1.

92 Compare *The annals of Ulster (to AD 1131)*, ed S Mac Airt and G Mac Niocaill (1983), 859.3 (the alienation of Osraige to Leth Cuinn) with 851.5 (Ulster in the narrower bounds, east of the River Bann, is distinguished from Leth Cuinn).

93 *Bechbretha*, ed TM Charles-Edwards and F Kelly (1983), §32; *Corpus genealogiarum Hiberniae* i, ed MA O'Brien (1962), 8–9.

94 *Bechbretha*, ed Charles-Edwards and Kelly, §33 and note on pp 133–4.

95 In the legal tract *Din techtugud* the Ulster judge Senchae is corrected by the female judge of the *Féni*, Bríg: *Corpus iuris hibernici*, ed DA Binchy (1978), 209.

96 J Carey, 'An edition of the pseudo-historical prologue to the *Senchas már*', *Ériu* xlv (1994), §8; *Corpus iuris hibernici*, ed Binchy, 240.21–4, 529.1–5.

97 For a clear and authoritative outline see J Carey, *The Irish national origin-legend: synthetic pseudohistory* (1994).

by successive adaptations made to fit new circumstances. For this tradition, then, the unity of the Irish was a matter of descent: the story offered a single dynastic stock onto which the ruling lineages of numerous kingdoms could be grafted. The entire conception – both legend and genealogies – fitted a society in which descent was a pervasive principle of social order. Yet the earliest version of the legend was probably designed primarily for the *Féni* in the narrow sense. It expressed the inner shape of the alliance led by the Uí Néill, formed by a closer link with the Connachta west of the Shannon and a looser one with the Éoganachta of Munster. The scheme was, in essence, as follows:

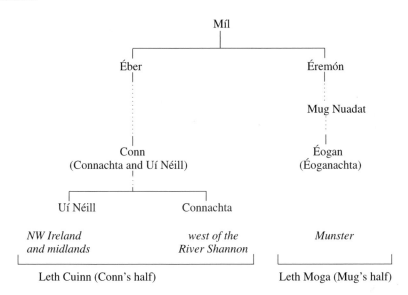

Whether any reality lay behind this scheme other than the alliance of the seventh and eighth centuries is uncertain. What the scheme meant during the hegemony of the Uí Néill is, however, best shown by one of the loose ends that remained. The division between Éber and Éremón, both sons of Míl Espáine, was intended to validate a division of Ireland between Leth Cuinn (Conn's half) in the north and Leth Moga (Mug's half), namely the south. From a Munster point of view this division should have been along a line approximately from Dublin to Galway, but that was not the prevailing reality.[98] Leinster, the south-eastern province, was normally subject to the Uí Néill rather than to the Éoganachta of Munster. In the genealogies, therefore, their ancestors were said to be descended from Éber, the legendary ancestor of the Uí Néill and the Connachta. Crucially, this assertion was accepted in Leinster: their version of the origin legends interpreted the genealogical link to their own advantage rather than denying it outright.[99] When Osraige, earlier part of Munster but adjacent to Leinster, was formally alienated by the king of Munster to Leth Cuinn in 859 the royal genealo-

---

[98] *Corpus genealogiarum*, ed O'Brien, 206.
[99] *Orgain Denna Ríg* in *Fingal Ronáin and other stories*, ed D Greene (1955); for a summary and partial translation see M Dillon, *The cycles of the kings* (1946), 4–7.

gies followed suit, linking Osraige to the Leinstermen and so to Leth Cuinn.[100] On the other hand, one of the principal boasts of a later king of Munster, Brian Boru, when he successfully dismantled the hegemony of the Uí Néill, was that the boundary between Leth Cuinn and Leth Moga was redrawn where, in the Munster view, it should always have been: along the line between Dublin and Galway.[101] Leinster became, for a short period, a dependency of Munster, within Leth Moga; and Brian Boru would die in the battle of Clontarf in the struggle to maintain Munster power over Leinster and Dublin.

The genealogical image of the unity of Ireland under the hegemony of the Uí Néill existed alongside another conception – in literal terms incompatible yet serving the same ultimate end. According to *Auraicept na n-éces* ('The primer of the poets'), originally composed about 700 but progressively elaborated over several centuries, the unity of the Irish was not one of race or descent but of language.[102] It derived not from the pedigrees of kings but from the schools of poets and grammarians. Irish had been invented a few years after the original language of mankind had been destroyed by God in punishment for man's pride in building the tower of Babel. Irish was not, unlike all other languages, one of the children of pride; instead it was put together in the school of the grammarian called Fénius (*Féni* with the Latinate ending *–us*) out of the best elements of several languages. In a world divided between mutually incomprehensible languages it was the closest possible approximation to that primitive language that Adam and Eve had brought from paradise, where they had spoken with God. The kernel of the Irish people was thus formed by the pupils in Fénius's school; and they came from several nations, a mongrel people speaking a mongrel – and therefore superior – language.

The significance of this story perhaps turns on the nature of Old Irish, a standard literary language and the sole attested form of Irish from about 600 to the tenth century. Old Irish, therefore, was contemporaneous with the hegemony of the Uí Néill. Although the dominance of this literary standard was so complete that we have hardly any evidence of regional dialects, most scholars think that such dialects existed.[103] For most speakers and writers of Old Irish, those whose native dialect was not the standard, it was a form of the language that they had to learn. The notion that Irish came from a grammarian's school in Egypt was not so strange when, for many, it may indeed have been mastered in a school. Unlike its late medieval counterpart, Classical Modern Irish, Old Irish did not encompass regional variety; it is thus a reasonable inference that it began life as a regional dialect and that its elevation to the status of a national language was associated with the hegemony of the Uí Néill.[104]

The two conceptions of Irish unity – either royal and dynastic or linguistic – are on the face of things incompatible, one asserting the claims of descent, the other refuting them, almost as if to illustrate that proverb of the early Irish lawyers, *ferr fer a chiniud*

---

100 *Corpus genealogiarum*, ed O'Brien, 16, 101.
101 *The annals of Inisfallen*, ed S Mac Airt (1951), 997.2.
102 A Ahlqvist, *The early Irish linguist: an edition of the canonical part of the Auraicept na n-éces* (1982).
103 A Ahlqvist, 'Remarks on the question of dialects in Old Irish' in J Fisiak (ed), *Historical dialectology, regional and social* (1988); P Kelly, 'Dialekte im Altirischen?' in W Meid, H Ölberg and H Schmeja (eds), *Sprachwissenschaft in Innsbruck* (1982).
104 Cf the origins of standard late Old English: H Gneuss, 'The origin of standard Old English and Æthelwold's school at Winchester', *Anglo-Saxon England* i (1972).

(a man is better than his descent).[105] Moreover the Milesian legend was initially concerned as much with Ireland as with the Irish, with Leth Cuinn and Leth Moga and thus with the territorial shape of a political hegemony. This hegemony was confined to the island of Ireland; it was linked with the kingship of Tara, in aspiration always and in fact sometimes a kingship of Ireland.[106] Similarly Armagh claimed a primacy over Ireland, not over the Irish outside Ireland.[107] Yet the Milesian legend came to embrace the Irish as a whole: even the ruling families of the Irish in Scotland were attached to the line of descent from Míl Espáine.[108] Even interpreted literally this opposition is not quite so harsh as it may seem: the legal validity of adoption meant that descent was not necessarily biological. And the two stories spoke to different audiences: there was both a vision of the unity of Ireland that made kings and their dynasties central and another that gave that position to poets, scholars and grammarians. One justified the current political elite – the Uí Néill, their allies and principal clients – and the other asserted that all the Irish, of whatever descent, outside as well as inside Ireland, could participate in a language in which, and a culture by which, the power of the Uí Néill was confirmed and celebrated. The secret of this hegemony was thus its openness and flexibility. True, the *Féni* might be contrasted with the Ulaid and the Laigin, yet to *Fénechas*, the law of the *Féni*, and to their language, invented by Fénius, all might subscribe.

The Scots

Irish national identity was not attached to Ireland in the way British national identity was attached to Britain. As the creation of Brittany shows, even the strong territorial component in the identity of the Britons was compatible with its extension outside the homeland, but there were no such difficulties in the way of the Irish.[109] Whether language was taken as the primary defining characteristic of Irish identity, as in *Auraicept na n-éces*, or descent, as in the Milesian origin legend, Irishness was only loosely connected with Ireland. The most enduring expansion of Irish settlement was into north-western Britain; it was the basis from which a new nation, that of the Scots, was eventually formed. The construction of a separate Scottish identity was, however, a long and complex process, not completed until the later middle ages.[110] I shall only

---

105   *Corpus iuris hibernici*, ed Binchy, 2263.28.
106   *Annals of Ulster*, 642.1, 703.2, 862.5.
107   *The Patrician texts in the book of Armagh*, ed and trans L Bieler (1979), 138–9 (Tírechán, *Collectanea*, §18), 188–9 (*Liber angeli*, §21). Thus *Hibernenses* may in this context mean 'inhabitants of Ireland' rather than 'Irish': ibid §28. For the connection between the kingship of Tara (Ireland) and Armagh see for example *Annals of Ulster*, 859.3. The interests of Armagh thus tended to advance the geographical notion of Ireland, whereas those of Iona tended to advance the national and linguistic notion of the Irish; once Cenél nÉogain, allied with Armagh, had dislodged Cenél Conaill, allied with Iona, from primacy in the north, it was more likely that the Irish settled in Britain would be distanced from those of Ireland. For a different account see M Herbert, 'Rí Éirenn, rí Alban: kingship and identity in the ninth and tenth centuries' in S Taylor (ed), *Kings, clerics and chronicles in Scotland, 500–1297* (2000).
108   *Corpus genealogiarum*, ed O'Brien, 329.
109   Brittany was a *Britannia* beyond the sea, already so called in Gregory of Tours, *Hist*, 5.26; in *Hist*, 5.16 the first instance is clearly Brittany, while the second may refer to Britain.
110   As demonstrated in great detail by D Broun, *The Irish identity of the kingdom of the Scots* (1999). See also TO Clancy, 'Scottish saints and national identities in the early middle ages' in A Thacker and R Sharpe (eds), *Local saints and local churches in the early medieval west* (2002), which is best read alongside Watson, *Celtic place-names of Scotland*, ch 10.

be concerned with the earlier stages, those that ensured that the Irish (*Scotti, Goídil*) of Scotland had a partially distinct identity from the Irish of Ireland.

After the Irish settlement in Argyll, traditionally dated to the post-Roman period, and even more so after the foundation of Iona in 563, the Picts came under strong Irish influence, through the church and through Irish aristocratic settlement within Pictland.[111] The latter may be compared, in a broad way, to the settlement of families of Norman or Breton background (speakers of French) in twelfth-century Scotland. In the mid-ninth century, however, the relationship between the Irish and Picts changed fundamentally with the enduring establishment by Kenneth mac Alpin (Cináed mac Alpín) of an Irish dynasty as kings of the Picts.[112] Yet, though the dynasty derived from Dál Riata (Argyll and north-eastern county Antrim), the kings continued to be 'of the Picts' until the reign of Kenneth's grandson, Domnall mac Caustantín (889–900) or his less well attested predecessor Eochaid son of Rhun (878–89). Thereafter, the title changed to king of Albu (later Alba).[113]

What this change meant at the time must be distinguished from the complex shifts in the meaning of Alba in subsequent centuries. The significance of the new regnal style is best shown by contemporary late ninth-century annalistic entries, namely entries for the generation immediately before the annals of Ulster first attest the style 'king of Alba' in 900. In 870 the same annals record the successful siege of Dumbarton (Ail Chluaithe) by the Northmen, led by their kings Amlaíb and Ímar (Óláfr and Ívarr). Dumbarton was the capital fortress of the Britons of western Scotland. In 871 the annals of Ulster include an entry on the return of Amlaíb and Ímar 'to Dublin from Alba with two hundred ships; and a huge booty of men, English and Britons and Picts, was brought away to Ireland in captivity'. Here the vernacular *Alba* and the Latin *Hibernia* are opposed, very much as in 873 the annals of Ulster term Ímar 'king of the Northmen of all Ireland and Britain' (*Hibernia* and *Britannia*). One

---

111 For the latter see K Meyer, 'Conall Corc and the Corco Luigde' in OJ Bergin, RI Best, K Meyer and JG O'Keeffe (eds), *Anecdota from Irish manuscripts* (5 vols 1907–13) iii.59; 'Conall Corc and the Corco Luigde', trans V Hull, *Proceedings of the Modern Language Association of America* lxii (1947), 897 (Uí Charpri among the Picts). This text is dated to *c*700 and appears to have been composed at Cloyne: *Corpus genealogiarum*, ed O'Brien, 196 (148 a 31–2).

112 For different views see MO Anderson, 'Dalriada and the creation of the kingdom of the Scots' in D Whitelock, R McKitterick and D Dumville (eds), *Ireland in early mediaeval Europe: studies in memory of Kathleen Hughes* (1982); AP Smyth, *Warlords and holy men* (1984); BT Hudson, *Kings of Celtic Scotland* (1994), 34–6; P Wormald, 'The emergence of the *regnum Scottorum*: a Carolingian hegemony?' in BE Crawford (ed), *Scotland in dark-age Britain* (1996); D Broun, 'Pictish kings 761–839: integration with Dál Riata or separate development?' in SM Foster (ed), *The St Andrews sarcophagus: a Pictish masterpiece and its international connections* (1998), 71–83.

113 *Rex Pictorum* in *Annals of Ulster*, 858.2, 862.1, 876.1, 878.2, but *rí Alban* ibid 900.6. Similarly *regio Pictorum* ibid 865.2, *Picti* 875.3, *Cruithentúath* (the Irish vernacular term for the Pictish people) 866.1, but *fir Alban* 919.3. It is important that the change is marked almost (but not quite) simultaneously by the *Annals of Ulster* in 900 and by the early regnal chronicle of the Scottish kings generally called 'the Scottish chronicle': 'The Scottish chronicle', ed MO Anderson, *Kings and kingship in early Scotland* (1973, 2nd edn 1980), 251, line 6 versus line 10, and 'The Scottish chronicle', ed BT Hudson, *Scottish Historical Review* lxxii (1998), 149.11 versus 150.1. In other words *Albania* (*Albu*) here appears slightly later, in the reign of Caustantín mac Áeda (900–*c*940). For discussion see D Broun, 'The origins of Scottish identity' in C Bjørn, A Grant and KJ Stringer (eds), *Nations, nationalism and patriotism in the European past* (1994), which argues that it was a deliberate change of regnal style made shortly before 900 (the obit in the *Annals of Ulster*) and after the reference to Viking devastation of *Pictavia* apparently towards the beginning of his reign ('Scottish chronicle', ed Anderson, 251.6).

effect of the taking of Dumbarton seems to have been to bring the Britons closer to the Irish of Scotland: Eochaid son of Rhun, who according to the Scottish chronicle was king (probably 'of Picts') from 878 to 889, apparently belonged to the royal dynasty of the Britons.[114] When 'the men of Alba' fought Vikings from Waterford at the River Tyne, they faced opponents who had 'left Ireland' to attack 'the men of Alba'. The site of the battle and the scale of the events (Niall Glúndub, 'king of Ireland',[115] would fall in battle against the Vikings at Dublin the next year) suggest that Alba meant more than just the immediate kingdom of Caustantín mac Áeda, centred on Forteviot and Scone (close to modern Perth). The Irish of Alba were claimants to a hegemony in northern Britain, such as that held by the Pictish king Óengus mac Forgusa in the previous century.[116] The Scottish chronicle suggests that claims to such a hegemony were not just a consequence of the destruction of Dumbarton, but that they had been actively pursued by Kenneth mac Alpin himself.[117] A possible interpretation of the change of regnal style depends on perceiving two early phases of this striving for hegemony in northern Britain: for half a century after Kenneth mac Alpin took control of Pictland about 842 the prime aim of the dynasty, initially most securely entrenched in Fortriu, was to strengthen its grip on Pictland as a whole; but the highly unstable military conditions exemplified by the destruction of Dumbarton in 870 and the campaigns of the Viking great army in England may have impelled Domnall mac Caustantín to declare openly that henceforth he and his successors were to be regarded as kings of Alba, that is, of Britain. What he meant by that title was what Óengus mac Forgusa had probably claimed – that he, as king of northern Britain, would be the partner of an overlord of southern Britain. As Æthelbald of Mercia had been the partner of Óengus, so Domnall may have been, or hoped to be, the ally of Alfred.[118]

These ambitions were very imperfectly realized, and the very term Alba came to be restricted: to the Irish of northern Britain, and even to the heartland of the kingdom, between the Forth to the south, the River Spey to the north and the mountain watershed dividing Alba from Airer Gaídel, Argyll, 'the coastland of the Irish', to the west.[119] This contraction of Alba was also a contraction of its new Latin counterpart, no longer *Britannia* but *Scotia*. In the early middle ages 'Scot' meant simply 'Irish'. It came to be applied to the people we know as Scots because it was employed for the Irish in Britain. Bede distinguished (leaving aside Latin) four 'languages of nations'. All four were present within the geographical area that we know as Scotland – all of them with a presence in, or on the edge of, the central lowland belt. Of these four, one,

---

114 Assuming that he was the son of Rhun ap Arthial, whose pedigree is given in the so-called Harleian genealogies: *Early Welsh genealogical tracts*, ed PC Bartrum (1966), 10, §5. Eochaid is described in the Scottish chronicle as Kenneth mac Alpin's grandson through a daughter (presumably married to Rhun): 'Scottish chronicle', ed Anderson, 250, ed Hudson, 149; cf the prophecy of Berchán, stanzas 134–5 in BT Hudson, *Prophecy of Berchán: Irish and Scottish high-kings of the early middle ages* (1996), 44 (ed), 85 (trans). According to the *Annals of Ulster* Eochaid's grandfather Arthial (Artgal, 'king of the Britons of Strathclyde') was killed at the behest of Caustantín mac Cináeda in 872.
115 *Annals of Ulster*, 919.3.
116 Charles-Edwards, 'Continuation of Bede'.
117 'Scottish chronicle', ed Anderson, 250.3–4 and n127, ed Hudson, 148.
118 The partnership of Æthelbald and Óengus is implied by the continuation of Bede under the year 750: *Bede's ecclesiastical history*, ed and trans Colgrave and Mynors, 574.
119 For its application to the Irish of northern Britain see *Annals of Ulster*, 952.2; for the narrower use see Broun, 'Origins', 46–7.

Pictish, was almost certainly extinct by the twelfth century; another, the dialect of British often known as Cumbrian, was by then moribund. Whereas in Britain as a whole three of Bede's languages of nations – English, British and Gaelic, the descendant of Old Irish – have endured into the third millennium, Pictish may hardly have survived the first. From the fifth to the eighth century the English nation was the beneficiary, in terms of population, of the greatest ethnic assimilation of the day within Britain; from the ninth to the eleventh it was the Irish.

Yet at the same time the kingdom of the Scots, the kingdom of the Irish in Britain, did not always include all Irish-speakers in Britain. The minimal definition of Alba or Scotia excluded Argyll, whose very name (*Airer Gaídel*) proclaimed it as a territory of the *Gaídil*, the *Scotti*; it also excluded Moray, ruled by a dynasty which claimed a royal origin in pre-Viking Dál Riata as ancient as that which dignified the dynasty of Alba.[120] Even more decisively, it excluded Galloway, the land of the *Gallgaídil* (foreign Irish), part Scandinavian, yet speakers of Gaelic down to the early modern period.[121] In spite of these exclusions the rulers of Alba continued to think of their subjects as the Irish (of Britain). The chronicle of the Scots suggests a policy of active hibernicization: God deprived the Picts of their lands for their sins, just as he had punished that other victim-people, the Britons; Kenneth mac Alpin fostered the cult of St Columba, while in the reign of his successor and brother Domnall 'the *Goedeli*, with their king, enacted in the palace of Forteviot the laws of the kingdom of Áed mac Echdach' (Kenneth and Domnall's grandfather, king of Dál Riata).[122] Similarly Caustantín mac Áeda, 'together with the *Scotti*, vowed to preserve the laws and disciplines of the faith and also the rights of churches and gospels'.[123] It was important to assert a primacy among the Irish of Alba for two reasons: hegemony over the other Irish dynasties was a prerequisite for a wider hegemony over northern Britain; and the claim to be *the* Irish of Alba was also consistent with a policy of linguistic and cultural assimilation of the Picts. A kingdom and people that was self-consciously Irish might more easily accept the legitimacy of a dynasty whose pedigree went back to Dál Riata, to Ireland and to Míl Espáine.

From the twelfth century there was a further change of direction. The Pictish identity and language had been eliminated, through assimilation to the Irish of northern Britain. In the twelfth century, however, Scotland became not just a polyglot kingdom (with Picts and Irish it had been that in the tenth century) but one in which national

---

120 *Corpus genealogiarum*, ed O'Brien, 329–30; the genealogy, as given, is not credible; whether its deficiencies were due to failures of record in the ninth and tenth centuries, in the worst period of the Viking threat, or to a purely fictitious connection of an eleventh-century dynasty with the Cenél Loairn of the pre-Viking era, is unknown. Cf A Woolf, 'The "Moray question" and the kingship of Alba in the tenth and eleventh centuries', *Scottish Historical Review* lxxix (2000).

121 WL Lorimer, 'The persistence of Gaelic in Galloway and Carrick', *Scottish Gaelic Studies* vi–vii (1949–53); J MacQueen, 'The Gaelic speakers of Galloway and Carrick', *Scottish Studies* xvii (1973). The laws of Galloway were long distinct: HL MacQueen, 'The laws of Galloway: a preliminary survey' in RD Oram and GP Stell (eds), *Galloway: land and lordship* (1991); HL MacQueen 'The kin of Kennedy, "Kenkynnol" and the common law' in A Grant and KJ Stringer (eds), *Medieval Scotland, crown, lordship and community: essays presented to GWS Barrow* (1993).

122 'Scottish chronicle', ed Anderson, 249–50, ed Hudson, 148.

123 'Scottish chronicle', ed, Anderson, 251, ed Hudson, 150 (my translation differs a little from that of Professor Hudson, 156). For another interpretation see TO Clancy, 'Iona, Scotland and the *Céli Dé*' in Crawford, *Scotland in dark-age Britain*, 122; but perhaps his understanding of the passage would have required *Hibern(i)enses* rather than *Scotti* (cf *rex Hiberniensium*, Anderson, 251.16, Hudson, 150.7).

identity ceased to be linked with a process of linguistic assimilation. From the ninth to the eleventh century the Scots, the Irish of northern Britain, were linguistic assimilators. From the twelfth century they were, like the Franks of the post-Roman era, the leading people within a kingdom that allowed different identities to persist (Galwegians, like Burgundians). It offered a home to Normans, Bretons and Flemings; and from the thirteenth century it finally ceased to make Gaelic a ticket required for full incorporation within a Scottish nation that now also included the descendants of the former Cumbrians and the English of Lothian.

The nationalities of Britain and Ireland in the early middle ages fall into three groups. First, there were the colonial nations, the English and the Scots, unabashed that they had only recently taken the land in which they lived, and correspondingly convinced of the sins of the defeated Britons and Picts. For both, nationality was bound up with a process of ethnic assimilation on a grand scale; and for both, therefore, their nationality was intimately related to that of their victims. We can say this with certainty for the English and the Britons, but we can also infer it with some confidence for the Scots and the Picts of the ninth and tenth centuries. Yet, whereas English identity was constructed in its new promised land, that of the Scots was always attached to the Irish of Ireland. The Scottish situation offers clues as to what might have happened if the English had been Saxons, one people with their cousins on the continent. Second, then, there were the victim nations: the Britons from the start and the Picts from the ninth century. Territory mattered most for the Britons, partly because they had lost so much of it, partly because, throughout the entire period, they were thought to be the original inhabitants of Britain. Whether they were colonial nations or victim nations, for Bede language was what defined them best. Yet this was only so because of the time at which Bede was living, when things had changed fundamentally from the period of bilingualism in which Gildas could still say that Latin was 'our language'. And, finally, the Irish stood between the two groups: they were like the English rather than the Britons in that they were conscious of being the last settlers of the island rather than the first. Although they might fear an English invasion, they never suffered from one except for that of a single year, 684, and then only in one province, Brega.[124] There was a tension between a political and ecclesiastical order for which the territorial unit, the island of Ireland, was crucial, and ethnic reality, in that the Irish were also settled in Britain, and were indeed expanding their lands 'in the east'. That tension, together with the different context and thus somewhat different meaning of Irishness in Britain, was enough to prepare the way for a split between the Irish of Ireland and a new nation, that of the Scots, even though in the early middle ages the separation was still only very partial.

---

[124] *Annals of Ulster*, 685.2; Bede, *HE*, 4.26 (24). For the fears aroused see *Patrician texts*, ed and trans Bieler, 164, 165, ch 52; *Críth gablach*, ed DA Binchy (1941), 20–1, lines 522–3.

2

Social Change in Early Medieval Byzantium

JAMES HOWARD-JOHNSTON

Byzantium was the most Roman of the sub-Roman successors of the Roman empire.
There was no permanent intrusion of a superior military power into its territory, no
sudden disruption of the administration, no dismantling of an age-old constitutional
structure, no subsequent partial recovery in the cultural sphere as a new non-Roman
ruling elite and the mass of its followers were gradually irradiated with Roman values.
The Roman empire survived in the east. Emperor and court (centred on a politically
emasculated senate), secular and ecclesiastical authorities, in Constantinople and the
provinces, continued to exercise their powers in traditional ways, as well as to display
their status in the elaborate minuet of established ceremonial. The infrastructure of a
developed polity was maintained – a relatively high level of literacy, an efficient and
reasonably fair justice system, a network of all-weather roads, grand public buildings,
a flexible monetary system. The apparatus of government retained the capacity to
reach out into the provinces and down inside even the smallest of remote localities.
The resources of society could be and were efficiently tapped by a state which faced a
crisis unprecedented in scale and duration. Above all there was no cultural hiatus, no
sudden weakening in ideological drive, no relinquishing of imperial pretensions nor
of a claim to special status as God's principal political agency in a world of flux.[1]

Observations such as these may be banalities to Byzantinists, but, for a wider read-
ership, it must be stressed that at the very beginning of the middle ages, in the seventh
century, there were fundamental differences of structure between the nascent
Germanic states on former Roman territory in the west and what remained of the east
Roman empire, after Islam, in a first phase of ultra-dynamic expansion, had lopped
off its rich near eastern provinces and the Slavs had infiltrated into much of the Balkan
interior. It should cause no surprise that the two cultures, despite so much shared
inheritance, should diverge markedly in their social and institutional development
over subsequent centuries.

The crucial point is that the Byzantine state never lost its fiscal grip over its
subjects and never lost control over those appointed to manage its affairs in the provinces or to command its armies in the field. Indeed it may well be that its powers were
enhanced in the first two centuries of its existence, as it strove to cope with repeated
mortal threats from an adversary, the caliphate, with greatly superior resources. It can

---

[1]   The following may be picked out from an abundant literature: G Ostrogorsky, *History of the Byzantine
state* (1968); C Mango, *Byzantium: the empire of new Rome* (1980); M Whittow, *The making of orthodox Byzantium, 600–1025* (1996); N Oikonomidès, *Fiscalité et exemption fiscale à Byzance (IXe–XIe
siècles)* (1996); M Mullett, 'Writing in early mediaeval Byzantium' in R McKitterick (ed), *The uses of
literacy in early mediaeval Europe* (1990); and G Dagron, *Empereur et prêtre* (1996).

be argued that fiscal efficiency was increased (with a finer calibration of individual tax liabilities and full monetization of the main taxes) and that what remained of the late Roman nobility was transformed into an aristocracy of service, far more dependent than before on the favour of the monarch.[2]

There were, however, many detailed organizational changes as Byzantium adapted to loss of empire and committed itself to a desperate struggle for survival, which was to last for over two centuries. Resources were concentrated on the war against the Arabs. Financial control was tightened. The central administration was restructured to reduce costs and improve coordination. The navy was developed into a major strategic force, capable of launching counter-strikes and of defending the long, exposed coast-line and many islands of Byzantium. Four great military commands were established in Asia Minor, between them embracing almost all of the core territory of the reduced state. *De facto* rather than *de jure* the generals in charge acquired near-plenipotentiary powers over all aspects of administration in their commands. The crown merely did what it could to bolster the civilian authorities, hiving off the judiciary and fiscal ad-ministration and eventually amalgamating civil provinces into larger, more equipollent units. Fixed defences were improved or constructed from scratch, special subvention from the centre funding work at places of strategic importance while the provincial authorities built castles to control passes or to secure designated refuge zones. The army itself abandoned orthodox methods of warfare, resorting instead to ultra-elastic defence and guerrilla counter-attacks on invading forces. Soldiers, no longer barracked in cities when not on campaign but dispersed over the countryside, were integrated as never before (at least since the days of the Roman republic) into rural society. Civilian and soldier cooperated effectively to implement a defensive strategy designed ultimately to minimize damage to the resources, human, animal and material, civilian and military, of the state.[3]

There is no denying then that there was wholesale institutional change, forced on Byzantium by brute circumstance. Admittedly the evidence is scanty and much of it circumstantial. For we suffer from a virtually complete documentary silence from the critical period of change, the reign of Constans II (641–669). There is no connected chronological account of it in any secular Byzantine source. Of the two chronicles which cover the seventh century, each written a century or more after Constans's death, one, the *Short history* of the patriarch Nicephorus, simply leaps over the whole reign, while the other, the *Chronicle* of Theophanes, tries to plug the hole with snip-pets of information taken, in the majority of cases, from a single Syrian chronicle. Only meagre material can be extracted from extant contemporary Byzantine sources, namely records of the trials of two recalcitrant churchmen, accounts of miracles worked at a Constantinopolitan shrine specializing in disorders of the male genitalia,

[2]   Oikonomidès, 24–151; Whittow, 104–13. In both respects Byzantium was a world apart from contem-porary states in Latin Christendom: cf C Wickham, 'The other transition: from the ancient world to feudalism', *Past and Present* 103 (May 1984).

[3]   The general account of JF Haldon, *Byzantium in the seventh century* (1990) can be supplemented by H Ahrweiler, *Byzance et la mer* (1966), 7–92 (naval build-up); JD Howard-Johnston, 'Studies in the organization of the Byzantine army in the tenth and eleventh centuries' (Oxford DPhil thesis 1971), 1–62, 188–237 (military deployment and strategy); JD Howard-Johnston, 'Thema' in A Moffatt (ed), *Maistor: classical, Byzantine and renaissance studies for Robert Browning* (1984), 189–97 (relations between civilian and military authorities); and M Whittow, 'Social and political structures in the Maeander region of western Asia Minor on the eve of the Turkish invasion' (Oxford DPhil thesis 1987) i.51–73, 128–30 (centrally funded fortifications).

and a partisan local history of Thessalonica. We would be hard put to gain any sense of the atmosphere of the time or of the many measures taken in a desperate struggle to survive, but for the reports about Constantinopolitan affairs which a distant Armenian observer (conventionally called Sebeos) writing in the 650s included in the contemporary section of his *History*.[4]

We cannot establish the sequence and absolute dating of the various institutional reforms enumerated above. Sebeos only enables us to witness, from the wings, one critical phase, when the Roman state was taking the strain of sustaining the war effort from a much reduced resource base in the early 640s (creating a deep but temporary fissure at the apex of government), and to place the reorganization of army commands after the early 650s (so probably in the respite offered by the first Arab civil war, 656–61).[5] For the rest we must rely on retrospection once the narrative sources resume their coverage, from the late seventh century. Most of this later information which we can retrieve is limited to specific posts, military and civilian, in Constantinople and the provinces, held by notable individuals who feature in the political/military narrative of the two indigenous sources. Similar material can then be extracted from a large corpus of legends (giving name, rank and post) on lead seals used to secure and authenticate official correspondence. A great deal of intricate work is required to reconstitute from this mass of discrete small pieces of information military and bureaucratic staff structures, and to trace their evolution back into the blank period of the mid-seventh century. But the task is feasible because the main structural features of the Byzantine administrative system in its fully developed form are revealed by two extant skeletal lists of posts in ranking order, dating from the ninth century.[6]

We are much, much worse placed when it comes to the investigation of the Byzantine social order. The narrative sources yield all too little information, since they are primarily concerned with the political manoeuvrings of elites, clerical and lay, and with foreign affairs. Seals can tell us absolutely nothing, and lists of rank are equally irrelevant. Archival documents only come on stream in reasonable quantities in the eleventh century and are largely confined to monastic landholdings (and in the peculiar conditions of Byzantium, where rural monasteries tended to huddle together away from the lay world, on holy mountains, it is debatable how much may be extrapolated from them about rural society at large). The social historian has to rely chiefly on material of two sorts, both tricky to handle: lives of saints which are set, in whole or in part, in the countryside, and prescriptive legal texts. No wonder there has been an earnest debate about the social order in Byzantium, a debate which is as vociferous now as it was one, two or three generations ago.

---

4   Nikephoros, patriarch of Constantinople, *Short history*, ed and trans C Mango (1990); *Theophanis Chronographia*, ed C de Boor (2 vols 1883–5), trans C Mango and R Scott as *The chronicle of Theophanes Confessor* (1997); W Brandes, ' "Juristische" Krisenbewältigung im 7. Jahrhundert? die Prozesse gegen Papst Martin I. und Maximos Homologetes', *Fontes Minores* x (1998); *The miracles of St Artemios*, trans VS Crisafulli and JW Nesbitt (1997); *Les plus anciens recueils des miracles de Saint Démétrius*, ed P Lemerle (2 vols 1979–81); *The Armenian history attributed to Sebeos*, trans RW Thomson and JD Howard-Johnston (1999).

5   *Armenian history*, 140–1, 142–3, 162–3, with historical notes 58, 60, 66.

6   The two earliest lists of rank, known as the *tacticon Uspensky* (842–3) and the *cletorologium* of Philotheus (899), are edited and translated, with commentary, by N Oikonomidès, *Les listes de préséance byzantines des IXe et Xe siècles* (1972), 41–235. The best modern analysis of seventh-century institutional reforms is Haldon, *Byzantium*, 173–253.

At its heart lies the issue of whether or not the late Roman social order survived the seismic shocks of the seventh century. Did the owners of large estates – ranging from magnates, who combined high office with extensive landholdings and exercised immense influence in their home provinces, to the leading and ordinary members of city elites, whose status ultimately rested on landed wealth and their reputation in the eyes of their peers – in general retain through a century of warfare and disruption their estates and, no less important, the agricultural labour on them? Or, if we look from the social base up, was there no change of fortune for many of the agricultural workforces of large landowners, barracked in labour-settlements and deployed as estate-managers saw fit on land kept in hand by the landowners, supporting themselves from allotments made over by their landlords, forbidden from marrying outside the estate? Did other intermediate categories survive in roughly the same proportions as in late antiquity: first, peasants owning land of their own but needing to work for others to make a decent living; second, peasants able to live independently off their own property; third, members of village elites, owning more, perhaps much more land than they needed to feed their households and necessarily employing additional labour to work it; and fourth, a whole range of urban rentiers, below the level of the urban elite, with smaller and larger estates in their city's territory?[7]

Byzantinists have been unable to conceive of this elaborate, graded social order enduring into the middle Byzantine period (ninth to twelfth centuries). They envisage wholesale change, in which the peasant villager emerges as the dominant element in the social order at the expense of the traditional landowner. This thesis was propounded with admirable clarity and force by Ostrogorsky: for him a slow-moving social revolution took place in the course of the seventh and eighth centuries which left the large landowner a virtually extinct species. This rather dramatic picture was modified by Lemerle, who invested his main effort into a careful re-evaluation of the principal sources and then pieced together an outline social history out of material extracted from them. He concluded that a rump of the old landed aristocracy managed to keep hold of their estates and to maintain their high social status but that independent peasant proprietors increased greatly in numbers and formed a major social component of the Byzantine state in its early phase. His view has gained general acceptance and has recently been reiterated at length in Kaplan's massive work on Byzantine rural society.[8]

A new social order can then be invoked in part-explanation of the extraordinary resilience which Byzantium displayed in the face of the forces of Islam. There was no

---

[7] The comprehensive survey of AHM Jones, *The later Roman empire 284–602* (4 vols 1964) ii.767–823 has been qualified subsequently in many ways. His gloomy picture of demographic decline and a consequent perennial shortage of labour throughout late antiquity has been replaced by one of steady demographic and economic recovery through the fourth, fifth and early sixth centuries, until the bubonic plague of 542: see for example JP Sodini, 'La contribution de l'archéologie à la connaissance du monde byzantin (IVᵉ–VIIᵉ siècles)', *Dumbarton Oaks Papers* xlvii (1993). A thoroughgoing reappraisal of the late Roman social order, based principally upon Egyptian estate documents and imperial legislation, has been carried out by P Sarris, 'Society and economy in the age of Justinian' (Oxford DPhil thesis 1999).

[8] G Ostrogorsky, 'Agrarian conditions in the Byzantine empire in the middle ages', *Cambridge Economic History of Europe* i (2nd edn 1966); P Lemerle, *The agrarian history of Byzantium from the origins to the twelfth century* (1979); M Kaplan, *Les hommes et la terre à Byzance du VIᵉ au XIᵉ siècle* (1992). Lemerle and Kaplan cannot be faulted for their documentation of the phenomena, but their emphasis on fiscal factors as the prime agents of social change is open to question.

slackening of the war effort for some three and a half centuries, first in defence of Asia Minor, then in a series of carefully directed counter-offensives which resulted in the annexation of a broad buffer zone in the east and south-east.[9] A single moment of hesitation in 654 when, after twenty years in which Islam had been carrying all before it, the whole population of Asia Minor, from the interior plateau and its fringing highlands to the coastal plains, submitted to the future caliph Mu'āwiya as he marched at the head of a formidable army on Constantinople, was never repeated.[10] An ideology capable of standing up to that of the new Islamic superstate was needed, as was an efficient governmental system, but no less important was the concentration of social forces on the struggle for survival. Implicit in Ostrogorsky's thesis, with or without Lemerle's modification, is an assumption that the peasantry who formed the bulk of the population of Byzantium committed themselves resolutely to its defence because they were fighting for their own lands, because they knew that ultimately the state was their state. To which it might be added that both the remnant of the old aristocracy and a new nascent court-centred elite were probably exceptionally dedicated to the performance of their official duties in the apparatus of government and thus less likely than usual to divert their energies into self-aggrandizement.

Such a picture makes good historical sense, but does it correspond to reality? Is there enough evidence, circumstantial and direct, to demonstrate social change on the scale envisaged by Ostrogorsky and Lemerle? The traditional approach has been to fasten on to the few pieces of direct evidence to hand. Attention has been attracted above all by a short legal text dealing with village affairs, the *nomos georgikos* (usually called the farmer's law by anglophone scholars and the rural code by their francophone colleagues). The problem, though, is that it is hard to pin this text down, to determine a date of composition and to associate its production with a particular milieu. The text is definitely post-Justinianic, much of its material having no analogues in the *corpus iuris* (contrary to the supposition of the medieval scribes who added such an attribution when they amplified the original title). Although the great majority of modern readers take it to be referring to a village of independent peasant proprietors, this is not the only possible reading. So it can be doubted whether the text, even if it can be dated and viewed as emanating from the governing centre, can be used to demonstrate the prevalence of such villages in early medieval Byzantine rural society.[11]

Leaving aside the tenurial status of the peasants and the relative importance of such villages, even the internal structure and functioning of the *nomos georgikos* village remains obscure. Nothing can be said about its constitution (the existence or not of a headman or of a panel of village elders) since nothing is reported. Nothing useful can be inferred about social stratification within the village (of which there are only hints in the text), about the impact of outside landowners (mentioned only in clauses 9 and

---

9   Howard-Johnston, 'Byzantine army', 188–298; Whittow, *Orthodox Byzantium*, 175–81, 310–27.

10 Mu'āwiya's offensive involved two fleets and a second, reserve army: *Armenian history*, 170–1, with historical note 75.

11 See the first edition with English translation by W Ashburner, 'The farmer's law', *Journal of Hellenic Studies* xxx (1910) and xxxii (1912), and the modern critical edition by IP Medvedev, *Nomos georgikos* (1984). The suggestion by N Svoronos, 'Notes sur l'origine et la date du code rural', *Travaux et Mémoires* viii (1981), accepted by Whittow, *Orthodox Byzantium*, 113–16, that it may be pre-Justinianic was firmly rebutted by L Burgmann, 'Ist der Nomos Georgikos vorjustinianisch?', *Rechtshistorisches Journal* i (1982) and Medvedev, 22–3, 138–40.

10) or about the presence or absence of craftsmen or clergy or soldiers (the only non-agricultural activity mentioned is milling, in clauses 81–3). For the text is very narrowly focused on one aspect of village life – the relations of villager to villager as owner or possessor of neighbouring property, fixed and movable. The impression is given that their holdings are jumbled up together and that all manner of disputes may arise, above all from animals straying into cultivated plots. From this one substantive conclusion may perhaps be drawn, with the aid of what is known of the sternly partitive inheritance law of Rome and Byzantium: namely that each individual holding was fractured into a number of small, differentiated plots and that the resulting mosaic-like pattern of intermixed, dispersed holdings imposed a high degree of social cohesion on members of village communities. For only the collective social will could effectually prohibit disputes between neighbours (for which the potential was virtually infinite), the law code being a weapon of last resort to resolve such disputes as arose as swiftly as possible. This solidarity of the locality was a social force of some significance of which both the state (in its fiscal procedures) and potentially predatory large landowners had to take note.

It may well be more profitable to turn first to the circumstantial evidence before returning to the *nomos georgikos* and such other snippets of material as cast a fitful light on rural society. There is an obvious starting-point – the provincial city, the basic unit of social, cultural and political life in the late Roman empire. It was embedded in the landscape. It was the focal point for the rural population living in its territory, both as a market centre which stimulated active economic exchange throughout its hinterland and as the basic, local administrative agent of imperial government, responsible in the first instance for tax-collection from its territory. It was also the normal place of residence of landowners.[12]

Rather more can be learned of the fate of provincial cities from the seventh to the ninth century than of their rural hinterlands, and from the changing fortunes of the city inferences may be drawn about social change in the countryside. Written sources are relatively unforthcoming. They attest the continued existence of a large number of settlements which were classified as cities and had resident bishops. But it is not possible to gauge the degree of their urbanism from simple listings (in tables of episcopal sees) or from incidental appearances in military or hagiographical narratives. Archaeological research comes to the rescue, patchy though it may be and traditionally preoccupied with classical antiquity to the detriment of the middle ages. Enough is now known to make it clear that most cities survived as settlements and clung to their ancient sites. There was no wholesale migration to new, elevated, naturally better-defended sites. But it is equally clear that there was a massive shrinkage of population and that a premium was put on defence. Thus, for example, the greatest city of the western seaboard of Asia Minor, Ephesus, halved in size, its defensive circuit contracting and incorporating several of the massive public buildings of its monumental centre. Nearby Miletus was reduced to a quarter of its former self, while Sardis split into a skeletal lower city and a heavily fortified acropolis. Similar contraction, to massive hard-point citadels, is attested in the interior of Asia Minor – at Cotyaeum and Ancyra for example. Only rarely was the whole of an ancient city

---

[12] On cities and their elites see Jones ii.712–66 and M Whittow, 'Ruling the late Roman and early Byzantine city: a continuous history', *Past and Present* 129 (Nov 1990). A case study which illustrates the intensity of exchange between town and country in late antiquity is C Foss, 'The Lycian coast in the Byzantine age', *Dumbarton Oaks Papers* xlviii (1994).

secured by its old defensive perimeter, as seems to have been the case at Amorium (perhaps because it doubled as a military base).[13]

Yet more significant are the scraps of evidence which point to a sharp drop in building standards, suggesting that whatever remained of the late antique urban population was impoverished in the subsequent era of prolonged warfare. Quarrying and recycling of material from ruined structures (chiefly for use in fortifications), adaptation and patching up of existing buildings, extensive use of mud brick and timber were the norm. Only very exceptionally were new public buildings erected before the tenth century. The familiar urban elites of late antiquity, who could negotiate as an independent social force, strengthened by mutual solidarity, with the imperial and local authorities, vanish from sight. They only begin to resurface in the sources from the end of the tenth century.[14] Everything suggests that war, unending war, generation after generation, and the damage that it caused, both to lives and to property, gradually wore down and impoverished the cities, the Byzantine fiscal authorities playing an important auxiliary part as they mopped up surplus resources to fund the defensive war effort. Thus Byzantium's institutional *romanitas*, manifest above all in its fiscal capability, can be said to have fed off and destroyed its social *romanitas*, evident above all in the cities.

This decline of cities, in both population and resources, inevitably had serious repercussions in their rural hinterlands. The bases from which the great majority of the landowning elite had managed the countryside crumbled beneath them. Many probably took to their heels when enemy forces approached (a familiar phenomenon, well attested in the case of Balkan cities).[15] It may be suspected that fewer and fewer returned after each successive crisis, that the collective social power of those who did steadily diminished with the decline in their numbers, and that consequently their ability to control their landholdings weakened remorselessly. The position of those who stayed away was weaker still. It was hard to maintain property rights and retain labour, however tightly contracted, from a distance in times of general confusion and administrative disruption.

There is no alternative but to resort to conjecture, given the paucity of evidence, unless one is ready to assume that shocks as severe as these to the central component of the Roman social system caused no long-term disturbance to that system, and that a fundamental weakening in the power of the landowning elite had no effect on its relations with its agricultural labour forces. The Byzantinist, who is perhaps naturally predisposed to seek out lines of continuity, must beware of assuming that a complex social organism, however set in its ways, however firmly controlled by custom and law, could not suffer fatal damage if vital parts were struck repeated blows and were

---

13 In general see Whittow, 'Maeander region' i.25–265; Whittow, *Orthodox Byzantium*, 89–95. For individual sites see C Foss, *Ephesus after antiquity: a late antique, Byzantine and Turkish city* (1979); Whittow, 'Maeander region' i.46–71, 118–26 (Sardis, Miletus); C Foss, *Byzantine and Turkish Sardis* (1976); C Foss, *Survey of medieval castles of Anatolia* i *Kütahya* (1985), 12–85 (arguing, unconvincingly to my mind, for a ninth-century date); C Foss, 'Late antique and Byzantine Ankara', *Dumbarton Oaks Papers* xxxi (1977); preliminary reports on the Amorium excavations published in *Anatolian Studies* xxxviii–xlvi (1988–96).

14 M Angold, 'Archons and dynasts: local aristocracies and the cities of the later Byzantine empire' in M Angold (ed), *The Byzantine aristocracy, IX to XIII centuries* (1984); P Magdalino, *The empire of Manuel I Komnenos, 1143–1180* (1993), 150–5.

15 See for example *Miracles de Saint Démétrius* 2.2.197, 200, ed Lemerle i.180–1, 185–6.

gouged out bit by bit, the fibres and filaments connecting them to the surrounding tissue gradually stretching and eventually breaking.

We must never forget that it was a time of war, that Arab armies regularly raided the interior of Asia Minor and launched three massive attacks on Constantinople itself (in 654, the 670s and 717–18).[16] While cities may have been their prime targets, extensive damage was done in the countryside, the estates of larger landowners with more conspicuous installations and storage facilities probably suffering disproportionately. Meanwhile the peasantry were not standing idly by, but were enlisted in large numbers as infantry in the army.[17] Their social power grew markedly relative to that of landowners. They were formed into tight-knit groups, whether on active service in their units or at home in their villages, and they were armed. General demographic decline, slight perhaps but sustained probably into the early ninth century, was also steadily increasing the economic power of labour.[18] There was no question of old elites maintaining their position in the longer run in the localities. Control of labour, it can be argued, was always more important than ownership of land in a landscape like that of Asia Minor where there is a superabundance of potential arable. Even in late antiquity landowners had been helped by public authority to maintain a firm grip on their labour forces.[19] In the era of war public authority was otherwise engaged and labour, we can be sure, haemorrhaged steadily away from landowners' estates.

Such is the case that can be argued on the basis of circumstantial evidence. A strong one, to my mind, since I find it hard otherwise to understand how Byzantium managed to fight a guerrilla war of defence against apparently overwhelming odds for two centuries. It is time, though, to turn to specific pieces of evidence, to see whether or not they provide corroboration. Given constraints of space, I shall refrain from scouring the hagiographical dossier from the seventh, eighth and early ninth centuries, although it can yield highly suggestive material,[20] and shall concentrate on the two most important pieces of evidence: the *nomos georgikos*, because thanks to intensive research carried out over the last thirty years, chiefly in Germany, much more is now known about the rich tradition of Byzantine legal manuscripts in which it is transmitted and about the wider legal context of its production; and a letter written by Ignatius, metropolitan bishop of Nicaea, to a senior provincial official early in the ninth century, which casts a revealing shaft of light on social and economic conditions and which has been published in a critical edition only very recently.[21]

Ignatius's letter, one of three written during a crisis in relations with the local authorities, documents the changed relations between large landowners and the peas-

---

[16] W Brandes, *Die Städte Kleinasiens im 7. und 8. Jahrhundert* (1989), 51–78.

[17] Howard-Johnston, 'Byzantine army', 30–1.

[18] Contra Lemerle, *Agrarian history*, 48–51.

[19] For example *Iustiniani novellae*, ed R Schoell in *Corpus iuris civilis* iii (1954), 17.13–14, 54.1, 156, 157, 162.

[20] Thus several cases of collective antagonism between the main body of villagers, termed *georgoi*, and a landowning elite within the village, termed *oikodespotai* (literally masters of households) are documented in Galatia at the beginning of the seventh century in *Vie de Théodore de Sykéôn*, ed and trans AJ Festugière (2 vols 1970), chs 43, 114–18, with commentary by S Mitchell, *Anatolia: land, men, and gods in Asia Minor* (2 vols 1993) ii.133–4, 139–40.

[21] *The correspondence of Ignatios the deacon*, ed and trans C Mango (1997), letters 1–3. Ignatius's tenure of the see fell either between 815 and the mid-820s, or between the late 820s and 843: ibid 6, 19, 23.

antry on whom they relied for labour. The church at Nicaea was better placed than most large landowners to uphold its title to land and to retain agricultural labour, for the city's secluded geographical position, far from the frontier and close to Constantinople, enabled it to survive the storms of the seventh and eighth centuries relatively unscathed.[22] It seems to have owned plenty of land in the early ninth century but relied for its cultivation on an agricultural workforce designated *paroikoi*.[23] These *paroikoi* were far from downtrodden agricultural labourers. They could show great independence of spirit (to the extent of withdrawing their labour when aggrieved). They, not the church, owned the draught-animals and equipment necessary for the cultivation of the bishopric's estates. They were remunerated with a share of the harvest, their share being that laid down in the *nomos georgikos*.[24] The reference, unquestionably, is to clauses 9 and 10 of that text, where circumstances are envisaged in which a *georgos* cultivates land belonging to a large landowner (termed *chorodotes*, grantor of land). The *georgos* works as a sharecropper (*mortites*) and is entitled to nine tenths of the crop. This reduction of the landowner's share to a bare minimum of one tenth provides the most striking evidence of changed relations between landowner and agricultural labour.[25]

So sharp a change in the balance of economic power testifies to a major shift in social relations, in favour of the peasantry. No less significant is a change in the common usage of the word *georgos* by the early ninth century, when, as we now know thanks to Ignatius, the *nomos georgikos* was in existence (and probably in general use). Strictly speaking *georgos* means 'land-worker' and gives no indication of economic or social status. But it had a narrower meaning in the common legal parlance of the sixth century: it was used as the Greek equivalent of the Latin *colonus*, to designate peasants who were contractually obliged to work on land belonging to others and who might or might not own small plots of their own. In the sixth century the *georgos* was distinguished from the independent proprietor, great or small (the *ktetor* or *kektemenos*).[26]

As has been noted above, it is possible to view the average peasant of the *nomos georgikos*, despite his evident economic self-sufficiency, as possessing his landholding as a tenant or latter-day *colonus* rather than owning it in his own right. Even on this hypothesis, however, there had been a marked improvement in his status from

---

22 Brandes, 124–6.
23 The *paroikoi* of charitable institutions, churches and monasteries feature in a highly polemical account of the fiscal policies of Nicephorus I (802–11) included in the *Chronicle of Theophanes Confessor*, 486–8.
24 'For regarding the event that has taken place, I have received a report that some of the *paroikoi* who had gone away protested frantically against our Church that they had suffered injustice at her hands on account of the produce that they, like hired laborers, had raised on her lands. Surely, your God-loving Prudence is aware that our Church does not nourish a single ox that pulls the plow; that she has never yoked a plow, be it of one piece or compacted of several, nor has she thoroughly greased a plowshare after singeing it in the fire. Nay, she parcels out her land to those who till the land and awaits the crop from God, the provider of harvest, which she justly enjoys with them according to the farmer's law.' *Correspondence of Ignatios*, trans Mango, 29.
25 *Nomos georgikos*, clauses 9–10: 'If a *georgos mortites* (sharecropping farmer) reaps without authorisation from the *chorodotes* (grantor of land) and carries off his sheaves, he shall be deprived, as a thief, of all his crop. A sharecropper's portion is nine bundles, while that of the grantor of land is one bundle; he who divides outside these limits is accursed.'
26 See for example *Iustiniani novellae*, 17.13–14, 128.8, 14, 144, 157. Cf Sarris, *Society and economy*, chs 6 and 9.

that of the agricultural worker housed in a landlord's settlement and deployed at the
direction of an estate manager in late antiquity. But the cumulative evidence of individual clauses in the *nomos georgikos* points rather to peasant proprietorship: the
georgos is *kyrios*, 'lord', of his land (clauses 2, 15–17, 20, 21); his land is described as
idios, 'his own' (clauses 1, 18, 19); individual parcels (vineyards, gardens) may be
fenced or ditched (clauses 50, 51, 58, 66, 85); permanent exchanges of land may be
agreed by *georgoi* in the presence of two or three witnesses (clause 3); permanent,
profitable installations (mills) may be built on individual holdings (clauses 81–3). All
of this suggests ownership, as does the absence of references to an outside landowner
in any of these clauses (although he would surely expect to be informed of permanent
transactions and to give them his approval). The *georgos* should be taken, then, to be
an independent peasant proprietor, who may, as is indicated by clauses 9 and 10, strike
deals in his own right with an outside landowner (the *chorodotes*, 'grantor of land') on
highly favourable terms. On this natural reading of the text there had been change in
the meaning of *georgos*. Such a semantic shift points to widespread change in society
at large and suggests that there had been an upward social and economic movement of
much of the agrarian workforce between the late sixth and early ninth century.[27]

Confirmation of this change, tantamount to the emancipation of a large part of the
peasantry, would be obtained, if the *nomos georgikos* could be shown not only to have
been a practical document, part of the current legal framework governing rural affairs
from the early ninth century at the latest, but to have been issued originally by the
imperial authorities. For this would demonstrate that the peasant village was so
important a component of the medieval state that the central government took an
interest in regulating the minutiae of its internal life.

An official, imperial provenance may be conjectured on the basis of the authority
ascribed to the *nomos georgikos* by Ignatius (and, presumably, by his correspondent).
It can also be argued that it was not composed as a free-standing legal text, its scope
being so restricted that it does not deal with many important aspects of village life
(including land transactions associated with the great rites of passage, marriage and
death, as well as land sales and rural debt). It may have been free-standing in the rich
manuscript tradition of Byzantine legal texts, but as a piece of substantive practical
law it presupposed the existence of a comprehensive legal code. On this line of
reasoning, tenuous but not entirely without force, it is tempting to associate it with the
ecloga of Leo III and Constantine V, the first post-Justinianic legal code, short, admirably well organized, lucid and practical, issued in 741 for use in courts throughout
the empire. As has long been remarked, the *nomos georgikos* employs the same legal
style (principle is presented in practical, down-to-earth terms), recommends similar
penalties and is close in phrasing and vocabulary to the *ecloga*.[28] The social concern
for the main body of the emperor's subjects which it presupposes is openly and force-

---

[27] There is some corroboration of the semantic shift to be found in the scanty sources of the period. First,
the cavalry soldier, who belonged to a distinctly higher category than the subsistence peasantry and
was part-owner of the family landholding, is classified implicitly as a *georgos* in the heading to chapter
16.2 given in the table of contents of the *ecloga*, a law code issued in 741. See *Ecloga: das Gesetzbuch
Leons III. und Konstantinos' V.*, ed and trans L Burgmann (1983), 157; the table of contents was added
to the text at a very early stage in its transmission (ibid 128). Second, it is equally clear that a well told,
semi-fictional saint's life composed early in the ninth century uses *georgos* of independent peasant
proprietors: 'La vie de S Philarète', ed and trans MH Fourmy and M Leroy, *Byzantion* ix (1934),
114–25.

[28] *Nomos georgikos*, ed Medvedev, 140–1. Medvedev, who would have the text originate in the sixth

fully expressed in the preamble to the *ecloga*, issued for the benefit of those whom the emperors termed the poor, those without influence in society. Together the *ecloga* and the *nomos georgikos* would, in the hands of honest magistrates, provide the peasantry with the justice promised them by the emperors.[29]

Such is the meagre haul of evidence from the most Roman of early medieval states about its social structure – a piece of concrete evidence extracted from a dossier of letters, various corroborative snippets of hagiographical and chronicle material (not considered in detail here but long subjected to close analysis by Byzantinists) and an apparently free-floating legal text for which a specific date and provenance may be suggested and from which far-reaching conclusions may, with effort, be teased out. Those conclusions, converging as they do with those obtained from circumstantial evidence, point in the direction of Ostrogorsky's more extreme rather than Lemerle's more moderate version of social change.

In this scenario the late Roman aristocracy and local provincial elites, residing in cities and basing their power ultimately on landed wealth, were eroded away in the generations following the initial Arab conquests. By the second half of the eighth century when the uppermost reaches of a new governing elite can be seen, in the near-contemporary part of the chronicle of Theophanes, the prime source of its power was different – not land but office, in the army and the civil administration, in Constantinople and the provinces.[30] It was an aristocracy of service, centring on the court and the person of the emperor, relying ultimately on preferment and government salaries to sustain its status. Undoubtedly elements of the older elite installed themselves within the new, but the links with the past were severed; aristocratic families laid no claim to pedigrees reaching back into the Roman past.[31] Undoubtedly landed property was sought to provide a more durable, supplementary base for a family's position. But as has been seen, relations between large landowner and peasant were transformed, and the old legal framework of land tenure, both that dealing with lease-hold and that binding agricultural labour to landlords, probably fell into disuse. Market forces, economic and social, now determined tenurial relations.

The most important change of all, that with the most profound long-term effect on the social order, was the shift of residence of the elite from city to country. Members of the Byzantine aristocracy who secured and perpetuated high status in the course of the eighth, ninth and tenth centuries did not simply buy estates. They lived on them, when they were not in post or attending the court in Constantinople. The country house became the nodal point of aristocratic life, where power was made manifest in stone, furniture and decoration, in the size of the household and the number of its retainers, and in munificent entertaining. In the countryside the new elite, termed the

---

century (between the publication of the *Digest* in 533 and 572) suggests that it may have gained official recognition at the time of the promulgation of the *ecloga*.

29 *Ecloga*, ed and trans Burgmann, 160–7. It must be stressed, though, that there is nothing in the manuscript tradition to suggest a closer association with the *ecloga* than with several other, later, legal compilations. It has been conclusively demonstrated that the *nomos georgikos*, which several manuscripts include in extended versions of the appendix to the *ecloga*, was not part of the original core of the appendix as it had taken shape by the middle of the ninth century: IP Medvedev, 'Preliminary observations on the manuscript tradition of the *nomos georgikos*: manuscripts of the 10th–12th centuries', *Vizantijskij Vremennik* xli (1980), 201 [in Russian]; L Burgmann and S Troianos, 'Appendix eclogae', *Fontes Minores* iii (1979), 69, 82–3.

30 *Chronicle of Theophanes Confessor*, 449–503.

31 JC Cheynet, *Pouvoir et contestations à Byzance (963–1210)* (1990), 249–59.

dynatoi (powerful) whether in post or not, set about extending and intensifying their power and influence until solid, ramified nexuses of clientage were formed. This was the second phase in the development of the new Byzantine social order.[32]

By the beginning of the tenth century, the 'powerful' had acquired the will and the wherewithal to subvert the peasant village, tight-knit though it was. The new provincial elites consolidated and extended their hold on the localities, despite a fierce legislative counter-offensive from the imperial government which began in the 920s and was sustained until the end of the century. Tenth-century emperors continued the policy of protecting the peasantry, whom they, like Leo III and Constantine V, called the poor. For they too regarded the peasant village as the basic building block of the state. The battle was long and hard-fought. The outcome remains a matter of debate.[33]

We too should recognize this fundamental truth about Byzantium, and should acknowledge that social and institutional continuity did not go hand in hand, that the most Roman of early medieval states underwent almost as dramatic and thorough-going a social transformation as that off-shore island in the far north-west, where a new Germanic order, with scarcely a tinge of *romanitas*, took shape on one-time Roman soil.

---

[32] JD Howard-Johnston, 'Pouvoir et contestation', *Europe* 822 (October 1997); P Magdalino, 'The Byzantine aristocratic *oikos*' in Angold, *Byzantine aristocracy*; Cheynet, 261–301.

[33] For the texts see E McGreer, *The land legislation of the Macedonian emperors* (2000). For discussion see R Morris, 'The powerful and the poor in tenth-century Byzantium: law and reality', *Past and Present* 73 (Nov 1976); A Harvey, *Economic expansion in the Byzantine empire 900–1200* (1989), 35–79; Kaplan, *Les hommes et la terre*, 359–444, 546–73; JD Howard-Johnston, 'Crown lands and the defence of imperial authority in the tenth and eleventh centuries', *Byzantinische Forschungen* xxi (1995).

3

The Annals of St Neots and the Defeat of the Vikings

ERIC JOHN

The collaborative edition of the Anglo-Saxon chronicle undertaken by a group of Cambridge scholars seems likely to be one of the great scholarly undertakings of our time. Something of the quality and value of the edition is shown by the first Latin texts to be published, in a volume edited by David Dumville and Michael Lapidge.[1] The main part of the book is devoted to Dumville's edition of the annals of St Neots. This is a Latin translation of an exceptionally good text of the chronicle, which, unusually, has quite a lot of information about Francia. It is clear that the annals are an important text previously neglected by scholars put off by the atmosphere of confusion that has surrounded their publication. Dumville has rescued the text and made it accessible. However, I cannot agree with his suggested dating of the text or his view of the purpose for which it was written. These are not trivial questions, but have a significant bearing on the relationship between late Anglo-Saxon England and the continent.

Dumville claims, in my opinion correctly, that the annals of St Neots depend on a Bury St Edmunds manuscript written between about 1120 and about 1140, that is almost certainly in the reign of Henry I of England. Although a product of Bury it is generally styled the annals of St Neots because the unique manuscript was taken from St Neots priory by the antiquary John Leland at the dissolution. Dumville devotes very little space to the dating of the manuscript, perhaps considering it to be obvious. He thinks the scribe may well be the author, and the date of the book the same as that of the writing of the book down. The reason for this is that much of the continental information seems to come from various Norman annals that cannot have reached England before 1066. He is handicapped, as is any student of the period, by the lack of decent, let alone reliable, editions of the Norman annals and the consequent difficulties scholars have in using them. One of the curious features of the annals of St Neots is that they end in 914 with the conversion of Rollo of Normandy and the treaty he made with Charles the Simple, king of the West Franks, that legitimated the status of the French Danelaw, Normandy. This is presented as a kind of parallel with the conversion of the 'English' Viking leader, Guthrum, and a change for the better in the status of East Anglia some years earlier.[2] Dumville thinks that these entries completed what the annals' compiler, as he calls him (reasonably enough, in view of the small amount of information of his own he contributed), had to say. He thinks that the

[1] D Dumville and S Keynes (general eds), *The Anglo-Saxon chronicle: a collaborative edition* (1983–) xvii *The annals of St Neots with Vita prima sancti Neoti*, ed D Dumville and M Lapidge (1985).

[2] Annals of St Neots, ed Dumville, under the year 890: *obiit Gvthrum, rex paganorum, qui et Athelstanus nomine in baptismo suscepit. Qui primus apud Orientales Anglos regnavit post passionem sancti regis Eadmundi; ipsam regionem divisit coluit atque primus inhabitavit.*

compiler was interested in the legitimacy of the Anglo-Norman kings of England. This depended on the one hand on the treaty Rollo made with King Charles and on the other the 'crusade' Alfred of Wessex led against the Vikings that finally identified the house of Cerdic with the kingdom of England.

It seems to me that Dumville's talk of the Norman annals is misleading. The annals of St Neots end with the creation of Normandy, and the abbeys that produced the Norman annals were once great West Frankish houses; the information is Frankish – West and East Frankish – not Norman information. This not a mere quibble. With one partial exception the annals contain no specifically Norman information at all.[3] When the northmen come into the picture their treatment is always hostile.[4] The enemy were *pagani*, that is Normans. It is impossible to know how quickly the Normans took to their new religion or how quickly they identified with their former enemies and new neighbours but I do not think a Norman writer would take the tone these annals take about the wars between Normans and West Franks in the late ninth and early tenth centuries. The point is that though we are dependent on Norman texts for the annals, their contents had a history that must go back before the foundation of Normandy. In fact if we read Dumville's introduction, substituting Frankish and West Frankish where he writes Norman and French, the results look rather different.

Dumville suggested that a concern to demonstrate the legitimacy of the Anglo-Norman royal family lay behind the compilation of the annals. But legitimacy is a very subjective concept. Some regimes of very doubtful legitimacy have never been in the least concerned with their lack of it. If their legitimacy, however dubious, is unchallenged why ever should they? No-one was going to challenge the legitimacy of the Anglo-Norman dynasty by Henry I's day. That legitimacy stemmed from Edward the Confessor's bequest of the crown to Duke William, sealed by a decisive victory in battle and the elimination of almost the entire challenging family, which in any case had sparse roots in English history. The Anglo-Norman establishment seems to have had little interest in, or sympathy with, the English past unless property rights were involved. It is worth noting that no post-conquest king called his sons by traditional English names until Henry III in the thirteenth century called two of his Edward and Edmund. When Edward succeeded his father he was known as Edward the first although he was the third Edward to rule the English. It is fair to point out that while no-one connected with the king or the court was likely to be concerned about the dynasty's legitimacy, an English monastic author from a traditionalist community might be. But the main objection to legitimacy providing the motivation of the compiler is the form, the very remarkable form, his book takes.

There is nothing like this book in the corpus of Anglo-Saxon literature, with the partial exception of Asser's life of Alfred. Although Asser used annalistic material his work is basically biographical, a panegyric of Alfred (849–99). But there is a great

---

3   The *Visio Rollonis*, included in the annals, is the partial exception. Under 876 occurs the first mention of the Viking leader Rollo, and the annalist shows that he knew that Rollo would become the ruler of Normandy with the title of duke. This doesn't make him any the less hostile to the Normans.

4   For example annals of St Neots, ed Dumville, under the year 898: *Eodem anno Rollo cum exercitu suo Carnotensem civitatem obsedit; sed episcopus eiusdem urbis, Walthelmus nomine, vir religiosissimus, Ricardum Burgundie ducem et Ebalum Pictavensium comitem in suo auxilio provocans, tunicam sancte MARIE virginis in manibus ferens Rollonem ducem divino nutu fugavit et civitatem liberavit.* Or under 882: *Loduuico, filio Loduuici regis, primum exeunte ad pugnam Deoque donante potiti sunt victoriam et pars innumerabili eorum maxima cecidit.*

deal of Frankish information. The deposition of the Carolingian emperor Charles III in 887 and his replacement by the East Frankish king Arnolf of Carinthia get a whole chapter (chapter 85), and this appears to be the source of the account in the annals of St Neots. It seems to me that Dumville might have asked why Asser and the compiler of the annals should be interested in this turn of events. Rosalind Lavington thought that Asser visited Flanders and may well have written his life there, in which case many of its puzzling features could be easily explained. She suggested that Asser had been sent on an embassy to Baldwin II, count of Flanders, by Alfred to negotiate an alliance, which must have been aimed against the Vikings, and that the negotiations culminated in the marriage of Alfred's daughter to Count Baldwin. The life was a sort of testimonial to Alfred – that he was father-in-law material – and a demonstration of Asser's own *bona fides* as ambassador. Her explanations of Asser's peculiar treatment of placenames are more convincing than most, and she has some surprising suggestions as to where Asser found insular material to hand in Francia. On this reading of Asser there is a striking resemblance between the concerns and interests of Asser and those of the compiler of the annals of St Neots.[5]

There is the sheer volume of information about Francia, made manageable because of the compiler's intimate understanding of the Frankish world. The earlier entries drawn from the West Frankish annals are general enough. They include under 424 a bare note of the death of St Augustine: was this, like some other items of general ecclesiastical interest, not otherwise known in Anglo-Saxon England? Under 860 the death of Æthelbald of Wessex is announced together with a Viking attack on Winchester. Under 865 the West Frankish annals are cited (*venerunt Normanni in Franciam medio Iulii*). Under 870 an extract from Asser is neatly combined with one from Abbo of Fleury's *Passio sancti Edmundi*. From then on the compiler makes a lively enough account of the Viking invasions, on both sides of the Channel, out of the Anglo-Saxon chronicle, Asser and the West Frankish annals. He is skilful at blending his various sources together and the result is a unique synoptic view of the Viking invasion and its progress. All his continental information, or nearly all, comes from the Frankish annals, but my impression is that the compiler was not simply doing a scissors-and-paste job on his various sources but that he was already familiar in outline at least with the world he was depicting, a world that ranged from Wessex to Bavaria.

The compiler had a taste for vision literature. This is shown by the three visions he takes from Bede. More interesting and more revealing are the three Frankish visions he cites. Each has what the Germans call a *Tendenz* relating to a particular crisis in Frankish history. The *Visio Eucheri* concerned the infernal punishment of Charles Martel for his way with church property. The *Visio Rollonis* certainly had connections with Normandy and, as Dumville points out, a special interest in the church of Rouen. Its *Tendenz* is concerned to elicit new grants of land to the church, perhaps to the church of Rouen in particular, over and above the restoration of what had been lost in the time when the Normans were pagan. Dumville thinks this would fit the Norman situation in the middle of the eleventh century. I cannot agree.[6] Rollo and his people

---

5   I am indebted to Mrs Lavington for letting me use her Manchester MA thesis on Asser.
6   Dumville relies on D Bates, *Normandy before 1066* (1982), 189ff. Bates points out that considerable revival of the Norman church began about 1020 and was consolidated by the advent of Duke William II (William the Conqueror). But is not the point of the *Visio Rollonis* to herald and promote this revival which it necessarily prefigures?

had become Christians at the beginning of the tenth century: for all that they had forced their way into north-west France they were not all-powerful. They did manifestly less well than their kinsmen in England. The West Franks were not powerless before them even if they could not eliminate them. On the other hand the northmen had got as much as they judged they could. But they had to accept Christianity and I do not believe that the Norman churches would have waited one hundred and fifty years before they raised the question of church property.

The *Tendenz* of the third vision, the *Visio Karoli*, has to do with the situation following the deposition and almost immediate death of Charles III. Dumville is content to show that the *Visio Karoli* was known in Normandy, which it certainly was, but this does not prove that the compiler could not have got it from somewhere else. Dumville writes: 'Hariulf's source is believed to have been a manuscript of St Wandrille, and excellent evidence for the availability of the text there already in the tenth century is provided by Saint-Omer, Bibliothèque municipale MS 764 written at that abbey.' In other words the manuscript was around in the tenth century. The difficulty here is that Dumville depended on the older literature for his knowledge of the *Visio Karoli* rather than what seems to me the best discussion of the work, that by Eduard Hlawitschka.[7]

The *Visio Karoli* is now thought to have been written either by, or in the circles around, Archbishop Fulk of Rheims. Its *Tendenz* was the promotion of the candidature of Louis of Provence, a direct descendant of Lothar, eldest son of Louis the Pious (*d.* 839), to rule the undivided Carolingian empire. It must have been written after the death of Charles III and before the murder of Fulk on 17 June 900. The oldest manuscript stems from St Omer and the abbey of St Bertin, of which Fulk was abbot from 878, when he succeeded Hincmar as archbishop of Rheims, until 883; he was again abbot *in commendam* with Rheims from 892 until his death. Now Archbishop Fulk had English acquaintances and correspondents, so it is hazardous to exclude the possibility that the *Visio Karoli* was known in England quite early in its history.[8] The three political visions are overwhelmingly Frankish in orientation. Hlawitschka points out, as earlier German historians had done, the crucial importance in Frankish history of the *coup d'état* that replaced Charles III as emperor by Arnolf of Carinthia. It is interesting to see that the St Neots compiler had grasped the point too.[9] The two main East Frankish sources, two recensions of the royal annals from Mainz and Regensburg, are neither as full nor as balanced as the annals of St Neots.

This was Fulk's point of view more or less. He did not want the empire divided. He detested the non-Carolingian 'usurpers' as he would have called them. That Louis of Provence – whose impeccable pedigree was only matched by his lack of resources –

7   E Hlawitschka, *Lotharingien und das Reich an der Schwelle der deutschen Geschichte* (1968).

8   FM Stenton, *Anglo-Saxon England* (1943, 3rd edn 1971), 271. Fulk's letter to Alfred is printed in S Keynes and M Lapidge (trans), *Alfred the Great: Asser's life of Alfred and other contemporary sources* (1983), 182–7.

9   Annals of St Neots, ed Dumville, under 887: *Karolus imperator viam universitatis adiit; sed Arnulfus, filius fratris sui, sexta antequam defunctus est ebdomada illum regno expulerat. Quo statim defuncto quinque reges ordinati sunt et regnum in quinque partibus conscissum est. Sed tamen principalis sedes regni ad Arnulfum iusto et merito provenit nisi solummodo quod in patruum suum indigne peccavit. Ceteri quoque quattuor reges fidelitatem et obedientia Arnulfo – sicut dignum erat – promiserunt. Nullus enim illorum quatuor regum hereditarius illius regni erat in paterna parte nisi Arnulfus solus. Quinque itaque reges confestim, Karoli moriente, consecrati sunt. Sed imperium penes Arnulfum remanserit. Talis ergo regni diviso fuit.*

offered a real possibility we can see with hindsight, as perhaps some of his contemporaries could with foresight, was pure illusion. (Louis did in fact gain imperial consecration after Fulk's death; the only result was that he was blinded at Verona in 905 and thereafter counted for nothing.) But the Carolingian empire had stood for something for a very long time: it represented peace, stability, legitimacy and its dissolution was unthinkable to men of the old establishment, of whom Archbishop Fulk, the successor of the great Hincmar, was as great as any. He could not in fact have done much about it, but it was not foolish, let alone ignoble, of him to try.

It is instructive to look at the crisis of 887 from the front angle as well as the back. When Charles was deposed he was already ailing and it must have been obvious that he had not long to live – he survived his deposition by only a few weeks. The reasons behind the coup must, then, have been pressing. In the forefront of them must have been the question of the succession. Charles had an illegitimate son who was totally unacceptable to the magnates – and the pope – because his mother was of low birth.[10] Arnolf, his actual successor, was also canonically illegitimate but his mother was a lady, so he was acceptable. Charles was at complete variance with his magnates over the succession, so that it was important he should not die in harness before they had resolved the situation. But the Vikings were also a factor. The Frankish royal annals were at this time being kept up in two recensions: the northern annals, being written at Mainz, and the southern annals located at Regensburg. The Mainz annalist is very hostile to Charles while the Regensburg annalist is more favourable. Charles's reputation had been sinking since his accession, and his inability to deal with the Vikings was an important factor. What the Mainz annalist particularly disliked was the fact that Charles was prepared to treat with the Viking enemy, which Mainz thought treasonable. It is easy to see that Charles wasn't just an incompetent fool. His power-base was Swabia, which was not troubled by the Vikings. Had he taken an active role against them as Mainz wanted, he might have failed to do much unless he could rally his southerners to follow him in a war that did not affect their interests. The magnates thought that Arnolf, who also it should be remembered had a southern power-base, was the better bet (which he was). What I think we can see is that the empire was coming apart at the seams. This was an epoch-making event, even if it is one that leaves most English medieval historians cold. The compiler however did grasp something of the gist of what was happening.

It is widely known that there were threads connecting England and Francia at this time. The migration of St Ursula and her multitude of virgin companions from England to Cologne and the gifts or loans of important illuminated manuscripts that so influenced Anglo-Saxon art are obvious examples. They have been seen merely as threads, but I think they were more, that they made up a pattern, and an important pattern at that. I have come to see the English tenth-century reformation as coming to a head in Edgar's reign but really beginning much earlier, in Æthelstan's. In an important paper Michael Wood has shown how Frankish, notably East Frankish, clerks penetrated England and the English church in that reign.[11] The first contacts between

---

10 According to R McKitterick, *The Frankish kingdom under the Carolingians* (1983), 262, Charles's failure to have his illegitimate son Bernard recognized as his heir was 'not necessarily because he was illegitimate but more likely to have been a reflection on his ability'. But Hlawitschka, *Lotharingien*, 2–8 points out that the sources emphasize that his mother was a concubine of low birth and the magnates, especially the bishops, would not have him at any price.

11 M Wood, 'The making of Æthelstan's empire: an English Charlemagne?' in P Wormald, DA Bullough

Fleury and senior English churchmen were made in the same reign: contacts that were to have such fateful consequences. What drew these threads into a pattern was the Vikings.

At least it can be said of the northmen they were never guilty of racial discrimination. The ancestors of English, Germans, Dutch, Belgians and French were plundered indifferently. The Vikings cared nothing about them or their traditions, only about their property. They turned the English Channel and the North Sea into a lake from which they could attack all the surrounding shores wherever and whenever it suited them. It is obvious that the fleets mentioned in the English and Frankish sources were sometimes the same fleet; and the Vikings did not see their operations as divided into two halves.[12] The same interconnection between the invaders of England and Francia is shown in the prelude to the *Visio Rollonis* under 876.[13]

No less obvious is the fellow-feeling the compiler had for the Frankish world and the way he closely identified with it especially from the intimate information he records and the way he does it. It is to be noticed for example how sensitive the compiler is to Frankish protocol in the differentiation he makes under the year 879 between the obit of the emperor Charles and that of his son King Louis.[14] The intimate blending the compiler achieved of Frankish and English sources is shown well by the continuation of the same annal. This reveals the compiler as an author whose world ranges from Chippenham to Bavaria via Fulham, and who moves in easy familiarity all over it.[15] This fellow-feeling was above all created by the Viking threat. We should expect cooperation where that was possible, and at the least shared intelligence. There is plenty of evidence of this in the pages of the annals of St Neots. But there is also evidence of shared intelligence at a rather deeper level.

The Anglo-Saxon chronicle has a puzzling entry under the year 853: 'The Lord Leo was then pope in Rome, he hallowed him [Alfred, youngest son of Æthelwulf, king of Wessex 839–58] as king and accepted him as godson.' Alfred was only four years old at the time and the annal has met with puzzlement and dismissive scepticism.[16] It has been suggested that the pope confirmed Alfred and the chronicle mistook this for coronation. The sacrament of confirmation has its mysteries but it

and R Collins (eds), *Ideal and reality in Frankish and Anglo-Saxon society: essays presented to JM Wallace-Hadrill* (1983).

12 Annals of St Neots, ed Dumville, under 879: *Et eodem anno magnus paganorum exercitus de ultramarinis partibus venit navigans in Tamensem fluuium.* Under 885: *paganorum exercitus divisit se in duas turmas: una etenim turma in Orientalem Franciam perrexit; et altera, ad Angliam veniens Cantiam adiit civitatemque que Hrofesceastra dicitur . . . obsedit.*

13 *Eodem quoque anno Halfdena – rex illius partis que in Nordanhymbris erat – totam regionem sibimet suisque divisit; et illam cum suo exercitu colunt. Rollo cum suis anno eodem Normanniam penetravit xv kal. Decembris. Idem Normannorum dux Ról, cum in Antiqua Brytannia sive Anglia hiemaret militaribus fretus copiis.*

14 Annals of St Neots, ed Dumville, under 879: *xii nonas Octobris praecellentissimus imperator Karolus sancte recordationis insignisque memorie temporalem finiens cursum feliciter – ut credimus – ad gaudia migravit eterna . . . Ipsoque anno obiit Hlodovicus rex Occidentalium Francorum, frater Iuditte regine Adhelwlfi regis Anglorum.*

15 *Eodem vero anno praefatus paganorum exercitus, de Cyppanhame – ut promiserat – consurgens, Cyrenceastram adiit que est in meridiana parte Hwicciorum sita ibique per unum annum mansit. Et in eodem anno magnus paganorum exercitus de ultramarinis partibus venit navigans in Tamensem fluuium et adunatus est superiori exercitui; sed tamen hiemavit in loco qui dicitur Fullanham iuxta flumen Tamensis. Loduuicus rex Saxonum adhuc fratre suo Karlomanno vivente Bauuariam ingreditur.*

16 D Whitelock, DC Douglas and SI Tucker, *The Anglo-Saxon chronicle: a revised translation* (1961, 2nd edn 1965), xxiii.

seems unlikely that it had so great a hold on the contemporary imagination as to drive Æthelwulf to send a four-year-old boy on the perilous journey to Rome simply to be confirmed by the pope. I suggested many years ago that the business had to do with Æthelwulf's will, which gave a plausible reason why it was important to him to have Alfred consecrated by the pope.[17] We know from Asser (chapter 16) that Æthelwulf made a will, but the text has not survived. Its terms were rehearsed however in Alfred's own will.[18] According to Alfred, Æthelwulf bequeathed the inheritance to the three brothers Æthelbald, Æthelred and Alfred with the proviso that whichever lived the longest was to succeed to everything. This resembles a form of insurance called a tontine in the early modern era, now for obvious reasons illegal.

I suggested that Æthelwulf was trying to overcome the traditional, customary, law that required that the kingdom should be divided between the deceased king's surviving sons. He was seeking to achieve what Gerd Tellenbach, writing about the attempt by Henry I (*d.* 936) to do the same in East Francia, called *die Unteilbarkeit des Reiches*, the impartibility of the kingdom.[19] It cannot be said that historians have taken much notice of what I wrote.[20] Scholarly attention has been given to explaining away the chronicle annal and a cognate document, an alleged letter to Æthelwulf from Leo IV printed by Stevenson in his edition of Asser. One scholar cast doubt on the letter by pointing out that Leo IV's name was much used by forgers of papal letters as a convenient attribution. But as Leo IV was the pope of the day, had any other papal name been used we should have to dismiss the letter out of hand as a forgery. So if it is attributed to Leo IV it is a forgery and if it isn't it is a forgery too. This is catch-22 diplomatic, the sort that should warn any scholar tempted to use it that he or she is barking up the wrong tree. In other words it is a device for ignoring the letter and the annal. The annals of St Neots have not been cited in this connection: they need to be. Under 853 they read: 'At this time the lord pope Leo IV occupied the apostolic see, and he confirmed the aforesaid child Alfred and received him as his son by adoption and also consecrated him with oil as the anointed king.'[21] That seems to be that.

The custom of partitioning the kingdom on the decease of a king seems to have been strongly entrenched in Francia, as the problems raised by the succession to Louis the Pious show. Louis had, unusually for the men of his family, several sons who survived into manhood. By custom he must provide for each. Agreement was reached when he was in the prime of life and the nature of his own views is suggested when he exempted the empire from the partition. This was to remain indivisible and was entailed on his eldest son Lothar. Then Louis sired another son who had to be provided for too. His half-brothers would not agree to any revision of the agreement that meant less for themselves. The dangers these partitions could create must have been obvious to anyone. But revision meant disinheriting younger sons and a reduction in their expectations of status. Thus was created a vast vested interest of younger

---

[17] E John, *Orbis Britanniae and other studies* (1966), 37ff.

[18] *Select English historical documents*, ed FE Harmer (1914), no xi; also conveniently available in Keynes and Lapidge, *Alfred the Great*, 173–9.

[19] G Tellenbach, 'Die Unteilbarkeit des Reiches' in his *Die Entstehung des deutschen Reiches*, ed H Kämpf (1956).

[20] With the honourable exception of the late Michael Wallace-Hadrill, in his Ford lectures of 1970. Cf JM Wallace-Hadrill, *Early Germanic kingship in England and on the continent* (1971).

[21] *Quo tempore dompnus Leo papa quartus apostolice sedi preerat, qui prefatum infantem Alfredum confirmavit et in filium adoptionis sibimet accepit et etiam unctum oleo consecravit in regem.*

sons and younger brothers. Only a great external threat could overcome this combination of vested interest with the inertia of tradition, and that did not exist as yet in Louis's day. The same practice certainly existed in England.[22] Æthelwulf, who was married to Louis's granddaughter, had every opportunity to learn about Louis's problems in Francia (if he needed lessons in this matter). But he ruled an England in which he and his family offered the only prospect of preventing a complete Viking takeover. His magnates could see what this would mean for them in expropriations when they looked at England outside Wessex. Partly for this reason Æthelwulf was successful, partly because only his two youngest sons left heirs. When Æthelred succeeded near to the darkest time of the war, Alfred tells us, the two brothers renewed and confirmed the agreement. In spite of this one of Æthelred's sons refused to accept it and joined the Vikings to no very great effect.

We left East Francia ruled by the emperor Arnolf, who was succeeded by his shadowy son Louis the Child (king 900–11), who died too young to do anything anyone thought worth noting. Louis was succeeded by the first non-Carolingian king of East Francia, Conrad I, duke of Franconia. This is what it is usual to say but it may be doubted if Conrad would have agreed. He was quite closely related to the Carolingian family on his mother's side – he was as closely related to the Carolingians as Louis of Provence – and for most of his reign (911–19) tried to rule in a high Carolingian style with disastrous results. At the end of his life Conrad realized that the Carolingian order had gone for ever – though it left a residual legacy that was to give the tenth-century kings of the East Franks a great deal of trouble. Conrad therefore arranged that he should be succeeded by the most powerful of the East Frankish magnates, Henry the Fowler, duke of Saxony (Henry I of East Francia 919–36).

At this point we must look at another reversal, not so much of custom, but of what was usual practice. At this time most kings married the womenfolk of their magnates. There were exceptions. In England in the sixth century Æthelberht of Kent married a Frankish princess. Æthelwulf married the sister of the king of the West Franks and after his death his son married the same lady (and after his death she married the duke of Bavaria). This was really all. Æthelred II's marriage to Emma of Normandy and Cnut's marriage to Emma after Æthelred's death don't really count. Emma was not a princess although she was foreign; the marriages fitted more into the pattern of magnatial politics than international relations. But Edward the Elder, king of Wessex 900–24, had several daughters and Frankish royalty queued up to marry them. This is easy to explain. The compiler had already noted that of the five kings who replaced the emperor Charles III only Arnolf was of royal birth. The new royal families were woefully short of pedigree and one legacy the Carolingians had left was the importance of pedigree. The house of Cerdic had pedigree in abundance.[23] According to their traditions they went back to the earliest Merovingian times and without any doubt they were royal earlier than the Carolingians. Marriage to an English princess was an asset in this world, and not only upstarts joined the queue. The only remaining Carolingian king, Charles the Simple of West Francia, married one of Edward's daughters and ended up burdening Æthelstan with the need to support, in every sense, his son, Louis (IV) d'Outremer (king of the West Franks 936–54). The most striking marriage, although technically to an upstart family, was that of a West Saxon princess

22 Stenton, *Anglo-Saxon England*, 66ff.
23 Æthelweard, *Chronicon*, proem.

to Otto, the son and eventual heir of Henry I, the future emperor Otto (I) the Great (912–73). From this union the Salian dynasty that succeeded the Saxon derived its pretensions and this English connection was to have important consequences in the last generation before the Norman conquest of England.

It is interesting therefore to note that Henry I of East Francia followed in the footsteps of his daughter-in-law's great-grandfather, Æthelwulf. Henry did not have to deal with the Vikings – Arnolf had seen to that – but he did have to deal with the Hungarians, who from the point of view of East Francia were worse. Because of their geographical position they could raid every part of the kingdom. They almost never attacked directly from Hungary through the mountains and forests that protected southern Germany. Instead they swept through what is now Poland but was then a flatland ruled by a disparate *mélange* of Slav tribes without even a semblance of unity and attacked Saxony and Thuringia, which were then in the front line. This danger gave Henry the power to force his magnates to accept the *Unteilbarkeit des Reiches* and appoint his eldest son, Otto, as his sole heir. He did not follow Æthelwulf's precise example: he had no need to. His youngest son Brun (*d.* 965) was dedicated to the church from an early age; he was always a strong supporter of his brother Otto and became archbishop of Cologne and duke of Lotharingia. The disinherited son was Henry (*d.* 955), who took years to accept his disinheritance. He was for a long time a thorn in the side of his brother but he never quite gathered enough support to threaten to overturn Henry I's arrangements. In the end Henry realized that whatever sympathy he aroused in traditionalists could not overcome the feeling that the policy was right for the time.[24] In the event he accepted his reduced position and Otto made him duke of Bavaria where, loyal, he was at least as much trouble as he had been disloyal. It is impossible to tell whether Henry I took Æthelwulf as his model but it seems likely he knew about what had happened in Wessex.

There is another parallel between West Saxon and old Saxon policies for dealing with invader-raiders. King Alfred introduced the policy of surrounding Wessex with fortified garrisons called burhs. Most of the people of Wessex lived within twenty miles of a burh and it was difficult to escape the burdens the burhs entailed. The point of the system is obvious: the countering of the Vikings greatest weapon, mobility. The burhs had to be built, supported and garrisoned locally. They exercised considerable control over their dependent districts through the *burhgemot*, a court that met twice a year. After defending Wessex successfully they were imported into the midlands by Alfred's daughter and his son-in-law, Æthelflaed the lady of the Mercians and Æthelred the ealdorman of Mercia. In Saxony in the 920s Henry I had by a great stroke of luck – contemporaries would have called it providential and who is to say they were wrong – secured a truce with the Hungarians that let him build a similar system round Saxony and probably Thuringia. Some, if not much, information survives about both systems, and there is enough to suggest a certain family resemblance, as Maitland noted long ago.[25] I think we are entitled to think that Henry knew about what happened in Wessex and followed its example. Whatever it cost the local people – and the evidence suggests the burdens were onerous – it was worth it. In both

[24] Even Henry's partisans, led by his mother, did not wholly reject Henry I's policy. Queen Matilda argued that the Byzantine rule of porphyrogenitus, that is the succession of the son born first after his father had attained the purple, should apply. There is no precedent for this and I think that Matilda realized there was no hope of partitioning the kingdom, so she sought the whole lot for her favourite son.

[25] FW Maitland, *Domesday book and beyond* (1897, 1965 edn), 231.

cases the invasions were decisively checked. When the Hungarians tried a last large-scale invasion, the one that was finally ruined at the Lech in 955, they were forced to attack southern Germany directly. The mountains and the forests were less formidable than the *Burgen*.

It is easy to see that interest in what was happening on both sides of the North Sea was mutual. It is equally easy to see why the Anglo-Saxon chronicle, Asser and the annals of St Neots should have such an interest in Frankish affairs. Given the compiler's interest in and understanding of the contemporary situation, it was natural for him to end where he did. He saw that the conversion of Guthrum and Rollo meant a sea-change in the politics of his world. I do not suppose he thought that conversion in itself would bring an immediate amendment of manners, but that is not the point. In England and West Francia the northmen had become part of the body politic, and that was to make a tremendous difference. How soon after the chronological ending of the annals did the compiler set to work? I think that the realization that the conversion of Guthrum and Rollo and their followers was crucial implies that a certain lapse of time was necessary before the full story could be put together. One of the compiler's sources suggests this was indeed the case.

This is Abbo of Fleury's *Passio sancti Edmundi*, which the compiler knew well and quotes at length and verbatim. Abbo wrote this work while in temporary exile from his home monastery, Fleury, where his 'host' Oswald, archbishop of York, bishop of Worcester and abbot of Ramsey had received his monastic education. It seems that Abbo had got his information about St Edmund and a sort of commission to write his life from St Dunstan. The book can be dated to the mid-980s. There is no doubt that the compiler used the *Passio* that has come down to us. He quotes verbatim on some scale and he quotes bits of Abbo's characteristic theology that Ælfric, abbot of Eynsham, leaves out of his English version.[26] Thus the annals of St Neots cannot be earlier than the tenth-century reformation. That movement was part of a development common to England and Francia. The great Frankish centre that so influenced England was the abbey of Fleury. The event that started that connection off has already been mentioned. Æthelstan had taken his nephew Louis d'Outremer, the son of the Carolingian king of the West Franks, under his protection. When Louis was invited to take the West Frankish crown Æthelstan sent him back under the escort of Bishop Oda of Ramsbury, later archbishop of Canterbury. Bishop Oda visited Fleury on his way home and received the tonsure there. Under the circumstances this could have been little more than a gesture of solidarity with the new Benedictine monasticism. But Oda's nephew was St Oswald and he was sent to Fleury for what seems to have been a protracted monastic training. The relations and contacts of the late ninth and early tenth centuries were still developing and bearing fruit and I think history of the kind represented by the annals of St Neots would have been of interest to the new monks.

---

[26] Another sign of the times is provided by Ælfric's hagiographical writings. Had they been written in Latin and survived in an anonymous manuscript there would have been considerable difficulty in determining where they came from and the milieu of the author. The vapid life of St Swithun – included only because he had been bishop of Winchester – and the powerful life of St Oswald derived from Bede might have given clues. On the other hand the life of St Maur with its traditional if legendary account of the foundation of Fleury, told at some length, and the strongly Frankish orientation of much of Ælfric's writing would have counted against any English origin.

This might well fit in with another source, the first *Vita Neoti*. The compiler mentions the life of Neot by name and tells the story of King Alfred and the cakes. Michael Lapidge, its latest editor, thinks for what seem sound reasons that it is certainly pre-conquest, but dates it no more precisely than between the third quarter of the tenth century and the conquest. But is the life Lapidge has edited the one the compiler used? Lapidge thinks it is, and his case is a powerful one. If this is so, as it may well be, it fits pretty well with the compiler's use of the life of St Edmund. Dumville raises important doubts however.[27] The verbal differences between the story of Alfred and the cakes in the life and the annals are considerable. They have, in fact, only a two-line verse in common. The interpolation of verses into his text is typical of the hagiographer but not the compiler. Dumville points out that a number of the compiler's sources can be identified and the only one he rewrites so drastically is the life. The only wording the two works have in common is the aforementioned two-line verse and there is a considerable alteration in the storyline. One may add this is the more telling when one notices he introduces the passage by: 'And in the life of the holy father Neot it is written' (*Et, in vita sancti patris Neoti legitur*). Dumville is inclined to think that the compiler was using 'an intermediate source'. Lapidge, on the other hand, thinks that the alterations 'are nothing more than the attempt to make the Neot-centred narrative of the *Vita* 1 square with the Alfred-centred narrative of Asser'. But even so a total rewriting, in which some of the rewriting does not seem specially relevant to what Lapidge thinks the compiler's aim was, does seem rather drastic. I incline to Dumville's view here, but one must admit that at the moment this is an insoluble dilemma. If there were an intermediate version of the life it would most probably be earlier than the life Lapidge edited, but in any case there is really little of importance for the dating of the annals of St Neots to be got from the *Vita Neoti*.

There is a point worth throwing in here. One of the compiler's sources was Flodoard. One could not claim with any certainty that Flodoard was unknown in early tenth-century England. But I have pointed out there are signs that his writings and views were known and had influence in English reforming circles in the late tenth century.[28] So Flodoard, Abbo of Fleury and perhaps the life of St Neot point to the time of the tenth-century reformation. To which one might add that it seems unlikely that the annals of St Neots were written after the full scale of the Danish invasions of the last decade of the tenth century had been disclosed. I have already suggested the evidence of the continuity behind all this. Although the Carolingian empire had passed away, members of the Carolingian family ruled West Francia until 987 and the head of the family in 987 survived to make trouble for some years to come in West Francia. The last known member of the Carolingian family survived to bring the body of Otto III (*d.* 1002) back from Rome to East Francia (the fact that his Christian name was Otto cannot be without significance). The concerns of the annals were still sufficiently relevant to justify the labour of their composition. In the reign of Henry I – of England and Normandy – it was possible that an antiquarian-minded scribe in an antiquarian-minded community might wish to copy the text but not I think compose it.

---

[27] *Vita prima sancti Neoti*, ed Lapidge, cxviii–xix; annals of St Neots, ed Dumville, lxiv. Lapidge and Keynes, *Alfred the Great*, 197–202 conveniently gathers together the texts relating to Alfred and the cakes. It does seem that the story of Alfred and the cakes is earlier than has been supposed. I remember the late Sir Frank Stenton, who was of course compelled at that time to believe that the written texts were post-conquest, expressing the opinion that the story was based on much older traditions.

[28] *Orbis Britanniae*, 289 n1.

The exaltation of Norman power, the Norman triumph in England and probably too the consequences of Harold Godwineson's great victory at Stamford Bridge had rendered the northmen marginal. It used to be a favourite examination question whether England only became part of Europe in 1066: the answer it seems is no it did not, but also that what happened in 1066 was rather the exclusion of the northmen from Europe outside their native Scandinavia. This was a new and very different world from that reflected in the annals and no longer a very recent world when the manuscript was written, about 1120–40. I cannot see that they belong to this new world and I opt for the old one. The conversions of Guthrum and Rollo either side of the year 900 and their consequences had opened the way for new polities with new policies. An end had been put to the periodic collapses of civility, and the tenth-century reformation, largely rooted in Francia and England, was one of the first fruits.

It seems to me that the compiler was a man intelligent enough to have grasped this: not a man of any originality, he proceeded to lay before his readers an account of what had happened and how it had happened by a process of selection, largely from the writings of others. His principles of selection were not insular. They indicate a man of European perspective. Precisely because he was not original and confined himself very largely to selection we cannot argue that his was a lone voice. The fact that he took the trouble to make the annals of St Neots must suggest he thought an audience for this sort of thing existed. It has been suggested – by Patrick Wormald – that a successor to Wilhelm Levison's marvellous Ford lectures is called for and would be entitled 'England and the continent in the tenth century'.[29] The annals must be an important primary source for such an enterprise. Another such source would be the anonymous *Encomium Emmae reginae*, probably written in Flanders in 1041 – the projected study could not be entirely confined to the tenth century – and a complementary work in that here a continental writer comments to some effect on English affairs. Again he is writing from the milieu of a house reformed as part of the tenth-century reformation. In the encomiast's day the compiler's world had come apart but not in the fashion of the dark days of the first Viking age. Quite a lot was left, notably the reformed houses that could now survive the havoc created by Sweyn, his son Cnut and their henchmen; it was in one of these houses that the compiler must have been working. But it does seem that the mental world of the encomiast is quite different from that of the compiler. For the compiler the English had triumphed and absorbed the Vikings. For the encomiast the Danes had come and in a way absorbed the English. It seems to me that a reading of the two works strongly suggests that the compiler wrote at least a generation earlier than the encomiast. At the very least the view of late Anglo-Saxon England as a lot of homespun peasants waiting to be taken into Europe by William the Conqueror is a load of codswallop.

---

[29] Cf W Levison, *England and the continent in the eighth century* (1946).

4

Cola's *tūn*: Rural Social Structure in Late Anglo-Saxon Devon

ROSAMOND FAITH

The small region discussed here is part of the South Hams district of south Devon.* It is essentially the peninsula bounded on the east by the Kingsbridge ria, the long inlet of the sea running up to Kingsbridge, and on the west by the shallow tidal estuaries of the Avon and the Erme. It has a rocky coastline with steep cliffs, at their highest and most dramatic at Bolt Head. Its northern edge linked the lower reaches of the Avon and Erme to the top of the Kingsbridge ria. Each river had an important beach-port: Bantham at the mouth of the Avon, where Mediterranean wares were still imported in the seventh century, and Oldaport on the Erme, with an associated Romano-British defensive work. Both were served by roads kept up in the ninth century, and it is hard to resist thinking of a possible connection with the Dartmoor tin trade, undocumented though that is for the Anglo-Saxon period. So although the area was at the county's edge it was for perhaps eight hundred years on an important trade route.[1] The uplands at its centre are crowned by tumuli at Malborough (110m) and Sorley (137m), and the major present-day nucleations at Malborough, Churchstow and West Alvington catch the eye from a good distance across an open landscape. From these uplands steep-sided valleys drop down to the sea or to join the two major rivers: this is WG Hoskins's 'characteristic Devonian landscape . . . the lanes, the small irregular fields, the great hedge-banks, the isolated farmhouse at the end of a track'.[2]

Most of the farms and hamlets are on or near the spring-line around 40–80m and the most typical site for the farmstead is at or near the head of a small valley.[3] The importance of the water-supply in their location is shown by the fact that several incorporate Old English *wielle*, spring or stream, in their names. One farm is called Collaton, today a hamlet in Malborough parish. Collaton is one of twenty-three manors recorded in domesday book in the area shown in figure 1. In King Edward's time it had belonged to Cola, from whom it took its name: Cola's *tūn*. After the conquest the manor of Collaton had been swept up into the large barony of Judhæl of

---

* This is a version of the paper awarded the John Nichols prize for 2002.

[1]   A Fox, 'Some evidence for a dark age trading station at Bantham, near Thurlestone, south Devon', *Antiquaries' Journal* xxxv (1935); M Todd, *The south-west to AD 1000* (1987), 260–1; D Hooke, *Pre-conquest charter-bounds of Devon and Cornwall* (1994), 106, 108.

[2]   WG Hoskins, *Devon* (1954), 55.

[3]   This may be an ancient pattern: see WLD Ravenhill, 'An analysis of the dwelling sites established in Cornwall and Devon between the fifth and the eleventh centuries, and their contribution to the modern settlement pattern' (University of London PhD thesis 1950).

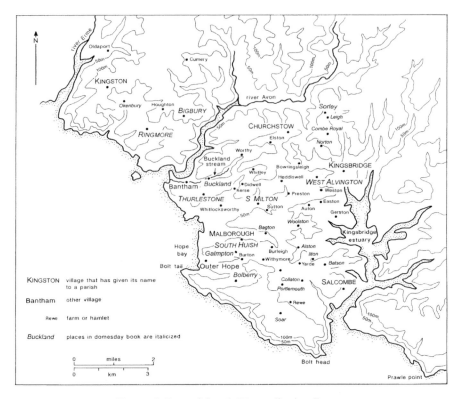

Figure 1 Part of South Hams district, Devon

Totnes and he had granted it to Turgis. If Cola was at all typical of south Devon
farmers of the eleventh century, investigating his resources in land and livestock and
the neighbourhood in which he lived and farmed may illuminate a small corner of the
world of an important class of late Saxon people.

Names formed like Collaton from a personal name in the genitive with the suffix
-tūn are common in this area, as they are in much of Devon.[4] They generally record an
earlier generation of Saxon owners who had been replaced by others before 1066. In
our area Eadhild of Ilton, Afa of Auton, Wulfsige of Woolston, Bacca of Bagton,
Ægel of Elston, Ælfa of Alvington do not appear in domesday book among those who
had land 'in the time of King Edward', that is at the time of the Norman conquest.
Cola at Collaton was unusual in owning a farm in 1066 which bore his own name and
Alwine of Alston is a lone example of the eponymous owner still being in possession
in both 1066 and 1086. The combination of information given in the main 'exchequer'
domesday book and in the more detailed returns for the south-west preserved in what
is known as Exon domesday (*liber exoniensis*) about the landholders in 1086 and
1066 with minor placenames such as these gives us a rare opportunity to look back

---

4   JEB Gover, A Mawer and FM Stenton, *The place-names of Devon* (2 vols English Place-Names
    Society viii–ix 1931–2) ii.680. Unless otherwise indicated, all placename derivations given here are
    from this source.

beyond 1066 to an earlier stratum of local landholding, although it is a stratum as yet impossible to date any more precisely.[5] However, the survival of a charter of the mid-ninth century, whose boundary clause has recently been interpreted by Della Hooke, makes possible a glimpse into a more remote past.[6] In 847 a charter was drawn up for Æthelwulf, king of the West Saxons, concerning twenty hides *om homme*, taken to mean 'in the South Hams'. In this charter these twenty hides were to be 'booked' to the king himself and the result of this odd transaction would be to make the land – or rather the people who lived on it – exempt from all dues to the king except for two of the common burdens of public service (army service and bridge work).[7] What formerly could be taken from the land and its inhabitants for the king's benefit could now go to whomever he chose to grant it to. No subsequent grantee is known, but large grants of bookland were the common way of endowing a minster, and a possible candidate might have been a putative minster at the royal manor of West Alvington. The church there later had dependent chapelries nearby at Sorley, South Milton, South Huish, Salcombe and Malborough and was evidently a church of superior status. The placename Preston indicates the presence of a body of clergy, although it has to be borne in mind that Buckfast Abbey had an interest in the area, as it owned Norton by 1086. As will appear, there are indications that West Alvington had also been the centre of some kind of 'multiple estate'.

What Æthelwulf 'booked' was a large territory. It comprised virtually the whole of the Bolt Head peninsula and its hinterland. It is essentially the land between the Kingsbridge 'estuary', known then as the *hunburgefleot*, and the Erme. This estate had probably once been much larger. Of two hides at North and South Huish only South Huish is included in the grant and the boundary is drawn in such a way as to exclude the whole of the present-day parish of Thurlestone which possibly, as it includes Buckland – 'bookland' – had already been granted out. It looks very much like the southern part of what Hoskins described as a 'riverine estate', a large early land unit with rivers as its boundaries.[8] Six of the south Devon hundreds, long units with their heads on Dartmoor and their feet in the sea, have such boundaries; Æthelwulf's South Hams estate represents the southern part of two of them, Stanborough and Ermington hundreds.

Manors and parishes

Æthelwulf's twenty hides can all be 'assigned to their own places and names' in the words of a charter of his forebear Ine, thanks to Hooke's work. That is to say that the individual hidages recorded in domesday book of the places within the area described by the charter's boundary amount to twenty. By the time that domesday book was compiled the hidage of a place represented the base for calculating the amount of geld it owed. It is by virtue of its appearance in domesday under its own name, and with the

5   *Domesday book, seu liber censualis Wilhelmi primi regis Angliae* [ed A Farley] (2 vols 1783); *Liber exoniensis* in *Libri censualis vocati domesday-book additamenta* [ed H Ellis] (Record Commission 1816).
6   Hooke, 105–12.
7   P Sawyer, *Anglo-Saxon charters: an annotated list and bibliography* (1986), no 298; FM Stenton, *Anglo-Saxon England* (1947), 304–5.
8   WG Hoskins, 'The highland zone in domesday book' in his *Provincial England: essays in social and economic history* (1963), 40–3.

number of hides for which it 'answers to' the geld, that a place, irrespective of size, may be reckoned a 'manor'. The hidage was distributed among the 'manors' of the area in very small amounts, from a half to two hides. Such low assessments were characteristic of this part of Devon.[9] Not all the places in the area appear in domesday book. Neither Churchstow nor Malborough is there, yet both are today the centres of parishes and were evidently sites of early cultural importance: *Mala's beorg* tumulus gave its name to Malborough and a British site at *cruc wiel* (Churchill) is nearby. Churchstow is 'church place'. Some places like Yarde (yard, or yard of land) or Rewe (row or rough) were perhaps too small to be assessed and were included under larger places. Places in another category may not have been hidated because of their function and their relationship to a major estate centre. Easton, Weston, Sutton, Norton, Gerston, Burton and Bowringsleigh (east, west, south and north *tūnas*, grass *tūn*, *geburas' tūn* and *geburas' leah* respectively) all have names which by either their location or function relate them to an estate centre. If they were part of the inland of an important estate, land directly exploited for the landowner, they are likely to have been exempt from geld and thus will not have had a geld rating or hidage.[10] The distribution of these placenames points to West Alvington as a likely estate centre. A royal manor before the conquest and after, it had a large amount of arable by local standards – enough for ten teams – some of which may have been at the king's *tūn* at Kingston (also unhidated).

It is less easy to account for the non-appearance as manors of individual farms or hamlets with names much like Collaton: Elston (Ægel's *tūn*), Auton (Afa's *tūn)*, Heddeswell (Hiddi's *wielle*), Whitlocksworthy (Wihtlac's *worthig*, farm) and Didwell (Dudda's *wielle*, spring or stream). Not only are their names similar, with a Saxon personal name as their first element, they occupy very similar locations and like Collaton each is today simply a farm, or perhaps a couple of farms. To explain these we might fall back on Maitland's definition of a manor, 'a house against which geld is charged', and imagine the inhabitants of these other places paying their tax at their neighbour's house. But that leaves us with a puzzle: why was Collaton chosen to bear a geld rating and thus appears in domesday as a manor while these others were not? This question is pursued below.

Puzzles about the qualifications for manorial status are paralleled by puzzles about parochial. Some places within the territory of Æthelwulf's charter became parishes (West Alvington, Malborough, South Huish, Churchstow, Bigbury, South Milton, Ringmore, Thurlestone and Kingston) but others did not (Salcombe is a modern not a medieval parish). Despite great advances in our understanding of the evolution of the English parish and its chronology the process by which one place attained a church and parochial status and another did not remains rather mysterious. In parts of England church and manor are now seen to have 'kept company from the outset', the landlord's church having started as his private chapel and coming to serve the people on his manor which thus evolved into a parish. The conformity of many manorial and parochial boundaries has substantiated this.[11] But in this part of the South Hams this model will not serve. As Collaton shows, a manor could be tiny, with no seigneurial centre, and not nearly all the manors in domesday became parishes. Nor were all

---

9   J Hatcher 'New settlement: south-west England' in *The agrarian history of England and Wales* ii *1042–1350*, ed HE Hallam (1989), 238–40.

10   RJ Faith, *The English peasantry and the growth of lordship* (1997), 48–55.

11   J Blair, *Minsters and parish churches: the local church in transition 959–1200* (1988), 1–19.

parishes manorial in origin, as the examples of Malborough and Churchstow show: both were parishes, both are absent from domesday book. A possible explanation for their parochial status may be their cultural importance within the settlement hierarchy: that is to say that they were revered holy sites, rather than seigneurial centres. Devon churches are often remote from centres of population, representing early cult sites rather than being closely tied to settlement.[12] More likely they became parishes to serve a growing post-conquest population: Malborough has a substantial medieval church, and both Malborough and Churchstow became significant nucleated settlements. If a place was to achieve parish status it is likely to have done so by the twelfth century. But the roots of the development which culminated in parish formation may well be earlier, and these roots surely went down into the character of an area, its landscape, its social structure, its economy and the lives of its people. With these factors in mind, and with Cola and his *tūn* as our starting point, we can begin to explore Æthelwulf's territory in the South Hams before the conquest.

Topography and farming systems

The South Hams as a whole was 'a fertile region underlain by Devonian sandstones with an above-average density for the county of both population and ploughteams by the time of the Norman Conquest'.[13] The deeply cut landscape meant that the areas where those teams could work were limited to the uplands between the little valleys and to the less steep of the valley sides. These uplands were probably also under pressure from livestock and were probably more used for pasture than they are today: domesday book records considerable acreages of pasture on the coastal manors Soar ('sorrel', where there was a 'steer stream'), Bigbury and South Huish. There were small amounts of meadow at all but three of the twenty-three domesday manors in this area. Woodland is recorded at only five, mostly in the north part of the area where it had been either cleared or penetrated by small clearings and where the charter records an 'old swine enclosure'. It is likely that by the eleventh century there were no longer any substantial woods in the district except those clinging to the valley sides. Because farms needed to include a spread of resources the local topography dictated that they be both large and dispersed. Today they are about a mile or two apart and Hoskins, in pioneering work linking the farms of his day to their possible domesday and Anglo-Saxon predecessors, reckoned that these had been of about two hundred acres and that 'one would have seen four or five farmsteads scattered over every square mile of the landscape other than the moors'.[14]

This raises the question of the size and nature of the working group needed to operate farms of this size before the era of mechanization. A larger group than the nuclear family and a larger settlement than a single farmstead has been suggested as typical of early medieval farms, especially in the highland zone. While there are local variations according to the terrain there is a striking similarity in the descriptions of these, whether on Bodmin Moor, the Scottish western highlands, the chalk downs of Hampshire or the Chiltern hills: a tiny hamlet or cluster of farmsteads surrounded by

---

[12] SM Pearce, *The archaeology of south west Britain* (1981), 214.
[13] Hooke, *Charter-bounds*, 110–11.
[14] Hoskins, 'Highland zone', 31.

its own small subdivided field system with access to considerable areas of open grazing beyond shared with other communities.[15] These seldom developed fully fledged large-scale common-field systems, which are rare in Devon. Rather, in the eastern part of the county at least, the post-conquest pattern was of hamlets shrinking to form the single isolated farms of today. Where villages did develop they had sub-divided fields, but these were not worked in a common-field system.[16] Therefore, while a shift to common-field farming is often cited as a crucial impetus to the development of the English village, the possibility must be left open that other processes contributed to the development of the three major nucleations in this area, Churchstow, Malborough and West Alvington.

Collaton is today a tiny hamlet, with vestiges of at least one other farmstead on the site. Lower and Higher Collaton lie down tracks less than a quarter of a mile away and the layout of the roads suggests that there was once another farm as well. Collaton lies at the head of a mile-long combe which runs between steep wooded sides: these 'hangers' are likely to have been the six acres of woodland recorded here in 1086. It then widens through a little marsh to a small sandy bay. This is the 'salt combe' from which the later Salcombe took its name and no doubt once had a saltern as did Bigbury in 1086. The stream running down the combe, which rises just above the farmstead at Collaton and periodically floods the meadow just below the house, used to power Hangar Mill at the foot of the steepest part of the combe. Less than a quarter of a mile to the west of the salt combe another runs down to the sea and is likely to have been part of the farm at West Portlemouth, so their boundary will have run along the ridge between the two. To the east a boundary knoll, *gemære cnoll*, now Maryknowle, and beyond that 'Bata's stone' marked the boundary of the adjoining farm at Batson.

Domesday book reckoned the assets of Collaton as land for three ploughteams, half an acre of meadow, two acres of pasture and six of woodland. Only one team was at work; there were three cattle in addition to the team, and a small flock of eleven sheep. The essential winter feed for the team must have come from the valley meadow and from the woodland. The livestock's summer grazing may have been marsh pasture, along the boggy stream bed where in a hot summer the cattle love to stand in the shade up to their bellies in mud, but could also have been on the high ground behind the hamlet, now notable for its larger modern fields. These are under the plough nowadays, but similar land nearby is called 'down' from *dun*, a flat-topped hill. These 'downs' (Broad Downs, Furzedown and so on) look like grazing land, perhaps shared between the farms which abutted on them. It is difficult to make a plausible suggestion about the likely location of the land for three ploughs, but the upper valley sides were ploughed by horses during the second world war and could, with difficulty, have been ploughed by oxen.[17]

Cola would have had some powerful neighbours. To the north-east were valley farms much like his own, whose names record earlier owners, Eadhild, Afa, Alwine, Wulfsige, Bacca and Ægel. Several of these had been replaced before the conquest by influential men who had been picking up farms in the area. Two in particular were Algar and Heca the sheriff. Algar had land at Soar which occupied most of the Bolt

15 N Johnson and P Rose, *Bodmin Moor: an archaeological survey* i *The human landscape to 1800* (1994), 81, 86–7; Pearce, 179–85.

16 HSA Fox, 'Field systems of east and south Devon' pt 1 'East Devon', *Devonshire Association Report and Transactions* civ (1972).

17 Information from Mr G Ayre of Collaton.

Head headland and four other manors in the South Hams: Ilton, Bagton, Sorley and South Huish. Beorhtric son of Algar had another at Leigh. Algar had land in seventeen other places in the county. Heca the sheriff, who held Ringmore and West Portlemouth, had five other Devon manors. Woolston had gone to Uhtræd who had three further Devon manors. Woolston's former owner, the eponymous Wulfsige, survived the conquest property upheaval better than these powerful Saxon lords: none of them remained in possession of their local properties but he was still farming in the neighbourhood at Batson.

Table 3.1

Holders of manors in the South Hams in 1066 and 1086

manor	1066	1086
West Alvington	king	king
Bagton	Algar	Osbern, from Judhæl
Woolston	Uhtræd	Colbert, from Judhæl
Bolberry A	Eadmer	count of Mortain
Bolberry B	Wado	count of Mortain
Buckland	Eadgifu	Hugh
West Portlemouth	Heca	Judhæl
Soar	Algar	Judhæl
Collaton	Cola	Turgis, from Judhæl
Ilton	Algar	Judhæl
Alston	Alwine	Judhæl
Batson	Wulfric	count of Mortain
Norton	Buckfast Abbey	Buckfast Abbey
Combe Royal	Ælfric	Robert
Leigh	Beorhtric son of Algar	Walter de Claville
Sorley	Algar	Judhæl
Thurlestone	John	Judhæl
Ringmore	Heca	Judhæl
Okenbury	Tovi	Judhæl
Bigbury	Ordwulf	count of Mortain
South Milton	2 thegns	Tovi
South Huish	Algar	Judhæl
Galmpton	Alweard	Judhæl

Did the diversity of landowners in the area before the conquest, from magnates like the sheriff to small landowners like Cola and Wulfsige, lead to a parallel diversity of farm management? We can investigate this to a certain extent from the information domesday gives, helped by the fact that Exon domesday provides more information about livestock, and the ratio of demesne to *villani* ploughs, than does the exchequer domesday. However, both record the situation in 1086, not that in 1066, and there are obviously dangers in using their information retrospectively. We do not know how much difference a new Norman lord could have made to a place in the twenty years since the conquest. Looking further back we can observe some major differences between manors that may have resulted from their management in the hands of the last generation of Saxon owners, but may equally have had deeper roots. Looking forward we can speculate with a little more certainty as to whether any of these differences were to be a factor in the processes that led to the formation of parish and village.

Landowners and their properties in 1086

One inquiry we can make about the South Hams manors as they appear in domesday is to ask how seigneurialized they were, in the sense of being organized to support a lord. Were they heavily demesne-oriented with a large home farm and dependent manorial tenants, were they large farms kept in hand with no tenants, were they loose agglomerations of farms of roughly equal status yet related to a manorial centre, or were they single-family yeoman or peasant farms?

Large pasture farms with absentee owners

As we have seen, two men had dominated the local land market before 1066, Heca and Algar. With property and preoccupations elsewhere they are likely to have been absentee landowners, as were their Norman successors. They would have had to put in a reeve as manager, or leased their manors to a tenant. In spite of the wealth and power of their owners, both Saxon and Norman, several of the manors look more like substantial pasture farms or granges than centres of seigneurial authority over a local tenantry. They cannot have sustained a large arable element: none had more than a couple of teams at work on the home farm and most had small overall populations with few teams in the hands of 'the men'. As Peter Sawyer pointed out long ago, raising sheep for the market was by the eleventh century an important source of Devonshire wealth.[18] Algar and his son and Heca had held manors with large areas of grazing land and their successors had sheep and goat flocks large by the standards of the area.

Although their manors were valuable in terms of these economic assets, this value was not reflected in the manorial values, nor their size in their hidage assessments. Three – Bagton, Woolston, Ilton – had formerly been family farms of the Collaton type, albeit farms with a good supply of grazing land, and had perhaps been rated accordingly. This raises some problems of domesday interpretation. We are accustomed to taking the *valet* figures in domesday as rough indicators of economic value: much of our thinking about the eleventh-century economy would be impossible unless this approach were broadly viable. But it is not easy to adopt this approach to hidages and values in the area considered here. Both are low, both are strikingly uniform. Hidages range between half a hide and two hides, and only two values, of Bigbury and the royal manor of West Alvington, reach £7, generally being much lower. Bigbury was one of the principal stock-rearing manors, but the others with high stock figures had insignificant valuations. One possible explanation may be that these manors had not been considered to be worth much when first hidated, nor valued highly in 1086. Their hidation may date back to the time of Æthelwulf's grant, when their values may have been calculated with an eye to their arable rather than their pastoral potential. There is a strong suggestion that by 1086 these old-fashioned criteria

18 P Sawyer, 'The wealth of England in the eleventh century', *Transactions of the Royal Historical Society* 5.xv (1965).

Table 3.2
Manorial values and assets in 1086

This table shows for each manor: value in £.s.d; land for how many ploughteams; ploughteams in dominio: ploughteams of the villani; number of slaves, villani, bordars, sheep in demesne, other demesne stock.

	value	land for pt	d:v pt	slaves	villani	bordars	sheep	other
West Alvington	7.5.0	10	1:5	4	10	5		
Bagton	15.0	30	½:½	2	3	3	20	15 pigs
Woolston	10.0	3	1:2	3	3	3		
Bolberry A	1.10.0	4	1:1	1	1	19		
Bolberry B	1.7.0	4	1:1½	1	3	1		
Buckland	0.4.0	1½	1½:0	0	2	2		
West Portlemouth	2.0.0	4	1:1½	1	0	3		
Soar	2.0.0	4	1:1½	2	1	3	240	
Collaton	1.0.0	3	½:½	0	3	1	11	
Ilton	1.0.0	3	0:1[a]	1	1	4		
Alston	1.0.0	2	1:½	0	0	3		
Batson	1.15.0	4	1:1	1	3	3	30	
Norton	1.10.0	10	1:5	6	9	12	70	
Combe Royal	0.3.0	3	1:1	1	2	2		
Leigh	1.10.0	4	2:3	4	7	6	80	
Sorley	0.10.0	3	1:2	1	3	4	125	18 cattle, 12 pigs
Thurlestone A	4.0.0	6	2:6	5	15	6	0	also 4 cottars
Thurlestone B	0.5.0	1	0:½[b]	0	2	3		
Ringmore	1.10.0	6	2:3	2	6	6	67	
Okenbury	2.0.0	3	1:2	1	5	2	40	
Bigbury	7.0.0	12	2:3½	0	12	12	107	
South Milton	3.0.0	12	2:3	1	8	6		
South Huish	1.5.0	4	1:3	2	6	6	143	
Galmpton	2.0.0	5	1:4	1	8	6		

[a] at Ilton there was no demesne team, while the villani had six cattle to a plough
[b] at Thurlestone B there was land in demesne for one plough but no demesne ploughteam, while the bordars had half a ploughteam

had been overtaken by a new reality. It looks rather as if the forays which late Saxon landowners had made into the local land market had been made with an eye to acquiring farms with under-exploited potential which they could develop as large-scale pastoral enterprises.

Large absentee landlords with arable farms

Other manors owned by important absentees before the conquest present a different picture. Leigh was owned by Algar's son Beorhtric, Bigbury by Ordwulf; Ringmore was another manor of Heca the sheriff; Buckfast Abbey had Norton and the king West Alvington. In comparison with the pastoral manors just considered these had in 1086 more arable, more teams on the home farm and high manorial populations, also with considerable numbers of teams. In short they were run more as arable enterprises, although Bigbury was an important stock manor too. As arable farming was more labour-intensive than stockraising this meant that they were run with a larger workforce. Although almost all the manors in the area had at least one slave – Devon being a county with a high slave population – these manors had between two and six. What is probably an equally important indicator of an important demesne arable sector is that they had larger numbers of bordars, a category of people closely involved with the work of the home farm (twelve at Norton and Bigbury).[19] This must have given them a distinct centre, with the buildings of the home farm and housing – and very probably allotments – for the slaves and bordars. Some of these large pre-conquest home farms are recognizable today as 'bartons': Leigh Barton, Court Barton at South Huish, Portlemore Barton at West Portlemouth.[20] Bearing in mind their absentee owners, we should probably envisage a reeve or tenant in charge of their day-to-day management.

There were between six and twelve *villani* on these manors. In Devon as elsewhere *villanus* is a difficult term to translate, but there is no need to choose between apparently conflicting interpretations, for each represents a distinct aspect of the people in question. Maitland considered that the *villanus* was a member of the vill, in Old English a *tūnman*, a person belonging to a *tūn* or township, and this proves to be a very helpful way of interpreting the domesday *villani* of the South Hams. Hoskins took the Devon *villani* to be independent farmers, and his course is followed here too.[21] Domesday was interested in the number of ploughteams the *villani*, and sometimes the bordars as well, had at their command: perhaps it is the contribution these teams would make to the productivity of a manor that was of interest to the commissioners, and it is of interest to us too. Finally the Devon *villani* were geld-payers, and their heads, not just their ploughteams, were probably counted with that in mind. We do not know what relationship *villani* had to the owner of the land, and the term may well have had different implications for social relationships in different parts of the country. At its most minimal however it must have indicated the number of people making a living in the vill or township, and on these manors of important absentee landlords there were more *villani* than on the rest. If they were tenants – and this is by no means certain – their manorial lords would have been receiving rents and services of some kind from them. Even if they were simply neighbouring farmers, they were also geld-payers. Larger arable demesnes and larger manorial populations: either or both of these factors had pushed the valuations of West Alvington and Bigbury far above the local average.

Smaller seigneurialized landholdings

It is possible to identify Heca, Algar and Ordwulf as large absentee landowners because they, and their other landholdings, can be identified elsewhere in domesday book. But we cannot find out anything about most pre-conquest landowners, either because we cannot safely identify them with their namesakes elsewhere, or because they have none. Their manors can be analysed though, and several fall into the cate-

---

19 Faith, *English peasantry*, 70–5.
20 Hoskins, 'Highland zone', 33.
21 FW Maitland, *Domesday book and beyond* (1897, 1965 edn), 86–7; Hoskins, 'Highland zone', 20ff.

gory usefully conceived of as 'small seigneurialized landholdings'. These have a home farm with at least one ploughteam and farm workers (slaves and bordars) but with less land under the plough than the large arable-oriented manors discussed in the previous section. Both manors at Bolberry (here designated A and B), Combe Royal, Batson, Sorley, the main Thurlestone manor (Thurlestone A), Woolston, Okenbury and South Huish fall into this category. Some but not all were to become parishes. Leigh is an example. In 962 King Edgar granted to his *minister* land 'at Sorley' consisting of 'a hide less one eighth' or just over three yardlands.[22] The bounds, even as explained by Hooke, are difficult to understand on the ground, but seem to describe a narrow piece of land, mostly bounded by streams and roads, in the steep and wooded territory between Kingsbridge and the Avon. Although only a small place in its overall extent and its arable capacity (land for four teams) it had ten people at work on the home farm in 1086 and has a fine medieval farmhouse, Leigh Barton. It seems that here the successors to a newly endowed royal official of the tenth century had by the eleventh set up an estate which was small but run on seigneurial lines. Higher and Hope Barton at Bolberry possibly originated in a similar way as the centres of Wado and Eadmer, who had each had land there before the conquest.

Family farms or small hamlets

Cola's Collaton was one of a handful of manors which seem on examination to have been little more than single farms: Ilton, Alston, Thurlestone B, Bolberry A and B, and Buckland being very similar. Their overall population consisted of five families or fewer. These families might include one that were slaves, and up to three that were bordars or farm workers. Small though they are, they were counted as manors, and the formula of '*x* plough teams *in dominio*, *y* teams of the *villani*', was applied to them too. Their home farms had a single team or less, and their *villani* the same number. Exchequer domesday, which gives the number of ploughteams on both the land *in dominio* and that of the *villani*, shows that there were similar amounts of each.[23] It has already been suggested that there were in the neighbourhood – and are there today – many other places which seem from their names, distribution and topography to have been very similar but which, having no hidation and therefore not being regarded as manors, do not appear in domesday. It is possible that they could have come into existence between the time of Æthelwulf's grant of 847 and 1086. This would be the likely explanation if all the farms in the district had received their hidage ratings at the time of the grant and these particular farms were omitted from domesday because they were created after 847. They were certainly in existence by the eleventh century, for their names are firmly Saxon: Eadhild of Ilton, Afa of Auton, Wulfsige of Woolston, Bacca of Bagton, Ægel of Elston, Ælfa of Alvington.

Another explanation is pursued here: that these farms are subsumed in the domesday entries under a neighbouring manor, and that the domesday *villani*, the men of the township, were their farmers. This is substantially the kind of analysis that Hoskins applied to domesday when describing the Saxon farms of the highland zone.[24] On most the overall hidage, seldom more than two hides, is divided equally between the demesne and the land of the *villani* (and sometimes of the bordars as well) who pre-

---

22 Hooke, *Charter-bounds*, 165–8; *pace* Hooke this corresponds to the hidage of Leigh, not Sorley, in domesday.

23 *Domesday book: Devon*, ed C Thorn and F Thorn (2 vols 1985) ii, appendix L.

24 Hoskins, 'Highland zone', 21.

sumably would have divided the geld obligation among themselves. We do not know what lay behind the equal division of the hidage liability between both elements in these little 'manors'. Nor do we know when it was done. It is possible that when the overall hidage for each part of Æthelwulf's grant was allotted it was not thought necessary, or possible, to divide the public obligations of each little neighbourhood in this way. Perhaps it was not until the domesday commissioners came around, or possibly when geld came to be levied systematically from the 990s, that it became necessary to divide the liability more systematically too.

Topography, which dictated the dispersed settlement pattern, would have made it difficult to call every farm a manor and give it its own entry in domesday. The entry for West Alvington, with its comparatively high recorded population of ten *villani*, five bordars and four slaves could well have covered nearby Heddeswell (Hiddi's *wielle*) and Auton (Afa's *tūn*); their farmers, and perhaps also the *geburas*, the dependent unfree peasants, of Bowringsleigh, could have owned the five non-demesne plough-teams. It has already been suggested that its dependencies at Easton, Sutton and so on were unhidated and included in its entry. A similar situation on the ground may underlie the entry for South Milton in the western part of the locality, which two thegns had held freely and jointly (*in paragio*) before the conquest. This was a valley-head site with an impressive later barton and more meadow than the average. It was rated at two hides – high for the area and on this basis has been treated here among the manors of large absentee landlords with arable farms. That something more than a seigneurial centre was involved is suggested by the large extent of its potential arable (land for twelve ploughs) and comparatively high recorded population of six bordars and eight *villani*, all apparently unconnected with the demesne farm but with three teams among them. Possibly we should envisage South Milton as comprising an area with the 'middle *tūn*' as its centre and including the farms or hamlets of Wihtlac's worthy (Whitlocksworthy), Dudda's *wielle* (Didwell), and possibly Burleigh and Withymore, all part of the parish today. This would allow each farm a team and a fair amount of ploughland and, if we include the bordars, a couple of farm workers with smallholdings as well.

Thurlestone's entry too, with its high overall population of thirty, of whom fifteen were *villani*, and its six teams beyond those on the demesne, may include neighbouring farms.[25] Thurlestone is an area, and was later a parish, but never apparently had a nucleated centre of any kind: its name comes not from a *tūn* but from the *thyrelan stan*, the pierced stone, at Thurlestone Rock. Its centre, with land for two demesne ploughteams and housing for five slaves, is likely to have been at West or East Buckland. One of these was added to the manor of Bolberry.[26] Thurlestone was discussed above as a smaller seigneurialized landholding and, possibly like Leigh, this *bocland* had been the subject of a grant to a royal official. The remaining six teams could have worked at Worthy, Whitley and Kerse, all valley farms with pre-conquest names. There may well have been other farms as well: there are fifteen *villani*, six bordars and four cottagers to account for. The geld obligation of two hides on this manor, we learn from Exon domesday, was equally divided among demesne and the rest; this equal division, or something very near to it, is found on most of the manors. There was another manor in Thurlestone. It had been leased by a thegn from

---

25 Thurlestone was excluded from Æthelwulf's grant but is discussed here as clearly topographically part of the area under consideration. Hooke, *Charter-bounds*, 107–10.

26 *Domesday book: Devon*, ed Thorn and Thorn, 15.38.

the manor's pre-conquest owner, and the new owner Judhæl had granted it to a knight. It had a small demesne with a single team and two *villani*; three bordars had half a team and a couple of other cattle, perhaps milch cows. This double structure may account for the east and west settlements which were to develop along Buckland stream.

Bigbury, Bicca's *burh*, is one of two manors with this suffix, which suggests some kind of centre distinguished from the more usual *-ton*. The other is Bolberry, named from the peninsula hillfort at Bolt Head. A high-value manor with a large livestock element as well as a considerable demesne workforce, Bigbury was discussed above as being in 1086 the property of an absentee landlord, Ordwulf. On the one and a half hides outside the demesne, however, there were twelve *villani* with three and a half teams at work, very likely at Huga's *tūn* at Houghton, the *worthig* at Cumery (origi-nally a name with a *-worthy* suffix), and possibly others as yet unidentified. The *gafolmanna-tūn* (gafol-payers' *tūn*) at Galmpton, with eight *villani* and six bordars, was a distinct settlement from South Huish, in whose parish it was, and separate too from its little appendage at Burton (perhaps the *geburas' tūn*) on the other side of the small stream which runs down to the bay at Outer Hope (Old Norse *hop*, bay). This pair of places looks rather as if they were originally home to two very distinct kinds of peasants: the free gafol-payers and the unfree geburs, both perhaps defined by their relationship to a seigneurial centre at South Huish.

These examples raise the question of the relationship between the places identified as manors and the neighbouring farms or hamlets which are invisible in domesday book because they are subsumed in the manorial entry. It has been suggested here that these were the farms of neighbouring *villani* and ploughed by their teams. Were these people tenants of the holder of the main manor, itself a small place? Or simply their neighbours? One possible explanation is that even these small farms could have formed a hierarchy that was recognized locally and within which it was the better provided farms that were chosen to be the places 'where geld is demanded and paid'.[27] Hidages must always have been a very rough and ready guide to area and value. But if we take them at face value as reflecting the real division of the two elements in a manor, then they can be useful. In these terms they show that the demesnes of the manors had more ploughteams per hide or yardland than did the land of the *villani*. All the demesne farms had at least one team and supported the families of the slaves and other farm workers. Considering that each of the *villani* farms too had a family to support, then a further disparity begins to appear. The *villani* families had fewer teams at work for them than did the demesne families: most had less than half a team per family (between a tenth and a third of a team per family if we include the bordars).[28] Even when the 'manor' farm was small, as was Collaton with half a team in demesne, its family was better off than the three *villani* with half a team at work between them.

These ploughteam figures are strikingly small, even taking into account the likeli-hood that arable played less of a part in the South Hams farms than did livestock. In fact it is hard to envisage the economy of a farm run on a fraction of a team. In places like Collaton some kind of co-aration seems likely; given the exigencies of the terri-tory this would be co-aration between people who were close neighbours in the small

---

[27] Maitland, *Domesday book and beyond*, 159.
[28] RV Lennard, 'The economic position of the bordars and cottars of domesday book', *Economic Journal* lxi (1951); Hoskins, 'Highland zone', 23.

hamlet, or huddle of farms, that was suggested earlier as typical of early settlements and their field systems. Perhaps at Collaton the 'demesne' or the main farm, with its small flock of eleven sheep and half a team ploughing its yardland, was closely linked with the yardland and half-team of its three *villani* and one bordar: literally so, in that their oxen may have been yoked together to do the ploughing. Where the *villani* of a manor were farmers on land a good way off from the demesne manor this explanation will not do. It was suggested that West Alvington's entry could have covered Heddeswell, Auton and perhaps Bowringsleigh, which between them owned five non-demesne ploughteams. These are over a mile away and must surely have been independent farms, each with a team or more. Similarly the farms or hamlets of Whitlocksworthy, Didwell, Burleigh and Withymore, possibly entered under South Milton, must have been substantial farms each with a team and a fair amount of ploughland. Thurlestone's Worthy, Whitley and Kerse, all valley farms with pre-conquest names, again look like independent units.

Settlement hierarchy and parochial status

This brief survey has revealed a wide range of landholdings in the South Hams from the sheep farms or arable demesnes of powerful absentees, through the seigneurialized manors of smaller lords, the *tūns* and 'worthys' of independent peasant farmers, down to the small and poor places like Cola's *tūn* at the bottom of the hierarchy. The question of the parish system and its local origins may now be clearer with this hierarchy in mind. No single explanation is likely to do. The link between manor and parish, so clear in other parts of England, cannot explain why here certain, but far from all, manors became parishes. Churchstow and Malborough parishes may reflect the fact that both were places of early cultural importance. For the rest, population seems the obvious element to single out: the more churchgoers the greater need for a church. The manors with the highest recorded populations in 1086 were Thurlestone, Norton, Bigbury and West Alvington, with between nineteen and thirty families, followed by Leigh, South Milton, South Huish, Galmpton and Ringmore, with between fourteen and seventeen. Of these only West Alvington, South Huish, Bigbury, South Milton, Ringmore and Thurlestone became parishes. So it seems that while a comparatively high population was a necessary condition for becoming a parish, it was not by itself sufficient.

Population was associated with, perhaps dependent on, another factor: the importance of arable farming. Of the manors with considerable amounts of arable, or what was considered to be potential arable, all but Norton became parishes. Bigbury, South Milton, Norton and West Alvington had land for ten or more teams, Ringmore and Thurlestone six, the rest two to six. Of the manors which score highly both for large populations and large arable, only Norton did not become a parish (and Norton may in fact have operated as the working home farm of a royal centre at West Alvington). It does not seem as if parish status followed the establishment of an impressive home farm and associated seigneurial residence as it did elsewhere. None of the South Hams manors had large demesne arable operations, to judge by the small numbers of their teams *in dominio*, generally one or two, and the remaining teams were at work on the scattered farms described above. Nevertheless it is hard to shake off the idea that a church was likely to be established at an already nucleated and seigneurialized centre. West Alvington is one candidate for this category: a royal manor, possibly the site for a proposed or actual minster.

Arable cultivation is very labour-intensive in comparison with pastoralism. One element that could have been important in establishing a centre was the presence of a large workforce serving the home farm, driving its ploughteams, caring for its working livestock, labouring on its fields – what I have described elsewhere as an 'inland workforce' of slaves and bordars. It is not always possible to distinguish these in Devon domesday from the slaves and bordars of outlying *villani* farmers, but in comparison with the six or fewer on the other manors there do seem to have been significant concentrations of them at West Alvington (9), Norton (18), Leigh (10), Ringmore (8), Bigbury (12), Thurlestone (11), South Milton and Galmpton (7) and South Huish (8). Of these, all but Leigh and Norton became parishes; and while Norton may have served as a home farm for West Alvington, Leigh is likely to have been too near to Churchstow to gain independent parochial status. There must have been other factors now quite unknowable which influenced the decision to found a church on a manor, and which raised that church to the status of a parish centre, but one category of landholding which may have contained the seeds for growth of this kind in the future were those manors with a substantial inland – a home farm and several families living and working there – in territory with more than the average potential for arable cultivation.

It may be significant in this context, though it does not apply to any of the parish names considered here, that in Devon places with the suffix *-tūn* were those most likely to gain parochial status, far more likely than those with the suffix *-worthy*. A *tūn* could be a different kind of place in different regions – in Devon 'farm' is the favoured translation, just as it is of worthy – but the term always seems the have connotations of enclosure and some Devon farmsteads to this day have walls which would justify the suffix.[29]

Conclusion: local social structure before the conquest

It was in the nature both of Anglo-Saxon lordship and of the demands of the strong local topography of the South Hams that what Æthelwulf 'booked' by his charter in 847 had never been, and could never be, a consolidated unit. Rather it was a stretch of territory containing a number of dispersed farms and settlements. By turning his royal 'folkland' into bookland the king transferred its traditional obligation to provide the royal *feorm* to the benefit of any new owner, and gave him the power to alienate (perhaps a minster at West Alvington benefited from the transaction). Nevertheless some elements remained of what had once been a 'multiple estate': a centre at West Alvington with its arable-oriented demesne farm at Norton and (unhidated) dependencies at Easton, Sutton and so on. An active land market developed in which entire farms changed hands, because no smaller unit was viable in this region where a farm could, in fact virtually had to, comprise an entire little valley. In this land market the upper ranks of the peasantry no doubt participated, with the result that the people whose 'names were on the land' no longer held it in 1066. There were opportunities too for accumulation by powerful men with interests elsewhere in the county. They had demesne centres at Leigh, Ringmore and Bigbury and were raising livestock, principally sheep, on their pastoral manors on a larger scale than their neighbours.

It is important to note here that domesday's valuations and hidage figures were far

---

[29] Gover, Mawer and Stenton, *Place-names of Devon* ii.680.

from being the indicators of real wealth for which they are sometimes taken. The hidations, which were low and with remarkably little variation, may well date from the time of Æthelwulf's grant. The valuations, while they may represent a conventional figure for which a property could be leased, seriously undervalued its prime non-arable asset: its pasture. They had not caught up with the fact that raising sheep was coming to be profitable in south Devon. Algar and Heca and others like them were able to profit from this fact, buying up farms and rearing large flocks while paying little for the land or in geld. Their wealth and position cannot be calculated by the methods conventional among domesday scholars of counting their manors, or calculating the number of hides they owned and what values were put on them.

The question has recently been raised, 'Was there an Anglo-Saxon gentry?'[30] In so far as gentry is as much a quality of culture and lifestyle as of economic status, this is not a question our documents will ever answer. The concept of the manor has given the entire landholding class recorded in domesday an air of superior social status in our eyes, for we are very well aware of what a powerful signifier of social status the manor, and everything associated with it, was to be. But it is important not to read back into the eleventh century social developments which were then only in embryo. After the conquest Devon certainly had its gentry, and several of the small manors of domesday can be seen reincarnated as knights' fees in the thirteenth century.[31] But it also had a large class of respected franklin or yeoman farmers to whose position in society the trappings of 'gentry' were virtually irrelevant. Undoubtedly some of the small manors of domesday were the foundations of these later substantial families. Hoskins identified in bartons with their fine farmhouses acquired in the great rebuilding of the sixteenth century the 'lineal descendants' of the smaller seigneurialized landholdings discussed above. The bartons were the homes of franklins in the fifteenth century, of lesser gentry in the sixteenth, but the social position of their owners did not rest on their manorial connotations, which tended to drop away.[32] And Collaton is a good example of how fragile a distinction there might have been between a manor and any other independent farm, a distinction which may date back to the vagaries of ninth-century hidation. There must have been in eleventh-century Devon, and perhaps in other counties too, many farmers who were economically virtually indistinguishable from their manorial neighbours at the house at which geld was paid, employing about the same number of people and with about the same resources. This broad class of free farmers attended the same courts of shire and hundred, traded in the same markets, probably intermarried. Cola had lived in a society in which powerful interests had been able to make their considerable mark. Yet the yeoman class remained firmly rooted. Their farms are still in business, or were until very recently when forces outside their control have driven so many small farmers to the wall. Collaton is now a guest house.

[30] J Gillingham, 'Thegns and knights in eleventh-century England: who was then the gentleman?' *Transactions of the Royal Historical Society* 6.v (1995); Faith, *English peasantry*, ch 6; P Coss, 'What's in a construct? the 'gentry' in Anglo-Saxon England', below; P Coss, *The origins of the English gentry* (2003), ch 2, 'Roots'.

[31] O Reichel, 'The hundred of Stanborough and Dippeford in the time of *Testa de Nevill* 1243', *Transactions of the Devonshire Association* xlv (1913).

[32] Hoskins, 'Highland zone', 23; Hoskins, *Devon*, 58–78.

5

The Ancestry of English Feudalism

TREVOR ASTON

Until a few years ago there seemed little enough to discuss further about the general subject of this paper.* Now, with the work of Hollings, John, Powicke, Prestwich, and most recently Richardson and Sayles, the genesis of Anglo-Norman feudalism is one of the liveliest points of debate in English medieval history. I am not going to attempt to cover anything like the whole ground. I am going to talk about late Old English landlordship in the light of what seem to me the salient aspects of what we know as feudal society in England. And further, I shall limit what I have to say more or less to the southern and west midland parts of England. There is some justification for this geographical limitation. Many of our notions of Anglo-Norman feudal society are in fact based on evidence from this large area and a bit beyond. By contrast most of our ideas on the nature of Old English lordship – on commendation and so on – derive from quite different regions, from the areas of so-called Danish influence. Not surprisingly we find profound contrasts: on the one side – Anglo-Norman England – we see large estates, knights' fees and all the paraphernalia of the first century of English feudalism; on the other we see freemen and sokemen commending themselves in a bewildering fashion, tiny holdings going this way and that, petty thegns and the rest. By confining our attention to the southern and midland parts of England in the last generation or so of the Old English period we may hope to see more clearly the similarities and the differences between upper-class society before and after the Norman conquest.

I cannot however begin to talk about Old English lordship and feudalism even in this one half of England without, as a brief preliminary, saying something of our

* It seems that this paper was first delivered by Trevor Aston in 1964, and was read to a learned society on at least one subsequent occasion. It is much to be regretted that it was not published soon after its composition, when it might have had a very great impact as a groundbreaking study of difficult and important issues. Scholarship in this field has advanced considerably since the 1960s, and historians now working on the same topics might reject some of Trevor Aston's hypotheses and are much better placed to approach some of the questions that were obscure in his time. They might, for instance, wish to amend his treatment of Anglo-Saxon commendation or his pessimism about the possibility of reconstructing pre-conquest lordships. Nonetheless it has been decided that so much of what this paper says is still stimulating and relevant to current historical concerns that it justifies publication in its original form, even without references. In particular it is remarkable for its identification of the distinction between personal and tenurial dependence in pre-conquest England, and of the prevalence of dependent tenure on ecclesiastical estates; also notable, for example, is its analysis of the distinction between the principles on which military obligation was assessed and the way in which it was actually enforced. The question of the relationship between lords of all kinds and their dependants, so perceptively raised in 1964, is still inadequately explored. We are grateful to Stephen Baxter, Sally Harvey and Patrick Wormald for their comments on this paper.

received notions of feudalism. Our ideas are very narrowly defined and they stem directly from the work of Round. There is something altogether just and right in Round being the father of English feudalism – for as a historian he was in fact something of a mounted warrior making short, decisive forays into this or that occupied territory. Appropriately enough he left a good deal of devastation around – and he also left an idea that mounted warriors and the military service they owed were the determining features of Anglo-Norman society. We can indeed be more precise than that. To Round the baronial *cartae* of 1166 were the epitome of Anglo-Norman feudalism. His forceful advocacy of the variable knight's fee against those who had held that the five-hide unit was the basis of Anglo-Norman feudalism, as well as the attractive simplicity of so neat a social index as a short run of round figures for the most part drawn up in a single year and taken in at a glance, made certain military features the hallmark if not the whole of post-conquest feudalism; and correspondingly made their absence the measure of the lordship it replaced. And even Round's recent critics have in effect accepted this basic premiss by adopting Round's battleground as their own. The rather jaded look of some of Round's military institutions, even of the feudal army itself, is one good reason for wondering if the concentration on military factors has not been rather excessive. Another reason, and one that any collection of twelfth- and thirteenth-century charters will emphasize, is that feudalism – I mean here tenure by knight service, scutage and so on – could later be used as little more than a convenient vocabulary in which to conduct what were in fact perfectly straightforward land transactions, a vocabulary by which one could maintain a formal overlordship much as we might by some petty ground rent over a lease for, say, 999 years. What any study of upper-class society in the twelfth and later centuries makes clear is the need to approach feudal and pre-feudal history on much broader lines than did Round and his successors. We must deal with the structure of lordship and estates rather than merely with the precise military service which estates or any other units owed.

All this, however, is a long way from the subject of this paper. It is relevant only because of the need it implies for approaching feudal history and pre-history on broader lines, as Maitland and Bloch did, or as Lennard has done; for approaching it through the feudal estate rather than the precise military service it owed. English feudal estates were characterized first and foremost by their elaborate proliferation of dependent tenures, involving at least a degree of personal dependence. In time kings, lawyers and others made sharp distinctions between one tenure and another, but in many respects the later differences between tenure by service and tenure by a rent are less significant than the early similarities, especially as rent and service, even military service, could so easily be combined in a single tenure. And secondly, feudal estates were marked by the existence of rights and duties of a public nature which, whether by royal grant or general custom, went with the lordship and which were enmeshed in the tenurial dependence of one person on another – even to the point of constituting its sole tangible bond as in the case of tenure by military service or suit of court to the shire and hundred. If therefore we are to get properly to grips with lordship in the late Old English period we must first disentangle the estates themselves and assess the importance of all kinds of dependence within them and on their fringes; if we can do this over a wide area we should be able to trace with more assurance some of the ways in which public obligations may have become involved in estate organization. The most I can hope to do here is to give a few facts on the first point and a few suggestions on the second.

I am going to spend most of my time on the first task but I will also say something of the second, which brings us closer to established debates on lordship and feudalism. Since I shall be saying much about dependence I must make quite clear one point of terminology. I shall use the phrase *dependent tenure* only of those cases where the holder of an estate could not withdraw it from his lord's lordship, a simple enough situation which of course domesday book renders in a variety of formulae which have provided historians with many happy hours of technical debate. I shall use the phrase *personal dependence* to cover those landholders who had a lord from whose lordship they could withdraw their land. This too is a situation described by a variety of phrases, for example *X* holds of (or *sub*) *Y* and can go elsewhere, recede, or whatever; or *X* the thegn, the housecarl, the man of *Y* holds, and can go, and so on. And I shall use the word dependent to cover both these types as well as all indeterminate cases – for example *X* holds *in alodium* or *in paragio* of *Y* – there being this much in common between all dependence, that the dependent man was commended to the lord in respect of the estate or holding in question.

Dependent tenure on ecclesiastical estates had a long ancestry, but I do not think that the impression the evidence gives of an increase in such tenures, both in volume and variety, in the last century or so of the Old English period is altogether false. For, viewed overall, such an increase was in a sense socially and economically necessary as the counterpart to the lavish scale of lay piety and the marked expansion of ecclesiastical landholding from the mid-tenth century onward. Still, as a whole, we must wait until domesday book in order to measure at all accurately the importance and distribution of such dependent tenure. This evidence has been used often enough, at least for one or two ecclesiastical estates, but I do not know that it has been generally appreciated just how large a part dependent tenures played in 1066 on many ecclesiastical estates, nor how similar in layout and amount they often were when measured against those of the immediate post-conquest period. I suppose that when we think of the effects of the conquest on church estates we seldom get out of earshot of contemporary complaint and dispute, and that by and large the subinfeudations of 1086 appear as invasions of the demesne lands of the church. It has thus been necessary to argue at length to show, for instance, that it was not the demesne lands but the thegnlands, the dependent tenures, of the see of Worcester which formed the basis of the so-called subinfeudations in the generation of the conquest. So too in the case of Ely, where William's policy of safeguarding the abbey's demesne lands could hardly have been as broadly successful as it was but for the extensive pre-conquest thegnlands which were open to occupation by Anglo-Norman lords, in theory on the abbot's own terms. These two estates have perhaps lost their power of general persuasion by their very familiarity. But some of the other cases are no less striking. On the estates of Abingdon Abbey domesday book confirms the Anglo-Saxon chronicle's impression of extensive Old English thegnlands. In Berkshire, where the bulk of the abbey's lands lay, there were in 1066 dependent tenures on about half at least of the separate estates recorded as being in the abbey's lordship, such dependencies occupying the whole of about eleven of the separate holdings. In all, using the 1066 hidation as the basis of calculation, something of the order of 21–2 per cent of the abbey's Berkshire lands were held by subtenants; in 1086 the percentage was only slightly higher, and most of the Anglo-Norman subtenants had merely taken over from Old English dependants. In Oxfordshire, the only other county where the abbey had substantial lands, about 13 per cent was held by dependent tenants in 1066, and though here its losses seem to have been greater over the conquest, the 1066 figure is impressive enough. It was the same on the estates of the bishop and monks of Winchester. In Hampshire (excluding the Isle of Wight) there were dependent tenancies on approximately half of the twenty-one or so separate estates which belonged to the bishop in 1066, and they amounted to almost exactly a quarter of the 280 or so hides. On the monks' estates there, if we exclude the manor of Meon held by Stigand, dependent tenure was less important, but even so it is found on at least nine of the twenty-six or so separate estates, and totalled about one sixth of the whole, as it did in 1086. On the Wiltshire and Somerset estates of the see the pattern was similar. Or again nearly a fifth of Malmesbury Abbey's Wiltshire lands, nearly a fifth of Glastonbury Abbey's in the same shire and over a quarter of Romsey Abbey's two large estates there were held by subtenants, not to mention other similar instances in Wiltshire. The greater part of the quite extensive Cornish estates of the church of St Petroc were held 'of' it, and in fact only about six of its twenty-eight or so properties were held in its own hands. In Worcestershire well over a half of the abbot of Westminster's great estate of Pershore was in the hands of dependent tenants, who held some or all of the land in twenty or so of the twenty-six or twenty-seven separate properties listed under Pershore, the distribution of subtenancies being very little different from what it was twenty years later.

It would be easy, though tedious, to multiply such cases. But the essential points are clear enough. On these and other ecclesiastical estates dependent tenure of one kind and another was an important element in 1066. It was, moreover, either as important as in 1086 or nearly enough so for the estate structure to be properly regarded as broadly similar. And in a very large number of cases – on some estates in the majority of individual subtenancies – the subtenant of 1086 has merely stepped into the shoes of his 1066 antecessor.

On the other hand there are of course many ecclesiastical estates on which, if we are to believe domesday book, dependent tenure was either a novelty of the immediate post-conquest period or was very nearly so. For instance, though just over a quarter of the bishop of Chichester's Sussex properties were held of him by subtenants in 1086, none of these was so recorded under 1066; and in fact it is very hard indeed to find any lay subtenants on Old English ecclesiastical estates in domesday book for Sussex. Or again, though the archbishop of Canterbury had many subtenants on his Kentish properties in 1086, I think only two are listed under 1066. It is not easy to know what to make of these and many similar instances – especially in the Canterbury case if we are to make sense of the later story about Lanfranc converting his drengs into knights, since the drengs would presumably, like their northern namesakes on for instance the bishopric of Durham's estates, have held land. It is not easy because it can readily be shown that domesday book does not record all dependent tenancies existing in 1066. For instance domesday book records a large number of dependent tenures on the abbey of Glastonbury's extensive Somerset estates, but it certainly did not record them all, for Exeter domesday shows at least four others, totalling 9½ hides. In the nature of the case it is impossible to estimate the extent of domesday book's unreliability in recording 1066 subtenures; but in view of the evidence I have already cited a good case could be made out for the view that in many counties and on many estates it was considerable, amounting sometimes to wholesale lack of interest in any subtenancy at all, in others to casual and apparently inexplicable omission of information certainly available at an earlier stage of the inquiry. If so then the estate structure revealed on for instance the estates of the abbeys of Abingdon, Glastonbury, Ely, Bury and Westminster, or the bishoprics of Winchester and Worcester will be emphatically the rule. And even if domesday book's omissions are put at their lowest, the net of tenurial dependence will still be very wide, often – for we need a yardstick – wide enough to accommodate most of the immediate demands of the Anglo-Norman lay aristocracy.

The only common denominator in the subtenancies I have been describing is, as I have mentioned, that the tenant was a man of the ecclesiastical lord of whom he truly held his land – that is he could not remove it from his lord's lordship. In all other respects there is infinite variety: infinite variety of social and economic standing among the subtenants, with a corresponding variety no doubt in their obligations, security and length of tenure, origins as dependants and so on.

The subtenants – most if not all of whom were of the legal status of thegns – reflected, as did their Norman successors, the whole society of which they were a part, from the very greatest lords down to persons of the humblest standing. Of the five named subtenants on the abbey of Malmesbury's Wiltshire lands three are not named as holding other land in the shire, one held two properties of the abbey in adjoining parishes and perhaps held elsewhere, while the last, to whom the abbot had leased an outlying portion of his large manor of Bremhill, was Ælfstan of Boscombe, the richest of the Wiltshire thegns and holder of about 230 hides scattered through eight shires. Ælfstan also held a £10 estate of the bishop of Sherborne in Wiltshire, and in this he, like many other ecclesiastical subtenants, reflected a more particular and very marked feature of late Old English estates, what we may call heterogeneity of tenure, that is one man holding estates by a variety of titles and perhaps of more than one lord. For instance the Hampshire subtenants of the bishop of Winchester, though often very lowly persons, included a certain Cypping of Headbourne Worthy who held in all twenty estates in the shire worth nearly £130, with urban properties in Southampton and Winchester. Of these twenty estates he held three worth £9 of the bishop and monks of Winchester, fourteen variously of King Edward, worth nearly £100, one 'of' Earl Harold, worth £5, and two others worth about £15. The heterogeneity of his estate as a whole was epitomized in his relations with the see of Winchester: two properties he held 'of' the bishop, not being able to withdraw from the lordship; the third he held for life only; and there was a fourth which his immediate predecessor had bought altogether out of the church's lordship for the term of three lives and which Cypping was now holding, presumably as a result of commendation, 'of' King Edward. Land which was on lease or thegnland and could not be separated might be found with its holder commended to another lord (whether by agreement or not we usually don't know), as for example with some of Stigand's men (*homines*) in Hampshire who held non-separable land of St Albans or Westminster.

Dependent tenure was in no way an occasional or superficial element in church estates. It was deeply embedded in the whole organization and exploitation of an ecclesiastical lordship and in its relationships with the secular lordships around it. It was, for instance, often a condition of its growth: many new estates came to the church initially in the form of dependent tenancies, as with the arrangements known as *precaria remuneratoria* or *precaria oblata* and many testamentary benefactions. It was by *precaria oblata* that a thegn named Osulf and his wife granted the abbey of St Albans their estate at Studham in return for a subtenancy for life, the new subtenants agreeing to pay 20*s* per annum as a recognition rent. And I am inclined to think that the alliance of personal interest and piety which such arrangements allowed was a very important element in the growth of dependent tenures on ecclesiastical lordships. It was a condition too of a lordship's relationship with the secular society on which it largely depended for its recruits, servants and supporters. The nepotism of bishops and abbots, the need to pay and reward servants, local landlord pressures extending from arbitrary seizure to less drastic measures to obtain hold of an estate: these and similar necessities and emergencies were most readily, and at least in the late Old English period most often, accommodated to the church's overriding desire to maintain its lordships at least formally intact by resorting to loans for a life or lives. Esgar the staller, familiar as one of the greatest Old English lords because his estates founded the fortunes of the de Mandevilles, held the manor of High Easter of the abbey of Ely for life, a subtenancy which was in fact a compromise in the face of his arbitrary seizure of the estate from the monks. Similarly, dependent tenure was a convenient way to raise ready money by way of sale or mortgage: of course money could be raised by outright sale, but more normally sales and mortgages were effected with a reservation of the church's lordship. In Wiltshire the powerful thegn Wulfweard White, who held extensively in ten or eleven shires, had bought three hides to hold for life of the bishop of Sherborne's demesne manor of Potterne.

But more important than these particular transactions where dependent tenure can clearly be seen as a necessary compromise between ideas of inalienability and social and economic needs, was the intimate relationship between dependent tenure and the year-to-year exploitation of an estate. For as we now know, very few ecclesiastical properties were really managed, as we would say, in demesne. Estate management was normally by 'farming out', that is by installing a deputy of sorts responsible for rendering to the church some predetermined return or service. Between these deputies – reeves, farmers, thegns, great lords and so on – and their lord there was for long a continuum of relationships, all the deputies being in some sense dependent tenants, all the estates being in some sense demesne. It is only slowly and rather artificially that the unity of the whole estate is broken by our familiar dichotomy between demesne lands on the one hand and thegnlands, reevelands and the like on the other; and it is not easy to see on what basis this cleavage was made, or when. In part it must have arisen from the fact that the church was sometimes given not land but rights over the land-lords on it, so that it was presented ready made with property rights which, for the time being at least, it could only absorb as thegnlands: as for instance when Edward the Confessor ordered all the thegns belonging to Pershore and Deerhurst to pay the abbey of Westminster the dues and recognitions due to him. But by that time, as domesday book shows, most churchmen had accepted the fact that not all their land was, even ultimately, equally their own. Earlier they may have seen things rather differently: for, if John is right, among the Oswaldslow thegnlands which Bishop Oswald uniformly claimed as prospectively the church's demesne there were some which had not ever been so. The contribution of grants of this kind to the emergence of the dichotomy between demesne and dependent lands must therefore, for the moment, remain uncertain. So too must that of other obvious factors: for instance there was the sheer practical difficulty of really recovering possession of a property leased for, say, three or more lives; there was the evident difference between those deputies who owed their lord little or nothing and those who owed heavy, more or less economic renders. And there was the need to concentrate the church's defences in the realm of theory as well as practice against permanent loss on those estates from which it derived its supply of food and clothing. At all events the erstwhile theoretical unity of the church's lordship was severed, and a fundamental step taken. And even if we allow that ecclesiastics of William's reign may have exaggerated the doctrines of King Edward's day for the better defence of demesne properties in their own, numerous references show that by and large the severance had been made in the Old English period, though by no means in its final form. Once made, it left the dependent tenures freer to develop, for instance in the direction of greater security of tenure and ultimately hereditary right, and also, though this again is perhaps a process more gradual than we yet know, towards a lightening of obligations until these came to be often only the royal military service due from the land. By contrast rights over demesne lands were perhaps tightened – though not sufficiently to prevent dependent tenures of a kind appearing there too, not only after the conquest but before. 1066 was very much in the middle of these contrasting developments in what, in the technical talk of historians, go by the names of the demesne and the subinfeudated parts of feudal lordships. But so too was 1086. And, as we have seen, the internal structure of at least many great ecclesiastical lordships was broadly similar at the two dates, and in many individual properties identical.

When we turn to the estates of laymen, we are at once in what seems to me a different world, and certainly an infinitely darker one and one in which, with a few exceptions, we are completely at the mercy of domesday book. But to reconstruct those lay lordships from the domesday entries for individual properties, which are of course listed under the tenants in chief of 1086, is a large task even for one shire, let alone for the whole kingdom. It is also a most frustrating one which can never be more than partially completed. For, even apart from domesday's habit of recording as land-owners in 1066 persons who had been dead a decade or more, we can never hope to identify all – and perhaps not even most – of the men who are said to have held in King Edward's day. If Harold is fairly easily traced – the name being rare and usually qualified by the title – Godwine is not; and I cannot think that any amount of ingenuity will sort out those men with common names such as Alwine or Alweard whom domesday book's confused orthography even further confounded. It is not hard therefore to see why so few historians have tried to write about these men and their lands or why, for instance, most writers in the introductions to domesday book in the Victoria county histories have left them, as Round called them, 'mere shadows in the land' whose 'deep obscurity does but enhance [their] pathos', and have sought easier refuge among Anglo-Norman lords and in prolonged discussion of hides, ploughlands and the like. But a start must be made and, though with considerable misgivings, I will try to outline some of the preliminary conclusions which seem to me to emerge from an incomplete study of most of England south of the Thames and in the west midlands, with one or two shires beyond: in all fifteen shires or so.

I do not know that this great area had much secular homogeneity, except perhaps that by and large it was an area of thegnly estates, with what one might call an economically independent peasantry playing a very minor role. This is an elementary enough proposition, though one worth remembering since so much of the study of dependence, of commendation and the like, on Old English estates has been directed to regions of a different and for the most part humbler social texture. But these thegnly estates were, of course, of the greatest diversity in their size and topography, whether we view them within the confines of a single shire or, yet more conspicuously, when we view them more widely. If few shires were so completely dominated by a single landowning group as was Sussex by the house of Godwine which held over a third of the land, there was in most if not all a small group of lords who held a very large proportion of the land, and also a fairly numerous body of minor thegns. Not less than two-thirds of the wealth of Cornwall in the hands of private lay lords in 1066 was held by a mere eleven or twelve persons, while something like one hundred or more shared the remaining third – and of these one hundred, not fewer than twenty-eight and poss-ibly as many as seventy or more held only a single property there worth ten shillings a year or under. Or, to take an altogether richer shire, there were in Kent somewhere between 100 and 180 different lay lords. Of these somewhat under forty had land worth less than £5, usually a single estate – and of these forty at least about eleven and probably over twenty had no other property at all, and the remainder at most very little. At the other end of the economic scale, between sixteen and twenty-two persons held estates worth £25 or more and together controlled estates worth about £1000, that is something of the order of a quarter of the total value of Kent in 1066. This small, powerful Kentish group was itself very heterogeneous. Leaving aside its richest member by far, Earl Godwine, and also the queen, the archbishop as a private lord, and Godwine's son Leofwine, at least three held no estates outside Kent, these including a certain Molleve who had seven Kentish properties worth about £40; three more held little if anything outside the shire, whereas by contrast Æthelnoth Cild's lands, though concentrated there, extended into six other shires including Oxfordshire. Most of the members of the group held their Kentish estates either independently or in dependence on the king, but a certain Thorgils (Turgis) held nearly half his in dependence on Earl Godwine, as well as having Earl Harold and the abbot of Chertsey as his lords in Surrey.

The pronounced social differentiation among the noble class as a whole which such an analysis brings out, the juxtaposition of poverty-stricken thegns and great lords who were not infrequently possessed of considerable administrative power and special privileges, would certainly seem fruitful ground for the development of widespread dependence in the ways so often sketched by modern writers. And yet, over the area I am considering, dependence of any kind, that is to say personal or tenurial or of an indeterminate nature, was far less developed than we have seen it on many ecclesiastical estates, and indeed in most counties quite insignificant in importance. Furthermore, such dependence as is recorded is almost entirely confined to dependence on very great men, or at least men of great local power; there is nothing of that intricate net of clientage in which quite minor thegns might achieve personal overlordship such as is found in some other areas of England. To take Kent again, there are only twenty-five certain cases of dependence of any kind, and the overlords were Earl Godwine with eleven, Æthelnoth Cild with five, Earl Harold and his brother Leofwine, earl of Essex and Kent, who had respectively three and two, and Queen Edith and three locally important lords who had one each. In Sussex dependence is more common, more so than in any other shire in the area I am considering, but if we exclude dependence on the earls Godwine and Harold which together made up a great part of the total, we are left with a mere sixteen cases of lay dependence, the lords being the queen, Earl Godwine's wife, two of Harold's brothers, a certain Azor whom I shall be mentioning more than once and who held very extensively in Sussex and almost certainly elsewhere, and two other locally important lords: and of these Sussex overlords only three had more than one recorded dependant. In Hampshire and the Isle of Wight there are only thirty-one instances of dependence in all, and in some shires dependence was even rarer: in Staffordshire there are only five cases, and in Cheshire, apart from unnamed radknights inside lay manors, only one. Again, if we look not to the tenurial fabric of particular shires but to that of particular great estates, it is only those of Godwine and Harold which had more than a handful of dependants. For instance Eadmer Atule, otherwise called Edmeratorius, who held in the region I am considering about fifty-four estates totalling some 116 hides concentrated in Devon, Somerset and Dorset and whose estate is several times called an honour in the Exeter domesday, had only eight recorded dependants, while Eadnod the staller, who held twenty-three estates scattered over five shires, is not recorded as having any at all.

The overall contrast with the ecclesiastical estates I was describing earlier is therefore clear. But it becomes even more notable if we attempt to distinguish in this lay dependence the personal from the tenurial – it being the latter to which my figures from ecclesiastical estates related. This is unfortunately not often possible, domesday book merely recording that the dependant held 'of' the lord or was his 'man'; and it is partly because of this doubt that I have given figures for dependants of all kinds. But the descent of estates over the conquest establishes a presumption that many, probably the majority of the dependants were personal dependants only, and for some areas the domesday book entries themselves allow one to be certain in particular cases. For instance, though the nature of thirteen of the thirty-one dependencies in Hampshire is uncertain, ten of the remainder were tenurial, and the rest were *in alodium* – a phrase which, though not altogether incompatible with dependent tenure, almost always indicates the existence of a purely personal bond of dependence. In Sussex we know nothing of Harold's dependants, but we can be fairly confident of the position of at least eight of Godwine's – two were almost certainly tenurial, while the other six were probably personal. Only in the radknights of certain western shires do we find dependent tenure at all frequently.

But before we go any further we should face the suspicion which these facts from lay estates must arouse: that the evidence of domesday book is not to be relied upon, and that a record which may have omitted many dependent tenures on ecclesiastical estates with an uninterrupted history over the conquest is even more likely to have omitted dependence on lay estates. Now it is certainly true, as a comparison between domesday book and its associated so-called satellite texts shows, that domesday book omitted some cases of dependence. For instance on the Devon honour of the considerable west-country lord Ordwulf it omits two of the five dependencies given in the Exeter text. And it might be argued with some force that in general the most that could be expected in domesday book would be a note of such dependence as it materially affected the descent of an estate, which would not be so in the majority of cases of mere personal dependence. On the other hand there are some shires in which domesday book cannot have omitted much in the way of personal dependence since all or most of the landholders are clearly and fully accounted for. Most conspicuously is this so in Middlesex. There all private lay estates not held by an earl or other very elevated person were either held in dependence on a private lord or in dependence on the king: there was no unattached person of ordinary rank. The same is more or less true in Kent, Surrey and Hampshire, and to a very considerable extent in Berkshire and Sussex. And yet, if we leave out of account dependence on Godwine and Harold, the evidence of these shires is not materially different from that of others. In Berkshire, apart from five dependencies under Earl Harold, there are only about four others on lay estates. Even in these shires, of course, there remains the possibility that domesday book conceals dependent tenure within particular manors, as opposed to dependence by one manorial lord on another; but with this reservation, we may conclude that the evidence of domesday book is unlikely to be seriously misleading in its picture of lay dependence.

When we come to consider the dependants themselves we find something of the same variety of economic condition that has already been noticed on ecclesiastical estates. Earl Godwine's twenty-nine or so named dependants in Sussex were a fair cross-section of Sussex and indeed Old English society. No fewer than thirteen had no other Sussex property, and of these thirteen at least four or five had no other estate at all; but the thirteen also included at least one person who was more than a local lord, a certain Cuthwulf who held three Hampshire and three Wiltshire manors, his whole property being worth over £33. Another dependant in the middling ranks of society, but unlike him a purely Sussex lord, was Haiming who held a discrete manor of Godwine, and also three other Sussex estates bringing his total holding to a value of £13 10s 0d. And then Godwine's twenty-nine dependants included from among the great lords of south-eastern England that Azor I have already mentioned who, as part of his lordship, held three estates of Godwine and another three of Harold, on one of which he had a dependant of his own. Finally there was one rich priest who held land worth £40 in dependence on Godwine, this apparently having been filched from the church of Bosham's manor. Earl Harold's fourteen named dependants in Herefordshire were of a similar complexion, while his four in Berkshire included the wealthy priest Blacheman and Eadnod the staller. But lay dependants of the standing of Eadnod or Azor were uncommon and their presence no doubt reflected the great prestige of the house of Godwine. In general dependants on lay estates belonged as one would expect to the ranks of the middling and lesser thegns. Even a great lord such as Beorhtric son of Ælfgar, who dominated lay society in Herefordshire with estates worth over £100 and dependants including radknights with land worth well over £50, does not seem to have had among his dependants any very important person, and certainly had some very minor ones.

Apart from variety of social standing, several of these examples show how common it was for persons who held dependently in one place to hold independently in another. One does indeed come across dependants with more than one manor who were holding all their property in dependence on one lord, as probably did the Beorthmær who held three Sussex manors under Azor. But such cases are, I think, rare, and even where a thegn held more than one manor under a particular lord and where dependence looks fairly pervasive, the dependant more often than not held other land not under his lord's lordship. Thus Thorkell who held no fewer than seven properties in dependence on Earl Harold, six in Herefordshire and one in Gloucestershire, held at least three other Herefordshire estates independently and probably a good deal more – for he was probably the Thorkell White who, along with his wife Leofflæd, held extensive western estates. Or again, at least two and probably four of Earl Edwin's five dependent thegns in Worcestershire held other land in the shire not of him. The lack of what one may call comprehensiveness in dependent relationships which such estate structures reveal is still further emphasized by those instances where a man held in dependence on more than one lord. I have already mentioned the Hampshire thegn Cypping who held dependently under the king, Earl Harold and the bishop of Winchester, and it is quite common to find heterogeneity of this kind where the second lord is either a church or the king. Less common, if we exclude those cases where the two lords were Harold and Godwine, are dependants with two private lay lords; but such cases can be found. For instance the Særic who held a half-hide estate as a thegn of Earl Harold in Herefordshire also held one of the many estates dependent on Queen Edith's manor of Leominster, as well as two or three other Herefordshire properties independent of any lord. Now it has sometimes been remarked, as if it were a sign of the fragility and superficiality of the ties of dependence in late Anglo-Saxon England, that a man might – as Særic did – have more than one lord. And the other examples I have quoted might prompt the suggestion that evidently lordship was not what it once had been. Perhaps not. But a moment's reflection will suggest that, until the tie of lord and man has been rendered non-exclusive, until it has been given flexibility, it is liable to be confounded fairly quickly once it leaves the close quarters of the household or following for the more complex environment of the estate. And similarly commendation between one land-holder and another becomes a more not a less useful element in developing social relationships as and when it has jettisoned its exclusiveness and comprehensiveness and can be entered into or enforced as the case may be, piecemeal, manor by manor as particular interest or pressure dictates; when, in other words, it is viewed from the beginning not indeed as a tenurial relationship but in a strictly tenurial context. The adaptation of the futile tradition of personal lordship to the hard and mobile facts of a complex economic and tenurial framework with scattered estates, and the heterogeneity of tenure and lordship to which this often gave rise, were thus signifi-cant steps in the direction of feudalism in England. For feudalism, at least in its English variety, matures with a weak not a strong sense of the loyalty of one man to another.

This was, however, a change in men's thinking about affairs, not necessarily in the affairs themselves – and in fact, as we have seen, dependence was rare, and dependent tenure rarer still. Why this was so will not be known until all the lay estates of the Old English period have been carefully studied, but there are one or two points which further work is, I think, unlikely to modify.

I said earlier that dependent tenure was deeply embedded in the organization and external relations and, as it were, theory of an ecclesiastical estate. Contrariwise, absence of lay dependent tenure was equally founded in the attitude of lords towards their properties. Lay estates had little of that rigidity and permanence, or at least search for permanence, which characterized most ecclesiastical estates, particularly in the tenth and eleventh centuries, and which did so much to mould dependent tenure on them. We need but look at an Old English will to see that domesday book's familiar insistence that particular persons were free to give or sell their land was no idle turn of phrase on the part of the scribes, but a real reflection of the frequency of land transfers of one kind and another and of a whole attitude of mind as well. Where, for instance, the abbot of Ely gives his twelve-hide manor of Milton in Cambridgeshire to his *dapifer* Albert or, further back, Bishop Oswald wishes to endow one of his *cnihtas*, they do so by making dependent tenures; when, by contrast, Leofgifu for instance wished to reward her stewards and knights she did it by outright gift. Or when again the same abbot wished to enrich his brother Guthmund to facilitate his marriage plans, when the abbot of Glastonbury wished to provide for his mother or the abbot of Ely for his uncle, this was done by a normally dependent tenure; whereas on lay estates family needs were normally met by outright gift or subdivision, and even arrange-ments for ultimate reunification of a lordship usually made no provision for a unified overlordship in the interim. And this lack of permanence meant too that, though no doubt lay estates like ecclesiastical ones were frequently administered by leasing them out, there was not time for these lessees to establish a real hold and convert themselves into what we would call dependent tenants; a lease for three lives, for instance, is not really at home in the world of lay estates. Now outright alienations of this kind did not spring from any lack of the idea of dependent tenure: laymen must have been fully familiar with it on ecclesiastical estates, often as tenants themselves, and occasionally a lay lord did indeed retain lordship when he granted away an estate. They sprang from an indifferent regard for the integrity and permanence of the estate. And in the contrast between this willingness to alienate and the church's longstanding quest for the inalienability of its land lies one of the chief reasons for the facts we have found.

No such psychological factor stood in the way of the elaboration of purely personal dependence, especially if it had been adapted to a tenurial context in the way I have suggested. And yet it too was rare. The contrast with some other regions is here, of course, pronounced. In part this rarity was, I think, due to the simple fact that our area was an area of landlords, the poorest of whom was legally and in most cases economically in a relatively strong position. As the piecemeal nature of personal dependence shows, such men did not readily come under another's lordship, still less completely so. And though there were no doubt occasions when their independence was overridden, by arbitrary pressures and seizures, we have no evidence that such cases were either frequent or of lasting consequence. And then secondly there was in at least six or so of the shires in question an obstacle, which may in practice have been serious, to the development of private dependence by lawful or unlawful means. This was that extremely widespread dependence on the king himself to which I have already referred. Admittedly this dependence was for the most part personal not tenurial, leaving the dependant free to change his lord. But backed up as it was not only by rights of jurisdiction but, for instance in Kent, by other royal rights, it must have acted as something of a bar to the development of dependence at a lower level. It may have been a barrier which only those who, like the great earls, administered royal rights on the king's behalf or in their own name on their comital manors or who, like Queen Edith at Leominster apparently, exercised them by some royal grant, could hope to breach at all easily on any scale.

These are however merely intended as tentative suggestions towards an explanation of the rarity of dependence, and especially tenurial dependence, on lay lordships in the half of England that I am considering, and of the contrasts we have found between the highly developed dependent tenures on ecclesiastical estates and their spasmodic and almost casual occurrence on lay lordships. I do not doubt that further inquiry into the details of estate structure will yield additional explanations, and will equally emphasize regional variation. Until that inquiry is complete it will certainly be hazardous to launch on a discussion of what I have suggested is the second large ingredient of the feudal estate in England: that is the assumption or delegation of certain military, financial, judicial and other responsibilities to private lay and ecclesiastical lords, and the involvement of these responsibilities in the frame of tenurial dependence.

We can, of course, easily see that this assumption or delegation proceeded at no uniform pace and, in the event, never reached a uniform conclusion. Thus I doubt if anyone would dispute that many jurisdictional rights were in private hands by 1066 – though we may be inclined to underestimate the scope of such private jurisdiction by having regard solely to that which passed by specific royal grant, to the neglect of those rights which custom accorded a landlord over his dependants and which we would later think of as manorial or honorial as opposed to franchisal jurisdiction. By contrast delegation of the duty and right of collecting the geld levied by the king was a rarity outside the unit of the individual manor where, probably, the lord had complete control. Lordly responsibility for the collection of the geld came, for the most part, only some time after 1086 when the conqueror's great survey was drawn up in a way that assumed some such general delegation of tax-collection to baronial lords would be made within each shire and on the basis of the general reassessment to geld that was the inquest's overriding purpose. And I am inclined to think that the delegation or assumption of tax-collecting functions before – though not after – the conquest followed a course not dissimilar to that followed by the delegation of military recruiting functions to which I will devote the remainder of this paper.

Here I draw heavily on recent work, particularly by Marjory Hollings, Eric John and Warren Hollister. They have, it seems to me, established three vital points, though they disagree on a fourth and equally important one. First, whatever military service may have been owed by the king's intimate personal followers – and I am not sure that for example a landowning king's housecarl should be reckoned as such, and I am quite sure that an ordinary landowning king's thegn should not – the rank of thegn in the late Old English period did not itself involve military service of any kind. There has indeed never been any evidence that it did – a point demonstrated by Hollings in 1949. Second, the basic fighting obligation, whether for sea or land service, was due from the land – we should here, clearly, leave room for a good deal of flexibility in the rate at which such service might be levied at different dates and for some regional variation too; but the rate of one man (a mounted man, a *miles*) from five hides is by no means limited to the one county for which domesday book categorically records it. Third, this service was, at least in some areas and maybe generally, for a period of sixty days and could on occasion be commuted for the current two-month wage of the Berkshire *miles*, that is 20*s*. This military service thus looks very like that which was owed from Anglo-Norman lordships, sharing with it a firm basis in the land or other real property. It has been argued that, despite this similarity, Anglo-Norman military service was something additional to the Old English military obligations I have been describing and that, for a time at least after the Norman conquest, the two types of obligation existed alongside one another on the same estates. I do not find the evidence cited for this is in any way convincing. It is far from clear that the famous incident in 1094 when 20,000 men, having been mustered at Hastings for service abroad, were sent back home minus their pocket-money has any direct bearing on regular Old English military arrangements; and it can hardly relate to what Hollister calls the select fyrd, since it was evidently a body of footsoldiers and not mounted warriors. While the other evidence cited by Hollister from the abbey of Peterborough is susceptible of a far more plausible explanation than the one he gives. But, if we may conclude that Anglo-Norman feudal service was a direct continuation of Old English military obligation of the type recorded for Berkshire, this does not mean that the precise liability – number of men, even period of service – remained unaltered. I am very ready to believe that the *servitia debita* of the ecclesiastical lordships were born in circumstantial bargainings between the conqueror and the new incumbents of his bishoprics or abbeys, perhaps at or soon after the time they received their appointment and lands from him – though in the case of, for example, the bishopric of Worcester no such occasion arose in William's reign. Anglo-Norman lay lordships, unlike most ecclesiastical lordships, were the conqueror's own creations. Their military obligations must have been new bargains. It would have been far beyond the capacity of the king or his administration to do anything but make a new bargain: to preserve the old arrangements of, say, one man from five hides while converting it into the mould of the new tenancies in chief would have demanded far more knowledge than the king had before the compilation of domesday book, and quite advanced arithmetic even after that. But I would not myself think the changes in the rates at which military service was demanded – or even in the period of military service – are of any particular importance for the questions we are discussing; they are indeed no greater than the very considerable changes in liability to the geld (both its rate and its assessment) which must for most contemporaries have been a much more pressing matter.

The crucial thing about Anglo-Norman *servitia debita* is not their precise arithmetic – which like geld assessments may not have remained constant – but their very existence. For what after all particularly characterized and determined Anglo-Norman military obligations was their general and inescapable canalization through the king's barons and their lordships. I do not know how far the shire or other administrative unit may have been used for actually mustering knights, but as units of assessment vills, hundreds and shires ceased to exist. In their place the assessment was now put on the lordship, and the recruiting and imposition of the military levy made an indisputable duty of the lord of the honour. We may, if we wish, say that these lords held their honours for so much military service. But I would prefer to say that they held their honours of the king, one of their public duties being to arrange the royal military service, the military tax that was due. It was this simple fact, as we know, which more than any other made for that intermixture of public obligation and private tenurial dependence in the upper ranks of society which we recognize as specifically feudal.

The real questions therefore to be asked of Old English military arrangements are: how far was there similar canalization of responsibility, how far were military levies bound into the fabric of private lordship; how far had a system which was based on public – or at least public-looking – administrative units (shires and hundreds) been modified by basing it in part on private estates. Here again Hollings and John have made a vital contribution. They have, it seems to me, shown that in the bishop of Worcester's triple hundred of Oswaldslow the bishop alone was responsible for levying and even leading the contingent due from the land during the last century of the Old English period. It seems certain too that the bishop of Winchester was similarly placed in his lordship of Taunton. Whether such instances were the exception or the rule we cannot yet say, but there are one or two other cases which seem in some respects similar. For example Edward the Confessor's grant of the two-hundred-hide lordship of Pershore and the large estate of Deerhurst to Westminster Abbey commanded the thegns there to be subject to the abbey – and we have seen them so subject in domesday book – and prohibited anyone other than the abbot having authority inside the lordship, phraseology which is not unreminiscent of some of that employed for Oswaldslow. More clearly, the bishop of Sherborne seems responsible for the naval and presumably also the military service from three hundred hides, probably the three hundreds of Sherborne, Yetminster and Beaminster found later in the hands of his successor, the bishop of Salisbury. In each of these cases the duty of military recruitment is intimately related to ownership and jurisdiction over a whole hundred – whether a pre-existing hundred specifically made over to the private lord or a block or group of his estates which is made into a hundred. This association of hundredal ownership and jurisdiction with the kind of lordly canalization we are looking for directs attention to other instances where, though nothing is said about military obligation, a lord owned all the land in a hundred with the hundredal jurisdiction. There are, even in the fragmentary evidence we have on Old English private hundreds, almost forty such cases, including those I have already mentioned. It must, I think, be reckoned likely that there was military canalization in them, for such canalization would have involved no jarring of the established assessment of military duties. And canalization is perhaps especially probable in the case of lords who, like the abbey of Bury in his eight and a half hundreds or the abbot of Ely in his estates in

Edward's reign, had the additional privilege of receiving the penalty for default of military service which Cnut had, as a general rule, reserved to himself unless specifically granted away.

But if these pieces of evidence suggest that some lords were militarily responsible for part of their estates they also suggest important contrasts with post-conquest arrangements. The Old English responsibility I have been mentioning was still, as it were, very much on a public basis; it was conceived in hundredal terms and operated through single or multiple hundreds. Equally important, it was part of a special and, in the only certain cases, highly elevated franchise. Anglo-Norman responsibility was not formulated in hundredal terms; and it was in no meaningful sense a franchise, being built into the customary framework of baronial duties. These two points are very closely interrelated. Lordly responsibility could only be general if military assessment was freed from at least its hundredal basis – the assessment could indeed have been kept within a shire fabric, as was the later geld, but in the event it was not. Now there is, so far as I know, no evidence that military responsibility was ever thus freed in the Old English period. What then are we to make of the famous entry in domesday book for Worcestershire, and the similar if rather garbled entry for Berkshire, which show that lords could, apparently if they wished, organize the military service from their lands to the extent of sending a deputy for a man who was due but who did not serve. It is, of course, tempting for those favourably disposed to ideas of general continuity to use these entries as the basis of the proposition that Old English lords could be – and therefore were – responsible for the military service from their lands. And we need not doubt that a lord who had, say, a twenty-hide manor, would organize the military service due, and even send deputies and so on. But I think it is on this so to say infra-manorial level that we should think of these Worcestershire and Berkshire customs as operating. There is a measure of feudalism here; but it is of a very humble kind, unless the manor is very large – say one hundred hides – or unless it is joined with other manors, as in the case of Oswaldslow, to form an even larger unit.

I find myself therefore rather on the side of the conservatives here. I find territorial military obligation, which Stenton so curiously missed. But I do not find its levying much in private hands. Where it is in private hands, this is on a smallish scale and for the most part – outside the bounds of levying within the manor – the hands are those of ecclesiastics. But it was there that we found what seems to me quite as important an ingredient of feudalism as the canalization of military and other responsibility through private lords, that is extensive dependent tenures. The conjunction of these two elements is here complete and striking enough for us to call these ecclesiastical estates feudal in the proper sense of the term. But it was a feudalism which was limited in its scope and perhaps more efficient in its operation than its ubiquitous successor. For the tenurial dependence and the military canalization were still contained within the fairly uniform administrative framework of the shire. The next step – which was William's and his successors' – destroyed all that. The silence of domesday book, which was arranged by shires, on the military arrangements of the conqueror's reign is something that it would have taken more than mere scribal enthusiasm to cure. But perhaps by then it was ceasing to matter all that much anyway.

6

What's in a Construct?
The 'Gentry' in Anglo-Saxon England

PETER COSS

In a formulation which has become famous – or infamous, according to one's stand-point – Patrick Joyce urged historians to accept the 'major advance of "post-modernism"'... namely, that the events, structures and processes of the past are *indistinguishable* from the forms of documentary representation, the conceptual and political appropriations, and the historical discourses that construct them'.[1] Notwith-standing the passion with which post-modernist historians advance their cause, and to some extent because of it, relatively few historians have been diverted from practising their craft in the traditional manner. This response is hardly surprising. Post-structuralism – the real foundation upon which this whole edifice is built – main-tains that language, being a self-referential system, gives no access to an external reality or, indeed, to anything non-textual that is anterior, logically or temporally, to itself. The past, then, is inaccessible. Most of us know, by instinct and by training, that this proposition is an absurdity. Hence few have taken up the challenge proffered by post-modernism, the majority preferring to remain aloof.

It is doubtful, however, whether this is the appropriate response, even from a defensive point of view. Those who see clearly realize just how naked the emperor post-structuralism actually is, but it may be a very long time before his post-modernist courtiers are brought to acknowledge the fact. Moreover post-modernist history gains some validity from the truths, or quasi-truths, that are embedded within its proposi-tions. As Richard Evans has said:

> drawing up the disciplinary drawbridge has never been a good idea... Historians should approach the invading hordes of semioticians, post-structuralists, New Historicists, Foucauldians, Lacanians and the rest with more discrimination. Some of them might prove more friendly, or more useful, than they seem at first sight.[2]

Hence Gabrielle Spiegel's generally applauded starting point: 'No historian, even of a positivist stripe, would argue that history is present to us in any but textual form.' She can acknowledge this while denying that it necessarily forecloses access to the past:

---

[1] P Joyce, 'History and post-modernism', *Past and Present* 133 (Nov 1991), 208 (my italics).
[2] RJ Evans, *In defence of history* (1997), 8–9. His introduction contains some interesting observations on the reception of post-modernism among British historians. See also, from a very different stand-point, P Joyce, 'The return of history: postmodernism and the politics of academic history in Britain', *Past and Present* 158 (Feb 1998).

'The problem, of course, is not whether there is a past "out there" . . . but how we reach it and what procedures permit us to do so in ways that respect its integrity'.[3]

My concern here will be not with textuality *per se*, but with the second half of Joyce's formulation, that is to say with the 'conceptual and political appropriations' and with the 'historical discourses' that, supposedly, construct the past; primarily with historical discourses and their interdependence. Keith Jenkins puts the post-modernist position in this respect as follows: 'what has gone before is *always* apprehended through the sedimented layers of previous interpretations and through the reading habits and categories developed by previous/current interpretive discourses'. Moreover:

> the differences that we see are there because history is basically a contested discourse, an embattled terrain wherein people(s), classes and groups autobiographically construct interpretations of the past literally to please themselves. There is no definitive history outside these pressures, any (temporary) consensus only being reached when dominant voices can silence others either by overt power or covert incorporation . . . Ideology seeps into every nook and cranny of history, including the everyday practices of making histories in those institutions predominantly set aside for that purpose – especially universities.[4]

One might want to reject this second proposition in the stark manner in which it is put. But it can hardly be denied that historical writing can be, and indeed very often is, an ideological battleground, nor that some interpretations become institutionally favoured over others. More broadly, while most of us would reject the proposition that the narratives historians construct are *determined* by the stories others have told before them, that is to say by the interpretative texts they have read, we must all realize that in the language we use we draw, implicitly if not explicitly, upon discourses that are anterior to our own. Those discourses bequeath their own assumptions and thought processes to us and are inherently inclined, as the post-modernists stress, to contain ideology and to reflect past power relations. We must respect the fact that every concept we borrow, every term that we share, has been historiographically shaped. This has both positive and negative implications. It carries benefits, but it also carries dangers. The challenge from post-modernism should cause us to reflect upon these implications. Thus when historians of a particular epoch begin to deploy a concept normally reserved for a later age, it is worth exploring what that novel deployment implies and contains. What discourse, or discourses, are they buying into, and with what effect? This is my concern here.

It is noticeable that in recent years historians of Anglo-Saxon England have increasingly been using the term *gentry*. A number of scholars have been struck by the similarities between the lesser landowners of the pre-conquest state and the gentry of later times. Introducing an edition of the Bedfordshire domesday in 1991, for example, Richard Abels wrote that in 1066 'the greater part of the shire belonged to a handful of wealthy king's thegns and a host of lesser landowners who *much resemble* the country gentry and yeomanry of later times', while in 1993 James Campbell observed that one 'general feature of English society as it appears in domesday is not at all likely to be new: that is the presence of major classes of what would later have

---

3   GM Spiegel, 'History, historicism, and the social logic of the text in the middle ages', *Speculum* lxv (1990), 76.
4   K Jenkins, *Re-thinking history* (1991), 11 and n5 (my italics), 19–20.

been called gentry and yeomanry'. In 1998 Henry Loyn wrote that 'Anglo-Saxon thegnage became *akin to* manorial lordship and the country gentry of later times'. Others have been less circumspect. John Blair, in particular, has been arguing for some time that the lesser landowners of late Anglo-Saxon England constituted a gentry. In 1991, for example, he referred to 'the appearance of a broad, locally based class of minor aristocracy: the proliferation between 900 and 1066 of the English country gentry'. In 1997 Rosamond Faith asserted that 'well before the Conquest smaller landowners with bookland . . . came to be a self-conscious class, whom there is no reason not to regard as gentry, however anachronistic the term'.[5]

There can be no doubt that the impetus behind this deployment stems, initially at least, from new directions in the study of later Anglo-Saxon England. Much emphasis has been placed upon the fragmentation of the great or 'multiple estates' and its consequences, including the growth of myriad small estates, the forerunners of the manors that are so familiar to students of medieval England.[6] With this fragmentation there developed a broader seigneurial class, much of it ministerial in origin, having achieved status by service, and including a great many thegns. Allied changes included the emergence of nucleated villages and their associated field systems and the steady proliferation of local churches.[7] The extent to which members of this broader landowning class were responsible for these developments is unclear, but it seems extremely likely that in all of them they played a very major part.

Consequently historians of Anglo-Saxon England have been paying considerable attention to the development of the small estate and its economy.[8] As Faith has stressed, lords who needed to support themselves from these small estates, being unable to draw on the extensive food-renders that greater landowners enjoyed, needed 'to adopt appropriate management strategies'. As a result 'the spread of the small estate is likely to have brought about an intensification of exploitation of inland arable and meadow, woodland and pasture, livestock and people'.[9] In this context, land tenure and landlord–peasant relations become matters of obvious concern. So, too, does the development of the 'defensible seigneurial centre' with its 'lord's hall and complex of buildings later known as the *curia*, the court'.[10] Such seigneurial

---

5   *The Bedfordshire domesday*, ed RP Abels (Alecto edn 1991), introduction, 34 (my italics); J Campbell, 'England *c.*991' in his *The Anglo-Saxon state* (2000), 168, repr from J Cooper (ed), *The battle of Maldon: fact and fiction* (1993); H Loyn, 'Thegnage' in PE Szarmach, MT Tavormina and JT Rosenthal (eds), *Medieval England: an encyclopedia* (1998), 731–2 (my italics); J Blair, *Early medieval Surrey: landholding, church and settlement before 1300* (1991), 160–1; RJ Faith, *The English peasantry and the growth of lordship* (1997), 126.

6   However the reality is likely to have been more complex than this process implies. The 'multiple estate' model too has been brought into question, and small estates were also created 'from below'. For a recent review of the literature and the arguments see DM Hadley, *The northern Danelaw: its social structure, c. 800–1100* (2000), 24–6, 85–8.

7   For a recent overview of work on settlement patterns see C Lewis, P Mitchell-Fox and CC Dyer, *Village, hamlet and field: changing medieval settlements in central England* (1997). On churches see especially J Blair (ed), *Minsters and parish churches: the local church in transition 950–1200* (1988), introduction.

8   Pre-eminent among recent studies is Faith, *English peasantry*, esp ch 6, 'The growth of small estates and the beginnings of the seigneurial life'. See too the comments in Hadley, *Northern Danelaw*, 159–64.

9   Faith, 168–9.

10   Ibid 163. See also A Williams, 'A bell-house and a burh-geat: lordly residences in England before the Norman conquest', *Medieval Knighthood* iv (1992).

complexes, whether one calls them manors at this stage or not, are being identified through placenames ending in *-tun* or *-burh*, and are often found to contain a proprietary church. Aspects of civilian aristocratic life, including hunting and hawking, are also receiving attention. In short:

> on the foundations of the security of tenure given by bookland, a long lease from a local monastic house, or part of their family's hereditary land, the lesser landlords of later Anglo-Saxon England were able to build their 'magnate farmsteads' and strike the roots of the seigneurial life.[11]

It is not altogether surprising, therefore, that historians have begun to import the term gentry into later Anglo-Saxon studies. The gentry, as I have stressed elsewhere, is a construct.[12] As such it can mean whatever we want it to mean. In its looser usage it can be little more than a synonym for smaller landowners, or for lesser nobility, and suggests a landed elite whose members possess (predominantly rural) estates, preferably with tenants. However, its long pedigree and historiographical usage endow the word with many, more specific, connotations. Willy-nilly, any historian who employs it is liable to be tapping into these.

This can be of benefit in raising new questions. For example it is encouraging current historians of Anglo-Saxon England to look beyond the vertical ties of association between lord and man that are so apparent in the sources towards the existence of horizontal ones. Now it is undeniable that lordship was an overwhelmingly powerful ingredient in the society of Anglo-Saxon England. Wherever we look – in the civilian as well as in the military sphere – we find vertical lines of association. Domesday book shows us that commendation, whether to lord or to landlord, was a vital element in late Saxon society. Moreover, the wealthier 'median' thegns had thegns of their own, and a hierarchy of tenures may have existed that was similar to the situation in post-conquest England.[13] Nevertheless the heavy preponderance of vertical over horizontal ties is to some degree a product of the evidence upon which the historian of Anglo-Saxon England has to rely, and if horizontal ties cannot easily be shown they can at least be surmised. Blair has pointed to one local scenario from which horizontal ties, based upon neighbourhood, can be deduced. Of the thirteen thegns who witnessed the lease of Great Tew by the abbey of St Albans to Tova, widow of Wihtric in 1050–2, five are linked by the preposition *aet* to Oxfordshire placenames. They were, suggests Blair, 'a group of gentlemen-farmers: Tova's friends and neighbours'.

> We cannot know if these people normally used toponymic surnames, but their names as stated in the lease are strikingly like those adopted by minor manorial lords in the twelfth and thirteenth centuries. The impression is of a gentry firmly rooted in the land.[14]

Such ties, it might reasonably be argued, are a natural consequence of neighbouring lordship.

There must surely have been horizontal ties, too, between members of the elite. Ann Williams has recently pointed to the existence of just such an elite who domi-

---

[11] Faith, 176.

[12] PR Coss, 'The formation of the English gentry', *Past and Present* 147 (May 1995).

[13] For this perspective see D Roffe, 'From thegnage to barony', *Anglo-Norman Studies* xii (1989), esp 161–4. Susan Reynolds, however, disagrees in her 'Bookland, folkland and fiefs', ibid xxiv (1992), 221–2. I owe this last reference to the kindness of Ann Williams.

[14] J Blair, *Anglo-Saxon Oxfordshire* (1994), 138–40.

nated the local society of Kent.[15] The Kentish folios of domesday book identify eight laymen whose men, together with those of three religious houses, did not owe heriot directly to the king, the implication being that they received the heriots directly themselves. To these can be added fifteen men from west Kent who enjoyed rights of sake and soke. Of the twenty-three laymen who held special privileges in Kent, four are identifiable as landowners elsewhere: Wulfweard White, Alwine Horne, Brihtsige Cild and Æthelnoth Cild. Of these the first two were major landowners across the home counties, with relatively little land, it seems, in Kent. Brihtsige and Æthelnoth, on the other hand, are better described as Kentish magnates. The others – men like Godric of Brabourne, Esbearn Bigga and Sired of Chilham – were men with more localized interests. In the words of Williams, on the eve of the conquest: 'Kent was dominated by a small group of powerful men. There were gradations of wealth, and perhaps of rank, within this group.' Wulfweard White certainly, and Æthelnoth Cild probably, 'operated at a "national" rather than a local level, and . . . had personal or ministerial relationships with the king and the royal household'. However:

> the rest of the group seem to have been local men. But all of them, whether magnates or local worthies, were king's thegns, serving their royal lord (*cynehlaford*) either at his court or within their own shire. They owed him military service . . . They were also obliged to attend the shire court (and were fined if they did not) but need go no further than Pennenden.[16]

There they witnessed transactions that involved the transfer of land and settled legal disputes. As lords they were responsible to the king for the behaviour of their dependants, both landed or unlanded, including the performance of the military service they owed to the king.

There was nothing unique about Kentish society in this respect and the situation described by Williams is replicated elsewhere. Indeed she herself describes a similar local society operating in Shropshire.[17] In Bedfordshire in 1066, to take another example, there was 'a coterie of thegns whose wealth and influence set them above their neighbours'.[18] That there existed horizontal ties between at least some of their number is hardly to be doubted. It is likely, too, that ties existed between men commended to the same lord, which at the lower levels in particular will have reinforced ties of neighbourhood. We generally lack the sources that would give us details of marriage alliances and of people acting as surety for one another in civil matters.[19] Nevertheless, though subordinate to lordship, horizontal ties must have co-existed with it, and sometimes even reinforced it.

This structure, with a group of landholders operating below the level of the truly national figures and the magnates with more regional interests, is one which the historians of later medieval gentry would easily appreciate and recognize. What is

---

[15] A Williams, 'Lost worlds: Kentish society in the eleventh century', *Medieval Prosopography* xx (1999).

[16] Ibid 73.

[17] A Williams, *The English and the Norman conquest* (1995), 89–96.

[18] Abels, *Bedfordshire domesday*, 34.

[19] For a marriage agreement between two Kentish thegns and for a list of sureties for the estates of Peterborough Abbey see *Anglo-Saxon charters*, ed AJ Robertson (1956), nos 40 and 77. See also R Fleming, *Kings and lords in conquest England* (1991), ch 2, 'Cnut's conquest and the destruction of the royal kindred'.

especially interesting in the present context is that Williams adopts the language of the county community with its resident elite:

> This paper is an attempt to analyse the shire community of Kent on the eve of the Norman Conquest . . . the members of that community (the *meliores*, 'better men' of the shire) included not only great lords but also 'lesser' men of primarily local importance. The problem is to find and identify the *meliores* of the shire.[20]

The concept of the county community originated within the historiography of early modern England and was adopted by later medievalists. Its applicability is now under fire from some of them, especially historians of the fifteenth century.[21] The point is that talking in terms of a gentry takes us not just to the shire – which was, as Williams puts it, 'the highest tier of English local administration and a vital link in the maintenance of royal influence in the English regions'[22] – but to a certain way of looking at the shire, namely as a gentry-led community.

Even when looking at the operation of lordship, however, historians of Anglo-Saxon England are now tending to stress the mutual advantage of both magnate and lesser landowner, with one eye not only on the post-conquest honour, where the tenants have often been deemed to constitute a community, but also, perhaps, on the affinity of later medieval England, where lord and retainer entered into a relationship of mutual benefit by means of a written contract.[23] In introducing Bedfordshire domesday Richard Abels, for example, writes:

> Having men in as many hundreds as possible was to the lord's advantage, since a thegn with five hides of land could represent his lord in the hundred courts. For the client, the protection of a great lord could prove decisive in disputes with other men or with their patrons.

The chief 'principle of association' at this level was geographical, and indeed 'it is likely that hundred boundaries helped determine the patterns of lordship'. As Abels points out, the hundred courts were particularly important to lesser landowners, because that was where they secured their title to land and acknowledged their military service. Not that all of those who had a free choice in the matter necessarily commended themselves to their most immediate strong man; far from it. There was a large measure of intelligent choice: 'The motives that lay behind an individual's choice cannot be uncovered from even the closest study of Domesday Book. Family ties, the commendation of parents, friendships, enmities, property disputes all played a part.'[24]

The issue of the local courts, most especially the shire court, opens up other dimensions. While most historians who have spoken recently of a 'gentry' in Anglo-Saxon

---

20 Williams, 'Lost worlds', 51.
21 See especially C Carpenter, 'Gentry and community in medieval England', *Journal of British Studies* xxxiii (1994) and JR Lander, 'The significance of the county in English government' in P Fleming, A Gross and JR Lander (eds), *Regionalism and revision: the crown and its provinces in England 1200–1650* (1998).
22 Williams, 'Lost worlds', 51.
23 For a recent discussion of the several ways of looking at aristocratic society in England see D Crouch, 'From Stenton to McFarlane: models of societies of the twelfth and thirteenth centuries', *Transactions of the Royal Historical Society* 6.v (1995).
24 Abels, *Bedfordshire domesday*, 38, 39, 40.

England have done so hesitantly and have proceeded by way of analogy with later periods, as a consequence of the re-focusing of Anglo-Saxon studies, John Gillingham, by contrast, has recently argued vociferously for the existence of an Anglo-Saxon gentry and has mounted a direct challenge to historians of later medieval gentry. His target is those 'scholars who regard themselves as historians of the gentry [but who] seem reluctant to admit that the phenomenon they study can have existed much before 1200, if then'. What is especially interesting is the sequence of argument. He begins, unsurprisingly, with what he aptly calls 'the new landscape of late Anglo-Saxon England' as recently redrawn by Blair and others. But he soon changes direction, focusing on three criteria 'widely regarded as crucial' for the existence of a gentry: 'first, the participation by local landowners in local public office; second, the existence of county solidarities; and third, the participation by some in national assemblies'. It is 'precisely these criteria', he argues, which suggest 'that the peculiarly English brand of the lesser nobility existed before 1066 and, in some respects, was re-created after it'.[25]

The words he uses are pregnant with historiographical associations, some of which are very old indeed. One dimension is of course the issue of continuity across the Norman conquest, and all that that continuity has implied. Another dimension is the 'peculiarity of the English'.[26] In short, the gentry has been grafted on to a much older historiography. Let us explore its implications.

In locating his gentry Gillingham invokes his fellow historian Campbell. Gillingham's gentry functioned in – indeed were an important constituent part of – what he calls 'Campbell's kingdom'.[27] The characteristics of this kingdom are well known. Late Anglo-Saxon England was a prosperous and highly centralized state in which relations between the central authority and the localities were extremely important and where many men, thegns and others, functioned as agents of the state.[28] Campbell has been much concerned with the origins and nature of this state, with the continuity of its institutions and with the differences between the English state and those of the continent. In many ways the key institution is the shire: 'The continuity of the shire units is part of the bedrock of English administrative history and of the long success of the English state.'[29] Now we don't read very far into Campbell's work before we realize that his approach to and interpretation of late Anglo-Saxon history have much in common with the views of the Victorian scholar William Stubbs. Indeed this is made explicit in his appreciation of Stubbs, written in 1989 and entitled, significantly, 'Stubbs and the English state'. In Campbell's words:

> Stubbs' leading ideas are easy to trace. The most important of them he summed up as follows: 'The great characteristic of the English constitutional system . . . the principle of its growth, the secret of its construction, is the continuous development of representative

---

[25] J Gillingham, 'Thegns and knights in eleventh-century England: who was then the gentleman?', *Transactions of the Royal Historical Society* 6.v (1995), 129, 131.

[26] To borrow a phrase used in a very different context by EP Thompson, 'The peculiarities of the English', repr in *The poverty of theory and other essays* (1978).

[27] Gillingham, 130.

[28] See especially J Campbell, 'Was it infancy in England? some questions of comparison' in M Jones and M Vale (eds), *England and her neighbours, 1066–1453: essays in honour of Pierre Chaplais* (1989); J Campbell, 'Some agents and agencies of the late Anglo-Saxon state' in JC Holt (ed), *Domesday studies* (1987); and J Campbell, 'The late Anglo-Saxon state: a maximum view', *Proceedings of the British Academy* lxxxvii (1994). These articles are reprinted in Campbell, *Anglo-Saxon state*.

[29] Campbell, *Anglo-Saxon state*, introduction, xi.

institutions from the first elementary stage, in which they are employed for local purposes . . . to that in which the national parliament appears' (*Constitutional History* I,
p 611). His theory of the development of the English state is both providential and teleological. The idea of necessity is important to him . . . For example, he says that in the
twelfth century the English acquired 'conscious unity and identity which made it necessary to act as a self-governing political body' (Ibid I, p 712).[30]

Conscious of the powerful modern criticism of the Stubbsian framework, Campbell, despite his admiration, falls short of endorsing it. But only just. Indeed there is
considerable ambiguity. Take the following, for example: 'That his view of social
change and historical progression is teleological is bound, I think, by that very token
to earn the disapproval of some.' And, again, the 'principal element in the rejection of
Stubbs has been a morbid fear of anachronism'. It is a charge from which, at least in
regard to parliament and to magna carta, Campbell seeks to free him. In the last analysis, 'much of what he argued about the debt of the English present to the English past
is right'.[31]

When he came to write the introduction to his collection of essays, entitled *The
Anglo-Saxon state*, in the year 2000, Campbell was prepared to be more forthright in
his Stubbsianism:

> The antiquity and long continuity of the shires made . . . them focuses of sentiment as
> well as units of government. Shire courts, which could be very widely attended, were, as
> one might say, local proto-parliaments. The development and rise of parliament from the
> thirteenth century Stubbs saw as built upon these local 'parliaments' sending their repre-
> sentatives to the centre . . . It is not anachronistic nonsense to see such assemblies as
> having representative characteristics. Equally valid is Stubbs' view that when the House
> of Commons appears it is largely as an assembly of representatives of other, older assem-
> blies. That representative institutions have their roots in the dark-age and medieval past
> is not an anachronistic view; rather it is fully demonstrable.[32]

Campbell follows Stubbs then in looking to Anglo-Saxon England for the roots of
later institutions. Far more is at stake here, however, than the mere question of roots.
In Campbell's own words:

> It is a question of how far the continuities of the state the Anglo-Saxons founded
> involved freedom, or constitutional rights, constitutional freedoms. A century ago it
> would have been accepted that this was indeed so; the matter would appear to have been
> settled by a series of distinguished historians. In more recent years it has been normal to
> avoid discussion of early arrangements in terms which might suggest approval or at least
> that such arrangements were the true ancestors of institutions and ideas which are now
> generally approved of . . . There is, at least in my mind, no sensible reason for avoiding
> studying history as, in part, the history of liberty. And it does indeed look as if the history
> of constitutional liberty has important beginnings in Anglo-Saxon England.[33]

Gillingham likewise stresses the continuity of institutions. For him, too, the
Anglo-Saxon shire was the focus of sentiment.

> [That men] met together frequently at either hundred or shire level or both seems reason-
> ably certain. That they met together often enough to form local solidarities articulated at

---

[30] J Campbell, 'Stubbs and the English state' in his *Anglo-Saxon state*, 252.
[31] Ibid 254 (my italics), 261, 267.
[32] Campbell, *Anglo-Saxon state*, introduction, xxviii–ix.
[33] Ibid xxix.

the shire level is implied by the comment of the Anglo-Saxon Chronicle on the break-down at the end of Æthelred's reign. 'In the end no shire would even help the next.'[34]

Both scholars refer enthusiastically to magna carta and its later history, and both employ John Maddicott's work in particular to show what they contend to be the Anglo-Saxon county at work in the thirteenth century. In one respect, however, Gillingham goes further than Campbell in arguing for the Anglo-Saxon antecedents of later institutions. For him the royal crown-wearings of the eleventh century have the ingredients of a parliament. Quoting the statement in the Anglo-Saxon chronicle for 1087 that the easter, whitsun and Christmas crown-wearings were attended not only by archbishops, bishops, abbots and earls, but also by thegns and knights, Gillingham envisages assemblies in which the lesser men made themselves heard.[35] We are drawing close here to Stubbs and to the representative principle, especially when we recall those three putative criteria for the existence of a gentry: participation in local office, county solidarities and attendance at national assemblies. It is this belief in an underlying and enduring sentiment which leaves these scholars most open to the charge of anachronism, however, for anachronism lies not merely in mistaking the content of institutions but in failing to distinguish the context in which those institutions operated. If we are to use words like freedom, liberty, constitution, or for that matter county community, local solidarity and the like, we need to ensure that we are using them in a way that contemporaries would have appreciated and not investing them with some later sense.

The underlying thought processes are those of William Stubbs, and the inherited discourse which Campbell and, through Campbell, Gillingham are locked into is essentially that of nineteenth-century romantic nationalism, found equally in the works of novelists like Sir Walter Scott and Charles Kingsley and serious historians like John Kemble and William Stubbs. It may well be true that, as Kathleen Biddick has recently said:

> In order to separate and elevate themselves from popular studies of medieval culture, the new academic medievalists of the nineteenth century designated their practices, influenced by positivism, as scientific and eschewed what they regarded as less-positivist, 'nonscientific' practices, labelling them *medievalism*.[36]

Nevertheless they believed equally in the virtues of the Anglo-Saxons and in the existence of a post-conquest 'Norman yoke'.[37] The influential Kemble, for example, much drawn on by Stubbs, believed that all that was best in English institutions had Saxon origins, albeit temporarily corrupted by the tyranny of the Normans.[38] Despite the differences, popular writers and professional historians shared a discourse. There are strong echoes, moreover, of even older discourses, primarily that of the English scholars of 1660–1730 whose achievement David Douglas resurrected so fully for us

---

34 Gillingham, 132.

35 Ibid 131. For a broader discussion of crown-wearings, and one which stresses their post-conquest incidence, see M Biddle, 'Seasonal festivals and residence: Winchester, Westminster and Gloucester in the tenth to twelfth centuries', *Anglo-Norman Studies* viii (1986).

36 K Biddick, *The shock of medievalism* (1998), 1.

37 For a good recent discussion see M Chibnall, *The debate on the Norman conquest* (1999), ch 4.

38 See P Levine, *The amateur and the professional in Victorian England, 1838–1886* (1986), 79–80, cited by Chibnall, 57.

and whose collections of primary sources proved so invaluable.[39] These in their time had been strongly influenced by earlier scholars who had looked to the Anglo-Saxon past for the prototype for the protestant church, for the origins of the common law, and for so much else, and by the early seventeenth-century discourse that gave us the myth of the Norman yoke.[40] As Douglas wrote: 'Strong tides of sectarian zeal, of pristine patriotism and of political conviction . . . swept through these men and gave to their research an ardour which it would never otherwise have possessed.'[41] It is revealing in this respect that Gillingham should have invoked Samuel Daniel, who produced his history of medieval England as long ago as 1612. Referring to the connections between the central authority and the localities Daniel wrote: 'these links thus intermutually fastened, made so strong a chaine to hold the whole frame of the State together in peace and order, as all the most politique regiments upon earth, all the interleagued societies of men, cannot shew us a streighter forme of combination'.[42] Make no mistake, these men were congratulatory. Daniel also urged his reader to 'looke upon the wonderful Architecture of this state of *England*'.[43] The assertion of English, of Anglo-Saxon, difference has a very long pedigree.

Anglo-Saxon difference persisted across the Norman conquest and beyond. Stubbs wrote of English constitutional history as 'a distinct growth from a well-defined germ to full maturity: a growth, the particular direction and shaping of which are due to a diversity of causes, but whose life and developing power *lies deep in the very nature of the people*'.[44] As his successor at Oxford, Edward Augustus Freeman, put it (rather more bluntly): 'we, the English of the nineteenth century, are the same people as the English of the fifth and sixth centuries, and not some other people'.[45] What Gillingham writes is not that far away from Stubbs. When comparing the societies of England and France he writes:

> at this point we have to add in the ingredient that was different – the institutions of a pow-
> erful royal government in England. It is certainly arguable that for a generation or two
> after 1066 great landowners had more power over their major tenants than had been the
> case at the end of the Anglo-Saxon era, none the less in the continuing network of shires
> and hundreds we have an institutional framework which allows us to see the 'lesser
> nobility' as a gentry – both before and after 1066.[46]

Gillingham's version is more sophisticated but it is not in the end greatly dissim-ilar. We even have a faint echo of Kemble's temporary eclipse under Norman tyranny.

---

[39] DC Douglas, *English scholars, 1660–1730* (1939; 2nd edn 1951).

[40] See especially C Hill, 'The Norman yoke' in his *Puritanism and revolution* (1958). Patrick Wormald has recently taken us back to the starting point of the early legal historians. In his view 'the story of the birth of the Common Law with which historians and lawyers have lived since Maitland told it is proba-bly – not certainly but probably – wrong . . . England's law is distinctive because it is as old as the English kingdom'. P Wormald, *The making of English law: King Alfred to the twelfth century* (1999), xi.

[41] Douglas, 23.

[42] Gillingham, 132.

[43] Chibnall, 33. Daniel, however, was not wholly in agreement with the legal historians. For him 'The main stream of our Common Law . . . flowed out of Normandy'. Wormald, 7.

[44] *Select charters and other illustrations of English constitutional history from the earliest times to the reign of Edward the first*, ed W Stubbs (1st edn 1870), preface (my italics); Chibnall, 58.

[45] Quoted in ME Bratchel, *Edward Augustus Freeman and the Victorian interpretation of the Norman conquest* (1969), 15.

[46] Gillingham, 144.

Here the continuity is both in the institutions and in the social structure. As we all know, the gentry are quintessentially English. In his deliberate deployment of social terminology considered more appropriate to later medieval and early modern England, Gillingham is consciously eliding the differences between these societies. He does this not merely to emphasize continuity but to contend, in effect, that the basic features of English society have not changed between the Anglo-Saxon period and modern times.

English difference is the underlying message of the discourse on which Gillingham draws. It lies at the very heart of 'Campbell's kingdom'. It is surely not by chance that Campbell applauds Alan Macfarlane's work *The origins of English individualism*. For Macfarlane the English were and are different from other nations in their attitudes towards property, enterprise and family. They were already in the thirteenth century market-orientated individualists, ego-centred rather than ancestor-centred, lacking the sense of a multi-generational family for which in other cultures the head was essentially the trustee. Set against his model of a 'classical' peasantry, which was derived essentially from eastern Europe, medieval England was simply not a peasant society. In fact 'England has been inhabited since at least the thirteenth century by a people whose social, economic and legal system was in essence different not only from that of peoples in Asia and Eastern Europe, but also in all probability from the Celtic and Continental countries of the same period'. Macfarlane, however, was conscious that his study had not actually found the roots of English difference. 'I have my own suspicions', he adds, 'as to where the "origins" were in time and space and they are similar to those of Montesquieu', that is to say the English took their land law and inheritance system, with their political system, from the Germans. 'In perusing the admirable treatise by Tacitus *On the Manners of the Germans* we find it is from that nation the English have borrowed their idea of political government. This beautiful system was invented first in the woods.' It is hardly surprising that Campbell dubs Macfarlane's interpretation 'a neo-Stubbsian one'.[47]

The most important point here is that the essential difference, the peculiarity of the English, lies deep in the social structure. As with the peasantry so with the aristocracy. Gillingham devotes the final part of his essay to the code of honour enjoyed and expressed by the Anglo-Saxon thegnage. Here, however, he employs another term of transhistorical resonance, *gentleman*. 'I turn to the word "gentleman" in the sense of someone who accepts a code of honour.'[48] This code comprises, naturally, the heroic values of loyalty, courage and prowess. But it has other dimensions too. These include 'urbane eloquence', 'upright conduct', 'fine appearance', 'aristocratic restraint' and 'gentleness of spirit'. In other words the Anglo-Saxon 'gentry' had a developed and appropriate code of behaviour, even if this was 'not yet a code of chivalry'.

Gillingham has to confront a serious difficulty at this point for he has already shown in previous essays that chivalry, in the sense of restraint towards other knights in the heat of battle, was introduced into England by the Norman conquest, a view strongly supported by other scholars of Anglo-Norman England.[49] Hence the

---

[47] A Macfarlane, *The origins of English individualism* (1978), 165, 170, 206; Campbell, 'Stubbs and the English state', 258–9.

[48] Gillingham, 144.

[49] M Strickland, 'Slaughter, slavery or ransom: the impact of the conquest on conduct in warfare' in C Hicks (ed), *England in the eleventh century* (1992); J Gillingham, '1066 and the introduction of chivalry into England' in G Garnett and J Hudson (eds), *Law and government in medieval England and*

Anglo-Saxon code is akin to, though not quite, chivalry. Chivalry, in this line of argument, becomes a subspecies of a wider code, a point made most strongly by Matthew Strickland.[50] Although Gillingham is tapping into a recent discourse among early medievalists which stresses the continuity between Carolingian and twelfth-century knightly values,[51] in reality what he is pointing up, once again, is the continuity of Anglo-Saxon attitudes. If chivalry, properly speaking, is French, the essence of the value-system it incorporates is Germanic, and as far as England is concerned Anglo-Saxon. Norman and twelfth-century dimensions to the code are seen as merely incremental; indeed in some respects they were reversible.[52] Students of aristocratic behavioural codes have to tread warily, for they know that chivalry is yet another word which contains later connotations and that its cavalier use can so easily elide differences.

This tendency to elide differences through the adoption of later terminology is actually in contention with another, and important, perspective offered by Campbell. This is to see Anglo-Saxon England as a type of Carolingian society.[53] One effect of this perspective is to play down the difference between Anglo-Saxon England and its contemporary societies, and to anchor the former more firmly in its own time. This, of course, is not in itself at variance with the Germanist tradition. As Stubbs said at the outset of his *Constitutional history of England*: 'The English . . . are a people of German descent in the main constituents of blood, character and language, but most especially, in connection with our subject, in the possession of the elements of primitive German civilization and the common germs of German institutions.'[54] Another effect, however, is to open up an evolutionary dimension. While 'Carolingian' society failed on the continent, it persisted and indeed was further developed in Angevin England. Societies change as they evolve, and do so as a whole and in parts. It is not my purpose here to argue directly against the existence of a gentry in Anglo-Saxon England, although I do so elsewhere.[55] It is rather to suggest that the gentry, too, can be seen in an evolutionary perspective. In this line of interpretation, while the gentry is itself a product of later times, some of its roots do lie in Anglo-Saxon England, as indeed do the roots of the institutions – most especially the county court – in which it later functioned. A stricter definition of the gentry might well stress, *inter alia*, its role in parliament and the articulation between county and parliament which developed with the constituencies, creating a forum for the expression of gentry interests, the

Normandy: essays in honour of Sir James Holt (1994); J Gillingham, 'Conquering the barbarians: war and chivalry in twelfth-century Britain', *Haskins Society Journal* iv (1992); M Chibnall, *Anglo-Norman England* (1986), 187–8.

[50] M Strickland, *War and chivalry: the conduct and perception of war in England and Normandy, 1066–1217* (1996), ch 1, 'The conquest and chivalry'.

[51] K Leyser, 'Early medieval canon law and the beginnings of knighthood' in L Fenske, W Rösener and T Zotz (eds), *Institutionen, Kultur und Gesellschaft im Mittelalter: Festschrift für J Fleckenstein* (1984), repr in his *Communications and power in medieval Europe: the Carolingian and Ottonian centuries*, ed T Reuter (1994); JL Nelson, 'Ninth-century knighthood: the evidence of Nithard' in her *The Frankish world 750–900* (1996).

[52] Concerning the murder of Simon de Montfort and his followers at Evesham in 1265 and the executions following Boroughbridge in 1322 Gillingham comments: 'In these variations in the prevailing ethic of the secular elite over many centuries there is little room for the notion of a straightforward advance from bloodier to more peaceful or human values.' Gillingham, 'Thegns and knights', 153.

[53] See J Campbell (ed), *The Anglo-Saxons* (1982), 241 and Campbell, *Anglo-Saxon state*, xv.

[54] W Stubbs, *The constitutional history of England: in its origin and development* (3 vols 1873–8) i.2.

[55] In *The origins of the English gentry* (2003), ch 2, 'Roots'.

collective control over the populace which came to be invested in them as local justices, and the social gradations of knight, esquire and gentleman, which heralded the triumph of a wholly territorial way of envisaging society.[56] In the meantime, beginning in pre-conquest England but extending through the twelfth century, a lesser nobility was steadily developing and with it an increasingly powerful elite culture. This was manifested in the development of toponymic surnames, for example, and in heraldry and the many other expressions of twelfth-century chivalry that were emerging in France and were being reflected in romance literature. It could be argued, therefore, that to speak of a gentry in Anglo-Saxon England is to elevate continuities while masking or devaluing change.

The borrowing of terminology can be invaluable in opening up new, or at least alternative, perspectives, and can be used, with care, to highlight continuities. At the same time, however, over-accentuating continuities can distort, by decontextualizing features which are found to be prominent later. As far as the employment of the word *gentry* in the analysis of late Anglo-Saxon England is concerned, possible distortions include elevating the thegnage above all others in terms of agency of the state and of public obligation, emphasizing horizontal associations within the aristocratic world to the extent of downplaying the predominance of vertical ties between lord and man, reducing the value of evolutionary developments, for example within codes of behaviour and conduct, and, perhaps above all, comprehending the life of institutions and of sentimental attachments to them in terms of their later history – the whig interpretation. Over and above this one runs the risk of entering, at least by implication, into a romantic and essentially redundant nationalist discourse.

---

[56] As I argue in my 'Formation of the English gentry', 47–50.

7

The State of the Demesne Manors of Glastonbury Abbey in the Twelfth Century

NE STACY

About 1140 Glastonbury's most eminent abbot, Henry of Blois, described the leasing of manors for set terms in return for rent as 'the custom of the country'.[1] It was indeed the preferred method by which lords in the twelfth century extracted income, either in cash or in kind, from that portion of their estates whose economic exploitation had not been handed over to military tenants – from their demesne, to use the word in its broadest sense. By the end of the century, however, many lords had begun to place their estates under their own direct management. This process had probably often been initiated in response to Henry II's expansion of royal justice, which threatened to give lessees the same immunity from a lord's control as that enjoyed by military tenants, but it would have been encouraged by the experience of the Cistercians in their directly cultivated granges, and have received added impetus from the rampant inflation of John's reign (1199–1216), as the real value of fixed rents plummeted.[2]

Until recently manorial lessees of the twelfth century have received a bad press. MM Postan saw them as agents of the decline in demesne husbandry which he believed overtook many large ecclesiastical estates in the twelfth century, and even Edward Miller stressed the negative features of leasing. But at the same time Miller sowed the seeds for doubt in 1971 by demonstrating that the twelfth century no less than the thirteenth was one of economic expansion: the population was growing, new land being colonized, towns expanding and costly building projects flourishing. How could it be in such a context that the economies of great estates were in decline? It had already been established by FRH du Boulay that the twelfth century was not a time of 'dramatic dissolution' for the demesnes of the archbishop of Canterbury. Nor was it for those of the abbot of Peterborough, who were shown by Edmund King in 1973 to

---

[1] Henry of Blois, 'Scriptura' in Adam of Domerham, *Historia de rebus gestis glastoniensibus*, ed T Hearne (2 vols 1727) ii.307 (*mos patriae*); also *English episcopal acta* viii *Winchester 1070–1204*, ed MJ Franklin (1993), 206. For the date of the 'Scriptura' see NE Stacy, 'Henry of Blois and the lordship of Glastonbury', *English Historical Review* 2.cxiv (1999), 1–2. Ralph Evans and Ros Faith have given me painstaking and expert help, and Barbara Harvey read and commented on an early draft of this paper. While recording my deep gratitude I also acquit them of responsibility for any remaining errors and infelicities, which are all my own work. I am also most grateful to the British Academy for permission to reproduce material which has already appeared in *Surveys of the estates of Glastonbury Abbey c1135–1201*, ed NE Stacy (2001) [hereafter *Surveys*].

[2] BF Harvey, *Westminster Abbey and its estates in the middle ages* (1977), 82; P Latimer, 'The English inflation of 1180–1220 reconsidered', *Past and Present* 171 (May 2001); cf G Duby, *Rural economy and country life in the medieval west*, trans C Postan (1968), 199.

have been able to recover from heavy losses of property at the time of the Norman conquest and stabilize their income throughout the following century. In 1978 AR Bridbury questioned the whole basis upon which Postan's twelfth century was built, reinterpreted the evidence from the estates of Ramsey, Durham and St Paul's to reveal active and prosperous organizations and emphasized the positive contributions made by lessees and the leasing system. The St Paul's estate has recently been examined in depth by Rosamond Faith, who has further repaired the reputation of twelfth-century lessees, and demonstrated how the effect of demesne leasing on demesne husbandry was not necessarily detrimental and how an increase in labour rent provides unequivocal evidence that demesnes were not run down.[3]

One great estate is conspicuously absent from the general picture. It is that of Glastonbury Abbey. This is a large omission, since Glastonbury was among the richest monastic houses. Indeed the abbey is frequently stated to have been the richest of them all at the time of the domesday survey in 1086. This is true only if account is taken of the entire lordship, but nearly 31 per cent of that lordship was in the hands of subtenants from whom the abbot would have received only an insignificant and incidental income.[4] The annual revenue generated by those manors which were kept in demesne was £564 14s, some £200 less than that enjoyed by the cathedral monastery of Christ Church, Canterbury.[5] Nevertheless there was only a handful of houses with incomes in excess of £500, and Glastonbury's landholding was enormous, taking in much of the Somerset levels and the foothills of Mendip, a swathe of north-west Wiltshire and south Gloucestershire, and extensive stretches of chalk upland on the Berkshire and Marlborough downs, on Salisbury plain, in central Dorset and in south Wiltshire, as well as a large manor in the vale of Blackmoor.[6]

Glastonbury has not therefore been overlooked because of its insignificance. Nor was it for lack of evidence. After the death on 8 August 1171 of Henry of Blois, who had been abbot of Glastonbury since 1126 and bishop of Winchester since 1129, Richard of Ilchester, archdeacon of Poitiers, received custody of both abbey and bishopric, and he commissioned Hilbert, precentor of Wells (a church with which he had close connections), to inquire into the value of Glastonbury's manors.[7] Hilbert's *inquisicio* gives details of manorial leases and stock and sometimes customary rents both in the early years of the late abbot's rule ('the time of King Henry the son of William') and at its end. Details for the time of Henry I (1100–35) may have been

---

3   MM Postan, 'Medieval agrarian society in its prime: England' in *The Cambridge economic history of Europe* i, ed MM Postan (1966), 586; E Miller, 'England in the twelfth and thirteenth centuries: an economic contrast?', *Economic History Review* 2.xxiv (1971); FRH du Boulay, *The lordship of Canterbury* (1966), 204; E King, *Peterborough Abbey 1086–1310* (1973), 144; AR Bridbury, 'The farming out of manors', *Economic History Review* 2.xxxi (1978); R Faith, 'Demesne resources and labour rent on the manors of St Paul's cathedral, 1086–1222', ibid xlvii (1994).

4   D Knowles, *The monastic order in England* (1950), 702 placed Glastonbury at the top of his table of monastic wealth. My figure for the lordship's total value is £816 10s 6d, some £11 less than his.

5   The demesne income of Christ Church in 1086 was £762 10s; next came the old minster, Winchester, with £569 14s; then Glastonbury, followed by St Augustine's, Canterbury (£557 14s), Westminster (£515), Ely (£484) and Bury St Edmunds (£423). The Westminster figures are from Harvey, *Westminster Abbey*, 55 and those of Ely from E Miller, *The abbey and bishopric of Ely* (1951), 94. Domesday does not give separate values for the demesnes of three of Glastonbury's Wiltshire manors, so figures for this county have been taken from the summary totals in *Liber exoniensis* in *Libri censualis vocati domesday-book additamenta* [ed H Ellis] (Record Commission 1816), fo 527b.

6   *Surveys*, 9 and map (pp xvi–vii).

7   Ibid 1–2, 70–6.

taken from a register of leases and have had limited relevance in 1171, as other leases could have intervened.[8] However, Hilbert was working for a royal custodian who had reached prominence in the service of a master (Henry II) who insisted that a cloak of illegitimacy be laid over all that had happened during the reign of his predecessor, Stephen (1135–54). If he wanted a benchmark, it had to be found in the time of Henry II's grandfather, Henry I.[9] The next description of the estate is much fuller; it was made in 1189 for Abbot Henry of Sully, who had just succeeded after a disastrous vacancy of nine years, during which the abbey had been rebuilt after being razed by fire in 1184. The *Liber Henrici de Soliaco* provided him with a detailed survey of fees, household and manorial tenements, services and stock, with occasional reference back to conditions under his two immediate predecessors. Henry of Sully exchanged Glastonbury for the bishopric of Worcester in 1192 at the instigation of Savaric, bishop of Bath, who sought to attach Glastonbury to his see. In 1198 a handlist was drawn up to give Savaric a summary of customary and leasehold rents paid from Glastonbury manors. The union of Glastonbury with Bath was confirmed in September 1200, and the abbey's estates were placed in the hands of trustees while the pope sought to effect a just division of them between monks and bishop. In 1201 Reginald de Fontibus, a clerk in the household of Hubert Walter, who was one of those trustees, drew up a synopsis of manorial rents, renders, labour services and stock.[10]

Such is the material for putting Glastonbury's demesne on the map of twelfth-century England, but its interpretation has been beset by controversy. Postan found evidence of declining demesne husbandry, commutation of villein services and the contraction of demesne acreage, to confirm a picture he had already drawn of the twelfth century in 1937. Reginald Lennard, however, questioned Postan's selective use of the material and his accuracy. He also warned that where manors were leased the record of stock was of that in the lease, which would not necessarily be the same as that in the fields. Postan responded by protesting his general accuracy and asserting that most Glastonbury manors were under direct management in 1171, so that the statistics indeed related to actual rather than contractual livestock. Lennard's brief reply, published posthumously twenty years later, made another plea for precision and questioned Postan's evidence for the radical administrative change he claimed had taken place by 1171. Postan issued his 'restatement'. The controversy appeared 'complex and inconclusive', and historians turned to other estates for evidence of what was happening in the twelfth century.[11]

---

8   For example there is evidence from another source that there was livestock at Butleigh and Shapwick during Bishop Henry's rule, whose numbers do not tally with Hilbert's figures either for *c*1135 or 1171: *Surveys*, 132, 143. There are similar details for East Brent, which did not receive an individual entry in Hilbert: ibid 167.

9   Cf GJ White, 'The myth of the anarchy', *Anglo-Norman Studies* xxii (1999), 328–30.

10   *Surveys*, 2–3, 79–238 (*Liber Henrici de Soliaco*); 3, 239–41 (1198); 4–5, 248–61 (1201).

11   MM Postan, 'Glastonbury estates in the twelfth century', *Economic History Review* 2.v (1952–3); cf M Postan, 'The chronology of labour services', *Transactions of the Royal Historical Society* 4.xx (1937). RV Lennard, 'The demesnes of Glastonbury abbey in the eleventh and twelfth centuries', *Economic History Review* 2.viii (1955–6); MM Postan, 'Glastonbury estates in the twelfth century: a reply', ibid ix (1956–7); RV Lennard, 'The Glastonbury estates: a rejoinder', ibid xxviii (1975), 520–3; MM Postan, 'The Glastonbury estates: a restatement', ibid 524–7. BF Harvey and E Stone's introduction, ibid xxviii.517–20, gives a full exposition of the debate. Cf Bridbury, 'Farming out of manors', 506 ('complex and inconclusive').

An attempt will here be made to indicate how Glastonbury can be fitted more satis-factorily into the general picture. Many of the detailed points at issue between Lennard and Postan can be resolved by establishing a reliable text of the Glastonbury surveys and by the correct identification of placenames. It is hoped that a new edition of the *Liber Henrici de Soliaco* and the publication of those surveys hitherto available only in manuscript have made such resolution possible. This paper seeks first to estab-lish the chronological framework within which the estate moved from indirect to direct management. It should then be possible to handle the livestock figures in the surveys with more assurance, since it is crucial to know whether they relate only to the stock for which a lessee was responsible (in which case they may be an unreliable indicator of actual demesne agriculture) or whether they relate to manors in hand. Even in the case of the latter, where one might expect an accurate reflection of the situation in the fields, evidence must be considered for the subletting of herds and flocks. Ploughteam statistics must also be analysed in the context of labour services owed by the local villeinage. Evidence for the commutation of such services shows that it was neither necessarily recent nor irrevocable. It could also be balanced by an increase in tenements owing customary works consequent upon a rising population. The question of how demesnes were affected by pressures to satisfy the land hunger of that population will be posed. Finally an attempt will be made to look more closely at those few lessees whose names are known to us, before a general assessment of the state of the abbey's demesnes at the end of the twelfth century is ventured.

Hilbert the precentor recorded details of thirty-eight manors for the time of Henry I. Thirty-three of them were explicitly stated to have been leased, or 'at farm', to use Hilbert's terminology, while another (Uplyme, a coastal manor on the Dorset–Devon border) owed weekly renders of fish, which presumably constituted a food-farm. Two manors were allocated to monastic offices. The only manors under direct management were Glastonbury itself, which, as the headquarters manor, was being run according to custom for the sake of its produce, and the small neighbouring fishing settlement at Meare.[12]

If leasing of Glastonbury manors was the local custom in the early years of the abbacy of Henry of Blois, it remained so in the year of his death. Postan simply misread Hilbert, whose evidence clearly shows that in 1171 only Street and Damerham had moved from indirect to direct management since 1135. Street was Glastonbury's immediate southern neighbour across the Brue, so the supervision of its direct cultivation would not have stretched the abbot's administrative resources, but Damerham was over forty miles away in south Wiltshire (it is now in Hampshire). It seems that Henry had brought this huge manor under direct control in order to consolidate a demesne which he had painstakingly recovered from the prebends into which it had been carved by members of the local collegiate church. Damerham's ex-perience did not signal a radical shift in general estate policy, and indeed the manor had been leased again before 1189.[13] It may be that Ashcott was also temporarily taken under direct supervision when Bishop Henry removed it from the hands of a military tenant and brought it into demesne between 1135 and about 1140, but by 1171 it had been fitted into a network of eight manors leased for food-farms.[14]

[12] *Surveys*, 17.

[13] Ibid 18–19; Stacy, 'Henry of Blois', 8–9.

[14] Stacy, 17–18; *Surveys*, 20, 71; cf PDA Harvey, 'The pipe rolls and the adoption of demesne farming in England', *Economic History Review* 2.xxvii (1974), 352.

By 1198 all food-farms had vanished. The properties from which they had been drawn were among the first to be moved into direct cultivation by the abbot himself. They all lay within a thirteen-mile radius of the abbey, within which most manors had been taken out of the hands of lessees between 1171 and 1198. The only direct management undertaken further afield was at the important Dorset complex of Sturminster Newton, some twenty-five miles south-east of the abbey, but over reasonably easy terrain and with ready access to the markets of Sherborne and Shaftesbury. The abbey was feeling its way towards the direct exploitation of its more distant properties, but until the middle years of the next century there would still be a significant place in its economy for indirect management.[15]

This was still so in 1189 even for a few manors close to home. At Blackford in Wedmore, which remained leased throughout the century, a series of damaging boundary disputes may have been a factor in leaving the task of exploitation to lessees. Also at farm in 1198 was the abbot's little manor of Meare, Glastonbury's immediate western neighbour, which seems to have been run directly in 1189, as it had been in the time of Henry I.[16] Its movement against the prevailing tide reminds us how little we know of the springs of action of twelfth-century estate managers.

Nevertheless the framework within which the Glastonbury estate entered direct management is clear, and it is possible to know whether statistics for ploughteams and other livestock relate to manors in hand or on lease. Except for Glastonbury and Meare in the time of Henry I, and additionally Street and Damerham in 1171, Hilbert's figures represent the stock received by lessees at the outset of their contracts and due to be returned, either in kind or in cash equivalent, at their termination. Some of the totals for oxen in 1171, unlike the earlier figures, are not cleanly divisible by ploughteams.[17] Henry of Blois died at the one time of year (August) when ploughing did not feature in the agrarian calendar, when old beasts would have been disposed of and replacements not yet made. Perhaps these are instances of contracts being offered by the incoming royal custodian, based on what remained of the previous lessees' stock.

However that may be, Lennard was surely right when he insisted that recorded details for ploughteams and other livestock were not necessarily the same as the number of animals a lessee might actually use to work the land.[18] To take an extreme example, the lessee of Cranmore (Somerset) paid £7 a year in Henry I's reign for a property stocked with sixteen oxen, two hundred sheep, an affer (draught horse) and a cow, but the stock had been completely removed by 1171, when the farm had been reduced to £5. This does not mean, however, that the demesne had been wound up.

[15] *Surveys*, 21–2. For evidence of the continued leasing of Glastonbury manors in north Somerset, Wiltshire and Dorset see *Interdict documents*, ed PM Barnes and WR Powell (Pipe Roll Society new series xxxiv 1960), 21–2, 29; *The great chartulary of Glastonbury*, ed A Watkin (Somerset Record Society lix, lxiii, lxiv 1947–56) iii, nos 1239, 1321; *Rentalia et custumaria Michaelis de Amesbury (1235–1252) et Rogeri de Ford (1252–1261) abbatum monasterii beatae Mariae Glastonie*, ed CJ Elton, TS Holmes and E Hobhouse (Somerset Record Society v 1891), 67.

[16] *Surveys*, 22, 75–6, 174–5, 239, 253. It is possible that Meare was leased in 1171, as the abbreviation of a now lost version of Hilbert gives it a 'value' of £2, which was its farm in 1198: ibid 75 n4.

[17] Ibid 70–5 (Street, Butleigh, Walton, Shapwick, Ham, Mells, Pennard, Batcombe, Baltonsborough, Uplyme, Ashbury). Ploughteams on Glastonbury manors could be of six, eight or ten oxen: RV Lennard, 'The composition of demesne plough-teams in twelfth century England', *English Historical Review* lxxv (1960), 200–1, 203–4.

[18] Lennard, 'Demesnes', 360–1; RV Lennard, *Rural England 1086–1135* (1959), 189–95.

The manor had been leased for life to a cleric based apparently in Winchester, who would have put in his own sub-lessees, either provisioning them himself or leaving them to make their own arrangements to work a demesne for which the abbey was once more to supply stock in 1201. It was not expected that demesne capacity would necessarily be fully stretched by the livestock in a lessee's contract: Hilbert recommended the addition of eight oxen and two hundred sheep to the stock at Idmiston (Wiltshire) in 1171, while the abbot advanced 33*s* 4*d* to the lessees of Nettleton (Wiltshire) in 1189 to add another hundred sheep to their existing flock.[19]

The records of an earlier survey, the domesday inquest of 1086, were of course concerned with stock on the ground rather than on parchment, but its evidence should not unhesitatingly be taken as a yardstick by which to judge later developments. Where figures are available for comparison between 1086 and 1082, when Thurstan of Caen 'received' the abbey of Glastonbury, leasable values can be seen to have risen by 75.5 per cent.[20] It is even possible that the increase took place within a year, since the improvement on the Somerset manors was said to have happened while they were *in manu Turstini abbatis*, and Thurstan was exiled in 1083.[21] Some may have reflected rises in actual worth caused by restocking and restoration after the departure of royal custodians, who had been in since 1078, but most were so sharp that it is hard to believe that they were caused by anything other than a severe racking of lessees' rents. Not all Thurstan's farms proved sustainable. By 1135 they had dropped back at Zoy, East Pennard and Wrington, and at none of these manors were so many ploughteams ever again present on the demesne as there had been in 1086, not even in 1259, after reclamation, assarting and the purchase of free holdings.[22] It is reasonable to suppose that they were employed in 1086 in an effort by lessees to meet exorbitant obligations.

Lessees' rents, however, did not always overtax a demesne. For example Walton (Somerset), whose arable was worked by thirty-two oxen in 1173–80 as it had been in 1086, when its farm was £15, had been leased with twenty-four oxen for £12 *c*1135, and with only seventeen oxen for £9 in 1171. Was this decline after 1086, prior to the sudden recovery in 1173–80, apparent or real? At Buckland Newton (Dorset) the ploughteams were reduced from five to three between *c*1135 and 1171, but here the farm doubled.[23] It is possible to find one manor provisioned with eight oxen and an affer, another with sixteen oxen, fifty sheep, twenty pigs, an affer and eight cows, and a third with twenty-four oxen, forty pigs, two affers, a bull, five cows and a flock of two hundred sheep, all owing identical farms of £10.[24] Sometimes the divergence

---

[19] *Surveys*, 72, 83–4, 84 n1, 250 (Cranmore), 74 (Idmiston), 197 (Nettleton).

[20] The rise was without parallel in the south-west, and is comparable to what was happening on royal manors and at Canterbury, where we know leasing was almost universal: Du Boulay, *Canterbury*, 201; RW Southern, *St Anselm and his biographers* (1963), 257; Lennard, *Rural England*, 155–7. Just as Faith has found Lennard's conclusion that farms lay behind many domesday values applicable to the estate of St Paul's, I find it applies also to that of Glastonbury: Lennard, *Rural England*, 113–28; Faith, 'Demesne resources', 659.

[21] *Liber exon*, fos 173, 528; William of Malmesbury, *De antiquitate Glastonie ecclesie*, ed J Scott (1981), 158.

[22] *Liber exon*, fos 162b, 167, 169; London, British Library, add MS 17450, fos 112v–13r, 137r, 151r–v. For Glastonbury's exceptional commitment to demesne agriculture in 1086 see S Harvey, 'Domesday England' in *The agrarian history of England and Wales* ii *1042–1350*, ed HE Hallam (1988), 107–8.

[23] *Surveys*, 71, 75, 148; for examples on the St Paul's estate of the number of demesne teams falling or remaining stable while demesne arable expanded see Faith, 'Demesne resources', 663.

[24] *Surveys*, 71–2, 76 (High Ham, Mells, Blackford).

between farm and real worth was great enough to cause comment in the records: Damerham's farm in 1086 was £16 too high according to 'the men' (*homines*); Wrington's farm was considered excessive in 1171, whereas Winscombe's was thought to be too low.[25] Many of these puzzles would doubtless be explained if we had details of the payments (*gersumae*) made by lessees when they took up their contracts.[26]

A paucity of livestock is remarkable in many of the leases recorded for 1171: apart from oxen, only an affer, for example, at Street, Butleigh and Ditcheat, and no other beast at all at Batcombe. The dearth, however, may sometimes have existed only on parchment. Two tenants at Street in 1189 were obliged to send a man 'to the cows' pasture', but no cow was actually recorded in the stock at Street at any time in the twelfth century.[27] Livestock was frequently sublet, not only by manorial lessees but also by the administrators of directly managed demesnes. Signs of this activity are lost in the brevity of Hilbert's survey, but emerge from the fuller details supplied in 1189 and 1201, when we are often told that 'there could be' or 'should be' certain stock which at the time was not in the hands of lessee or bailiff. For example at South Brent (Somerset) in 1189 'there ought to be fifteen cows priced at 3*s* but they are not there'. Where they were was with William Ster, who had rented fifteen acres of the demesne with fifteen cows for 50*s*, the lord providing pasture and hay. In the 1230s two dairy farms, each of twelve cows and fifty sheep, are revealed at Berrow (Somerset), where in 1189 'there could be one hundred sheep' and in 1201 'there could be one hundred sheep and twenty-four cows'. Similarly the counterparts of the twelve cows and hundred ewes apparently missing from Lympsham (Somerset) in 1189 and 1201 turn up in a couple of dairy farms (or wicks) in 1236.[28] Such husbandry was perfectly suited to the salt marshes of the Somerset levels, where cows and ewes produced a higher yield of cheese than on other pastures, at the same time utilizing land while waiting for the salt to be leached out of it.[29] Dairy farming involved intensive and specialist use of labour, and farmers not only in the levels but throughout Wessex persisted in renting out cows until the end of the nineteenth century, despite the condemnation of agricultural 'improvers'.[30] On the Glastonbury estate the custom also surfaces in 1189 at Ashbury in Berkshire, where Ailric *de Wicha* paid 40*s* for his yardland (*virgata*), ten acres and 'pasture belonging to the wick'; it was separately noted of the demesne stock that 'there could be four ploughteams and six cows', and these duly appear in 1201 sublet for 40s.[31] The fortuitous nature of this evidence is

---

[25] *Domesday book, seu liber censualis Wilhelmi primi regis Angliae* [ed A Farley] (2 vols 1783) i, fo 66bi; *Surveys*, 72.

[26] For example Mr Alan de Cretton paid five marks for the lease of Blackford in 1195x1203: *English episcopal acta x Bath and Wells 1061–1205*, ed FMR Ramsey (1995), no 219; cf Lennard, *Rural England*, 180–2.

[27] *Surveys*, 70, 73, 149–50. The fact that the lord's labour-rent was being used to service 'the cows' pasture' suggests that it was grazed by a manorial herd, albeit leased, not by villagers' stock.

[28] Ibid 157–8, 162, 171, 254–5; cf 167 and n2; *Rentalia et custumaria*, 39, 48, 51. The table for cows in 1201 in Postan, 'Estates', 364 is unhelpful: I recognize from the manuscript only 12 of the 38 figures it gives.

[29] Cf Walter of Henley, *Hosbondrye*, chs 87–8, in *Walter of Henley and other treatises on estate management and accounting*, ed D Oschinsky (1971), 332–5.

[30] JH Bettey, *Rural life in Wessex 1500–1900* (1977), 17–18. Compare the dairy farms keeping ewes and herds of six to twelve cows which flourished in the Tyrol and Styria 1200–1500: BH Slicher van Bath, *The agrarian history of western Europe AD 500–1850*, trans O Ordish (1963), 142–3.

[31] *Surveys*, 210, 212, 261.

obvious and inhibits any conclusion that the phrase 'there could be' certain livestock meant that it was in fact absent.[32]

These shafts of light throw into relief the importance of information we simply do not have for the great majority of manors under indirect management. Records of leases can be misleading when used for any other purpose than their own: to remind lessee and lessor of the terms of their agreement. Statistics drawn from them cannot by themselves provide a reliable guide to the state of agriculture on the Glastonbury demesnes in the twelfth century.

By the time we reach the surveys of 1189 and 1201, however, details become available for significant numbers of manors under direct management. Even when the farming out of livestock was practised on these too, as it clearly was on Brentmarsh in 1201, demesne stock recorded in surveys might be expected accurately to reflect at least the situation in the oxhouse, and at last it would seem that a comparison with figures in domesday book may be useful. On seven manors the total number of teams present or potentially present in 1201 (or 1189 where data recorded by Fontibus in 1201 are lacking) was the same as in 1086.[33] Ashcott had three teams compared with two in 1086 when it had been subinfeudated, but on another seven demesne manors the total had fallen: by one team at Ditcheat and Butleigh, by two at Glastonbury itself and at Zoy, by three at East Pennard, four on Brentmarsh, and by eight at Pilton.

Demesne arable, however, was not worked solely by demesne ploughteams. Lords or their lessees also had access to ploughing services due from the customary tenantry, and the availability of this resource would have had an obvious impact on the required number of demesne oxen. As Faith has warned, 'while it is safe to conclude that a large number of demesne ploughteams undoubtedly meant a large demesne, it is unsafe to assume that a small number of teams denotes a small demesne'. Postan was, of course, aware of the problem but concluded that labour services were commuted on such a scale on the Glastonbury estate in the twelfth century that its implications could be discounted.[34] So sweeping a conclusion is not, however, supported by the evidence.

One of the questions put to manorial juries by Henry of Sully's surveyors in 1189 was 'if any land has been made free in the time of Bishop Henry which ought to be worked (*que debuit operari*), by what warrant this was done, and to what degree it be free'.[35] If the jurors' answers can be taken at their face value they reveal that, out of about 220 hides and 3,700 measured acres covered by the surviving portion of the *Liber Henrici*, only 20½ hides and 121 acres had had weekly labour services commuted since 1126. In other words, it would seem that while the estate was still very largely in the hands of lessees only 10 per cent of villein tenements and a little over 3 per cent of cotlands and other holdings had been freed from liability to regular customary work.

This is not the whole picture, since every manor had some tenants, often large numbers of them, who paid higher *gafols* (money rents) and did fewer works than

---

[32] In 1185 a royal clerk emphasized that a list of livestock leased at Broughton in Lincolnshire comprised 'all the stock that is there', implying that such might not always be the case: *Rotuli de dominabus et pueris et puellis de xii comitatibus*, ed JH Round (Pipe Roll Society xxxv 1913), 20–1.

[33] Shapwick, Ham, Street, Doulting, Batcombe, Walton, Sturminster Newton: *Surveys*, 120, 148, 249, 251–2, 257. I have assumed that the twelve oxen at Batcombe represented a change in the make-up of the team from eight to six.

[34] Faith, 'Demesne resources', 663; Postan, 'Estates', 361–2, 364–5.

[35] *Surveys*, 103.

their fellows with identical holdings, without eliciting a comment in Abbot Henry's survey. Some such tenancies, particularly those on colonizing manors, may have been of recent creation and owed lighter services from the start, but elsewhere uniformity is found on a scale large enough to imply block grants of commutation. While it is possible that Abbot Henry's survey was sometimes negligent in one of its primary tasks, we cannot assume that it was consistently so, and it seems likely that much commutation of labour services pre-dated 1126.[36]

Only where it resulted in the creation of a free tenement was such commutation irrevocable. In the great majority of cases it was enjoyed 'at the will of the lord', and while no doubt it often continued from generation to generation, nevertheless it could be revoked in practice as well as theory. In 1189 five half-yardlanders at Ashcott paid 1*s* 3*d* and owed half the ploughing service of their six fellows who paid 5*d*. How long they had enjoyed this liberty is not known, but they did not enjoy it for much longer: in 1201 there were twelve half-yardlanders all doing the heavier service and paying the lower gafol, and the total for assized rents dropped accordingly.[37]

The consequent increase in the ploughing due from the tenantry at Ashcott between 1189 and 1201 amounted to a hundred acres *per annum*, and the removal of one ploughteam from Ashcott's demesne between those same dates can be seen as a direct result of that increase. Ploughing services must similarly have contributed to the situation at Pucklechurch (Gloucestershire) in 1189, where lessees were using only twenty oxen compared to the forty they had received, yet the arable 'is ploughed as well as if there were five teams'.[38] The importance of customary services in the ploughing of demesne acres is most strikingly illustrated in the case of Zoy. Here the two demesne ploughteams present in 1086, introduced perhaps by a lessee trying to fulfil an extortionate contract, had been removed by 1135, when the stock contained no oxen at all. Nor did it in 1171, nor thereafter when the manor was in hand. This means neither that the demesne had been wound up nor that beasts would have had to be hired to make up the deficiency. Customary works would have given farmers or bailiffs more tillage than they needed: 800 acres could have been ploughed in this way in 1189 and 1201, while the actual arable after extensive reclamation measured only 500 acres in 1259. There were no demesne oxen throughout the twelfth century any more than there were in 1259, because they were not needed.[39]

So far this attempt to understand the scope of Glastonbury abbey's demesne agriculture has depended on what can be inferred from livestock statistics and the services of the customary tenantry. More confident conclusions may perhaps be based on explicit statements that the demesne had been drawn upon to create new tenancies or enlarge old ones – that it had been 'placed outside' (*foras positum*) to use the contemporary terminology. This was one of Postan's central indicators of declining demesne husbandry. The jurors of 1189 were to report if demesne land had been occupied or let out in freedom or villeinage, and advise on any action that might be in the lord's interest.[40] While we should remember that jurors' own interests might be intimately

---

[36] Ibid 47–8.

[37] Ibid 48 and n277, 144–5, 253.

[38] Ibid 194.

[39] *Liber exon*, fo 162b; *Surveys*, 71, 140, 252; British Library, add MS 17450, fos 112v–13r; cf R Faith, 'Tidenham, Gloucestershire, and the history of the manor in England', *Landscape History* xvi (1994), 47.

[40] *Surveys*, 103.

involved, they recommended that lettings of three ferlings (quarter-yardlands), forty-seven and a half acres of arable and seven of meadow were 'useful'. The great majority of instances passed without comment. On most manors, as Lennard observed, the amounts involved were very small and indeed may simply have represented the shedding of inferior land.[41] Some manors had a reserve of ground known as *landbot*, which was used to compensate tenants whose holdings needed adjustment. For example two acres of *landbot* at Lympsham were 'exchanged' for land flooded by the sea.[42] Use of demesne acres was common 'to augment' holdings or bring them up to a standard size.[43] Such lettings were clearly an essential element in efficient manorial administration. More substantial inroads into the demesne had taken place on three manors, resulting in the creation of entire customary tenements: ten and a half ferlings at Glastonbury, seven yardlands at Kington Langley (Wiltshire) and five yardlands at Badbury (Wiltshire). The available land at Kington and Badbury had been reduced by enfeoffments since 1086, but seven of the Glastonbury ferlings were located 'on the new site' (*in nova placea*), an instance of reclamation being used not so much to extend demesne agriculture as to expand both rent-roll and labour force.[44]

The labour supply generally had increased between 1086 and 1189, as the population continued to grow.[45] This was especially true of that drawn from cotlands, smallholdings (often on the edge of a manor's arable) which had a particularly important function as service-tenancies, providing demesnes with ploughmen, herdsmen, carters, beadles, watchmen and the like. The area occupied by cotlands quintupled at Ashcott, quadrupled at Butleigh, tripled at Zoy and Pucklechurch, and doubled at Sturminster Newton, Nettleton, Wrington, Winscombe, Brentmarsh, Blackford, Walton and Street.[46] More control was exerted over the creation holdings based on the standard unit of the yardland (*virgata*) and its fractions and with a share in the arable, the *terra villanorum* of 1086. This remained stable not only at manors whose rise in population may have been modest (like High Ham and Walton), but also at some which had to cope with very large increases, like Ashcott, Street and Zoy. Thus, for example, the six yardlands at Ashcott occupied by six *villani* in 1086 develop into six yardlands held by twelve half-yardlanders in 1189.[47] Considering its size, remarkable tenurial stability was preserved on the vast manor of Damerham, where, despite a doubling in the number of tenancies between 1086 and 1189, and despite the enfranchisement of some three hides by Bishop Henry, the *terra villanorum* increased by no more than 12 per cent, rising from 108 yardlands to 121.[48] Those in control of many

---

41 Lennard, 'Demesnes', 359–60. For the release of unproductive land see Postan, 'Medieval agrarian society', 557–8. Cf *Surveys*, 111, where it is noted of an acre let out for rent: *sic est utilius quam esset in cultura quia longe est a dominico*.

42 *Surveys*, 170; for *landbot* (or *botland*) see ibid 36 n201.

43 For example ibid 151–2 (Street), where the recipients are to be found among the cottars (151).

44 Ibid 105, 109, 203, 214; note 68 below. Cf B Dodwell, 'Holdings and inheritance in medieval East Anglia', *Economic History Review* 2.xx (1967), 54.

45 R Bartlett, *England under the Norman and Angevin kings 1075–1225* (2000), 290–7; for evidence of growth before 1086 see *Surveys*, 30–1.

46 Their increased numbers were not accommodated by a division of existing holdings but by a real increase in area, since cotlands were generally of five acres throughout the Glastonbury estate in 1189, and this was the size of tenement associated with them in the mid-tenth century: *Surveys*, 37.

47 *Liber exon*, fos 163b, 164; *Surveys*, 143–4; for Street and Zoy compare *Liber exon*, fos 162b, 164b with *Surveys*, 135–9, 150–1.

48 *Domesday book* i, fo 66bi; *Surveys*, 220–7.

Glastonbury manors were evidently reluctant to reduce the demesne's share of the available arable, and accommodated the rising population by reducing the size of standard tenements. Consequently, of course, in these cases more tenants did not mean more ploughing services, as these obligations were adjusted in proportion to the tenement.[49]

Where reclamation was under way, however, we find both an increase in the area of tenements with a share in the arable and a corresponding increase in the ploughing services owed from them on the demesne. On the large manorial complex of Brentmarsh, in the levels between the Axe and the Brue, tenancies increased by 165 per cent, and although some free tenants held whole yardlands, the customary tenantry in 1189 made do with half-yardlands and ferlings, but assized land was allowed to expand by 40 per cent. Apart from two ferlings the survey of 1189 does not identify a consequent loss to the demesne. The presumption must be that new land was providing the new tenancies. The demesne of course shared in the development of the marsh, expanding its meadowland and leasing what it did not need to established half-yardlanders.[50] At Butleigh, south of Glastonbury, where new land was being won both from the moor and the wood, settlers were encouraged: the number of tenants increased by some 125 per cent, but the yardland was allowed to remain predominant, so the area of assized tenancies rose by 170 per cent, while the number of cotlands multiplied by four. If the demesne was called upon to supply any of this land Henry of Sully's survey did not notice it, and the vast increase in the number of working cottars does not suggest a demesne that was in any way run down, since that was where their services were concentrated.[51]

The ploughing due from these growing numbers of customary tenants could well have compensated for the low and sometimes contracting number of demesne teams. In 1086, in the unlikely event that every one of the ten yardlands which made up the *terra villanorum* at Butleigh had been subject to the heaviest labour services owed a century later, the total ploughing due would have covered 240 acres. In 1189 the expansion of villein tenancies was such that, although half of them were free of weekly ploughing, the lord could still call upon his tenantry to plough 336 acres in a year. Perhaps this was how the arable in 1189 could be 'well ploughed' with two and a half demesne teams of oxen, one and a half fewer than those employed a few years earlier under Abbot Robert (1173–80), when a cash option may have been taken from the villeins instead of week-work.[52] On Brentmarsh all the land sown to wheat at South and East Brent and Berrow in 1189 could have been ploughed twice over by the customary services available in the autumn on these manors with expanding tenant-ries. There is no figure for land sown at Lympsham, another member of Brentmarsh, but even so it is clear that the complex would be overstocked with the forty-eight oxen

---

[49] Divided holdings were, however, the source of some profit: *Surveys*, 29 and n155.

[50] *Liber exon*, fo 170b; *Surveys*, 152–71: some 100 acres of meadow were let, mostly in five-acre parcels. For a graphic account of reclamation on Brentmarsh see Henry of Blois, 'Scriptura', 307–8; for a translation see *English lawsuits from William I to Richard I*, ed RC van Caenegem (2 vols Selden Society cvi–vii 1990–1) i.222. The 20 acres of demesne meadow at Brentmarsh in 1086 had become 296 acres by 1259: British Library, add MS 17450, fos 120r, 124r, 129r, 132v. Cf M Williams, *The draining of the Somerset levels* (1970), 43–5.

[51] *Liber exon*, fo 165b; *Surveys*, 129–32 (note the tenants *de bosco* and *de mora*).

[52] *Surveys*, 132.

present in 1171 (the same as in 1086 and c1135), and both the lessees of 1189 and the bailiffs of 1201 could make do with half that number.[53]

Brentmarsh had owed food-farms in the time of Henry I and so had Butleigh in 1171. It seems that the proceeds from the rent-rolls on such manors passed not to the lessees but direct to the abbey.[54] It would be surprising if the running down of demesne operations suggested on these manors by ploughteam and livestock statistics were not more apparent than real, for the only profit available to lessees had to come from the efficient management of their demesnes. Doubtless lessees with short leases and those approaching the end of long ones which they did not expect to renew might be tempted to fell woods and overcrop the land, and that lessees with full control over the tenantry might in similar circumstances indulge in irresponsible cash transactions, commuting services and leasing parts of the demesne. Farmers whose own affairs were in disarray were an obviously bad risk. Roger de Mara, who leased an unspecified group of Glastonbury manors in the third decade of the century, fell foul of the king and when he surrendered his leases to Henry of Blois he owed £40 in deficiencies of stock and arrears of rent. However, like the domesday of St Paul's, when it comments on the conduct of lessees Henry of Sully's survey is more often complimentary than not. Although some outhouses at Nettleton were found to be open to the elements and a couple of cows at Lympsham to be 'too old', the buildings on two manors had been improved, as had the quality of stock on two others, while two woods had been notably well managed under their supervision.[55]

The historian of the estates of the archbishops of Canterbury has concluded that 'farmers must have been men with substance and with money to invest'.[56] The handful of Glastonbury lessees whose identity is known would have fitted into this category. The grandest was Peter de Leia, bishop of St David's (1176–98), who farmed the north Wiltshire grouping of Nettleton, Grittleton and Kington in the year of his death. He may not have been as distant an absentee as he looks, as Glastonbury could have been the English monastery in which he stayed when he left his diocese in the care of Gerald of Wales, but he would surely have sublet the manors.[57] So would the brother of Abbot Robert, who had a life lease of Cranmore in 1189.[58] Even a local man, Reginald of Walton, put in his own sub-lessees at East Brent. In 1189 Reginald had a freeholding of one and a half yardlands in the manor from which he took his name and another half-yardland for the custody of Sharpham Wood, but the source of his prosperity was a marshland development for which he paid 24s in annual rent to the reeve of Shapwick: seven miles to the north-west of that manorial centre and separated from it by five subtenanted vills, Reginald possessed at Withy in Huntspill level the facilities to thrive as a grazier and conceivably to supply livestock to manors he leased.[59] Thriving presumably as a townsman, Matthew of Shaftesbury leased

53 *Liber exon*, fo 170b; *Surveys*, 158, 162, 167, 171, 254–6; six oxen made up a team on Brentmarsh.
54 *Surveys*, 21.
55 Henry of Blois, 'Scriptura', 306–7; *Surveys*, 167, 171, 178, 194, 197, 207; *The domesday of St Paul's*, ed WH Hale (Camden Society 1858), 21, 28, 34, 73, etc.
56 Du Boulay, *Canterbury*, 202; cf Faith, 'Demesne resources', 659; Lennard, *Rural England*, 150–1; Bridbury, 'Farming out of manors', 515.
57 *Surveys*, 239; *Giraldi Cambrensis opera*, ed JS Brewer, JF Dimock and GF Warner (8 vols Rolls Series 1861–91) i.54, iii.162. For Peter see *St David's episcopal acta*, ed J Barrow (South Wales Record Society xiii 1998), 7–8.
58 *Surveys*, 84 n1.
59 Ibid 85, 143 and n1, 146 and n2, 166.

Badbury in 1189 and Damerham in 1201, as well as Liddington (Wiltshire) from the abbess of Shaftesbury in 1194.[60] An earlier lessee of Damerham, John the clerk, may have been the prosperous rector of Grittleton, while the lessee of Blackford at the end of the century was certainly the richly endowed bishop's official Alan de Cretton.[61] At about the same time a monk–farmer, who may have been expected to be zealous in his custody of the abbey's property, surfaces at Grittleton in the person of Robert Giffard.[62]

It seems that syndicates might be formed to reduce individual exposure to the financial risks of leasing, for the survey of 1189 uses the plural in relation to the lessees of a number of manors.[63] At Grittleton 'the men of the vill' themselves grouped together to lease the demesne in 1189, 1201 and 1236. This was no exercise in egalitarian communalism. The 'men of the vill', or at any rate those who answered for their actions in the royal courts, were the elite among the customary tenants, the holders of half-hides.[64] No stock was provided by the lord nor any equipment (*implementum*) nor any acres sown or fallow, but the demesne did not 'cease to function', as Postan thought. It was run down in one respect: the *curia* was a modest affair compared with those of its neighbours in north-west Wiltshire at Nettleton, Kington and Christian Malford. When the manor came in hand in the 1250s or 1260s it could boast only a hall and a granary, whereas the others had kitchens and storehouses as well. The integrity of the demesne, however, was still recognized in 1189 and 1236, and indeed the manor had been leased on at least two separate occasions to individual lessees from outside Grittleton in the interval between the leases to the *villata* of 1189 and 1201. All that happened surely was that the men of the vill used their own seed to sow the demesne arable and their own beasts to plough it, stocked the dairy farm with their own cows and the sheep runs with their own flock. In 1236 and perhaps earlier they paid their gafol direct to Glastonbury, so there was limited scope for them to profit from demesne lettings or grants of commutation.[65]

Where it made geographical sense groups of manors within the Glastonbury estate were sometimes farmed out together.[66] Similar considerations must have led some

[60] Ibid 215, 258; *Three rolls of the king's court in the reign of king Richard the first AD 1194–1195*, ed FW Maitland (Pipe Roll Society xiv 1891), 92. Matthew was also active in 1203 at Teffont Magna, part of the Shaftesbury manor of Dinton, Wiltshire, where he took for five years a free tenement that he had occupied as the mortgagee of the tenant's late father. Whether or not he was the abbess's manorial lessee is unknown but not unlikely. *Fines sive pedes finium . . . 1195–1214*, ed J Hunter (2 vols Record Commission 1835–44) ii.89; cf British Library, Harleian MS 61, fo 73r (William *filius Ailardi*).

[61] *Surveys*, 85, 224; *Chartulary* iii, no 1202; *Episcopal acta: Bath and Wells*, no 219 and p lvi (see note 26 above).

[62] *Rentalia et custumaria*, 66–7. Robert Giffard appears *c*1191 as prior of the dependent house of Bassaleg; he was a member of the convent at Glastonbury in 1200: *Chartulary* iii, no 1305; Adam of Domerham, *Historia* ii.377, 385; cf Knowles, *Monastic order*, 437–8, 443 n2.

[63] *Surveys*, 158, 162, 167, 194, 197, 203, 207, 211.

[64] One name is illegible, but seven of the eight men found guilty in 1194 of enclosing common pasture at Foxcote in Grittleton to the exclusion of the military tenant at Clapcot can be identified with half-hiders in 1189. As the number of such tenants was in decline (from ten in 1189 to six *c*1236) it is likely that those cited were the full complement of half-hiders in 1194: *King's court 1194–5*, 67; *Surveys*, 198–9; *Rentalia et custumaria*, 64–6.

[65] Postan 'Estates', 364; *Surveys*, 198, 260. For the protection of demesne pasture and for the remuneration of the reeve by the *villata* for taking the *gabulum* to Glastonbury 'while the manor is at farm in their hands' see *Rentalia et custumaria*, 67. Cf WO Ault, *Open-field farming in medieval England* (1972), 68–70. For the *curiae* in the 1250s or 1260s see British Library, add MS 17450, fos 181v–2r.

[66] For the association of Nettleton, Grittleton and Kington in north-west Wiltshire, and of Winscombe

lessees to acquire interests which overlapped the borders of the abbot's lordship altogether: lessees like Matthew of Shaftesbury, who is known to have been farming the
Glastonbury manor of Badbury in 1189 and the neighbouring Shaftesbury manor of
Liddington in 1194.[67] Such men's enterprises would have constituted truer if more
transient agrarian units than the abbey's own estate. But although it lacked cohesion it
was not in decay. Clear evidence for expanding demesne agriculture is wanting but
many home farms seem to have operated within the same territorial limits throughout
the twelfth century. Those which shrank had often been subject to pressures which
were not entirely economic. The grant of military and socage tenures could seriously
deplete demesnes, and the reduction of demesne at Badbury, Kington and Damerham,
and its extinction at Camerton and Podimore Milton, coincided with the establishment of such tenancies for reasons that had little to do with agriculture. Similarly a
factor which may have contributed to the contraction of Pilton's arable demesne was
the creation of an extensive park by 1236. If so this alternative use of resources should
be ascribed more to social than to economic trends.[68]

For the forty-five years between 1126 and 1171 the Glastonbury lordship was the
responsibility of Henry of Blois, whose interest in demesne agriculture is known from
the memoir he himself wrote, describing among other achievements his creation of a
new demesne complex at Ashcott and his restoration of an old one at Damerham.[69]
Despite his myriad responsibilities he is unlikely to have presided over a disinteg-
rating estate. Nor, when we look at the total revenue generated by Glastonbury's
demesne manors, is there evidence that he did so. A simple addition of the annual
values given in domesday book for property not in the hands of subtenants produces a
total of a little under £565 for 1086. This rises to £695 4s 4d by 1135, when rents and
other dues paid direct from certain manors are added to a leasehold revenue of £629
(of which £73 might be paid in kind). In the year of the death of Henry of Blois (1171)
a similar grand total amounts only to £618 11s 4d, but allowance must be made for the
profits accruing from the huge demesne at Damerham, leased in 1135 for £60 but now
in hand. Reliable estimates of income are difficult to make once manors came into
direct management in any number, as they began to do after 1171. Information about
receipts from the sale of wool, hides, grain and dairy produce is occasionally provided
by exchequer accounts for years in the 1180s and 1190s, when the abbey was in the
hands of royal custodians, and they indicate an annual income of between £600 and
£700 on the eve of the chronic inflation of John's reign.[70] In 1203, when that inflation
was well under way, judges appointed by Innocent III to suggest an equitable division

---

and Wrington in west Mendip see *Surveys*, 72, 239. During the interdict of 1208–14 Grittleton and
Nettleton had the same custodians: *Interdict documents*, 21. For *quaedam maneria* leased to Roger de
Mara see Henry of Blois, 'Scriptura', 307. Cf Du Boulay, *Canterbury*, 199–200.

67 Matthew is not given a toponym at Badbury but the presence of Matthew of Shaftesbury at Liddington
(where 126 loads of corn had been stolen from him) makes it very likely that he was the same man:
Surveys, 215; *King's court 1194–5*, 92. For his activities in the Shaftesbury manor of Dinton, six miles
from the northern border of Damerham and Martin, which he leased from Glastonbury, see note 60
above.

68 *Surveys*, 75, 81, 86–7, 88 n5, 200; Stacy, 'Henry of Blois', 10, 18, 24 n1, 30 n2. For Pilton park see
Rentalia et custumaria, 7, 12–15, 37, and *passim*. The fence stretched for 4.7 miles in 1259: ibid 237.

69 Stacy, 'Henry of Blois', 8–9, 17–18.

70 *Pipe roll 27 Henry II* (Pipe Roll Society xxx 1909), 15; *Pipe roll 28 Henry II* (PRS xxxi 1910), 114;
Pipe roll 29 Henry II (PRS xxxii 1911), 166; *Pipe roll 33 Henry II* (PRS xxxvii 1915), 27–8; *Pipe roll
6 Richard I* (PRS new series v 1928), 10, 20; *Pipe roll 7 Richard I* (PRS new series vi 1929), 48; cf
Latimer, 'English inflation of 1180–1220', 3–7.

of revenue between the monks and the bishop of Bath (under whom Glastonbury was to be reconstituted as a cathedral priory) reported that careful management of the estate should yield a gross income of £800 *per annum*.[71]

Progress from £565 in 1086 to £695 about 1135 to £800 in 1203 was outstripped by that made by the bishops of Ely, whose landed income doubled between 1086 and 1172, but it accords well with the experience of the archbishops of Canterbury, the bishops of Worcester and the abbots of Peterborough.[72] The estate existed to feed and clothe the community, extend hospitality, beautify its buildings, and provide cash reserves to meet the emergencies of taxation and legal action. If these objects were achieved there was no incentive, perhaps a positive moral disincentive, to strive for more. A relaxed approach to financial matters may also have been inculcated during the four decades in which the abbey could tap the vast resources of Henry of Blois, who greatly embellished its fabric and seems to have kept litigants at a respectful distance.[73] His abbacy, however, had seen civil war spread for about ten years throughout the area of the lordship, isolating much of it from his control, disrupting communications, and occasionally causing actual physical damage to manors.[74] Between his death in 1171 and the end of the century the abbey was administered by its own prelates for only eleven years. Sixteen years were spent in the hands of royal custodians, and for the last two years of the century its lands were at the mercy of Bishop Savaric of Bath, whose designs on them had been apparent since 1193. In this context the revenues being generated by its leases and by demesne agriculture in the 1180s and 1190s seem compatible with an economy that was stable rather than stagnant. The commutation of labour services and letting of demesne acres evidenced in 1189 and 1201 were not so much symptoms of declining enterprise as part of the normal workings of that resilient and deceptively adaptable organism, the medieval manor.

---

[71] *Chartulary* i.75, no 126.

[72] Miller, *Abbey and bishopric of Ely*, 94; Du Boulay, *Canterbury*, 243; C Dyer, *Lords and peasants in a changing society: the estates of the bishopric of Worcester, 680–1540* (1980), 53; King, *Peterborough Abbey*, 44.

[73] Stacy, 'Henry of Blois', 22.

[74] Ibid 21–2; *Surveys*, 73, 75, 127, 178, 214.

8

The Manorial Reeve in Twelfth-Century England

PDA HARVEY

We know a great deal about the manorial reeve from the first half of the thirteenth century onward. He stands before us in surveys, in court rolls and, above all, in manorial accounts: the villein tenant who ran the lord's demesne for him under the successive scrutiny of bailiff, steward and auditor and who had to account to his lord for every penny received, every peck of corn harvested, every egg laid. We may see him as an oppressed victim of the contemporary economic system or as peculiarly well placed to profit from it: this depends on our own point of view, on the particular records, perhaps on the particular reeve. But we are not short of the information we need in order to form our opinion.

This is not the case when we look at his twelfth-century predecessor. The document we now call *Rectitudines singularum personarum*, which originated perhaps in the mid-tenth century and which gives an account of the rights and duties of the various workers on a rural estate, may well have been written for the guidance of local reeves; the reeve is the one person left out. In the early eleventh century it was read by someone, possibly Bishop Wulfstan of Worcester, who saw that by supplying this omission it could be turned into a little treatise on rural society in general and he added a postscript on the duties of the reeve that is now known as *Gerefa*, the Anglo-Saxon word from which 'reeve' derives. This text, however, seems to owe more to classical literature than to contemporary English practice and we arguably learn more of the Anglo-Saxon reeve from the gap in the *Rectitudines* than from Wulfstan's – if it was his – attempt to fill it.[1] But this is the fullest, indeed the only, detailed picture of the rural reeve before the records of the thirteenth century: for the intervening period we have only casual references.

If we look at these as far back as the late eleventh century and domesday book we are largely breaking new ground. Vinogradoff makes some interesting comments, but he never looks at the reeve in detail.[2] Stenton devotes a paragraph of the introduction to his Danelaw charters to the reeves that they mention, and more recently DE Greenway has usefully brought together the references to reeves in the Mowbray charters she edited.[3] However, the only general discussion is in five pages of Lennard's *Rural England 1086–1135*, though for the reeves in domesday book this

1 PDA Harvey, '*Rectitudines singularum personarum* and *Gerefa*', *English Historical Review* cviii (1993).

2 P Vinogradoff, *Villainage in England* (1892), 356–8; P Vinogradoff, *The growth of the manor* (1904, 2nd edn 1911), 191–2, 271–2.

3 *Documents illustrative of the social and economic history of the Danelaw*, ed FM Stenton (1920), cvi–vii; *Charters of the honour of Mowbray 1107–1191*, ed DE Greenway (1972), xlv–vi.

has been valuably supplemented by James Campbell in his contribution to the essays commemorating the ninth centenary of 1086.[4] It is time to look at these reeves again in the light of other recent work on the period, in the light especially of Rosamond Faith's book which brings together so much recent exploratory work on the Anglo-Saxon and Anglo-Norman periods; with its new interpretations and insights it is a real starting-point for looking at the period afresh, through new eyes.[5]

The Latin records in which we meet the thirteenth-century manorial reeve refer to him as *prepositus*, or occasionally by the all-purpose word *serviens* (employee). *Prepositus* corresponded to one aspect of his work – he was set over his fellow villagers to command their services for their lord – but if he had first been given a Latin name in the thirteenth century he would more appropriately have been called *villicus*, a manager of rural property. But the translation of the English *gerefa* as *prepositus* goes back well before the thirteenth century and it is nearly always as *prepositus* that we meet the rural reeve in earlier Latin texts. Nonetheless in the Shaftesbury Abbey surveys of about 1130 and 1180 he is more often *prefectus* and is probably twice called *pretor.*[6] *Prefectus* occasionally occurs in other sources and in the so-called laws of Henry I at the beginning of the century we find *tungrevius*, a direct Latinization of the English *tungerefa*, reeve of the vill.[7]

The word occurs in the laws of Henry I in a list of those who are to attend the shire court, from the bishop downwards. The rural reeves have to be called *tungrevii* because both *prepositi* and *prefecti* have already been included in the list.[8] This introduces a problem in looking for these rural reeves in twelfth-century sources: they may have been nearly always *prepositi*, but so were other people as well.[9] The *prepositi* of the laws of Henry I were probably royal reeves, agents of the sheriff; they are often mentioned, usually *prepositi* sometimes *prefecti*, among them the reeves of hundreds who are sometimes distinguished from the others.[10] By the end of the twelfth century *prepositi*, royal reeves, were often included in the list of officers to which royal letters patent were addressed.[11] To ask whether the reeve of a royal manor is to be seen as one of these royal reeves or simply as a manorial reeve like any other is to make a distinction that might not have been understood in the twelfth century; the royal manor was after all in the sheriff's keeping. There were other *prepositi* as well. There were the reeves of a borough, royal or seigneurial.[12] The second-in-command of an abbey, the

---

4   R Lennard, *Rural England 1086–1135* (1959), 271–6; J Campbell, 'Some agents and agencies of the late Anglo-Saxon state' in JC Holt (ed), *Domesday studies* (1987), 205–7, 215–16.

5   RJ Faith, *The English peasantry and the growth of lordship* (1997).

6   London, British Library, Harley MS 61, fos 37r–89r passim (*prefectus*), 80r (*prepositus*), 59v, 69v (*pretor*; though Henry *pretor de operacione augusti* on fo 59v might suggest the *budel* of other entries rather than a reeve, this is presumably the same Henry who appears in the list of jurors on fo 59r as *prefectus*).

7   Thus *Domesday book, seu liber censualis Wilhelmi primi regis Angliae* [ed A Farley] (2 vols 1783) i, fo 218v and *Sir Christopher Hatton's book of seals*, ed LC Loyd and DM Stenton (1950), 243; *Leges Henrici primi*, ed LJ Downer (1972), 98.

8   'centenarii, aldermanni, prefecti, prepositi, barones, vavassores, tungrevii et ceteri terrarum domini'.

9   As Lennard, *Rural England*, 274 points out.

10 WA Morris, *The medieval English sheriff to 1300* (1927), 53–6; *Domesday book* i, fo 218v.

11 Thus *A formula book of English official historical documents*, ed H Hall (2 vols 1908–9) i.21 (letters patent of 1194).

12 Thus *The great roll of the pipe for the eleventh year of the reign of King Henry the second* (Pipe Roll Society old series viii 1887), 12 (Gloucester), 39 (Lincoln); *Earldom of Gloucester charters*, ed RB Patterson (1973), 37 (Bristol), 157 (Cardiff).

prior, might be called *prepositus* following the usage of the rule of St Benedict and so might the provost of a cathedral chapter.[13] A local official with some particular function might be called reeve, like the reeve of the market (*prepositus fori*) at Glastonbury.[14] Usually it is fairly clear what sort of reeve is meant, but some instances are ambiguous and it may be easier than it seems to fall into error.

Prepositus means the man set before or above his fellows and the laws of Henry I make the point by contrasting him with the *subditi* or *subjecti*, those who are under his authority.[15] Was the title *prepositus* more appropriate to the eleventh-century manorial reeve than it was to his thirteenth-century successor, or did he acquire it only by analogy because it was applied more realistically to other kinds of *gerefa*? This is an interesting question to bear in mind: the title may or may not reflect actual change in status. It is a question that underlies the three questions about the twelfth-century manorial reeve to be specifically addressed here successively in ascending order of difficulty: who was he? whose was he? and what did he do?

Who was he?

The reeve was probably always a manorial tenant. We meet him in this guise on every one of the thirteen private estates from which we have twelfth-century surveys.[16] He was a peasant, *villanus*, with usually a standard holding: a yardland (virgate), a half-yardland, two oxgangs (bovates). Occasionally he held more – two yardlands, half a hide – or he might supplement his holding by taking over the lord's mill or further lands and by the late twelfth century we see reeves participating in the local land market, acquiring and disposing of pieces of free land by charter.[17] None of this set the reeve apart from his fellow tenants. At Pittington, county Durham, about 1150 a reeve was put in place by a written charter: Baldwin was granted land and a mill in return for serving as reeve or, if he relinquished office, for 10*s* a year and two sestars of honey.[18] The surveys often acquit the reeve of part or all of the obligations due for his holding in return for his service; it would accord with thirteenth-century practice for this to happen even if not actually mentioned in the survey.[19] On three manors in

---

13 *RB 1980: the rule of St Benedict, in Latin and English*, ed T Fry (1981), 284–6; *Liber eliensis*, ed EO Blake (Camden 3rd series xcii 1962), 219, 290, 293, etc; EU Crosby, *Bishop and chapter in twelfth-century England* (1994), 346.

14 *An inquisition of the manors of Glastonbury Abbey of the year M.C.LXXXIX*, ed JE Jackson (Roxburghe Club 1882), 13.

15 *Leges Henrici primi*, ed Downer, 174–7, 194–5, 363.

16 Two additions should be made to the eleven non-royal estates listed in PDA Harvey, 'Non-agrarian activities in twelfth-century English estate surveys' in D Williams (ed), *England in the twelfth century* (1990), 101 n2. The first is Bury St Edmunds Abbey, whose early or mid-twelfth century surveys are in *Feudal documents from the Abbey of Bury St Edmunds*, ed DC Douglas (1932), 25–44; the second is Abingdon Abbey, whose surveys of 1185–90 are in *Chronicon monasterii de Abingdon*, ed J Stevenson (2 vols Rolls Series 1858) ii.299–309, 324–34. Douglas (*Feudal documents*, lxv) dated these Bury surveys to the late eleventh century, connecting them with documents that underlie entries in domesday book, but I do not doubt that they are significantly later.

17 Lennard, *Rural England*, 273; *Cartularium monasterii de Rameseia*, ed WH Hart and PA Lyons (3 vols Rolls Series 1884–93) iii.243 (two yardlands), 270 (demesne meadow); E Miller, *The abbey and bishopric of Ely* (1951), 284–5; *Documents of the Danelaw*, ed Stenton, cvii n1.

18 *Feodarium prioratus dunelmensis*, ed W Greenwell (Surtees Society lviii 1872), 129 n1.

19 Thus *Boldon buke*, ed W Greenwell (Surtees Society xxv 1852), 7, 10, 12 (fully remitted); *Inquisition*

the surveys of about 1195 from Ramsey Abbey the reeve's holding and services are the paradigm for the rest; on three manors in the Templars' survey of 1185 the reeve is the first tenant named.[20] In many other cases too the reeve is probably placed at the head of the lists of tenants, but without being identified; on many of the manors described in the surveys no reeve is named among the tenants but this does not mean that he was not there. On several manors of the Glastonbury estates in 1189 there was a reeve among the jurors who provided the information for the survey but not among the tenants – where, however, he probably appears without being thus identified.[21] Thus, to take an unusual name, the Sericus *prepositus* who was a juror at Christian Malford was presumably the same as the Sericus who had a cottage holding and one acre of demesne.[22]

In charters too we must meet many reeves without recognizing them. In a charter of 1174–81 quitclaiming three tenants, presumably at Maplestead in Essex, to the canons of St Paul's the witnesses include Hugh the reeve of Maplestead but in the actual grant of the same three tenants, a charter with a very similar witness list, we have instead simply Hugh of Maplestead.[23] We need not doubt that it was the same Hugh. That the reeve was sometimes so called, sometimes not, itself tells us something of the office and how it was regarded: it was important, significant in some contexts, but not so important that it must always be mentioned as its holder's outstanding characteristic. The reeve may occasionally emerge from anonymity, but he returns to it again all too easily.

Along with the estate surveys, charters are our best source of information on twelfth-century reeves. As in charters of the thirteenth century, the reeve is sometimes mentioned as the tenant of property adjoining the free holdings that are being conveyed but also, quite unlike the thirteenth century, he appears in the lists of witnesses to the transaction. There is no more cogent contrast between the manorial reeve of the twelfth century and his thirteenth-century successor than the fact that whereas he often witnessed charters his successor did not, even if this is no more than a simple but telling illustration of the development of the law of villeinage: not just the reeve but any villein tenant was now unable to attest a conveyance of free property. It is only rarely that we find someone who is apparently a manorial reeve witnessing a charter that can be firmly dated even a few years after 1200.[24]

Demonstrably neither surveys nor charters can be relied on to tell us when they are speaking of a reeve, so we can reasonably suppose that there may have been far more of them than these sources suggest. The note about the making of domesday book at the start of the related Ely survey, the *inquisitio eliensis*, tells how inquiries were made of the sheriff, the barons and their French retainers, the whole of each hundred and the

of Glastonbury, ed Jackson, 46–7 (half remitted); *Cartularium de Rameseia*, ed Hart and Lyons, 245, 246, 250 (no remission recorded).

20 *Cartularium de Rameseia*, ed Hart and Lyons, 245, 246, 250; *Records of the Templars in England in the twelfth century*, ed BA Lees (1935), 39, 46, 47.

21 *Inquisition of Glastonbury*, ed Jackson, 103, 112, 120, 127.

22 Ibid 112, 114, 115.

23 *Early charters of the cathedral church of St Paul, London*, ed M Gibbs (Camden 3rd series lviii 1939), 202–3.

24 Examples are in *Registrum antiquissimum of the cathedral church of Lincoln*, ed CW Foster and K Major (Lincoln Record Society 10 vols 1931–73) iii.325–6 (1203–4), vii.44 (1205–6); where, ibid vii.57, a *prepositus* witnesses a grant of c1215–19 we may wonder whether this can be a manorial reeve or even whether the date is correctly assigned.

priest, the reeve and six inhabitants of each vill.[25] Likewise the laws of Henry I rule that if the lord or his steward cannot attend the shire court or the hundred court the reeve, the priest and four of the best persons of the vill should go to represent everyone not summoned by name.[26] The assumption is that every vill will have a reeve. That this ruling was not mere theory is implied by a charter, probably of the late 1150s, in which Roger de Mowbray gave to the church of South Cave in the east riding of Yorkshire a house in the marketplace there. Fifteen important witnesses – the archdeacon of York, the abbot of Selby, canons and knights – are followed by six more 'of the vill of Cave' (*et de villa de Cave*): first was Hubert, the vicar, then four other names and finally Reginald, reeve of the same vill (*prepositus eiusdem ville*), that is the priest, the reeve and four others, just as the laws of Henry I required.[27]

David Postles has recently shown how seriously we should take the lists of witnesses to twelfth-century charters: they were not just names snatched from the air.[28] In this grant from Cave we can reasonably assume that we are looking at a transaction concluded in the hundred court where the local representatives were, sensibly enough, included among the named witnesses and in this case actually identified as such. How often they occur in other witness lists without being identified is almost anyone's guess: the conveyances recorded in charters must often have been made in the court and the reeve named among the other witnesses, whether or not he is actually called *prepositus*. Where a reeve does appear on witness lists he is often either right at the end or the last named but one, the last being sometimes specifically the writer of the charter, sometimes a clerk (*clericus*) who was probably the scribe.[29] In two late twelfth-century grants of land in Abney, Derbyshire, the first witness is a clerk who probably wrote the charters, the second a reeve.[30] This is unusual, but less unusual is the fact that the reeve, and the clerk too, came not from Abney but from Eyam, two miles away: a reeve who witnessed a conveyance may be the reeve not of the vill where the property lay but of a neighbouring vill. This example comes from the charters of Rufford Abbey and two others from the same collection are grants in Ollerton and Eakring, both Nottinghamshire, witnessed respectively by the reeves of Laxton and Winkburn, three or four miles away.[31]

However, we can reasonably follow Campbell in assuming that the *inquisitio eliensis* and the laws of Henry I were right to assume that in principle every vill had a reeve whom we often fail to recognize because our sources simply do not tell us that this was what he was.[32] Was this so throughout England? Witness lists to charters from eastern England name far more reeves than those from other parts of the country. Twenty-six of the Danelaw charters edited by Stenton name a rural reeve as witness, at

---

[25] *Libri censualis vocati domesday-book additamenta* [ed H Ellis] (Record Commission 1816), 497.

[26] *Leges Henrici primi*, ed Downer, 100–1; GC Homans, *English villagers of the thirteenth century* (1941), 334–6 discusses the occasions when the reeve and four or six men might represent the vill in the thirteenth century.

[27] *Early Yorkshire charters*, ed W Farrer and CT Clay (Yorkshire Archaeological Society 12 vols 1914–65) iii.438.

[28] D Postles, 'Choosing witnesses in twelfth century England', *Irish Jurist* new series xxiii (1988).

[29] Examples are in *Documents of the Danelaw*, ed Stenton, 219 (last name), 346 (last name apart from the writer of the charter), 294 (last name apart from a *clericus*), 214 (last name but one).

[30] *Rufford charters*, ed CJ Holdsworth (Thoroton Society 4 vols 1972–81) i.64–5. A similar case, where the first witness was specifically the writer, the second the reeve, is in *Documents of the Danelaw*, ed Stenton, 236.

[31] *Rufford charters*, ed Holdsworth ii.220, iii.430.

[32] Campbell, 'Agents and agencies', 205.

least 5 per cent of the relevant documents.[33] In collections from other parts of the country, such as the charters of the Redvers family or the earls of Gloucester, they are named much less often, though even here they appear and in these two collections we meet the reeves of Fleet in Dorset and of Winkleigh in Devon as addressees.[34] The preponderance of identified reeves among witnesses in eastern England may have no significance beyond regional scribal custom, which was clearly not very marked even there. Any suspicion that it points to an actual preponderance of reeves can be set at rest by domesday book. There reeves are seldom mentioned, but they do occur and nearly seventy are entered as manorial tenants in 1086 – of whom half are in Herefordshire.[35] Within Herefordshire their distribution follows no clear pattern: they are mentioned in manors of the king, the bishop and six other lords and occur in thirteen of the county's twenty domesday hundreds.[36] All this seems to point to little more than random naming of reeves in surviving records. It allows us to accept that there probably was a reeve in every vill and that his position, though significant within the local community, was not of such weight that one would expect it to be mentioned every time his name was recorded.

Might there be more than one reeve in every vill? Sometimes more than one reeve attests a charter. The last two witnesses to a grant to St Peter's hospital, York, of land at Swaythorpe near Bridlington in the 1160s are Swain the reeve and Godwin the reeve; in the 1180s or 1190s the witnesses to a grant in Hensall near Snaith include Reginald and William, named together as being then the reeves (*tunc prepositi*).[37] These pairs of reeves may, of course, have come from different manors or even from different vills: we have seen that charters might be witnessed by reeves of neighbouring places. However, the earl of Gloucester's letter to his officials at Winkleigh in the mid-twelfth century was not to his reeve but to his reeves.[38] A large manorial complex might well include a number of vills and hamlets, each with its own officials: Leominster, Herefordshire, with over two hundred ploughs, had eight reeves in 1066 and seven in 1086, while the possibly two reeves mentioned at Hanbury, Worcestershire, in the survey of about 1170 may reflect contemporary expansion of settlement there.[39] But we find more than one reeve as tenants of a single lord in what seem unexceptional manors of modest size. In the surveys they occur at Hemingford Grey (Huntingdonshire), Caddington (Bedfordshire), East Brent (Somerset), Idmiston and Tilshead (both Wiltshire).[40] To look further at this we have to turn to our second question.

---

33 *Documents of the Danelaw*, ed Stenton, 60, 90, 98, 122, 157 (x2), 184, 187, 201, 205, 207, 212, 214, 218, 219, 228, 236, 274, 285, 294, 327, 331, 346, 365, 369, 372.

34 *Charters of the Redvers family and the earldom of Devon 1090–1217*, ed R Bearman (Devon and Cornwall Record Society new series xxxvii 1994), 149–50; *Gloucester charters*, ed Patterson, 74.

35 See the five regional volumes of the *Domesday geography* of England, ed HC Darby, IB Terrett, IS Maxwell, EMJ Campbell and RAW Finn (1952–67), passim.

36 *Domesday book* i, fos 179r–87v.

37 *Early Yorkshire charters*, ed Farrer and Clay ii.189, i.383.

38 *Gloucester charters*, ed Patterson, 74.

39 *Domesday book* i, fo 180r; *The red book of Worcester*, ed M Hollings (Worcestershire Historical Society 1 vol in 4 1934–50), 186, 188; C Dyer, *Hanbury: settlement and society in a woodland landscape* (1991), 28–9.

40 *Cartularium de Rameseia*, ed Hart and Lyons, 243–4; *The domesday of St Paul's*, ed WH Hale (Camden Society old series lxix 1858), 113; *Inquisition of Glastonbury*, ed Jackson, 73–4, 76, 125–6; *Charters and custumals of the abbey of holy trinity, Caen*, ed M Chibnall (1982), 46–7. An intriguing

Whose was he?

Need the rural reeve have belonged to anyone? In an age when any office might become hereditary, from parish priest to sheriff, when the knightly tenant or the manorial lessee could effectively turn into the owner of the property, was the twelfth-century reeve at least some way along the road to making himself independent? Probably not. Two possible cases of a reeve being succeeded in office by his son are both ambiguous and there seems to be no recorded case of a woman serving as reeve, as one might expect would occasionally happen if a hereditary principle had become established.[41] Even in the fourteenth century a reeve might be succeeded by his son without the remotest hint of independent office.[42] No case has emerged of a rural reeve who paid to be admitted to office as the reeve of Abingdon did, and land that went with the office of reeve is rarely mentioned: the seven acres of *refland* and a small piece of meadow that belonged to the offices of reeve and forester at Hampton Lucy, Warwickshire, about 1170 are quite exceptional.[43] In the eleventh and twelfth centuries reveland more often meant an estate's inland, the area under the reeve's control.[44] We may be fairly certain that the reeve was not his own master.

If he was not, to whom did he answer? Was he the reeve of the vill or the reeve of the manorial lord? Stenton, Lennard and Campbell have all posed this question and all are agreed that there is no clear answer.[45] Oddly it is not, as one might expect, that there is insufficient evidence. It is rather that the evidence is clear and wholly contradictory. Even at the simplest level we find that those named as reeves among the witnesses to charters are sometimes called reeve of such-and-such a place, sometimes reeve of a particular person, usually the donor.[46] In a vill of single lordship the same reeve could and would indeed be both – it would be meaningless to distinguish him as one or the other – and he might well have been called either even in a divided vill, where he will have been the tenant of one or another manorial lord. But other, more cogent evidence points in both directions.

case appears in two late twelfth-century charters of Nigel de Mowbray, each granting away the lands and persons of some of his tenants at South Cave. The first included Gamel the reeve with his 2 oxgangs, the second, to a different recipient probably not long afterwards, included Gregory the reeve also with two oxgangs, but we cannot be sure they were in office simultaneously, and more than one explanation is possible. *Charters of Mowbray*, ed Greenway, 220–1, 231.

41 Swain the reeve of Nettleham, Lincolnshire, appears in *Pipe roll 12 Henry II* (Pipe Roll Society old series ix 1888), 10 and in *Pipe roll 13 Henry II* (ibid xi 1889), 48, while *Documents of the Danelaw*, ed Stenton, xxiii n4 cites a charter referring to land of Richard son of Swain the reeve of Nettleham: was 'the reeve' here Richard or Swain? William the reeve and William son of the reeve at Tilshead, Wiltshire, about 1170 are probably a single individual, but this may signify no more than loose description, the first step towards creating a surname separate from the office: *Charters and custumals of Caen*, ed Chibnall, 46–7.

42 PDA Harvey, *A medieval Oxfordshire village: Cuxham 1240 to 1400* (1965), 64–5.

43 *Chronicon de Abingdon*, ed Stevenson ii.306 (reeve may give gersum *pro tenenda villa*); *Red book of Worcester*, ed Hollings, 277–8; P Vinogradoff, *English society in the eleventh century* (1908), 372 n7 gives mid-twelfth-century examples of reveland with this meaning.

44 Vinogradoff, *Growth of the manor*, 225, 283–4; Vinogradoff, *English society*, 372–3; a late twelfth-century example of reveland with this meaning is in 'Charters of the earldom of Hereford', ed D Walker in *Camden miscellany* xxii (Camden 4th series i 1964), 71.

45 *Documents of the Danelaw*, ed Stenton, cvi–cvii; Lennard, *Rural England*, 274–6; Campbell, 'Agents and agencies', 206.

46 Thus on one Lincolnshire charter of Henry II's reign the witnesses include Alan the reeve of Walter and Ranulf the donor's reeve and on another Elias the reeve of Blyth: *Documents of the Danelaw*, ed Stenton, 212, 369.

There is no difficulty in finding cases where the rural reeve acts clearly as the manorial lord's local agent. We find instances of rural reeves exercising a good deal of authority in this role. In the mid-twelfth century an annual gift by Roger de Mowbray to the canons of Hirst of 30*s* and malt from the Isle of Axholme, Lincolnshire, was to be given to them by the reeves – who failed in this, so the canons were told they could collect it themselves from the Mowbray tenants. Other gifts from Mowbray manors, of sheaves and of wood, were likewise under the surveillance of the local reeves. In another Lincolnshire charter it was the reeve of Bourne, named as a witness, who gave seisin of a grant of land to its new owners.[47] At Kington St Michael, Wiltshire, in the 1180s Garwi, reeve of Robert de Courtenay, took 'by force and without judgement' a half-acre belonging to a yardlander tenant of Glastonbury Abbey and kept it for two years.[48] There is yet more telling evidence. A charter recording the grant to Rufford Abbey of land in Averham, near Newark, in the mid-twelfth century names as the last witness Gilbert, reeve of Ella, fifty miles away in Yorkshire, near Hull. The explanation is that the grantor at Averham, William Tison, was also the owner of Ella; although named there as reeve of Ella, Gilbert's appearance among the witnesses shows that he was Tison's reeve.[49] When Geoffrey de Mandeville gave Westminster Abbey the vill and church of Hurley in Berkshire, in 1085 or 1086, the land of Edric the reeve was excluded from the grant; a few years later William Warenne's grant of Heacham, Norfolk, to Lewes Priory went out of its way to say that the land of Payn, the reeve, was to be included.[50] Excluded – presumably to deal with residuary rights and neighbouring properties – or included in these grants of entire vills, the reeve is implicitly understood as the reeve of the grantor, his local agent: there would be no reason to make special mention of the reeve of the vill itself.

Some references are more ambiguous than may appear at first sight. Peterborough Abbey's chronicler tells us that William I 'granted his land on the hardest terms and at the highest possible price . . . He did not care at all how very wrongfully the reeves (*ða gerefan*) got possession of it from wretched men, nor how many illegal acts they did.'[51] These reeves may well have included those of individual royal manors, like Ælfsi, reeve of Sutton, Berkshire, whose claims to rights in local woods in William's reign were violently disputed by the abbot of Abingdon.[52] A little later, between 1107 and 1111, Swain, reeve of the royal manor of Fawsley, Northamptonshire, was ordered to return what he had taken from the adjacent lands of Thorney Abbey in Charwelton, and, as Campbell points out, the reeves whom Archbishop Anselm feared would oppress his tenants, if he himself did not visit the manors to hear their complaints, were clearly rural reeves.[53] These might seem obvious instances of local

[47] *Charters of Mowbray*, ed Greenway, 152–5 (Hirst), 200, 132–3; *Documents of the Danelaw*, ed Stenton, 345–6.

[48] Robert de Courtenay held two and a half hides of the abbey in Kington St Michael, five hides in neighbouring Grittleton: *Inquisition of Glastonbury*, ed Jackson, 107, 109, 111.

[49] *Rufford charters*, ed Holdsworth ii.167; *Early Yorkshire charters*, ed Farrer and Clay xii.134.

[50] *Westminster Abbey charters*, ed E Mason (London Record Society xxv 1988), 296–8; *Early Yorkshire charters*, ed Farrer and Clay viii.57–8.

[51] *The Peterborough chronicle 1070–1154*, ed C Clark (1958, 2nd edn 1970), 10; translation from *The Anglo-Saxon chronicle*, ed GN Garmonsway (1953), 218.

[52] *Chronicon de Abingdon*, ed Stevenson ii.10.

[53] *Facsimiles of early charters from Northamptonshire collections*, ed FM Stenton (Northamptonshire Record Society iv 1930), 14–15; *The life of St Anselm, archbishop of Canterbury, by Eadmer*, ed RW Southern (1962), 71; Campbell, 'Agents and agencies', 216.

reeves acting firmly and all too zealously in their lords' interests. However, they can equally, perhaps more convincingly, be seen as acting in the interests of the vill, extending its common rights at the expense of its neighbours, even – as Anselm hints – of their lord's other tenants.

Both the *inquisitio eliensis* and the laws of Henry I unequivocally speak of the reeve of the vill, not the reeve of the manorial lord. In the late thirteenth century the reeve was often chosen by the manorial tenants, not simply appointed by the lord, and this may well have been the ancient custom: as early as 1218–19 the tenants of the bishop of Winchester's manor of Burghclere were amerced for having made a bad choice.[54] We may see this as a vestige of a time when he was an officer of the community rather than of the manorial lord, and this same picture is given by some twelfth-century charters. We have seen the reeve being included or excluded in grants of entire manors. In the 1150s Peter Boterel gave to the church of St Melaine at Rennes just the reeve of Nettlestead, Suffolk, his heirs and all his lands; that the reeve was his tenant there can be no doubt, but it seems scarcely credible that he would want to give his own agent to a Breton church or that the clergy of St Melaine would find the gift a useful one without the rest of the manor.[55] This reeve was the reeve of the vill. But that he and his holding should have been singled out as the gift is interesting when we look at another grant of a single local tenant in Yorkshire: William Paynel gave the Hospitallers Gamel son of Arthur, his wife and all his boys, with warranty, failing which he would give them instead William the reeve with his family.[56] There is a hint here that the risk of losing the reeve as a tenant was a particular guarantee of the actual grant – that in ways that we can only guess, to have the vill's reeve among one's own tenants was a particularly valuable asset to a manorial lord.

Since the evidence is so clear both that the rural reeve was the reeve of the lord of the manor and that he was the reeve of the local community, should we envisage a dual system in which there were both? When a mid-twelfth-century grant of land at Hellifield, west riding of Yorkshire, is witnessed both by Richard the reeve of Peter des Arches (the donor) and Swain the reeve of Kettlewell (twelve miles away) we may well be looking at two different kinds of reeve.[57] This might explain how we sometimes find two reeves on a single small manor, as at Hemingford Grey or Caddington or East Brent: one was the reeve of the lord, the other the reeve of the vill. However, nothing we know of twelfth-century England could lead us to expect uniformity, so this does not preclude a norm that combined the two roles in a single person. When we look at the reeves of the thirteenth century we find not even residual traces of a dual system; the reeve who acted for the vill in certain circumstances was apparently the reeve of the lord of the manor.[58] Vinogradoff saw the reeve as an officer of the community on whom manorial duties came to be imposed.[59] To pursue this further we have to consider what the reeve's function on the manor was, what he actually had to do.

[54] Hampshire Record Office, 11M59/B1/7. I am grateful to Dr Katharine Stocks for telling me of this.

[55] DC Douglas, *The social structure of medieval East Anglia* (1927), 232. Another instance of the grant of a reeve is mentioned in *Registrum antiquissimum*, ed Foster and Major vi.175.

[56] *Early Yorkshire charters*, ed Farrer and Clay vi.243.

[57] Ibid xi.159.

[58] HM Cam, 'The community of the vill' in V Ruffer and AJ Taylor (eds), *Medieval studies presented to Rose Graham* (1950), 10–13; WO Ault, 'The vill in medieval England', *Proceedings of the American Philosophical Society* cxxvi (1982), 193–4, 205–6.

[59] Vinogradoff, *Villainage*, 356–7; Vinogradoff, *Growth of the manor*, 191.

What did he do?

We have already had several glimpses of the reeve at work: representing the vill at the hundred court, collecting rents of cash and of corn, supervising the lord's harvest and his woodlands, acting for the lord in giving seisin of land, extending his vill's or his lord's rights, whether legitimately or not, in neighbouring areas. These glimpses could be multiplied: here and there we see quite a lot of things that the reeve did. He was responsible for the waste land of the vill, let out lands and paid the vill's rents or amercements. He ordered the ploughing and winnowing, looked after the barn and granary and travelled on the lord's business. He held scotales for the tenants.[60] What we do not see so easily is the context in which he did all this: the seigneurial, the tenurial, the communal setting for his activities, and thus the overall picture.

It is reasonable to start from the premiss that this overall picture is unlikely to have been radically different in the mid-eleventh century from what it was to be in the mid-thirteenth: that there was no revolution in the reeve's position and function beyond what external circumstances dictated. The reeve-shaped gap in the *Rectitudines singularum personarum* points this way, so do what indications we have from domesday book onward. Starting, then, with the reeves of the mid-thirteenth century we see them acting as their lords' agents in operating manorial demesnes as home farms, extracting from the husbandry the maximum profit for the lord, profit that was handed over in its entirety to the lord himself, his receiver or steward. The reeve was the key local figure in the system of direct exploitation called demesne farming; in early manorial accounts he often accounts jointly with his superior, the bailiff, but it is always the reeve alone who carries the financial responsibility.[61]

This way of managing large estates became the fashion only in the late twelfth and early thirteenth centuries; it replaced what seems to have been widespread leasing of individual manors, with leases that got shorter in the course of the second half of the twelfth century, so that running the manor in demesne through the reeve, with annual accounting for profits, need not have seemed so big a change from a lease renewed annually.[62] What is not clear at all is how lords drew profits from their manors before the mid-twelfth century. For long it was an all but undiscussed question: historians wrote about manorial demesnes, their grant or sale, their expansion or contraction, as though everyone knew how they were run, how manorial demesnes were translated into seigneurial profits, when in fact no one really knew at all. Vinogradoff by implication and Postan more explicitly both assumed some form of demesne farming, seeing the frequent leasing of the later twelfth century as a temporary aberration.[63] On the other hand Lennard and, more recently, Edward Miller and John Hatcher have seen this leasing as the continuation of earlier systems, which one way or another

---

60 *Chronicon petroburgense*, ed T Stapleton (Camden Society old series xlvii 1849), 162, 164 (waste, letting land); *Pipe roll 14 Henry II* (Pipe Roll Society old series xii 1890), 202 (waste); *Feudal documents*, ed Douglas, 120, 128 (rent); *Pipe roll 17 Henry II* (Pipe Roll Society old series xvi 1893), 16 (amercement); *Red book of Worcester*, ed Hollings, 83, 148 (ploughing); *Chronicon petroburgense*, ed Stapleton, 163 (winnowing); *Inquisition of Glastonbury*, ed Jackson, 38 (barn and granary); London, British Library, Harley MS 61, fo 85r (travel); *Red book of Worcester*, ed Hollings, 37, 60, 85 and *Domesday of St Paul's*, ed Hale, cvii–ix, 144 (scotales).

61 PDA Harvey, *Manorial records* (1984, 2nd edn 1999), 30.

62 PDA Harvey, 'The pipe rolls and the adoption of demesne farming in England', *Economic History Review* 2.xxvii (1974), 353–4.

63 Vinogradoff, *English society*, 229–32; M Postan, *The medieval economy and society* (1972), 88–99.

drew a predetermined income from the demesne, leaving the hope of greater profit, the risk of loss, to someone closer to the locality.[64] Sally Harvey brought this question into the open in 1983 when she concluded, looking at domesday book, that we simply do not know whether or not lords mostly used some form of leasing to draw profits from their demesnes.[65]

Where there were relatively small estates consisting of a single manor or a single vill there need be no problem; it was presumably run by the owner who himself bore all risk and took all profit. The problem arises with larger estates. It is easy to see why some past historians assumed a system of demesne farming. So much of what we see before the mid-twelfth century is entirely at one with what we see in the thirteenth and early fourteenth: the listing of tenants' obligations in twelfth-century surveys, no different from the custumals of the thirteenth; domesday book's emphasis on the size of manorial demesnes; and the account of everyone's activities in the *Rectitudines singularum personarum* which with minimal alteration might apply to any late thirteenth-century manorial demesne. However, although we should keep our minds open to the possibility, it seems most unlikely that distant demesnes on large estates were run by direct management before the late twelfth century. We know so much about demesne farming in the thirteenth and fourteenth centuries because it was recorded in formal and elaborate manorial accounts; these were not generally adopted until the second half of the thirteenth century, though they appear on some of the largest estates much earlier. But this is not to say that demesne farming was otherwise conducted without written records; it is difficult to see how this would have been possible and some mid-thirteenth-century accounts from Bury St Edmunds provide a unique insight into the management of an estate by demesne farming before it adopted a system of fully formalized accounting, revealing a situation of chaotic complexity.[66] They show that the introduction of regular accounting, far from imposing bureaucratic forms, actually brought in a streamlined efficiency which was essential if the whole system was to work properly. Though it has become increasingly clear that written records played a significant part in Anglo-Saxon private administration, it seems unlikely that this can have been on a scale to make demesne farming remotely possible.

We have to look then to some form of leasing. Certainly domesday book often tells us that a particular manor was at farm, often indeed to a named lessee. This of course had the effect of converting the manor of the large estate into a single unit of production, as though the lessee was the owner of a single manor. But that domesday book particularly draws attention to this leads us to suppose that most manors were not at farm in this way. If we assume that some system of rendering predetermined amounts of cash or produce to the lord was everywhere the norm, what exactly happened on these other manors? How did they differ from those that were at farm?

There is plenty of evidence to show that on some large estates a well organized system of food-farms operated, a rota by which each manor of the estate contributed a

64 Lennard, *Rural England*, 106; E Miller and J Hatcher, *Medieval England: rural economy and social change 1086–1348* (1978), 204.

65 SJP Harvey, 'The extent and profitability of demesne agriculture in England in the later eleventh century' in TH Aston, PR Coss, CC Dyer and JI Thirsk (eds), *Social relations and ideas: essays in honour of RH Hilton* (1983), 45–9.

66 PDA Harvey, 'Mid-13th-century accounts from Bury St Edmunds Abbey' in A Gransden (ed), *Bury St Edmunds: medieval art, architecture, archaeology and economy* (1998).

fixed amount of produce in specified weeks, so that the central household was contin-
ually supplied week by week throughout the year. We find full details of the system on
several monastic and other corporate estates – Bury St Edmunds Abbey, Rochester
cathedral priory, St Paul's cathedral and others – and the 'farm of one night' that we
find in domesday book is seen as a vestige of a similar system on the royal estates.[67]
Some estates preserved a memory of the origin of the system: at Ely it was attributed
to Abbot Leofsige (1029–42), at Canterbury cathedral priory to Archbishop Lanfranc
(1093–1109).[68] But even if these memories were reliable, we need not suppose that
these reformers did more than create the rota. What they organized into a rational
system was what already existed: a fixed render of produce from each manor.

    Whether organized into a rota or unsystematically delivered on demand or at local
convenience, food-farms raise another question that has scarcely been addressed,
though Maitland touched on it long since.[69] What happened if the demesne failed to
produce the required farm? Who made up the balance? Or, if in a good year more was
produced than was needed for the farm, who kept the surplus? The answer might be
the reeve: if the lord had not brought in another farmer from outside should we see the
reeve as the effective lessee of the demesne, doing well in a good year when the crops
far exceeded the requirements of the farm, impoverished and starving in a bad year
when the farm took all that the demesne produced? This is possible. Certainly we are
sometimes shown the reeve as the alternative to a farmer: the early twelfth-century
Burton Abbey surveys mention either a reeve or a farmer on each manor.[70] This need
not imply that if there was a farmer there would be no reeve – there is far too much
evidence elsewhere to the contrary – but rather that if a particular manor had not been
let to farm the abbey would be dealing directly with the reeve. All the same it is difficult to see the reeve as an entrepreneur elected by the vill to make what he could from
the lord's demesne. It is much easier to see him certainly as responsible for supplying
the lord with the set produce due from the manor but to see this food-farm as an obligation not on him personally but on the vill as a whole. Much early evidence of
communal obligation of one kind or another points in this direction. In a good year the
whole vill would benefit, in a bad year the whole vill would suffer. Few will have been
as lucky as the tenants of Arlington and Chedworth, Gloucestershire, whose reeves'
recorded obligation in 1066 was, almost incredibly, to render 'what they wished'.[71]

    One objection to this can be dealt with briefly. There are references in domesday
book to manors being farmed by the local inhabitants, the men of the vill, and this
would be meaningless if the farm was already their communal responsibility. But
Hoyt showed that these references are few and more ambiguous than might appear,
and where the Burton Abbey survey of 1114–18 tells us that Abbots Bromley is at

---

[67] Ibid 134–5; RAL Smith, 'The financial system of Rochester cathedral priory' in *Collected papers by
      RAL Smith* (1947), 43–4; *Domesday of St Paul's*, ed Hale, xxxix; JH Round, *Feudal England* (1895,
      new edn 1964), 96–100.

[68] *Liber eliensis*, ed Blake, 152–3, 411–12; Miller, *Ely*, 37–9; RAL Smith, *Canterbury cathedral priory*
      (1943), 129.

[69] FW Maitland, *Domesday book and beyond* (1897, new edn 1960), 183–4.

[70] CGO Bridgeman (ed), 'The Burton Abbey twelfth century surveys', *Collections for a History of
      Staffordshire* 3.1916 (William Salt Archaeological Society 1918), 212–47. Both are mentioned only at
      Winshill in the 1114–18 survey (where the reference to Bristwi holding the manor for £4 may well be
      an addition) and at Willington in the 1116–26 survey: ibid 240–3, 236–8.

[71] *Domesday book* i, fo 164r.

farm to 'the men' (*homines*) the later survey of 1116–26 defines and names them as a group of five tenants – a small consortium, not a communal enterprise.[72]

A more serious and more obvious objection calls for longer consideration. If the annual renders were a communal obligation – the responsibility of the vill as a whole headed by the reeve, so that the food-farm was simply a charge on the local tenants – why should the lord cultivate lands himself as a manorial demesne? Here the new ideas that Faith brings together are particularly helpful. First is her demonstration, so convincing once it has been so clearly pointed out, that we should not equate the inland of the eleventh century with the manorial demesne of the thirteenth: it included tenant holdings as well, the lands of the peasant tenants whose services provided the labour, specialized or unskilled, for working the demesne. The inland was this entire complex; it was the reveland, the whole area that lay in the reeve's control.[73] Second, at separate points in discussing the Anglo-Norman countryside Faith quotes from two other historians whose comments have particular significance in this context. One is Nellie Neilson who wrote that heavy food-farms were of 'great influence in creating the rudiments of the demesne . . . the distinction between land used to produce the lord's food and lord's land being easily lost'.[74] The other is Barbara Harvey, writing of the Westminster Abbey estates in the twelfth century: 'The earlier the period, the more blurred does this distinction between demesne and tenant-land become . . . the notion that these two parts of the manorial estate were readily separable or that the one rather than the other should supply them with this or that kind of income lay in the future.'[75] Faith also mentions the suggestion that the mid-twelfth century saw peasant holdings 'territorialized', for the first time defined as specific quantities of arable and so on rather than as a simple share in the vill's resources.[76] If we bring these thoughts together we may wonder whether not only the holdings of the tenants but the holdings of the manorial lords as well were first defined on the ground between perhaps the late eleventh century and the mid-twelfth. It is all too easy to see earlier records through eyes that know the thirteenth century. When domesday book speaks of the lord's ploughteams *in dominio* we translate this as 'on the demesne': but are they not really the ploughteams 'in his control'? Is it not possible that domesday book expresses the lord's share in the manorial arable resources in terms of ploughteams simply because in many, even in most, cases this is the only way it could possibly be expressed?

Let us return to the reeve. If we assume the development of the manor on something like these lines many of the problems disappear. He did in the eleventh century just what he did in the thirteenth, look after the lord's resources in the vill, as part of the general oversight and organization of the inland. He was neither the vill's reeve nor the lord's but both: the distinction would be meaningless, and could be made only in the changing conditions of the twelfth century. What happened then in the vill of divided lordship? Presumably it had more than one reeve, but we may wonder just when and how the vill of divided lordship emerged. It is now generally accepted that

---

[72] RS Hoyt, 'Farm of the manor and community of the vill in domesday book', *Speculum* xxx (1955), 147–69; 'Burton Abbey surveys', ed Bridgeman, 223.

[73] Faith, *English peasantry*, 49–50 and passim.

[74] Faith, 186, quoting N Neilson, *Customary rents* (in Oxford Studies in Social and Legal History ii 1910), 18–19.

[75] Faith, 202, quoting BF Harvey, *Westminster Abbey and its estates in the middle ages* (1977), 129–30.

[76] Faith, 219, referring to PDA Harvey (ed), *The peasant land market in medieval England* (1984), introduction, 12–13.

parishes, nucleated settlements and common fields all developed late in the Anglo-Saxon period from an earlier pattern of dispersed homesteads or hamlets.[77] In a landscape of dispersed settlement, where parish, village and common fields were all unknown, what in fact determined whether a particular house and holding belonged to one vill or another if there was no dominating physical boundary? What defined the vill? The only possible answer is single lordship.

To sum up, the model proposed takes as its starting point a vill of single lordship where the inland, with its arable held in common just as its pasture was held in common, was worked by its tenants under the leadership of their reeve. He, on their behalf, delivered to the lord an amount of produce that was fixed in advance, unchanging from year to year. Convenience may often have dictated that cash replaced the food-farm, but in either form the render was fixed in tradition and in local custom. If the lord thought he might reasonably get a better return from any of his manors, we know from later experience that the strength of local custom would create difficulties in the introduction of any change. The answer was to hand the vill over to a farmer who, on the spot and with a direct personal interest in maximizing profit, would find it easier to achieve the increased returns that eluded the manorial lord.[78] It is likely that it was at this point that the demesne lands came to be separated from the tenants' lands, though the division of these among individual tenants may well have come later; simple fashion and pressure from tenants could have extended the separation of demesne lands to vills that were never set to farm. Thinking of the tenth-century leases of the bishop of Worcester's lands we may decide that the process began early, but if so it moved slowly and had still a long way to go by the time of domesday book.[79] Defining the demesne lands on the ground facilitated the division of vills into separate manors and opened the way to a peasant land market, though this could really take off only when the peasant holdings themselves had been defined on the ground. Later of course, in the second half of the twelfth century, long-term leasing gave way to short-term, then to demesne farming. Through all of this the work of the reeve will have undergone curiously little change, whether he was organizing the vill's husbandry to render the traditional farm to the manorial lord or running the now defined demesne lands to produce maximum profit, at first for the lessee on the spot, later for the distant lord.

This model needs to be tested against much more of the detailed evidence of what happened in individual manors before the mid-twelfth century. It cannot be said too strongly that we cannot expect to find great uniformity and it may well be that there was no such thing as a norm in the manorial development of this period. But however we interpret the evidence at our disposal we should never lose sight of the reeve. He is a key to our understanding of much that happened on landed estates in eleventh- and twelfth-century England.

---

[77] Faith, 165–7, 149–52, 143–7.

[78] *Domesday book* i, fo 16v records that the reeve of Tangmere, Sussex, was given 20*s* a year as a payment from the farmer; it is tempting to see this as a douceur to the vill for a break with custom that was to the community's disadvantage and it would be interesting to find any analogous case.

[79] C Dyer, *Lords and peasants in a changing society: the estates of the bishopric of Worcester, 680–1540* (1980), 17.

9

Stewards, Bailiffs and the Emerging Legal Profession in Later Thirteenth-Century England

PAUL BRAND

In Michaelmas term 1305 pleading took place in the common bench at Westminster in a case brought by John Royes against his lord, the abbot of the Norfolk Benedictine house of St Benet of Hulme. It is recorded in a summary version on the plea roll of the court. It is also recorded in rather more detail in six different unofficial law reports.[1] John was the tenant of a smallholding at North Walsham in Norfolk which he claimed to hold freely for fealty and a rent of three pence. The abbot was asserting that John was unfree. He had demanded merchet from him and attempted to make him pay tallage at will. He had also been trying to force him to act as his reeve and (according to two of the reports) demanding additional rent. John brought the relatively rare action of *ne vexes* to assert his freedom and the freedom of his tenement and the parties eventually joined issue as to whether or not John was a free man and whether or not his ancestors had always been free. Jury trial in the case was eventually scheduled to take place at a session at Norwich in late September 1306 before William Howard, one of the justices of the court whose own home county was Norfolk, and a local associate. John Royes did not, however, make an appearance on that day either in person or through an attorney. After the case had been adjourned back into the common bench judgement was given against John because of his failure to prosecute. The case is a puzzling one. How was a very minor Norfolk tenant like John Royes, on the borders of the dividing-line between free and unfree, able to take the initiative in bringing litigation against his lord in the main civil court at Westminster and to obtain the services of as many as three of the court's leading serjeants,[2] experts in presenting and arguing cases, in doing so? How did John Royes get to know that *ne vexes* was a suitable legal action for asserting his freedom against the abbot? *Ne vexes* was not an obvious way of doing this. It required good knowledge of the practical workings of this relatively rare form of legal action to know better. Why, having got so far, did John Royes then abandon his action?

---

[1] National Archives:, Public Record Office (hereafter PRO), CP 40/153, m 107; *Year books of the reign of King Edward the first*, ed and trans AJ Horwood (5 vols Rolls Series 1863–79), 33–5 Edward I, 11–15; London, British Library (henceforth BL), add MS 31826, fos 325v, 328v, Hargrave MS 375, fo 122r–v; London, Lincoln's Inn, misc MS 738, fo 43v; Oxford, Bodleian Library, Holkham misc MS 30, fo 32v.

[2] The three were Richard of Ashby, Richard of Willoughby and John of Tilton. The members of this legal elite were still sometimes called *narrator*, but by the late thirteenth century *serviens* or serjeant was coming to be the more common term for them; it was not until later that they came to be called serjeants-at-law. See P Brand, *The origins of the English legal profession* (1992), 48–9.

When the justices of trailbaston came to Norfolk in 1305 and 1306 one of the offences with which they were particularly concerned was conspiracy and they received a long list of presentments against local men accused of conspiring in various ways to pervert the course of justice. Particularly prominent in the list of local offenders was one Hugh Tyrel of Mannington and among the second round of presentments made against him in mid-February 1306 was one which linked him directly with the bringing of this case.[3] The presentment jury said that it was Hugh Tyrel himself who had instigated the litigation and that his purpose in doing so was to get bought off by the abbot. He wanted to secure for himself a money retainer and a livery of robes. When Hugh appeared to answer the charge, he did not deny that his was indeed the guiding hand behind the litigation. He claimed, however, that what he had done was no more than to give proper 'professional' advice to a client who had previously retained him as his counsel for an assize of novel disseisin John had brought against the abbot. He had seen that John would not be successful in his assize but that he might do better if he brought an action of *ne vexes*. No jury verdict is recorded on this presentment. Other presentments against Hugh Tyrel suggest that both stories may have been correct: that John Royes may indeed have come to Hugh Tyrel's attention when he had brought an assize of novel disseisin against the abbot and asked Hugh to act as his counsel and that Hugh may well then have advised him to bring the action of *ne vexes* and quite possibly given him financial assistance to help him bring the action and pay the serjeants, but that Hugh could probably have been bought off by the abbot. The action was abandoned in September 1306 either because Hugh was then still in gaol in London after his conviction for conspiracy or more probably because he had ceased to back John Royes, perhaps when the abbot acted on the earlier hint.

The legal historian investigating the early years of the English legal profession is almost spoiled for material when investigating the elite of that profession, the group of around thirty serjeants who by the second half of the reign of Edward I enjoyed a monopoly of practising on a regular basis in the main central royal court, the common bench at Westminster (or York) and who pleaded and argued in that court on behalf of litigants. By the late thirteenth century the same group of serjeants seems also to have dominated pleading at local sessions of the general eyre and in the itinerant court of king's bench and were active in other royal courts as well. The members of this group are relatively easy to identify from surviving law reports which record some (after 1291 a greatly increased proportion) of their professional activity in the common bench and in the general eyre, although much less of their activity in king's bench or other royal courts. A cross-check on who they were is provided, for the common bench at least, from late 1293 onward by entries on the plea rolls recording proffers for permission to levy final concords in the court (formal agreements generally about land made under the auspices of the court) and which from that time onward come to include a note recording that the parties have received their chirograph (their copies of the final concord) 'through' a particular, named serjeant. It is possible to establish the length of the careers of the members of this elite; to trace their geographical and social origins; to discover something about their professional training; and to track their

---

[3]   PRO, JUST 1/1334, m 55d (PRO will henceforth be omitted from citations of the classes JUST 1 and CP).

success at the bar through their property transactions.[4] It is a little more difficult to identify the members of the second, and much larger, group of professional lawyers active in the central royal courts, the professional attorneys. Their appearances in the early law reports are only fleeting and generally anonymous, but it is possible to identify them from their appointments to act for clients in individual cases which are recorded on the attorney appointment sections of the plea rolls. Not that all the attorneys whose appointments were so recorded are professionals. The professionals can generally only be identified through finding the appointment of particular individuals in multiple cases and over extended periods of time, although a relatively small number of professionals can also be identified from specific references to them as such in proceedings recorded on the rolls, generally of a disciplinary nature.[5] As yet there has been no investigation of the length of the careers of these early professional attorneys or of their geographical and social origins, but it is evident that there were by 1300 professional attorneys specializing in the business of the particular county in each county in England and that these were mostly drawn from that county. Rather more is known about the professional education available to attorneys in or close to Westminster in the last quarter of the thirteenth century; and from incidental references quite a lot is also known about the functions which professional attorneys performed on behalf of their clients in addition to the basic appearance in court on their behalf which was their core function.[6]

Given the quantity and quality of the surviving information about the members of these two groups and the relatively unproblematic nature of the relationship of both groups to the emerging legal profession it is tempting to ignore the various other people and groups in later thirteenth-century and early fourteenth-century England based in the localities who seem to be performing 'legal' functions but about whom the surviving information is much scarcer and much more fragmentary and whose relationship with the emerging legal profession is much more obviously problematic: men like the Hugh Tyrel of Mannington with whom this article began. They are indeed very largely ignored in my book on the origins of the English legal profession. I have now come to believe that this may have been a mistake. Neglecting these groups carries with it a real risk of distorting our picture of the emerging legal profession, of making it seem a much more centralized and Westminster-based, but also a much more superficial, phenomenon than it really was. In this paper I want to use the surviving evidence relating to the career of Hugh Tyrel as a way of trying to explore the nature of local legal practice during the final decades of the thirteenth century and the first decade of the fourteenth century, by looking at the variety of functions and roles which local lawyers can be found performing and the range of skills they might manifest and also at the kind of background from which such local lawyers might be drawn. It would be difficult, in the light of our current knowledge of local legal practice, to argue that Hugh Tyrel of Mannington is necessarily a typical figure; but it is only perhaps by undertaking a series of such studies that we will ever be able to reach any kind of reliable conclusions on this point. It is rarely possible, however, to know quite as much about a local lawyer as we do about Hugh.

---

[4] P Brand, 'The serjeants of the common bench in the reign of Edward I: an emerging professional elite', *Thirteenth Century England* vii (1999).

[5] Brand, *Origins*, 71–6, 87, 120–42.

[6] Ibid 117–19, 87–9.

Mannington is a small village in north-east Norfolk, about five miles north-west of the market town of Aylsham and less than twenty miles north of the county town of Norwich. Hugh was the second son of Walter Tyrel, also of Mannington. His father was still alive in the early stages of the 1286 Norfolk eyre but had died by July 1287.[7] His elder brother, another Walter, seems to have held the family lands only briefly in succession to his father before dying without issue, also by 1287.[8] Hugh inherited from his elder brother half a knight's fee in the adjacent villages of Mannington, Itteringham, Oulton and Little Barningham. By the middle of the fourteenth century that half knight's fee was held of the countess of Pembroke; in the late thirteenth and early fourteenth century it was probably held of William and then Aymer de Valence, successive earls of Pembroke, but there is nothing in our evidence to suggest that he had any other kind of connection with these men.[9] He does not seem to have acted for them or relied at all on their patronage. He may also have inherited other local lands. Incidental mentions show him holding land at Itteringham of Richard of Creeping and his wife Margery, and also holding land at Aylsham of the abbot of Bury.[10] But the half knight's fee seems to have been his main holding.

Hugh's status, once he had inherited the family lands, was that of a member of the local minor gentry. He possessed his own manorial court at Mannington and between 1297 and 1306 brought at least three actions of right there in the name of third parties for lands in Mannington and Itteringham.[11] These were free tenements and the tenants free tenants but he also had unfree tenants. In 1292 he was bringing litigation in the common bench claiming two brothers as his villeins through an action of naifty.[12] The 1305–6 presentments mention the fact that he possessed his own clerk, a man named William of Cawston, presumably from the Cawston four miles south of Aylsham.[13] He also had his own steward, Hugh Tyrel of Itteringham, who was not just a relative and namesake but had also made him the heir to his tenements.[14] Hugh also had a number of retainers, men who wore his livery and who are described in the presentments (like Hugh Tyrel of Itteringham) as acting as his confederates in various forms of alleged local wrongdoing. At least two of these four also came from the same small area of north-east Norfolk.

Hugh Tyrel seems to have been arrested in 1286 during the King's Lynn session held at the end of the Norfolk eyre.[15] Roger Loveday, who was not one of the justices of the

---

[7]   JUST 1/578, m 3; CP 40/75, m 67.

[8]   CP 40/75, m 67, 101, m 27d. For earlier evidence showing that Walter held lands at Itteringham and Oulton in his own right during his father's lifetime but was disseised of them by his father see JUST 1/1244, m 32d.

[9]   *Feudal aids* iii.486.

[10] CP 40/75, m 67 (Itteringham); JUST 1/1334, m 48 (Aylsham).

[11] JUST 1/1334, m 51–51d.

[12] *Year books*, 20 & 21 Edward I, 329–31; CP 40/92, m 59. Both the report and the record say that the acknowledgment was to his brother Walter but this seems likely to be an error for his father.

[13] JUST 1/1334, m 53. For other entries that couple his name with that of Hugh Tyrel of Mannington see JUST 1/1334, m 55d and JUST 1/591, m 13d. William of Cawston seems also for a while to have acted as bailiff of the hundred of North Erpingham: JUST 1/1334, m 15.

[14] JUST 1/1334, m 48–48d (*est de parentela sua et ipsum fecit heredem suum de tenementis suis et senescallus suus est*).

[15] The incident is known only from presentments made in 1305 before the trailbaston justices by the jurors of the hundreds of North and South Erpingham: JUST 1/1334, mm 15, 17. The arrest and bailing have not so far been found on the rolls of the 1286 eyre itself.

eyre but seems to have sat in on this session, attested that while he had been sitting as
an assize justice Hugh had brought a writ with a forged royal seal, purportedly
appointing an associate to act with Loveday and his colleague Robert of Ludham in
taking a particular assize. Writs of this kind were commonly brought into court by
lawyers acting for one of the litigants (generally for one of the defendants) and the
incident suggests that Hugh may already have been acting in a legal capacity at assize
sessions in or before 1286. Since Loveday and Ludham sat together on a regular basis
only between 1279 and 1284 the episode had probably taken place some years prior to
1286.[16] Hugh managed to secure his release on bail and the charge seems not to have
been pursued although it was to be resurrected in presentments made by the jurors of
the hundreds of North and South Erpingham in 1305.

The arrest seems not to have hampered his subsequent career. Hugh answered for
defendants as their 'bailiff' (*ballivus*) in three different assizes of novel disseisin
heard at Norwich in 1293 and 1300.[17] Answering as a bailiff in the assize of novel
disseisin did not by the later thirteenth century necessarily imply that the bailiff
concerned had anything to do with the disseisin for which the action was brought or
had even necessarily previously been in the service of the defendants. All it meant was
that he was employed or had agreed to answer in court in place of the main defendants
and to plead there on their behalf.[18] In one of the three cases Hugh's role does in fact
seem to have been wider than this, but in the other two there seems to be no evidence
of any such prior connection or action by Hugh and it looks as though he had been
employed specially for the assizes and because of his legal skills.[19] The clients who
employed him were prominent members of the local gentry and the holdings at stake
relatively substantial.[20] Nor was Hugh active in assize sessions only on behalf of
defendants. We have already noted Hugh's activity as counsel to John Royes who was
the plaintiff in an assize of novel disseisin against the abbot of St Benet of Hulme
some time prior to 1305. Other evidence from presentments made before the
trailbaston justices in 1305–6 shows him acting as counsel for John of Irmingland and
receiving money from Henry Cat to act as his counsel at an assize but once he had the
inside information on his case going over to act for his opponent, the defendant.[21]
Since the surviving record of Norfolk assizes in this period is incomplete and it is only
by chance that we ever hear of Hugh's activity as counsel for plaintiffs in assizes it
may well be that he was active in other assizes as well and that appearance on behalf
of litigants in local assize sessions was a significant element in the practice of at least
this one locally based lawyer. But it is also clear from other evidence that it was by no
means uncommon for members of the Westminster-based elite of the legal profession
(the serjeants of the common bench) to appear at assize sessions: so that assize
sessions were by no means a monopoly of local lawyers. Assize sessions were one

---

16 This may have occurred in the assize between his father Walter Tyrel and his elder brother Walter
which was heard by Loveday and Ludham, probably in 1282: JUST 1/1244, m 32d.

17 JUST 1/1298, m 30d; JUST 1/1311, mm 108, 110.

18 DW Sutherland, *The assize of novel disseisin* (1973), 44–5.

19 For the case in which he played a wider role see JUST 1/1311, m 108 (and cf JUST 1/1334, m 51).

20 Walter of Barnham and his wife Maud and their children John, Walter and Hamo, Margery widow of
Hamon Hauteyn and her daughter Alice Aungevyn were his clients in one case, Fulk Baynard in the
other.

21 JUST 1/1334, mm 53, 55d.

forum where the local and the national branches of the legal profession regularly met and mingled, perhaps to their mutual benefit.

The second 'legal' function which we saw Hugh Tyrel performing for John Royes was that of advising him as to an appropriate form of action for him to bring to assert his freedom. The presentments made before the trailbaston justices in 1305–6 show him giving similar advice to other litigants in a number of other cases. Two examples must suffice. Hugh had advised the master of the hospital of St Giles in Norwich to bring an assize of novel disseisin to challenge the seizure he had himself made on behalf of Roger of Calthorpe of land the master had acquired in breach of the statute of mortmain. He had also advised thirty-eight ancient demesne tenants at Aylsham to bring an action of replevin in the county court of Norfolk to uphold their freedom from being tallaged like normal villeins.[22]

In other cases Hugh Tyrel not merely advised on the choice of writ but is also known to have been responsible for arranging for the writ to be obtained from chancery or obtained it himself. In the case of a writ of right of reasonable share brought by John the chaplain in the earl of Norfolk's court of Hanworth against his brother, Hugh's defence specifically mentions John 'requesting him to get the said writ' (*rogavit eum quod predictum breve impetraret*). In this case we do not know who paid for the writ but in others we are told (or it is implied) that Hugh not only acquired the writs but also paid for them. This was true, for example, of the writ of right acquired by Hugh in the name of Richard son of Nicholas of Blickling for hearing in the court of Aylsham; it seems also to have been the case with a second plea brought by little writ of right in the court of Aylsham by Bartholomew of Bradfield against his brother, Master John of Bradfield.[23]

As has already been suggested, Hugh's assistance to John Royes may well have gone further than merely giving assistance in choosing and obtaining an appropriate writ. It seems quite likely that Hugh paid for the costs of the litigation and may also have played a major role in making the necessary arrangements for the case to be prosecuted. One of the presentments made against Hugh in 1306 described him in general terms as being 'a common undertaker and supporter of both false and other pleas'. Other presentments seem to show what this actually meant in individual cases. A writ of entry brought in the common bench by Walter Cleyt of Barningham was prosecuted 'at the cost of Hugh'. A 'champerty' agreement (under which the lawyer involved in the case paid the costs against a share in whatever he recovered) paid for the writ of right brought by Henry atte Grene of Baconsthorpe in the court of John of Coldham (and presumably also the connected writ of entry subsequently brought in the common bench).[24]

In another group of cases, a substantial payment was made in advance by the litigant or litigants concerned but in return for this payment Hugh Tyrel agreed to make all the necessary arrangements and to pay all the necessary costs as they occurred. Hugh 'prosecuted' a writ of right on behalf of a client in the court of earl Warenne at Gimingham in 1302 'at his own cost' but in return for a payment of ten marks

---

22 JUST 1/1334, mm 51 (St Giles), 48–48d (Aylsham).
23 JUST 1/1334, mm 51–51d (Hanworth, Aylsham), 53 (Aylsham).
24 JUST 1/1334, mm 48–48d (1306), 51–51d (Cleyt), 52d (Grene).

(*placitum illud falso et maliciose ad custus suos proprios pro x marcis sequebatur*); and prosecuted another action of right in the abbot of Bury's court of Aylsham at his own cost in return for a payment of one hundred shillings.[25] Arrangements similar to this are not unknown among the attorneys of the central royal courts.[26] Even these were not necessarily purely business deals, for the presentments commonly suggest that Hugh also had other motives for supporting the litigation: because he wanted to punish a juror who had refused to give the verdict Hugh wanted for a client; to cause trouble for a clerk involved in a dispute on some other matter with Hugh's clerk; or to cause sufficient trouble for the abbot of Bury that he would buy him off with a retainer (as the sacristan of Bury eventually did).[27] Sometimes Hugh's motive in paying for litigation was the simple one of trying to get the land for himself. Hugh brought a case in the name of Simon Selche in the court of Simon de Noers of Itteringham. The tenant had brought this on himself by his refusal to sell to Hugh nine acres of heathland in Itteringham next to heathland Hugh already owned. The case ended with Hugh purchasing the land for forty shillings though it was worth one hundred.[28] In other cases Hugh's motivation may from the start simply have been to be bought off: he was certainly said to have accepted fines from each of the three tenants whom he got Walter Cleyt of Barningham to implead by writ of entry, and shared with Henry atte Grene of Baconsthorpe with whom he had a champerty agreement the forty shillings he received for dropping the writ of entry Hugh brought in Henry's name against John le Chaloner of Little Barningham.[29]

Of his activities in support of defendants the presentments tell us much less but they do show that he was active here too. One crude, but effective, way of having an opponent's assize of novel disseisin quashed was for the defendant in possession to claim that he held the tenement in question jointly with a third party who was not one of the defendants named in the writ. For this to succeed all the defendant concerned had to do was to show a charter that indicated that they had been jointly enfeoffed of the land. The plaintiff was not allowed to counterplead the charter by alleging that it was not genuine but had to bring a second assize including the alleged joint tenant among the defendants. The presentments allege that Hugh Tyrel had been behind the production and use of such charters of joint feoffment in at least two (and perhaps three) different cases.[30] In one case he seems also to have attempted to secure yet further delay by getting the supposed joint tenant when he appeared in court to assert that he was Hugh's own villein and should not answer in a writ that had not named Hugh.[31]

Hugh Tyrel was certainly not the only local lawyer to make arrangements for litigation to be brought in a variety of courts and sometimes to pay for it and assisting defendants in resisting claims brought against them. Legal entrepreneurs of this kind were essential intermediaries between local clients and the wider world of litigation but the objects of considerable suspicion and hostility to their neighbours or at least to such of their neighbours as did not benefit from their services.

---

[25] JUST 1/1334, m 48–48d.
[26] Brand, *Origins*, 92.
[27] JUST 1/1334, mm 51–51d, 53, 48–48d.
[28] JUST 1/1334, m 53.
[29] JUST 1/1334, mm 51–51d, 52d.
[30] JUST 1/1334, m 54 (and cf JUST 1/1311, m 97); JUST 1/1334, m 55d.
[31] JUST 1/1311, m 97.

The trailbaston presentments only allow us to catch glimpses of Hugh Tyrel's activity in a third type of legal, or at least partially legal, role, that of steward. The position of steward commonly brought with it a number of separate responsibilities. The holding of the lord's courts was commonly regarded as one of his main duties. The author of the late thirteenth-century legal treatise *Fleta* mentions the holding of courts as the first of the steward's duties and, while conceding that he may often perform this duty through deputies, nonetheless advises that he should perform it in person in each manor at least two or three times a year.[32] That holding the lord's (manorial) courts was part of the generally accepted functions of a steward is also implicit in the written agreement made in 1281 between Nicholas son of Nicholas de Crioll and Philip of Great Thurlow.[33] Philip's services were engaged by Nicholas for a year for a payment of ten marks. His duties were to include holding (manorial) courts belonging to Nicholas at Benhall and 'Saldeford' and doing 'other business belonging to a steward' in Suffolk for Nicholas. In 1296 Isabel the widow of Robert de Ros sued John Wade of Uffington in the common bench for an account of the moneys he had received as her 'bailiff' (*ballivus*) at Belvoir (in Leicestershire) and at five other places (Woolthorpe, Tallington, Aubourn, Wragby and Melton Ross), all in Lincolnshire, during the period between Christmas 1293 and Christmas 1294. She alleged that he had been in control of all her movables in these manors (corn, horses, oxen, cows and so on) to the value of one thousand pounds and had left her service without rendering any account. The technical requirements of the action of account required him to be sued as her 'bailiff'. It is his defence that reveals that he had really been her steward. He admitted that he had been her steward but alleged that his only duties as such had been to hold her courts (and then to hand over the estreats to her bailiffs and receivers to levy what was due to Isabel from the courts) and 'to do the other things belonging to the office of steward' (*et alia que officio senescalli incubuerunt*). He denied that he had ever been a receiver of any of her money or goods.[34] That he had held her courts was evidently not in dispute; what was disputed was whether or not he had discharged additional responsibilities. If he discharged any responsibilities as court-keeping steward in the five Lincolnshire villages he must have been holding manorial courts there; but if he held Isabel's court at Belvoir this was probably the court of the honour of Belvoir.[35] There is other evidence to suggest that the steward was expected to hold a lord's other courts as well as his manorial courts. A plaint was made in the 1279 Sussex eyre alleging obstruction to the holding of a session of the hundred of Ashburne under an ash tree in the town of Midhurst earlier that year. The defendants (the lessees of the town of Midhurst) claimed that an earlier lord of the town (Franco de Bohun) had agreed to the holding of the hundred court within the town but only as a special concession while the same man (John of Arundel) was acting both as his steward and the steward of John Fitzalan, the lord of the hundred court. In 1279 the steward of the

---

[32] *Fleta* ii, ed HG Richardson and GO Sayles (Selden Society lxxii 1953), 241.

[33] JUST 1/375, m 8.

[34] CP 40/113, m 32.

[35] In 1291 Isabel was being sued for demanding suit to her court at Belvoir for a holding of two and one eighth knight's fees in seven Leicestershire villages: CP 40/87, m 33d. But note that in two cases of 1289 and 1291 Isabel's tenants asserted they had been distrained to perform suit of court at Wragby for tenements they held at Kettleby and Coleby: CP 40/80, m 16, CP 40/91, m 199.

bishop of Norwich held the court of the town of King's Lynn; and a presentment at the 1306 Cornish trailbaston session shows that it was a steward who presided over sessions of the town court at Lostwithiel.[36]

This was one aspect of the steward's job that Hugh Tyrel certainly performed. The 1305–6 presentments reveal him presiding as steward in the court of John Engayne at Blickling when he himself brought litigation in the court in 1303, and mention him ordering a distraint while steward of the court the same year.[37] This was probably only a manorial court though John Engayne was lord of half a barony elsewhere. The presentments also show him presiding as steward in the abbot of Bury's manorial court of Aylsham in 1305 while openly assisting one party and secretly assisting their opponents and then purchasing the land at stake in the litigation and ordering the bailiffs of the court not to deliver seisin of that land to the successful litigant.[38] This stewardship too was evidently only a local one and carried no wider responsibilities for the abbey's lands and courts elsewhere.

A second 'legal' function played by some stewards was that of performing suit to the local county court on behalf of their lords. This meant not just regular attendance at the county court but also participation in the making of the judgements rendered there: indeed, in a few counties the stewards of local magnates had come by the later thirteenth century to be regarded as the main (and perhaps the only) judgement-makers of the county court. The record of a replevin case heard in the county court of Northumberland in 1283 shows the stewards of the county alone making a judgement on whether or not an assertion had been conceded or denied and respiting judgement in the case. Other evidence shows a dominant role also being played by stewards in the county courts of Yorkshire, Nottinghamshire and Lincolnshire.[39] Even in counties where there is no evidence to suggest that stewards dominated proceedings in the county court, it might still be thought normal that magnates with local holdings be represented by their stewards in the county court and that they would play a significant part in its proceedings. In *quo warranto* proceedings of 1287 the king's serjeant alleged that Ralph de Beauchamp as a tenant in chief owed 'as of common right' suit to the county court of Bedfordshire either in person 'or through his steward' for 'the making of judgements and provision of justice there' so that 'the pleas of the county would not fail for lack of suitors'.[40] But if Hugh Tyrel did attend the Norfolk county court for his lords while serving as their steward there is nothing in the surviving evidence to tell us of this.

Although there is some evidence to suggest that the practice of using stewards to represent their lords and the lord's lands (and his tenants) at the county court goes back to at least the early years of the twelfth century, the immediate authority for the

---

[36] JUST 1/914, m 17d (Midhurst), CP 40/29, m 14d (Lynn; and cf m 27), JUST 1/119, m 7d (Lost-withiel).

[37] JUST 1/1334, m 52–52d.

[38] JUST 1/1334, m 48–48d (and for a follow-up complaint see JUST 1/592A, m 7d). For a second complaint about his conduct while presiding in the court at an unspecified date before 1306 see JUST 1/1334, m 53.

[39] CP 40/63, m 24d (Northumberland), CP 40/14, m 2 (Yorkshire), record from writ files, CP 52 (Nottinghamshire), CP 40/31, m 20 (Lincolnshire): cited by RC Palmer, *The county courts of medieval England 1150–1350* (1982), 124 n57, 128 n69, 126 n60, 127 n66. See *Placita de quo warranto temporibus Edw. I, II, et III in curia receptae scaccarii Westm. asservata* (1818), 414 (and cf ibid 429) for a similar suit against Roger de Mowbray.

[40] *Placita de quo warranto*, 3–4.

practice was the legislation of 1234 which permitted 'any free man who owes suit to county courts' freely to appoint his attorney before the bailiff 'to perform that suit and to claim the court of his lord and his franchises'.[41] A third 'legal' function performed by some (if not all) stewards was to assert and defend the lord's franchisal – and specifically jurisdictional – rights not only in the county court but also in other local courts as well. This side of the steward's duties is referred to in litigation in the 1263 Sussex eyre when Allard of Houghton was sued for an account of the time he had been John Mowyn's steward at Wittering in Sussex and at Hurst in Huntingdonshire. Allard agreed that he had been in John's service but claimed that his only duties as steward had been those of holding his (manorial) courts and 'claiming and defending his franchises'.[42] The two different forms of legal service clearly went together and were plausibly duties that might have been performed by a steward without having any further responsibilities. When John Sampson was sued by Roger Bigod, earl of Norfolk in 1290 for an account of the time he had been the earl's 'bailiff' in five places in Yorkshire between 1286 and 1289 he too claimed to have been in the earl's service as his bailiff and steward to hold his courts and to 'claim and defend his liberties' but to have exercised no wider responsibilities.[43]

A wider responsibility for overseeing (and perhaps on occasion themselves conducting) their masters' legal business seems to be indicated by other evidence. A passage from *Seneschaucy* talks of the steward needing to know 'the law of the country' so that he can 'defend actions outside the lord's estate' (*pur foreyn bosoynes defendre*).[44] The instrument appointing William of Barton as the steward of the lands of St Swithun's priory, Winchester in 1260 and the almost identical instrument appointing his successor Adam Stoke in 1292 mention among other responsibilities that of defending and supporting the 'rights and the liberties' of the priory at the priory's expense against all men and women 'both in the court of the lord king and elsewhere whenever was necessary', evidence that seems to indicate that these stewards were responsible for managing their masters' litigation.[45] When Thomas de Holm of Fridaythorp was sued by Denise de Mountchesney senior in 1290 for an account for a twelve-year period during which he had allegedly served as her bailiff in Sixendale and six other places in Yorkshire Thomas claimed only to have been her bailiff to hold her courts and to 'prosecute and defend her other business touching the law in the county of Yorkshire' but denied any wider responsibility for administering her property.[46] Again it seems likely that Thomas had in fact been employed by Denise as her steward but was described as her 'bailiff' in the litigation simply because of the technical requirements of the action of account; and we may assume that Denise did not deny that he had performed these functions for her as her steward but was asserting that he had also exercised other responsibilities as well. Managing the lord's litigation would have been a significant part of the steward's job. This was

---

[41] Palmer, 113; *Close rolls of the reign of Henry III preserved in the Public Record Office* (15 vols 1902–75), 1231–4, 551 (imperfectly summarized in chapter 10 of the so-called statute of Merton).

[42] JUST 1/912A, m 17.

[43] CP 40/86, m 160d.

[44] *Walter of Henley and other treatises on estate management and accounting*, ed and trans D Oschinsky (1971), *Seneschaucy*, 264/5.

[45] BL, add MS 29436, fos 40r–v, 41r–v.

[46] CP 40/93, m 19.

just the kind of activity at which (as we have seen) Hugh Tyrel was expert, though there is no direct evidence to show him performing this kind of activity for the lords for whom he acted as steward.

What looks to have been a further development from this wider responsibility for the lord's legal business is a still more general responsibility for the legal business of the lord's tenants, perhaps especially his unfree tenants. When William of Heywood and his wife Edith were impleaded in the 1293 Staffordshire eyre for land in Abbots Bromley which Edith's father had purchased of the abbot of Burton and for which the abbot was obliged under local custom to provide warranty they approached the abbot in the hall of Abbot's Bromley for assistance and he assigned his steward, Matthew de Vilers, to plead their case for them. They subsequently complained that they had mistakenly trusted his expertise 'as folk ignorant of the law' (*cum gens ignorans de la ley*) and had lost possession of their land because he had pleaded an inadequate exception.[47] Here the obligation to provide warranty may have played a part in securing the steward's legal services. But in other instances this was not the case. When the steward of the earl of Norfolk was accused of abetting a false appeal of murder against his predecessor in 1290 he pleaded in his defence that he had only acted in response to appeals from the widow of the murdered man. It was because she was one of the earl's villeins that he had asked the earl's serjeants (probably those retained by the earl) to assist her in making her appeal (*rogavit narratoribus ut ipsam Margeriam secundum formam legis in predicto appello adjuvaverunt*).[48] Although this story was not confirmed by the jury it seems likely that it was told because it seemed a plausible one and one that conformed to contemporary expectations about the assistance that a good lord and his steward might extend to one of his villeins under such circumstances. The same expectation seems to be reflected in the defence which Hugh Tyrel pleaded when accused of wrongfully bringing an action of right in the name of Richard son of Nicholas of Blickling in the court of Aylsham and of then harassing the suitors of the court of Aylsham with an action of false judgement when they gave a judgement against him. Richard had been a villein of John Engayne whom Hugh had then been serving as a steward. He had supported and helped Richard, Hugh alleged, because he had believed that Richard was entitled to the land he was claiming.[49]

More on the borderline between the 'legal' and the purely 'administrative' or 'executive' were the forcible actions (seizures of lands and distraints of chattels) that stewards might take or authorize for the extra-judicial enforcement of the rights or pretended rights of the lords whom they served. Even for this, however, legal skills and legal knowledge were of some relevance: a steward needed to know just how far to go and how to defend the forceful action taken on his lord's behalf. This is again a reasonably well attested part of Hugh Tyrel's activity for the lords whom he served as steward. It seems likely that he was acting not just as counsel to Roger of Calthorpe but more specifically as his steward when he seized land belonging to Roger's fee that had been acquired by the master of St Giles's hospital in Norwich on the grounds that the land had been alienated into mortmain in contravention of the statute. Another presentment alleged that while steward of John Engayne Hugh had extorted sums of between nine and forty shillings from four different tenants of John's. Hugh defended

---

[47] *Select bills in eyre, 1292–1333*, ed WC Bolland (Selden Society xxx 1914), 68–9.
[48] PRO, KB 27/123, m 9.
[49] JUST 1/1334, m 51–51d.

his action on the grounds that they were tenants of John's villeinage and the profits had gone entirely to John but a jury found that the money had been shared between John and Hugh.[50]

It would, of course, be wrong to suppose that most stewards performed only legal or quasi-legal functions. The description of the qualities expected of a steward in *Seneschaucy* mentions that the steward 'ought to be capable of administering the lands profitably' and required that he be capable of instructing and teaching 'the bailiffs who are under him in their duties'.[51] Stewards were commonly in overall day-to-day control of their lord's demesne farming: issuing orders to local bailiffs and reeves about the cultivation of the lord's arable and the sale, purchase, transfer and consumption of grain and other crops as well as livestock, and exercising a general supervision over these local officials in the interests of their masters. This is certainly the picture given us by the didactic treatises such as *Seneschaucy* as also by the relevant part of *Fleta*.[52] It is also the picture we get from other evidence. Successive stewards of St Swithun's priory, Winchester were responsible for 'taking care of everything to be done' in all the priory's lands as much as was appropriate for one bearing the office of steward. That this included control and oversight of the lesser officials in each manor is suggested by the care with which appointment and removal of bailiffs was reserved to the prior and other monastic officials.[53] A similar position and function for the steward is also indicated by an action of account heard in the 1263 Sussex eyre when we hear through the jury's verdict of a steward to whom the lord's reeves were answerable as to their superior and by whose orders they sold, received and disposed of the lord's property.[54] In an action of account brought by the archbishop of York in 1291 he sued John Morgan for an account of the two-year period he had been 'bailiff' of the archbishop's Gloucestershire lands. That this bailiff was in reality a steward (or might otherwise have been described as such) is suggested by John's defence in which he claimed to have had responsibility only for holding the archbishop's courts and of 'ordering and disposing' of what needed ordering and disposing but claimed that there were reeves and receivers in the manors who were accountable for the profits of the lands. The archbishop's answer did not deny this was the position but sought to make John accountable for exceeding his authority. John had apparently got reeves in the manors to sell corn and then converted the money to his own use: clear evidence that authorizing the sale of corn by local reeves had indeed been one of his functions.[55] But this does not mean that there were not stewards who specialized solely in the legal side of the steward's activities. We have already noted a number of cases of account in which men sued as 'bailiffs' claimed exactly this. It would also explain how it was possible for some serjeants of the common bench while practising in the common bench to act as stewards. The future royal justice William of Bereford, while still one of the leading serjeants of the common bench in the 1280s, is also to be found acting as steward to the abbot of Ramsey.[56] Another common bench

---

50 JUST 1/1334, mm 51–51d (Calthorpe), 53 (Engayne).

51 *Seneschaucy*, ed Oschinsky, 264/5.

52 Ibid 264/5–268/9; *Fleta* ii.241–3.

53 BL, add MS 29436, fos 40r–v, 41r–v.

54 JUST 1/912A, m 17.

55 CP 40/89, m 100. For another case which shows a steward being responsible for ordering the sale of corn by a local reeve see CP 40/96, m 141d.

56 *The earliest English law reports* ii, ed P Brand (Selden Society cxii 1996), xv–viii. For evidence that

serjeant, Edmund of Pashley, acted as one of the stewards of the archbishop of Canterbury in 1301–2, again while acting as a serjeant.[57] These men were not being used as general administrators but were being employed specifically for their legal expertise.

One further aspect of Hugh Tyrel's activity as a local lawyer that emerges quite strongly from our evidence is his aggressive assertion of his own property rights and claims both in the central and in local courts: the behaviour of someone who knows his way round the legal system and is intent on using it for his own profit and also of someone who is well aware of the use of litigation as a way of harassing opponents and making them buy off his claims. Take, for example, his assertion of his claims to the advowson of two local churches. The 1306 presentments tell us of him presenting his own candidate to the vacant local living of Erpingham and then of him suing a plea in court christian against the rival patron, Robert of Erpingham, until Robert's presentee bought him off by conceding him an annuity of one hundred shillings for life. Although the presentment jurors said that he had no right to the advowson he probably did have some kind of at least plausible title. The presentment jurors said something similar in passing about his presenting a candidate to another local living, that of Irmingland. Here, thanks to litigation about the right of presentation to Irmingland brought against him by John of Cockfield in the common bench in 1303 we can see that there was indeed some basis for his claim in a purported grant of the advowson to him even though the court eventually ruled against him.[58]

We can also find him generally successfully asserting his rights, or what he claimed to be his rights, to various, but generally small, holdings of land in his own local area in a variety of different courts: in the common bench at Westminster, in the court of Ralph atte Rothe of Oulton and in the court of John Engayne of Blickling.[59]

Hugh Tyrel was very much a local lawyer. The clients to whom he gave advice and whom he assisted financially (at least in so far as they were known to the presentment juries in 1305–7) all came from a relatively small area whose radius was no more than five to ten miles from his own home village of Mannington. It was within this area that he was so active in asserting his own rights and claims. It was in this same area that he can be found acting as a steward. Yet he did also have some contacts with a wider world. It was at Norwich that he appeared as a pleader for assize sessions. He also evidently knew men in the shrieval administration there, for he was able to trick an opponent by first getting the under-sheriff of Norfolk to come to the court of Aylsham for the purported removal of a plea into the common bench and then having the plea continued in the tenant's absence and awarding judgement against him by default and finally arranging at Norwich castle for the sheriff's administration falsely to return

---

he was still joint steward of Ramsey in 1293–4 after he had become a royal justice see AR DeWindt and EB DeWindt, *Royal justice and the English countryside* ii (1981), 555.

57 PRO, E 401/150; *Registrum Roberti Winchelsey, cantuariensis archiepiscopi, AD 1294–1313*, ed R Graham (2 vols Canterbury and York Society li–ii 1952–6) i.414, ii.1324–5.

58 JUST 1/1334, mm 52–3 (1306); CP 40/146, m 48 (1303).

59 CP 40/101, m 27d (a messuage and eight acres in Mannington and Little Barningham); CP 40/125, m 72 (a messuage and two acres at Itteringham) and JUST 1/1334, m 52 (follow-up to the recovery by default of one messuage and one acre in Itteringham), all in common bench; JUST 1/1334, m 52 (one messuage and one acre in Irmingland and Oulton); JUST 1/1334, m 52 (a messuage in, possibly, Blickling).

that the original writ of removal had come too late to be executed. He was also able to vex the suitors of John Engayne's court of Blickling by bringing an action of false judgement against them and (falsely) having a return made that the suitors had refused to record the plea. By 1309 Hugh had apparently himself entered the service of the sheriff of Norfolk.[60]

He was also evidently at home, or at least had contacts with, a much wider world than that. We have seen him acquiring writs for clients in chancery and channelling litigation into the common bench at Westminster, indeed paying for the cost of litigation there. If we can believe the allegations of John Engayne made early in Edward II's reign during the proceedings against Bishop Walter Langton, the former treasurer, Hugh's abilities had come to the notice of the bishop by the time of the trailbaston proceedings and it was as a man wearing the bishop's livery that Hugh supplied the 'great menaces' to the local presenting jury that ensured the false indictment of John at these sessions; and when Hugh Tyrel was convicted on a second occasion some time before March 1310 his eventual pardon (not granted until September 1310) was granted at the request of no less a figure than Piers Gaveston, earl of Cornwall.[61]

I have described Hugh Tyrel of Mannington as a local 'lawyer' and there is much in his pattern of activity to support that description of him. Yet there was also a much cruder, physical-force side to his activities as well. On at least two separate occasions the presentments ascribe his ultimate success in 'persuading' his opponents in litigation to surrender the land he was claiming for a payment that amounted to much less than the value of the land to threats from his associates; and 'common fame' in 1306 accused one of those associates, Roger of Oulton, of being involved in the killing of John de Syc of Irmingland, and Hugh of knowingly receiving him back into his company after the killing.[62] In 1311 Hugh and his servant (*garcio*) William Bigot were allegedly participants with Henry de Segrave, the former sheriff of Norfolk, and many men drawn from Essex, Suffolk and the Welsh marches in an attack on the manor of Walter of Barningham at Little Barningham, setting fire to the hall and terrorizing Walter's mother into revealing the whereabouts of his money and jewels and then taking all the money and jewels and goods there. It was probably in revenge for that attack that Hugh Tyrel met his end. An appeal brought by his nephew, John son of William of Itteringham, accused Walter of Barningham and a long list of other men including Hugh's own brother, John Tyrel, of involvement in his killing shortly after sunrise on the Saturday after trinity 5 Edward II (27 May 1312).[63]

Can a man like Hugh Tyrel be seen as part of the fledgling legal profession? He had certainly acquired what can only be described as specifically legal expertise: indeed two of the members of the local gentry who were accused along with him of various acts amounting to conspiracy to pervert the course of justice defended themselves on the basis of an implicit contrast between themselves, as men who acted on Hugh's

---

60 JUST 1/1334, mm 53 (Aylsham), 52 (Blickling); JUST 1/593, m 9 (1309).
61 *Records of the trial of Walter de Langton, bishop of Coventry and Lichfield, 1307–1312*, ed A Beardwood (Camden 4th series vi 1969), 259–61 (Engayne); *Calendar of chancery warrants preserved in the Public Record Office, AD 1244–1326* (1927), 311, 312, 317 and *Calendar of the patent rolls preserved in the Public Record Office, Edward II* (5 vols 1894–1904) i.277 (pardon).
62 JUST 1/1334, mm 51–51d, 52, 17.
63 PRO, KB 27/210, m 75–75d, 27/211, m 87d.

advice and in accordance with his plans but who were themselves ignorant of the law (*legis ignorantes*), and Hugh who gave that advice and made those plans and who was a legal expert. As we have seen, Hugh is to be found putting that expertise at the service of a variety of clients and using it in a range of different legal roles. But there is no evidence that any kind of public or semi-public authority had ever admitted him to practice. Nor is there any evidence that in his various activities he was subject to anything that could be described as professional discipline. There is no hint that when he was punished for 'conspiracy' in 1305–6 he was being punished for any kind of breach of specifically professional ethics. And as we have seen, Hugh was at least in part simply the local bully and thug, a man who used law and the legal system only as part of a range of tactics designed to secure success for his clients and profit and esteem for himself. Men like Hugh Tyrel do nonetheless seem to have played an important role within the English legal system by bringing litigation themselves and by advising and assisting others to do so as well as helping to run the lowest level of the legal system. If not themselves fully members of the legal profession Hugh Tyrel and others like him may have been an important part of the substructure that helped to support that profession and to make it possible.

10

Whose was the Manorial Court?

RALPH EVANS

The essence of a manorial lord's relationship with his tenants, most especially his unfree tenants, was exploitation.* His first concern was the preservation and extraction of rent – that is rent in its broadest sense, encompassing everything that he took from his tenants by reason of his lordship. This could vary greatly from manor to manor and included not only more or less regular renders of labour, produce or cash but also more irregular payments which would often be recorded, though not necessarily paid, at the manorial court. These might be the punitive payments called amercements – fines in the modern sense – or fines in the strict medieval sense of compositions which at least nominally were set by mutual agreement. There were also levies which amounted to a tax on activities as infrequent as marriage or as common as brewing for sale. A manorial lord might make many and burdensome demands of a peasant household, but he had no direct say in how it cultivated its land. By contrast the lord's cultivation of the portion of his land not occupied by tenants – the manorial demesne – could depend heavily on his exploitation of his tenants. And it is hardly possible to gauge a lord's influence over economic activity within a village, even when he was not exercising formal rights over his tenants; lordship may have left little room for a free economic market in land, labour or produce.

The ways in which English lords enforced, preserved and even extended their claims on their tenants are well illustrated in the surviving proceedings of manorial courts, a characteristically English historical record. The origins of the manorial court and of its written records have yet to be satisfactorily explained. Court rolls are of course a uniquely informative source for English medieval rural society, but they are not without difficulties of interpretation. The striking similarity in the form of documents from different manors is well known and can be related to the professional training and expertise of the clerks who compiled them.[1] Of the three main categories

---

* I am grateful to the warden and fellows of Merton College, Oxford, for allowing me to work on their archives. I am very glad to record my indebtedness to Trevor Aston for introducing me to the archives of Merton in particular, and for giving me the benefit of his deep knowledge of manorial documents more generally. I am grateful to Rosamond Faith for her comments on a draft of this paper.
[1] On the development of manorial documents in England see PDA Harvey, *Manorial records* (1984) and the introduction to *Manorial records of Cuxham, Oxfordshire, circa 1200–1359*, ed PDA Harvey (Oxfordshire Record Society 1 and Historical Manuscripts Commission JP xxiii 1976). On the origins of written records of manorial courts see Z Razi and RM Smith, 'The origins of English manorial court rolls as a written record: a puzzle' in Z Razi and RM Smith (eds), *Medieval society and the manor court* (1996).

of strictly manorial document court rolls display a greater diversity of form and content than either manorial surveys or accounts. The business recorded in the courts of two manors may vary because the manors themselves were dissimilar, for instance in the relative numbers of free and unfree tenants, or in the custom of the manor, which could differ significantly even within one locality. The policy of the lord and the efficiency with which his officers enforced it could affect the nature of the record in a way that is hard to detect, as too might local practice and convention in the writing down of the court's proceedings. Often the evidence of the rolls can support completely opposite interpretations equally well. This paper will illustrate arguments about the role of lord and tenant in manorial courts with examples drawn from manors of Merton College, mainly those at Cuxham in south Oxfordshire, at Thorncroft by Leatherhead in Surrey, and most especially that at Malden, also in Surrey, and will concentrate on the later thirteenth and earlier fourteenth century.[2]

Court rolls of this period are full of records of the efforts of the lord and his officers to protect his interests. The proceedings of the court of Malden held on 17 May 1288, chosen more or less at random, contain just twenty items of business. There are cases of unpaid money rent and of failure to perform fealty or to attend the manorial court. A day was set for a free tenant to show the charters which would prove he was not obliged to attend the manorial court. There was an amercement arising from the unlicensed marriage of an unfree woman, and arrangements for the custody of the livestock of a fugitive villein. The horses of various tenants had been seized in the college's pasture. The villeins (the unfree tenants of relatively substantial holdings) testified that the manor's woods, fields and meadows had been well kept and that one villein had damaged hedges and fences on his holding; the final details of their presentment, probably about the misconduct of the reeve, have been obscured by damage to the roll. Much of a judgement about the ploughing up of a ditch and bank and the boundary between Malden and Kingston has also been lost. With the possible exception of that last entry, and arguably those concerning attendance at court, all the recorded business of this court concerned the college's rights against its tenants or the care of its property.

Indeed the records of the courts of Merton's manors, like those of other lords, are full of procedures intended to assert the rights of the lord. They contain inquiries about the rent owed by whole categories of tenant, and also actions against particular tenants who have failed to pay some part of their rent (in money, kind, labour or other service) or who deny the obligation to do so. Some courts record actions arising from seigneurial monopolies, for example the requirement that unfree tenants should have their corn ground only at the lord's mill. There is much business about the holding and transfer of tenements: inquiries about the current occupation of a holding, or the admission of a new tenant and the terms of tenure. Some courts record the regulation

---

2   The surviving court rolls of Malden from the period 1280–1300 are in Oxford, Merton College, Merton College records (hereafter MCR) 4706–33. The court rolls of Cuxham from 1279 to 1358 are edited by Harvey, *Manorial records of Cuxham*. On Thorncroft see R Evans, 'Merton College's control of its tenants at Thorncroft 1270–1349' in Razi and Smith, *Medieval society*. On Merton's estate more generally see TH Aston, 'The external resources and administration of Merton College to *circa* 1348' in JI Catto and TAR Evans (eds), *The early Oxford schools* (History of the University of Oxford i 1984). Conditions in Surrey are described by J Blair, *Early medieval Surrey: landholding, church and settlement before 1300* (1991), which makes extensive use of the records of Merton College's manors in the county.

by the lord of his unfree tenants' maintenance of their holdings – which in feudal theory if not necessarily in popular perception were the property of the lord. Various occasional payments to the lord are recorded, including payments when a holding changed hands (either for a fixed term or indefinitely) or when the daughter of a villein married or a son entered the clergy. And there are numerous payments which shade imperceptibly from punitive amercements for misdemeanours into routine payments for activities which required the lord's formal consent.

Many transactions in Merton's manorial courts however involved no immediate revenue for the college but arose from its need to record and safeguard its jurisdiction. Any lord needed to know who was occupying his villein tenements, particularly if a tenant was personally of free status. Such tenants might well be more troublesome than those who were personally unfree, and there was always the slight risk that the unfree status of the holding might in time be disputed. Less rent was likely to be at stake where the manor's free rather than unfree tenants were concerned, but a careful lord would still go to great lengths to record changes in the occupation of free holdings. And because a lord was generally in no position to prevent the fragmentation of free holdings, and had less leverage against his free tenants, the trouble involved could be considerable. The rising population and demand for land in the thirteenth century meant that a quite substantial free holding could quickly dissolve into a multiplicity of free smallholdings. It could be hard for the lord to know who was the actual tenant of each fragment, and how the original rents had been apportioned between them. A large proportion of the proceedings of Merton's court at Thorncroft by Leatherhead derived from the need to register the changing occupation of fragmented free tenements, and there was much business of the same kind at Malden.[3] Very often the rents involved were tiny (cases in the court of 17 May 1288 concerned rents of only 1*d* or 2*d*) but failure to register them might ultimately have led to loss of title.

A common type of entry in court rolls is the presentment of those who have encroached on the lord's land in some way. The illicit cultivation by a tenant of small portions of adjacent demesne arable is not unknown. But it is damage to the lord's growing crops or pasture by tenants' livestock that is most often reported, and this is a category of offence which will be very familiar to most students of court rolls. The seizure of five horses found in the college's pasture was reported, for instance, to the Malden court of 17 May 1288. Much longer lists of trespasses in the lord's arable and pasture are to be found in some courts, though their number has to be set against the length of time elapsed between the courts at which they are reported. No presentment of the lord for allowing his animals to stray into the land of a tenant is to be found in the records considered here.

It is a particularly interesting aspect both of estate management and of manorial lordship that a lord was able to ask those who were required to attend the manorial court – its suitors – to report on the agricultural management of his manorial officers, or on their conduct in general. The use of this device at Merton's manor of Cuxham in Oxfordshire is well described by Paul Harvey in his classic study of that manor.[4] Such inquiries – which took the form of presentment under oath by some or all of the suitors

---

3 On free tenements at Thorncroft see Evans, 'Thorncroft', 228–31; on difficulties with a free man holding an unfree tenement see ibid 237–9.
4 PDA Harvey, *A medieval Oxfordshire village: Cuxham 1240–1400* (1965), 65–6, 69–70.

– could also extend to the local officers' handling of tenurial matters. The discovery in 1306 of several longstanding leases of demesne and villein land which had been made without authorization by the reeve or lessee of Thorncroft prompted a formal inquest in the manorial court.[5] There was a somewhat similar inquest at Malden on 29 October 1289. In some manors inquiries into the management of the demesne seem to have been occasional expedients. At Malden at the end of the thirteenth century formal inquiries into the conduct of the manorial officers were unusually frequent, and look like a routine aspect of estate administration.

It has been mentioned that in May 1288 the villeins of Malden testified about the care of the woods, fields and meadows. On 29 October 1289 an inquest found that 'all the lord's goods are well kept, whether in meadows, lands, woods or other places where they should be cared for, and that no fault was to be found in that regard in the reeve or hayward'. In the following February an inquest by free and unfree tenants as to the lands and woods reported nothing amiss, except that the reeve's daughter had taken a sheaf of oats when the reapers returned from the field one evening. At the court of 20 November 1290 the jurors said that the fields and pasture were well cared for, that the corn was duly looked after in the summer and that pasture had been leased according to its true value; as to the harvest they reported that two women who had received the reeve's permission to glean had done so improperly (*male*) in some way. They also presented that the reeve's animals had damaged the lord's wheat and pasture. On 8 June 1293 all the suitors (*tota curia*) of Malden were charged to inquire into damage to the woods and heathland. They found that the parker had felled four larger and nine smaller trees in the park; the steward added a further charge of improperly making and selling hurdles. The parker offered an explanation for the felling and called on the reeve to confirm that the hurdles were for manorial use. Significantly the issue was not settled by the decision of the steward, but had to be referred to a further inquest by the whole court, which upheld the original presentment of unjustified felling but not that of illicit disposal of hurdles.

It would be easy to multiply examples of the manorial court acting straightforwardly as the guardian of the lord's interests. It will be suggested shortly that the language of the proceedings and the way in which they were recorded tend to exaggerate the extent to which the court was the tool of the lord's will. It would also be possible – though not altogether easy – to argue that cases which touched the lord were significantly better recorded than others. We know very little of manorial courts or their predecessors before the middle of the thirteenth century, but it is abundantly clear that after that date, when we have copious records, their principal function in practice was to uphold the rights of manorial lords. There was after all an inherent conflict of interest between lord and tenant. In medieval England the manorial court was undeniably, first and foremost, the means by which manorial lords asserted and maintained control of their tenants. This is an important historical fact, which remains true whether or not it was recognized by lord or tenant in any particular medieval manor. But it is by no means the whole story, and the ways in which the manorial court was something other than the implement of seigneurial will is a particularly intriguing question, though one that is rendered especially difficult by the nature of the sources.

The origin of manorial structure in England was discussed in 1958 in a magisterial article by Trevor Aston that had the unintended effect of inhibiting further discussion

5   Evans, 215.

of a subject that has only recently been reopened and is once more receiving the serious attention it deserves.[6] We do not know when manorial or similar courts were first established in England, though the earliest extant accounts of the manors of the bishop of Winchester, those enrolled in the 'pipe roll' for 1208–9, give firm indirect evidence of their existence. The early twelfth-century legal text known as *Leges Henrici primi* refers to the court called *halimotum*: this may already have its later meaning of a manorial court, though this is not self-evident in the text itself. The presence of manorial or other very local courts even before the Norman conquest is sometimes assumed, but has not yet been clearly demonstrated. Thus the opening sentence of Doris Stenton's study of English justice between 1066 and 1215 speaks of 'the justice administered by peasant suitors in their immemorial local courts' in pre-conquest England. Maitland pointed out that at least one manorial court is recorded in domesday book but argued that it was mentioned precisely because it was then a novelty worthy of comment. In Anglo-Saxon England there could well have been a significant volume of very local business beyond that which could have been accommodated in the hundred or shire courts, and it is at least plausible that there was a layer of public courts below the hundred or wapentake court.[7] The Norman conquest is now once again seen as a truly significant point of change in English social conditions, bringing an intensification of seigneurialism and, very probably, manorialization; in the century following the conquest local courts that were essentially public may well have been transformed into courts which were dominated by lords and formed a central pillar of a newly rigorous manorial system. This remains a matter of speculation, but if the manorial court of later medieval England had emerged from an earlier system of public courts this would help to explain some of its more perplexing features.

Most obviously, manorial court rolls record litigation between tenants, actions to which the lord was not a party but which are among the most interesting aspects of the courts' proceedings. Litigation in manorial courts is receiving expert attention and will not be discussed here, but its very presence is noteworthy in relation to the questions now under consideration.[8] The volume of inter-tenant business could vary considerably between manors, sometimes but not necessarily in a way that can be

---

6   TH Aston, 'The origins of the manor in England', *Transactions of the Royal Historical Society* 5.viii (1958), repr with a postscript in TH Aston, PR Coss, CC Dyer and JI Thirsk (eds), *Social relations and ideas: essays in honour of RH Hilton* (1983); see too TH Aston, 'The ancestry of English feudalism' above. Cf especially RJ Faith, *The English peasantry and the growth of lordship* (1997).

7   For the Winchester pipe roll for 1208–9 and the later use of the word *halmote* see Harvey, *Manorial records*, 42–3. *Leges Henrici primi*, ed and trans LJ Downer (1972), 9.4, 78.2, and pp 319–20; cf *Select pleas in manorial and other seignorial courts*, ed FW Maitland (Selden Society ii 1888), xvii, lxxvi–vii. D Stenton, *English justice between the Norman conquest and the great charter, 1066–1215* (1964), 1 (cf ibid 14). FW Maitland, *Domesday book and beyond* (1897, 1960 edn), 112, 122. See too A Harding, *The law courts of medieval England* (1972), 15–16; PA Brand, *The origins of the English legal profession* (1992), 5–6; J Hudson, *The formation of the English common law* (1996), 40–1; Faith, 116–21, 255–9. On the courts of shire and hundred or wapentake see for example Brand, 6–7; RC Palmer, *The county courts of medieval England 1150–1350* (1982); Hudson, 34–40; Faith, 258; and PDA Harvey, 'The manorial reeve in twelfth-century England' above.

8   On litigation see for example JS Beckerman, 'Procedural innovation and institutional change in medieval English manorial courts', *Law and History Review* x (1992); PR Schofield, 'Peasants and the manor court: gossip and litigation in a Suffolk village at the close of the thirteenth century', *Past and Present* 159 (May 1998); LR Poos and L Bonfield (eds), *Select cases in manorial courts 1250–1550: property and family law* (Selden Society cxiv 1998), xxxix–lxxii.

easily explained. Merton's court at Cuxham dealt with a far higher proportion of actions brought by one peasant against another than did its court at Thorncroft. The small village and parish of Cuxham coincided exactly with the manor, while the college's manor of Thorncroft was merely the largest of the three main manors in Leatherhead: the manorial court of Cuxham may have provided a natural forum for the settling of local disputes, while the court of Thorncroft was more obviously an adjunct of lordship and less closely identified with a single unit of settlement and cultivation. An investigation of how inter-peasant disputes and genuinely communal matters were dealt with in settlements divided between two or more manors might reveal a good deal about the nature both of manorial courts and of local communities.[9]

Merton College held the only manor in the parish of Malden, to which were attached holdings in Tolworth besides the park of Chessington. Nonetheless inter-tenant business does not figure largely in the proceedings of the manorial court. Several of the cases which came to court in the early 1290s involved the villein Walter Brewer. Brewer held a yardland (Latin *virgata terre*, sometimes half-translated into English as 'virgate'), that unit of tenure whose nominal size varied greatly from place to place but which commonly included between sixteen and thirty acres of arable. In May 1290 Brewer acknowledged that he owed 5*s* 5*d* to John le Chaundeler, and he was given until the next court to settle up. In April 1292 it was reported that John Lombard had ploughed up Walter Brewer's meadow; the men of the court were ordered to go to view the meadow. The college had no direct interest in such cases. As the formal dispenser of justice, however, a lord would derive revenue even from business to which he was not a party. All amercements and fines at Malden went into the college's coffers. On occasion a suitor would seek an inquest to establish their right in some matter, and it was usual for the suitor to make a payment to the lord for the inquest. On 30 June 1282 the court of Malden found that half an acre in Merefurlong which rightly belonged to Emma the daughter of John Cook had been withheld from her by her father for two seasons against her will. John, the free tenant of half a yardland, was to pay not only a shilling to Emma in compensation, but also an amercement of 6*d* to the lord, though in reality this was not an offence against the college at all. Inquests by the court could perform a genuinely useful service for tenants, but it was the lord who drew an immediate financial benefit.

It is not obvious where peasants might have looked for the settlement of disputes of this kind if not to a manorial court. Neither the county nor the hundred court, whose suitors were the elite of the locality, was a suitable tribunal for the typical peasant disputes and inquiries found in manorial court rolls. There were serious restrictions on the appearance of villeins as parties to civil suits in royal courts, though the precise legal position is not altogether straightforward.[10] And it is to be doubted whether many free tenants would have had the resources to pursue an action there. Furthermore the manorial court was a convenient source of relatively inexpensive and probably even relatively speedy justice.

On 14 November 1296 John Phillips successfully brought an action in the court of Malden against William Finch for entering his house and assaulting him; Finch was

---

9   See for example PR Hyams, 'What did Edwardian villagers understand by "law"?' in Razi and Smith, *Medieval society*, 74.

10 See PR Hyams, *King, lords and peasants in medieval England: the common law of villeinage in the twelfth and thirteenth centuries* (1980), ch 9 (for example 132–5, 145–51) and 262–3; Hyams, 'Edwardian villagers', 70–3.

amerced 6*d*. On 25 April 1293 John Cook successfully brought five men to say under oath that he had not entered the house or barn of Peter le Keys; Keys was accordingly amerced 6*d* for bringing an unfounded action. Unlike John Phillips and his assailant, John Cook was a free tenant. Cases of this kind were not tenurial at all and did not directly affect the lord. They really concerned the keeping of the peace or petty criminal jurisdiction, even though Merton College did not at Malden exercise the leet or frankpledge jurisdiction which might otherwise have covered such cases.

Matters even more clearly divorced from the lord's concerns occasionally came before the manorial court of Malden. Thus on 25 April 1293 all the tenants at the court (*omnes tenentes curie*) were charged by the steward to make presentment under oath about two cows which had been given, along with pasture to support them, as an endowment for the fabric of the church of Malden. They found that the rent due from the keeper of each cow was in arrears by several years. Some eighteen months later the cow held by Henry Miller was transferred to the keeping of John Coleman, with the proviso that should he fail to pay he should be distrained (some of his goods would be seized to ensure his compliance) by the manorial bailiff after only a week. It is noteworthy that here the court as whole, the steward and the manorial bailiff were closely involved in an issue which was in no sense manorial.

On 29 June 1289 an inquest by the whole court of Malden found that by enclosing more than four acres with a ditch and bank Adam le Cros had obstructed a right of way and had deprived the college and its tenants of rights of common pasture there which they had enjoyed from time out of mind. The dispute was protracted, and was probably settled by the granting of reciprocal rights of pasture, as recorded in a sealed chirograph of 1293.[11] The fact that this was a dispute between a free tenant on the one side and the lord and his tenants on the other makes it seem that the court was here exercising more than seigneurial, manorial jurisdiction. And on 25 April 1293 a matter was reported to the manorial court of Malden which, remarkably, portrays the college simply as a landholder failing in its duty to its neighbours. An inquest presented that the bridge at the end of the village called Kingsford was broken, to the loss and grievance of the locality (*ad dampnum & gravamen patrie*) and that it ought to be repaired by the warden (the head of Merton College) without the help of the township (*sine auxilio ville*) because he had his demesne on both sides, that is presumably at both ends of the bridge. There is no suggestion that this finding was disputed by the college, and here the manorial court looks very much like a public court with the lord of the manor being simply one of its suitors.

This should remind us there is a certain amount of business in manorial court rolls whose essential nature might be either seigneurial or communal. It is entirely possible that the language of the rolls and their very nature as the lord's record of court proceedings tend to overstate the seigneurial and to downplay the communal aspect. And perhaps it is too easy for the historian to assume that it is the lord's interest that is at issue even when this is not explicit in the document. The lists of trespasses by animals which are so common a feature of court rolls are a case in point. The arable, meadow or pasture in question is not always described as being the lord's, and may not always have been so. Unless there were permanent closes or elaborate temporary fences a distinction between trespasses of this kind on the lord's land and that of his tenants would be unreal.

---

[11] The chirograph is MCR 918; see too the court of 29 October 1289.

It may well be that what were really communal rights and obligations are masked in the seigneurial language of the record, a tendency reinforced by the fact that it was the lord who received the amercements. An unusual case at Cuxham on 19 November 1295 records that Robert Waldrugge (a villein half-yardlander) was to be distrained to answer to the lord at the next court because he had received outsiders contrary to the lord's prohibition and because he had dug in the pasture of the township in contravention of the rights of the township (*fodiit in pastura ville contra libertatem ville*). This mixture of seigneurial and communal phrasing is uncommon, and another scribe might well have described the digging up of the pasture simply as an offence against the lord. Waldrugge's other offence, that of harbouring outsiders without permission, is found often in court rolls, and is also one where the interests of lord and community may be confused. At the same court another villein, Thomas Brian, was amerced for receiving outsiders at harvest against the lord's prohibition. It is likely that restrictions of this kind – possibly related to the so-called assizes of strangers of 1233 and 1253 – were particularly intended to regulate migrant harvest workers.[12] The implications were spelt out in some detail at Malden on 7 May 1290 in a case which involved not a harvest worker but a living-in worker. John Phillips had received into his house a woman named Joan ate Welde, and he was to be answerable for everything she did. There was to be an inquest as to whether she was trustworthy (*fidelis*) and worthy of remaining in the lord's liberty: all the freemen and villeins duly said on oath that she was good and trustworthy. No tenurial matter was involved, and the issue was rather one of public order. Here again it seems that the court's communal business was clothed in the guise of seigneurial jurisdiction.[13]

It is well known that manorial courts sometimes regulated agricultural regimes, though agricultural ordinances survive in far fewer numbers in manorial court rolls than might be expected. Warren Ault published in 1972 a valuable selection of agricultural by-laws from manorial courts.[14] He found two or three examples in the court rolls of Cuxham. On 5 August 1334, for example, it was ordered that no sheep should be allowed into the wheat field until all the grain had been removed, nor into the spring-corn field before Michaelmas. An interesting ruling is to be found at Malden on 10 June 1281, though it seems to be by way of the settlement of a dispute rather than a by-law in the usual sense. The jurors presented that by ancient custom the field of Adam of Chelsham, like other land in the township, was to be fallow and common pasture every third year; in the fallow year the tenants' arable was to be harrowed only if the college harrowed its land, and only if all obtained the college's permission. The court was insisting that Adam of Chelsham's field should conform to this pattern, and that it should be fallow and available as common pasture in the following year.

If these cases are of great inherent interest they are also notable for their rarity. Many of Ault's examples are from Great Horwood in Buckinghamshire, where agricultural ordinances seem to have been recorded in something like a systematic way,

---

12 For the assizes of strangers see *Court rolls of the Wiltshire manors of Adam de Stratton*, ed RB Pugh (Wiltshire Record Society xxiv 1970), 4, citing *Select charters and other illustrations of English constitutional history*, ed W Stubbs (8th edn 1900), 362, 375.

13 Cf RH Hilton, *The English peasantry in the later middle ages* (1975), 54–8.

14 WO Ault, *Open-field farming in medieval England* (1972). See too his 'Village assemblies in medieval England' in *Album Helen Maud Cam* (1960) and 'The vill in medieval England', *Proceedings of the American Philosophical Society* 106.3 (1982).

year after year. But the almost complete silence of the Cuxham and Malden proceedings is probably more typical of court rolls in general, and raises important questions about medieval agriculture and manorial courts. It may be thought that agricultural ordinances of the kind recorded in some places in a few years would have been necessary in every agricultural community every year. It could be argued against this that the provisions of the by-laws, including even the dates of access to pasture, were set by unchanging custom which did not need to be periodically proclaimed. And agricultural ordinances might not have been enacted or declared in the manorial court, though that would have been the obvious place where there was a single or dominant manor in a village. But where agricultural matters might be decided in a village divided between several manors remains a pregnant question. I know of no reference to alternative village assemblies, though there may well be some. The fact that sometimes by-laws were promulgated or their breach recorded in the manorial court implies that this was their natural forum. On balance the apparently random survival of by-laws suggests a lack of concern for their recording in writing. The clerks of manorial courts may well have considered them ephemeral arrangements not worthy of permanent record. Indeed more generally it is conceivable that any communal business transacted at the court may not have been systematically recorded in the rolls, which were written for the use of the manorial lord.

If we are interested in the role of the court relative to the balance of power between lord and tenant we will do well to give careful attention to the particular function of the various officers who appeared in court and of the generality of suitors to the court. The court rolls of the manors of Merton College do not normally record who presided over the court or who represented the lord. The warden of Merton College was very active as chief administrator of its estates, and sometimes was present at the manorial court. The fellows of the college too might be involved in estate administration, and sometimes presided at sessions of a manorial court, for example at the college's manors in Leicestershire. It is clear enough however that the officer who normally presided was the college's steward. The headings of the proceedings of the court of Cuxham for the years from 1343 to 1358 are unusual in consistently stating explicitly that the court was held before John le Bruyn, the college's steward. There is little doubt that this was the normal situation and that such a statement was really superfluous. The steward was a professional administrator who received an annual fee; he would have had some knowledge of agriculture and of royal administration and law, as well as familiarity with local custom and conditions on the college's manors. One of his crucial duties was the supervision of the manorial officers. He might for instance help the manorial reeves or bailiffs to compose their annual accounts, and would go with them to the audit, which for Merton's manors after 1300 normally took place at Oxford. And as already mentioned he could use the manorial court to make formal inquiry into the conduct of the manorial officers. And just as the steward was the court's president, so it was his clerk who wrote down its proceedings. Indeed in demonstrating that this was true at Cuxham, Harvey showed in addition that slight changes in the format of the rolls could be attributed to changes of clerk. Whereas the reeve may have found a local clerk to write his account, the court's proceedings were written by a clerk who followed the steward from manor to manor (and possibly from estate to estate when a steward was employed by more than one lord). The steward and his clerk probably carried with them for consultation the rolls of at least the immediately preceding courts. The rolls were stored more permanently at Oxford, in the stone muniment room built within the college about 1290. We should remember that the documents from which we reconstruct the proceedings of manorial courts were written and kept for the lord and his servants.[15]

Much business was presented to a manorial court by the local officers or by the suitors, but the steward came with his own agenda, quite possibly in written form. Such documents would have been of ephemeral importance, and regrettably few have survived. There is one however among the Cuxham records, in the form of agenda for the court of 4 July 1310. Most of its items relate to specific cases concerning named individuals which do in fact appear in the proceedings of the court. But there is also a note to inquire if anyone has without the lord's permission sold a colt or ox or allowed his daughter to marry or his son to be tonsured. No such case was recorded at the court of 4 July 1310, and this seems to be a speculative inquiry into certain obligations of the villeins. Perhaps checklists of this kind lay behind amercements like that of Henry the reeve of Malden in 1292 for failing to oppose the marriage of the daughter of Roger Cosin.

The relationship between the steward and the manorial officers out of court was clearly crucial. The local officers were probably the steward's principal source of information, but he was free to receive or seek out reports from other informants. It is likely that from time to time the reeve or bailiff might conspire with some or all of the tenants to conceal something from the lord. The inquest of the whole court of Malden which found on 29 June 1289 that an enclosure by Adam le Cros had infringed the rights of both lord and tenants has already been mentioned; it also presented that the tenants had concealed the offence since the preceding Christmas. An inquest at Thorncroft in 1333 declared that William ate Bergh had encroached on a small portion of the demesne arable; this verdict however was not accepted, and the jurors were ordered to view the land in question with the steward and bailiff. When they did so they accepted that Bergh had taken more of the lord's land than they had said, and for more than three years.[16] In such cases it remains a matter for speculation how the steward was made aware of the offence and its concealment. A tenant excluded from the benefits of a concealment, or with a grudge against a neighbour, might have been ready to tell the steward what was really going on. A shrewd steward might in any case have had his suspicions about what he was told, either informally or in court; and if he had doubts he could require the jury to reconsider.

Whether a case was brought to court by the steward, by a manorial officer or by a tenant, the facts of the matter were pronounced by the suitors collectively. The precise procedure might vary, but it was the suitors who were the essential repository of knowledge. In this fundamental respect the lord was dependent on his tenants. Holding land of a manorial lord generally implied the obligation to attend the manorial court – suit of court, *secta curie*, in the standard phrase of the documents – and was so normal a requirement that it might be omitted from the terms of tenure of villeins in a manorial survey. Most free tenants, including those who held by military tenure (holding all or part of a knight's fee), owed suit of court, though some might not have to attend every session of the court but only, for instance, twice a year; and some

---

[15] On the role of the college's warden, fellows and estate stewards see Aston, 'Merton', 331–5 and Evans, 'Thorncroft', 205–11; on the audit see Aston, 342–51; on the Cuxham clerks see *Manorial records of Cuxham*, ed Harvey, 82. On the legal background of stewards see P Brand, 'Stewards, bailiffs and the emerging legal profession in later thirteenth-century England' above.

[16] Evans, 210.

might have negotiated or simply arrogated exemption from attendance. The suitors who actually attended any session of the manorial court were likely to be a mixture of the resident free and unfree tenants, and the involvement of the free tenants in the court's procedure might vary from manor to manor. This is a question that would be worthy of further systematic analysis – as is the role in manorial courts of small-holders. Sometimes, in the courts of Merton's manors as elsewhere, judgements were delivered by all the suitors together, described variously, in a probably random mixture of tenurial and communal terms, as the whole court, the whole homage or the whole township. Sometimes a smaller group of suitors made a statement under oath, by reason of which they were termed jurors (*jurati*). The rolls of the manors discussed here do not normally record the number or the names of the jurors, but it is possible to find judgements delivered by some juries consisting entirely of villeins, and others which contained both free and villein tenants. Mixed juries are found presenting judgements about free tenements, though interestingly the succession to a free tene-ment could not be decided at Thorncroft in 1289 because not enough free tenants were present.[17]

Furthermore, although the amercements levied in the manorial court went to the lord, he did not directly determine their level. The monetary value of amercements was set by officers known as affeerors (*afferatores*). These officers are not often named in the rolls of Malden or Thorncroft, but from 1329 onward they are frequently named at Cuxham; there they were normally villein half-yardlanders, though a cottager is also recorded. Indeed the common assumption that manorial offices gener-ally were monopolized by the more substantial villein families is not entirely borne out by the Merton documents, especially those of Thorncroft. Nonetheless the possible oppression of free and unfree smallholders by the village's better endowed peasants must be considered alongside the exploitation of them all by the lord. The steward may have tried to influence the affeerors, but the level of fines tends to suggest rather a more or less customary and accepted scale for the common offences.

The relationship between the steward as the lord's representative and the tenants as the repository of custom is mirrored in the composition of manorial surveys (including custumals, extents and rentals of all kinds). The account of Thorncroft for 1333–4 records the expenses of the steward holding courts at Thorncroft and, with his clerk, making rentals of Thorncroft and Farleigh – another of the college's Surrey manors, south-east of Thorncroft. The heading of the 1333 survey of Farleigh says it was 'made by John of Aperdele, steward, and the whole homage'. The steward was the lord's officer best placed to know the tenurial position on each manor, but for its formal declaration he relied on the tenants. The Merton records rarely reveal exactly who provided the information for surveys. Surveys of the college's three Surrey manors in 1357 were said to have been made on the oath of worthy men (*probi homines*). Extant rentals of Thorncroft and of the college's manor at Gamlingay in Cambridgeshire probably date from 1279 and about 1280 respectively. It may not be unconnected that the accounts of those manors record that twice in 1279 at Thorncroft and three times at Gamlingay in 1280–1 the warden and certain fellows of the college entertained the worthy or good men of the locality or township (*boni viri patrie, probi viri patrie, probi ville*). Unusually the Farleigh extents of 1279/80 and 1289/90 appear

---

17 Ibid 233. On manorial juries see for instance R Lennard, 'Early manorial juries', *English Historical Review* lxxvii (1962); Beckerman, 'Procedural innovation'.

to give the names of four jurors. The lists are not identical for the two surveys, but all those named held villein holdings (one held small amounts both of villein and free land). They are termed respectively assessors (*taxatores*) and surveyors or valuers (*extentatores*) and it is conceivable that they were responsible only for the monetary valuations in the extents. The opinion of all the tenants was sought on one particular point, perhaps after the original composition of the Farleigh survey of 1279/80, for a note adds that 'the whole court says that it is the custom of the manor that they give the lord tallage from year to year at the lord's will'.[18]

It is likely that surveys were sometimes compiled at or following a session of the manorial court. It is probably significant that surveys are sometimes found among court rolls, perhaps written on the back of a membrane. On the back of the proceedings of the Malden court of 19 May 1290 is a list of contributions to scutage which amounts to a full rental, and there is a similar list on the back of the Thorncroft proceedings of 1 May 1279. The proceedings of the Cuxham court held on 9 October 1329 begin with what is in effect a full custumal, possibly arising from a dispute over labour rent. And it is likely that the survey of Thorncroft in 1357 was drawn up in court, as what appears to be the original is bound up with the contemporary court rolls; it is unheaded and differs slightly from the version enrolled with the surveys of Malden and Farleigh.[19]

Knowledge of the custom of the manor, as of other matters of fact which arose in court, resided in the suitors collectively. This was particularly pertinent to Merton College, for custom must have been firmly established on its manors when it received them in the 1260s and 1270s. And as its manors lay in different parts of the country and had been held by a variety of lords there was no uniformity of custom across the newly assembled estate. Merton may have had more reason than most lords to inquire into the custom of each manor. Even the existence of a written survey of a manor which recorded rents in full did not alter the fact that it was the tenants themselves who remained the fount of such information. A full extent of Malden was compiled in 1279/80. Nonetheless when the admission of a new tenant to a villein holding was registered at the court of 11 November 1294 an inquest by all the villeins of the court (*nativi tocius curie*) formally declared its money and labour rents in full.[20]

It is understandable that the court should be asked for clarification of custom in the earliest years of the college's lordship. The first entry in the proceedings of the first court of Cuxham which has survived, that of 27 January 1279, reads: 'The whole court says on oath that after the death of any of the lord's customary tenants the lord shall have the best beast, even if that be the only beast.' This question of villeins' heriot was probably raised by the death of a particular tenant, as reported in the next item in

---

[18] MCR 5448 (rental of Gamlingay, *c*1280), 5777c (rental of Thorncroft probably composed about 1 May 1279), 5779a, 5779d (survey of Thorncroft, about 1 August 1333), 4889, 4890–1 (extents of Farleigh, 1279/80 and 1289/90), 4893–4 (survey of Farleigh, 1 August 1333), 4783 (surveys of Thorncroft, Malden, Farleigh, June 1357), 5690, 5717, 5344 (accounts of Thorncroft 1278–9, 1333–4 and Gamlingay 1280–1). The surveys of Thorncroft to 1357 are tabulated and described in Evans, 258–9.

[19] MCR 5786v (Thorncroft scutage list), 5791 (Thorncroft court rolls of 1349–61, with survey); copies of the survey in MCR 5779b and 5778 follow the enrolled text, not that filed with the court rolls.

[20] MCR 4782 (survey of Malden of 1279/80). On the endowment of the college see *The early rolls of Merton College, Oxford*, ed JRL Highfield (Oxford Historical Society ns xviii 1964), 40–9; TH Aston and RJ Faith, 'The endowments of the university and colleges to *circa* 1348' in Catto and Evans, *Early Oxford schools*, 295–9. On the college's surveying of its manors see Aston, 'Merton', 313–21.

the proceedings. It is harder to see why some points remained doubtful long after the college had received a manor. As late as 27 August 1330 an inquest found that none of the non-hereditary cottage holdings of Cuxham was liable for heriot, though this was not the first time since the college had received the manor that a cottager had died. And it is somewhat surprising that when the death of a villein yardlander was reported to the court of Malden of 24 June 1289 an inquest was needed to establish that heriot and relief were payable but there was no entry-fine when the heir succeeded to a villein holding.

Manorial documents generally tend to give an impression of unchanging custom, but practices treated as long established may in fact be recent innovations. Only rarely are there traces of the conflict between lord and tenant which determined the exact shape of manorial custom, and even then it may be impossible to know which side has been seeking to introduce change and which striving to preserve the status quo. By the later thirteenth century the main points of custom on most manors would have been firmly fixed, and disputes are most likely to have focused on relatively marginal obligations – which might nonetheless have been of considerable significance to the tenants. Most often court rolls record decisions in the lord's favour, but from time to time it was the claims of the tenants that were upheld. An inquest by the villeins of Malden on 20 November 1290 found that for several years previously the free half-yardlander John Cook had performed ploughing worth 1½d at the lord's boon ploughing (*benerþe*). It was at first ordered that Cook was to be distrained in respect of the current year's ploughing, but a note adds that the same inquest, 'at length better informed' (*tandem melius verificata*), said that freemen and villeins were only obliged to plough at the lord's boon if it was at the lord's cost, and they did not have to pay money in place of such ploughing. What was at issue here was probably not the obligation to plough nor its valuation, but the college's failure to provide the customary food, or perhaps an attempt to extract cash in lieu.

An important custom that was defined at the first recorded Cuxham court, held on 27 January 1279, was the villeins' liability to transport the lord's corn. 'All the customary tenants say on their oath that they must carry the lord's corn only to Henley, Wallingford or Ibstone, and no further, nor was it their custom to carry it to other places.' This obligation was summarized in the custumal of the manor made in 1297/8 simply as 'carrying', a good example of how even detailed surveys do not necessarily reveal all that contemporaries, or historians, need to know about custom. In the surveys of Malden and Farleigh made in 1279/80 carrying services were recorded in the entries for individual tenants and also in separate lists. The Malden list, which included eleven named tenants, was headed 'the carrying services of Malden by the presentment of the villeins' (a separate list of eleven tenants owing carrying services is also to be found on the back of the court roll of 13 June 1287). It was noted on the Farleigh survey that in addition to the declared carrying services the steward was claiming further services that had been concealed. Whatever the truth of the matter, in the survey of Farleigh made ten years later the total of carrying services allocated to six villeins had risen from twenty-seven to thirty-six. Their usefulness elsewhere may have encouraged the college to attempt to introduce carrying services at Thorncroft. In 1307 two villein half-yardlanders were amerced for not responding to a summons to perform carrying-service, which in one case was described as customary. But nothing more is heard of this service at Thorncroft, and it does not appear in the surveys of 1333 or 1357. The evidence is fleeting, but it may be that the villeins of Thorncroft successfully resisted the college's attempt to standardize services across its Surrey manors in contravention of local custom.[21] There may well have been an attempt by the college to override custom at its manor of Barkby in Leicestershire – or perhaps the tenants were attempting to steal a march on their new lord. On 15 November 1287 the tenants petitioned the steward to maintain the provision that no villein should pay for the marriage of his daughter unless she married a stranger outside the township. The college's steward, Richard of St John, replied that they were asking for something which was wrong (*iniuria*) and which he was unwilling to support. The matter was brought up at several subsequent courts without being formally resolved.[22]

A difficult point of another kind was put to the Cuxham court in 1296. On other ecclesiastical estates tenants might be required to make a payment known as recognition when a new bishop or abbot took office, and the corresponding occasion for Merton College would be the election of a new warden. No such claim seems to have been made in 1286 when Richard of Worplesdon succeeded the first warden, Peter of Abingdon, but the college did not neglect the opportunity presented by the election of John de la More as third warden in 1295. On 29 April 1296 the whole court of Cuxham was given until the next session to say whether they should pay recognition to the warden on his first visit to the manor. They said, unsurprisingly perhaps, that they should not pay, but the matter was nonetheless to be held over; no final decision is recorded. A few days earlier, on 25 April 1296, the villeins of Malden had also been asked for recognition and had asked for respite until the following court. At the court held on 4 July the tenants utterly denied (*dedicunt penitus*) the obligation; even so the question was held over until the warden could be present in person. It appears that the new warden did indeed attend the next court, on 14 November, but the claim to recognition seems to have been dropped, as there is no mention of it in those proceedings.

Much of what is said here is of a speculative nature, and may perhaps be incapable of proof one way or another from the surviving records. Nonetheless it is important to remember that lord and tenants may have seen the court – and indeed the tenure of their land – in quite different ways. The very high degree of compliance with the decisions of the manorial court, and the infrequency with which its fundamental authority was questioned, is very striking.[23] The main function of the court, or at least the one best recorded in the documents, was clearly to protect the interests of the lord. But the tenants had good reason to consider it as in some ways their court, and it was arguably their best defence against new demands by the lord.

---

[21] Evans, 250.
[22] MCR 6565.
[23] Cf Evans, 226–8.

11

Poaching and Sedition in Fifteenth-Century England

IMW HARVEY

For a long time historians found the activities of medieval poachers no more inter-esting than those of foxes in henhouses. An activity so common and so widespread carried all too easily the appearance of an entirely routine aspect of rural life. However, work on the subject over the last couple of decades has revealed that any easy assumption that poachers were the village poor hunting for food is in some instances simplistic and in many cases plain wrong.[1] 'Medieval poachers' is to be seen as a label covering different individuals and groups whose motives for poaching were often quite distinct. This article makes a brief survey of the poaching spectrum and, more particularly, describes the way in which that spectrum was taken to its widest extent in the fifteenth century to include those who poached partly on principle in order to defy and deny the law. It made a difference to the political atmosphere of the fifteenth century, especially in the upper ranks of the peasantry, that, following the introduction of some legal restrictions, men who in the fourteenth century would have been called hunters found themselves redefined as poachers. The anger created by this new exclusiveness with regard to hunting can be most easily perceived in the south-east of England in the actions of its vigorous and demanding yeoman class.

The poacher trespassed on territory very close to the aristocratic heart. The primary sources and the scholarship are unanimous in their evidence of hunting as the great noble medieval passion, be it the pursuit of deer, whether red, fallow or roe, at that time the animal of preference for all English hunters, or of the less prestigious boar, hare, fox, otter and badger.[2] Among royalty and the aristocracy it was a passion shared by men, women and children.[3] The chronicler John Hardyng, writing during the 1450s, declared that fourteen was the appropriate age at which to begin hunting. But there is evidence that some royal children were too impatient to wait that long. At the age of twelve Henry VI went hunting hares and foxes when staying at Bury St

---

[1] J Birrell, 'Who poached the king's deer? a study in thirteenth-century crime', *Midland History* vii (1982); J Birrell, 'Peasant deer poachers in the medieval forest' in R Britnell and J Hatcher (eds), *Progress and problems in medieval England: essays in honour of Edward Miller* (1996). I am indebted to Dr Rosamond Faith for her comments on a draft of this paper.

[2] J Cummins, *The hound and the hawk: the art of medieval hunting* (1988) is one of the best book-length treatments of the subject; see also R Almond, 'Medieval hunting: ruling classes and commonalty', *Medieval History* iii (1993) and JM Gilbert, *Hunting and hunting reserves in medieval Scotland* (1979).

[3] For poaching as 'a game that reinforces male gender identity' see BA Hanawalt, 'Men's games, king's deer: poaching in medieval England', *Journal of Medieval and Renaissance Studies* xviii (1988).

Edmunds during the winter of 1433–4.[4] Hard on the heels of their social superiors, the gentry of fifteenth-century England were also keen hunters. Towards the end of the century the lure of the deer hunt made a poacher of the knight who was serving as sheriff of Wiltshire. In 1463–4, while still a schoolboy, John Hopton, the son of a Suffolk gentleman, spent two days killing deer for the vicar of Covehithe.[5]

When on a Saturday in June 1496 four poachers with dogs drove and killed a stag at Lanhadron in Cornwall the value of the animal was reckoned at 30*s* – the price of fifteen sheep, more than the value of a good ox and certainly the price of a good horse.[6] However, to talk in terms of price was usually irrelevant; animals of the hunt were not commodities like other livestock. A deer park and its beasts were not there primarily for the making of money (although as Jean Birrell has shown income from deer husbandry was not disdained).[7] The deer park was primarily a matter of display, an accoutrement of wealth and position. That is why the sport of the hunt could never be only recreation; it was also a social activity with strict rituals, subtle etiquette and a highly technical vocabulary. Even the hounds were addressed in courtly language – *mon amy*, *douce amy*. As an exclusively upper-class privilege it defined social standing, and venison was the food of feasts. It had little to do with commerce or with the need for food, even though deer caught in the hunt were eaten. If the king or lord wanted mere food for the table then he sent his own professional hunters to catch a stated number of deer.[8]

The nobility, however, found it difficult to maintain the exclusivity of their favourite sport. They resented bitterly that in practice, although not in theory, they competed for wild animals and fish (angling was now an upper-class sport) with illegal hunters drawn from all ranks of lower society – for as Almond has argued hunting was 'practised by the whole rural community'. Some poachers may have found excitement in being both hunters and hunted and have treated the whole enterprise as a thrilling sport, but it was so risky that most poachers were not principally sportsmen.[9] Fish poachers fished with linen or canvas sheets or they drained ponds to ensure that nothing escaped them, such as poachers who in 1457 broke into the earl of Arundel's park at Littleworth in Sussex, drained his lake there and so carried off its entire contents. This was the loss of a large investment for the earl. The records of the restocking of demesne fisheries elsewhere show it to have been a costly exercise.[10]

---

4 N Orme, *From childhood to chivalry: the education of the English kings and aristocracy 1066–1530* (1984), 192–3.

5 HC Brentnall, 'Venison trespasses in the reign of Henry VII', *Wiltshire Archaeological and Natural History Magazine* liii (1949); C Richmond, *John Hopton: a fifteenth-century Suffolk gentleman* (1981), 133.

6 Cornwall Record Office, AR2/348, m 4.

7 J Birrell, 'Deer and deer farming in medieval England', *Agricultural History Review* xl (1992).

8 R Hands, *English hunting and hawking in the Boke of St Albans* (1975), 66–7; N Saul, *Scenes from provincial life: knightly families in Sussex 1280–1400* (1986), 187–92; A Rooney, *Hunting in Middle English literature* (1993), 1–20; CM Woolgar, *The great household in late medieval England* (1999), 115, 160.

9 Almond, 147; J Bellamy, *Crime and public order in England in the later middle ages* (1973), 80–1; RC Hoffmann, 'Fishing for sport in medieval Europe: new evidence', *Speculum* lx (1985).

10 For an example of fishing with a linen sheet see National Archives: Public Record Office (hereafter PRO), SC2/219/12, m 19; for the Littleworth poachers see PRO, KB9/287, m 95. See too A Watkins, 'Landowners and their estates in the forest of Arden in the fifteenth century', *Agricultural History Review* xlv (1997), 28–9.

Although of course poachers existed for a variety of reasons and it is unlikely that any poacher acted from a single motive, it is helpful to consider the five principal motives which sent men out to steal game and fish. First, and most obviously, some poachers were motivated by a desire for food, in a century when the villager's diet was improving and expectations were rising.[11] These were often solitary poachers or those who worked in twos or threes: men such as a Hampshire servant and a labourer at Hurstbourne Priors who together, in the spring of 1443, broke into the local park of the prior of St Swithun's, Winchester, and killed a doe. They may well have been motivated largely by a desire for food. Likewise with a husbandman from Tottenham in Middlesex who in October 1443 netted partridges at Enfield and Edmonton. The solitary poacher could be an effective hunter if he provided himself with the right equipment and animals. Such a man as, for example, Henry Copwode, another Middlesex husbandman, who in the pursuit of hares and rabbits went out to Edmonton equipped with dogs, ferrets, nets and snares. The jurors of the hundred of Edmonton who presented the indictment against him in 1444 estimated that over a period of time he had taken twenty hares and forty rabbits from the vicinity.[12]

That category soon shades off into another: commerce. It is not a large step from providing something for one's own pot to providing something for one's discreeter friends and relations. There was no legal trade in game, so that to purchase it was to connive with the poacher. The lack of evidence means that it is necessary to speculate, but an expedition on the twelfth day of Christmas 1447 by a group of six men from four Suffolk villages which took an alleged hundred rabbits from the duke of Norfolk's warren at Eyke looks very much like a commercial venture. If the estimate of a hundred rabbits was approximately correct then each poacher's share was in the region of fifteen rabbits apiece, a large amount for one household of a flesh that does not keep well. The likelihood is that some of the night's catch was intended for sale or barter. Two years earlier, in December 1445, a group of six men from villages of the Sussex–Kent border broke into the park of Edward Sackville at Withyham and allegedly took twelve bucks and ten does. If the allegation is to be believed, this was a great deal of meat to carry away and dispose of, even divided among six men. All but one of the Sussex men were labourers but the Kentish man in the group, from just over the border at Speldhurst, was a butcher. It may be that this was a gang operating as a commercial venture, perhaps supplying a meat market via the Kentish butcher.[13]

A third category of poacher, not mutually exclusive with either the hungry hunter or the commercial hunter, was the man trying to rid his landholding of destructive vermin. This grievance is heard in the late fourteenth-century poem *Piers Plowman*, in which the ploughman expects that the knight should hunt the hares, foxes, boars and deer that break down his hedges and that he should use his falcons to take the birds that steal his wheat.[14] Whether or not the knightly class recognized this duty it was in any case powerless to touch the king's deer in districts designated as royal forests. Deer were free-range browsers that quite naturally made their way to the wheat, barley and meadow grass grown in the villages within a forest's bounds and in villages

---

[11] CC Dyer, *Standards of living in the later middle ages: social change in England c1200–1520* (1989), 151–60.

[12] PRO, KB9/243, m 54 (Hants); KB9/244, m 43 (Middlesex). All the king's bench files cited here are in the PRO, in the classes KB9, KB27 and KB29.

[13] KB9/257, m 42 (Eyke); KB9/252/2, m 36 (Withyham).

[14] Almond, 148; P Coss, *The knight in medieval England 1000–1400* (1993), 161.

neighbouring a forest's long perimeters. In such settlements villagers were prevented by forest law from building fences against the deer without special permission, something which was usually given only to the favoured and well connected. Occasionally the crown made compensation for deer damage, but again not to ordinary villagers. In 1365, for example, Edward III granted an annual payment to John de Appulby for the damage done to Appulby's land by the royal deer in Bernwood forest in Buckinghamshire. However, Appulby was also a royal household servant and so had the right connections.[15] Villagers who were not hampered by the proximity of a royal forest could nonetheless meet a similarly rapacious grazing pest in the form of rabbits escaped from warrens.

The fourth category of poaching is altogether distinct from the previous three varieties. This was the poaching which went on among large groups of magnates' followers or henchmen. The intention was to inflict spectacular damage on the parks, ponds and warrens of rival magnates. East Anglia in the mid-fifteenth century is a notable example of a region where poaching went on on a massive scale apparently as just one means of inflicting wilful harm on another man's prized property. When the dukes of this region feuded it was, naturally, their henchmen who did the dirty work. For example on the Monday before Christmas 1443 the land of Ralph Garneys, esquire, at Stockton in Norfolk (three miles north-west of Beccles) was broken into by a gang from Bungay, just over the border into Suffolk, who took, or so it was later claimed, twenty hares, a thousand rabbits, twenty pheasants and forty partridges. It was Ralph Garneys's misfortune or folly that he was engaged in a dispute with the duke of Norfolk and one of his most notorious henchmen, Gilbert Debenham. But Garneys could answer this sort of treatment in kind, and in March 1444 he, together with a gang of thirty-eight named individuals, fished the duke of Norfolk's great area of fishpond between Bungay and Beccles, taking an estimated one hundred pike, a thousand roach, fifty perch and four thousand eels, worth in total £66 13s 8d. This was a stretch of water which Garneys claimed as his own.[16]

A contemporary and adversary of Debenham, Robert Wingfield, knight, of Letheringham, two miles north-west of Wickham Market, also employed large poaching groups as one feature of his systematic terrorization of individuals in eastern Suffolk. On 11 January 1448 he and his accomplices allegedly broke into the park of the duke of Norfolk at Earl Soham and with bows and arrows took five deer worth 40s; then the following day he rode southwards and entered the free warren of the prior of Butley at Tangham where he took, it was estimated, twenty hares, six hundred rabbits, forty pheasants and two hundred partridges, worth a total of £10. If on occasion a target, the duke of Norfolk was not above employing such practices himself against his great rival in East Anglia, the duke of Suffolk. In February 1450 the duke of Suffolk's park at Eye was raided by a party headed by half a dozen of Norfolk's esquires from Framlingham. They killed twelve bucks and thirty does, carrying off the does but merely taking the skins from the bucks and leaving their carcasses behind. The impeachment and a few months later the death of Suffolk in May 1450 saw the unleashing of a spate of exceptionally violent raids upon the duchess's various parks by this same gang and also by more lowly opportunists. Huge numbers of deer

---

[15] J Broad and R Hoyle (eds), *Bernwood: the life and afterlife of a forest* (1997), 6.
[16] KB9/249, m 108 (1443); KB9/248, m 63 (1444); for Debenham see WI Haward, 'Gilbert Debenham: a medieval rascal in real life', *History* xiii (1929).

were carried off, sometimes over a hundred in the course of one raid. Attacks were made in February, June, July, August and October 1450, in July and August 1451 and again in August and December 1452.[17] This was both a symptom and a demonstration of the shift of power in the region away from Suffolk's circle in favour of the duke of Norfolk. During the years 1440–60 some fifty-five cases of poaching appear in the files of the court of king's bench. Twenty-one of these cases occurred, allegedly, during the years 1450–2; and it is the East Anglian raids marking the fading of the duke of Suffolk's regime which account for this sudden upsurge.

My fifth and final category of poacher is the politically motivated one. Sometimes deer stealing was a species of protest and sedition. More than two decades have passed since Thompson made this revelation about early eighteenth-century England in his study of the Black Act of 1723; more recently Manning has explored the notion in relation to the early modern period.[18] Yet although historians of the modern period have led the investigation of poaching as popular protest and social crime it was in the fifteenth century that poaching first really began to take on the possibility of a strong political colouring. The fifteenth century saw a change of circumstances which affected the nature of legal and illegal hunting: by means of a series of legal changes an alliance was formed between the nobility and the crown to make access to lawful hunting something forbidden to those of the yeoman class or lower. Earlier in the middle ages there had of course been severe restrictions on access to the hunting of wild animals, but these had been geographical rather than social. No-one, not a bishop or an earl, could legally hunt in a royal forest without royal permission. The royal forests, created to protect the king's hunting, his monopoly on hunting, were of very wide extent in their heyday but by the end of the thirteenth century it had become a political impossibility to maintain their size and exclusivity. By 1334 the area of England designated as royal forest had shrunk to about two thirds of what it had been in 1250.[19] Yet as the geographical extent of the royal forests waned a new form of social exclusivity among hunters began slowly to wax. Just as the king had once excluded aristocrats from hunting without invitation in his royal forests so the aristocracy began gradually to expel the lower ranks of society from access to hunting at all.

One means by which the nobility began to establish hunting as an exclusive pleasure was the proliferation of private chases, parks and warrens.[20] A chase was a kind of private forest, a privilege granted to a few great nobles and ecclesiastical lords and usually subject to common law rather than forest law. Hunting in a chase was restricted to the holder of the franchise and to those to whom the holder had granted permission. Examples of chases in the south-east were Arundel and Worth in Sussex and Enfield in Middlesex. Parks were smaller and more securely enclosed hunting grounds than the forests or chases, usually comprising some one or two hundred

---

[17] KB9/257, m 44 (Earl Soham, Tangham, Jan 1448); KB9/118/1, m 22, KB9/270A, m 29 (Eye, Feb 1450); KB9/118/1, mm 7, 12, 22, KB9/270, m 2, KB9/270A, m 29, KB27/778, *rex* side, m 28 (Feb 1450–Dec 1452).

[18] EP Thompson, *Whigs and hunters* (1975); KV Thomas, *Man and the natural world: changing attitudes 1500–1800* (1984), 49; RB Manning, *Village revolts: social protest and popular disturbances in England, 1509–1640* (1988), 284–305; RB Manning, *Hunters and poachers: a social and cultural history of unlawful hunting in England, 1485–1640* (1993).

[19] CR Young, *The royal forests of medieval England* (1979), 135–48; R Grant, *The royal forests of England* (1991), 133–69.

[20] For the definitions which follow see L Cantor (ed), *The English medieval landscape* (1982), 70–82.

acres. They were common features of the countryside and could usually be created without any special licence. Kent had two royal parks at Eltham and Greenwich but the rest of the county was peppered with the private parks of lay and ecclesiastical lords. It has been calculated that by the reign of Henry VIII Sussex had as many as a hundred parks.[21] Very much smaller than parks were rabbit warrens. Rabbits were introduced to England in the twelfth century from the Mediterranean and although in the later medieval period some had gone feral they were still regarded as a valuable commodity to be enclosed in purpose-built warrens. Some warrens had wooden watchtowers or stone lodges to house those guarding against animal predators and poachers, both of whom sought the rabbits for their meat, the poachers having an interest in their skins as well, particularly if the rabbits happened to be not the common grey but the rarer silver-grey or black.[22] Chases, parks and warrens were all forms of enclosure and were resented as such. In the early sixteenth century a speaker in More's *Utopia*, while on the subject of enclosures for sheep rearing, added 'as though they [the nobility and gentry] didn't waste enough of your soil already on their coverts and game-preserves'.[23]

Another means by which the nobility in the later middle ages limited access to hunting was by their enjoyment of the special right known as the right of free warren (not to be confused with the rabbit warren). A charter of free warren was a grant by the crown of the exclusive right to hunt the beasts of warren in a given locality. It was a privilege granted liberally to local landowners, permitting them to hunt smaller game such as the fox, hare, rabbit, badger, otter, squirrel, pheasant and partridge over their land. By the mid-fifteenth century the right of free warren seems to have been an almost standard aspect of manorial lordship.

A further means by which the rich took hunting away from the ordinary villager was by parliamentary legislation. In 1390 a statute of Richard II introduced a radical change in the law of hunting. As has been observed, up to this date hunting had been – outside the royal forests – a monopoly for the wealthy landowners who had obtained licences from the king for their chases, parks and warrens, and free to everyone in all other places outside those areas. No longer would this be the case. Now lay persons with lands or tenements worth less than forty shillings (£2) a year were forbidden to own greyhounds, or any kind of hunting hound, ferrets, nets or any device for taking deer, hare, rabbits or any other 'gentlemen's game' as the statute tellingly phrased it.[24] In the case of priests this ban applied to those with property worth less than £10 a year. Thus the king and wealthy landowners allied to protect their privileges from the lower ranks. By means of this statute ordinary people – the statute described them as crafts-men, labourers, servants and grooms – were excluded from hunting as a legitimate recreational or other activity. For such people this was not merely a ban from hunting in Sherwood forest or the New forest, it denied them the means of taking the feral rabbits in their own parish. Below a certain income it was now simply not legal to possess the means of hunting anywhere. Naturally the legislation did not have the effect of expunging all hunting by those of humble status: it just made humble hunters into poachers. It set apart further the poor from the rich and made the ownership of

---

21 *VCH Kent* i (1974), 472–3; *VCH Sussex* ii (1973), 298.

22 M Bailey, 'The rabbit and the medieval East Anglian economy', *Agricultural History Review* xxxvi (1988), 8, 12.

23 Thomas More, *Utopia*, trans P Turner (1965), 47.

24 *Statutes of the realm* ii (1816), 65.

chases, warrens, fisheries and parks an even more covetable privilege. The social divisiveness of the legislation was seen at its starkest on those occasions when the justices administering the statute upon the poachers were themselves the landlords whose game had been taken, as in 1446 when John, duke of Norfolk sat on an inquest at Ipswich into poachers who had taken rabbits from one of his own tenants.[25] In the fifteenth century fines were imposed for transgressions against the statute, often in the region of £2 – the kind of amount paid by those found guilty of insurrection.[26] So in the last decade of the fourteenth century a new chapter opened in the history of rural crime, legislation which has been called the beginning of the game laws which reached such a dramatic climax in the Black Act of 1723, under which the penalties for poaching were no longer imprisonment or a fine but hanging.

Thus by the fifteenth century the humble hunter found himself excluded from his pursuit. Those wild animals which were not behind park palings were now hedged about with legal protection. Like an insurgent the fifteenth-century villager–poacher was, almost by definition, a man with a grievance. Thus poaching slid closer towards protest. What is striking in the south-east of England is how very similar the procedures of poaching and protesting could be, following the same ruses and practices and at times being followed by the same individuals. An example of parallel practices was the adoption by both poachers and rebels of false names to mask their identities. During the second decade of the fifteenth century a Sussex chaplain under the assumed name of Friar Tuck led a poaching gang which made itself notorious for taking venison and burning foresters' houses in Surrey and Sussex. Early in 1450 there was an abortive rising in eastern Kent led by a Thomas Cheyne who went by the nickname the Hermit Bluebeard; the names of his rebel captains included King of the Fairies, Queen of the Fairies and Robin Hood. This was an example not only of rebels using the poacher's device of false names but the very names were similar to the kind poachers employed. The leader of the great south-eastern rebellion of the summer of 1450, Jack Cade, was known variously as John Mortimer, John Amendall and the Captain of Kent; one of his henchmen as the Captain's Butcher. Nicknames conferred the advantages not only of personality with anonymity but also of durability. Their wearers might be executed but the titles could survive as long as did rebel grievance: soon after Cade's death another Captain of Kent arose, his real name John Smith, and then another, his real name William Parmynter.[27]

The connection between the poachers and the protesters in south-eastern England in the mid-fifteenth century appears to be, first, that they were the same sort of people by and large, and secondly that in some instances they were precisely the same individuals. A significant proportion of poachers and protesters appear to have come from

---

[25] KB9/252/2, m 16.
[26] For an example of poachers fined £2 each see PRO, E372/297, *item Sussex*; for several followers of the rebel Henry Hasilden who were fined £2, although one individual was fined as much as £5, see PRO, E352/242, *adhuc item Sussex*.
[27] *Calendar of the patent rolls preserved in the Public Record Office, Henry V* (2 vols 1910–11) ii. 84, 141, *Calendar of the patent rolls preserved in the Public Record Office, Henry VI* (6 vols 1901–10) ii.1429–36, 10 (Friar Tuck); IMW Harvey, *Jack Cade's rebellion of 1450* (1991), 65 (Cheyne); PRO, E404/66, m 202 (Cade), E404/67, mm 38, 180 (Smith, Parmynter). The use in 1450 of Robin Hood's name agrees well with the suggestion that he might be seen as a 'yeoman hero for husbandmen': C Richmond, 'An outlaw and some peasants: the possible significance of Robin Hood', *Nottingham Medieval Studies* xxxvii (1993); but see also R Almond and AJ Pollard, 'The yeomanry of Robin Hood and social terminology in fifteenth-century England', *Past and Present* 170 (Feb 2001).

the same stratum of rural society. Neither group seems to have been primarily composed of village riff-raff or desperadoes. If one sifts through the names of persons accused in the central court of poaching at this time a variety of trades is to be found: weavers, fullers, dyers, tailors, drapers, butchers, grooms, carpenters, clerks, fletchers, husbandmen and servants. Yet among these a particular group stand out: the yeomen. It is rather striking that of those men indicted as poachers before the king's bench in the south-east during the 1440s and 1450s a quarter are designated yeomen. That is to say men who were likely to be the more prosperous and influential members of their parishes, a proportion of whom would have held property worth more than £2 a year and so be entitled to the ownership of hunting animals but who could not aspire to their own parks or rights of free warren. This was just the social group that seems to have led and inspired Cade's rebellion of 1450. They were not the poor, the outcast or the alienated, but were the village notables. This can be detected in the tone of a clause in one of their rebel petitions of 1450 in which they aired their grievance against the income generated by undersheriffs and bailiffs who made out false indictments against 'simple peple that usith not huntyng'. These appear to be a group on whose behalf the petition drafters wished to act, not to be the drafters alluding to themselves. They, indeed, were unlikely to see themselves as simple people and knew themselves to be hunters.[28]

Richard and John Weller, husbandmen from Shipley in mid-Sussex, are examples of men who appear to have been poachers one year and protesters another. They were charged along with another Sussex man with poaching rabbits and deer at West Grinstead in the autumn and winter of 1447–8 and they were also named on the pardon roll issued in July 1450 of those seeking a royal pardon for rising up in Cade's rebellion. Admittedly, finding their names on the pardon roll is not a cast-iron guarantee that the two Sussex poachers were supporters of the rebel Cade (some of those who were the rebels' targets took out pardons as insurance against future prose-cution), but there is a very strong likelihood that they were. William Fowyll, a dyer from Great Chart in Kent and constable of Chart hundred, who is recorded as offending against the hunting statute in early 1450 is likewise on the roll of those asking for a pardon after the revolt.[29]

An event which took place in the autumn of 1450 illustrates well the way in which the often separate activities of poaching and protest could on occasion conflate. On 22 October 1450 a large group of men entered the duke of Buckingham's park at Pens-hurst in Kent and carried off eighty-two deer.[30] Thirty-two men, nineteen of them yeomen, were named in the subsequent indictment which made clear that a good number had escaped by its claim that there had been a total of a hundred present (not a figure to be taken too literally). These armed men had charcoaled faces, wore long false beards and withheld their names, calling themselves servants of the Queen of the Fairies. There is a case for treating this as a straightforward poaching incident, if of a more than usually violent kind. The argument would largely rest on the fact that at least four of the men involved can be found in earlier records as alleged poachers. John Gourde, a husbandman, and Thomas Saxpays, a yeoman, both from Withyham

---

[28] Harvey, 187.

[29] KB9/258, m 21, *Cal patent rolls Henry VI* v.343 (Wellers); KB29/81, rot 15d, *Cal patent rolls Henry VI* v.339, 366 (Fowyll).

[30] FRH du Boulay (ed), *Documents illustrative of medieval Kentish society* (1964), 254–5; for the date of the raid see KB27/790, *rex* side, m 44d.

in Sussex, were accused of poaching in the mid-1440s. Two Kentish men, Robert Bailly of Chiddingstone, yeoman, and Richard Levyng of Edenbridge, labourer, were accused of having poached from the duke of Buckingham's park at Brasted during the late 1440s.[31] Yet despite this evidence there are further factors which tell against interpreting the incident simply as a deer-stealing raid. Factors such as the time and the place: 1450 was not just any autumn and Penshurst was not just any park. Only three months or so earlier Cade's rebellion had thrown Kent and Sussex into turmoil. Humphrey, duke of Gloucester, a great hero of the rebels for his combative war policy, had held Penshurst. Gloucester died in mysterious circumstances in 1447. Five days after Gloucester's death Penshurst was granted to the duke of Buckingham. In the over-excited atmosphere of Kent in 1450 it might well have been thought that Penshurst had been snatched from the good Duke Humphrey, who some indeed believed had been murdered for reasons of political expediency.[32] The political unpopularity of Henry VI's grant of Penshurst and other Kentish manors to the duke of Buckingham had already been signalled in parliament that May when the properties were listed in an act of resumption. Even the parliamentary commons wanted the manors in crown hands.[33]

Another factor which suggests that there was politics behind this poaching is that this group of poachers included insurgents, people who had rebelled earlier in 1450 and who went on to do so in the sporadic outbreaks of discontent in the early 1450s. Thomas Couper, a yeoman from Mayfield in Sussex, had been involved in Cade's rebellion and was at Penshurst on 22 October. His involvement with Cade was recorded when he was charged with house-breaking in Surrey in July 1450, apparently as the rebels dispersed homewards from London. In April 1451 he was one of the participants in an apparently coordinated rash of risings which took place over a broad band of country running from Mayfield, Rotherfield and Burwash in Sussex across the border to Tonbridge, Linton and Brenchley in west Kent and beyond to Eastry in the east of the county, a distance of well over fifty miles. Particularly noteworthy is the allegation that as Couper demonstrated at Rotherfield another man from the Penshurst raid of the previous autumn, Thomas Brodebrigge of Brenchley, was among the demonstrators at Brenchley who lay in wait to attack one of the constables of Brenchley hundred.[34] Is it possible that the men of Rotherfield knew the sympathies of the men of Brenchley and could coordinate their risings through the underground network of a poaching fraternity?

Although the mechanism by which the counties of the south-east were raised to ride up to London behind Cade appears to have been the county muster system it has never been clear how the men of a regional uprising knew of one another's shared grievances, how the inhabitants of one parish knew what another parish was thinking. Shared political songs and poems and letter-writing are only part of the answer. For farmers with livestock and grain to buy and sell the marketplace was an obvious

---

31 KB9/252/2, m 36 (Gourde, Saxpays); PRO, CP40/752, rot 155 (Bailly, Levyng).

32 C Rawcliffe, *The Staffords, earls of Stafford and dukes of Buckingham 1394–1521* (1978), 21; *Cal patent rolls Henry VI* v.45, 67.

33 PRO, E101/330/7, E357/41, Kent.

34 KB9/271, m 96, KB9/270A, m 8 (July 1450); KB9/122, m 52 (April 1451); KB9/47, m 19 (Brodebrigge). Couper was lucky to escape with his life that April as several men who rioted with him at Rotherfield were hanged; two years later he was still alive but in Maidstone gaol. KB9/271, m 96, KB9/270A, m 8, KB9/122, m 52; *Cal patent rolls Henry VI* v.117.

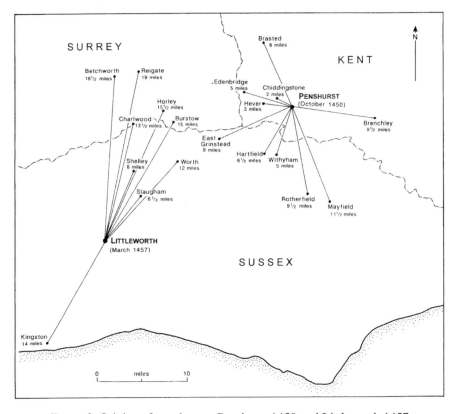

Figure 2 Origins of poachers at Penshurst 1450 and Littleworth 1457

meeting point, drawing men in to transact business and to gossip from a hinterland of villages – although horsefairs and horse-dealers were much less active during this period than they would become in the sixteenth century. For the woollen cloth weavers and finishers of the Sussex and Kentish weald the chapman travelling from artisan to artisan spread and perhaps canvassed opinion. However, in fifteenth-century England there were few inter-parish and especially inter-county groupings. Guilds and fraternities tended to be highly localized. Poachers, by contrast, appear to have come together over surprisingly long distances, crossing parish and county boundaries to work in groups tightly bound in all probability by the kind of oaths of secrecy and loyalty that rebels used. In 1450 the poachers converged upon Penshurst from parishes fanning out to the west and south, some over nine miles away. From Kent the indictment named one man from Brasted, three from Edenbridge, one from Chiddingstone, one from Hever and two from Brenchley. From Sussex it named two from East Grinstead, ten from Hartfield, five from Withyham, three from Rotherfield and two from Mayfield.[35]

---

[35] P Edwards, *The horse trade of Tudor and Stuart England* (1988); Manning, *Hunters and poachers*, 160. For an example of a rebel swearing loyalty see KB27/759, *rex* side, m 6d. For the Penshurst indictments see note 30 above.

An example of a poaching incident which drew on men from an even broader stretch of country is the attack in March 1457 on the earl of Arundel's fishpond at Littleworth in Sussex.[36] It is an incident which illustrates not only the inter-county, inter-parish nature of poaching groups but again that poachers were sometimes associated with protest. At least two of these masked and painted fish-poachers appear to have been rebel supporters of Cade in 1450.[37] The distances travelled by the poachers who came southwards from Surrey extended to as much as nineteen miles. The indictment named from Surrey one man from Burstow, one from Betchworth, one from Charlwood, one from Reigate and one from Horley. From Sussex were named one man from Kingston, two men from the parish of Crawley, five from Worth, one from Slaugham, the former parker from Littleworth itself and others unnamed to a total of thirty. It is hard to connect these men to a common town or trade or even a geographical district. Could they have had kinship ties, as did eighteenth-century poachers in Wychwood forest in Oxfordshire?[38] It would be illuminating to know how they communicated and organized their collective activity. However it was done it may well have been the channel by which on other occasions protesters organized themselves over broad stretches of country.

Not only were the poachers able to operate an inter-parish network but they apparently did so with their neighbours' collusion. 'Feeld hath eyen and the wode hath eres' went the medieval saying, for the countryside was never empty of watchers and listeners.[39] It would seem almost impossible that in these small communities poachers could have owned illegal animals and disposed of illegal game without their neighbours' knowledge. Even on isolated farmsteads it must have been difficult to shield the possession of hunting dogs from a neighbour's detection. The running dog, the greyhound, may have been relatively silent, but the scenting dog, more akin to the present-day bloodhound, was employed for its sonorous, bell-like voice as well as for its nose.[40] And yet it is evident that the illegal possession of hunting dogs was widespread; similarly with those other highly effective hunting animals, ferrets. In 1440 John Beket of Plumstead in Kent was in possession of four scenting hounds, two greyhounds and a ferret, yet he was someone who did not possess lands or tenements worth ten, never mind forty, shillings a year. Ferrets, of course, have the virtue of being largely silent but can be detected by a highly individual scent, pungent even by medieval standards. The rabbit poacher had to be mindful of any incriminating smell he might be carrying. Could it have been his own lack of sense of smell which caused Thomas Tiler, a yeoman from Ockley in Surrey, to be detected in possession of a ferret in 1447? The suggestion is made less fanciful by the fact that a fortnight later he was found selling a consignment of putrefied fish. Once in possession of illicit hunting animals their owners were more or less obliged to do some poaching merely in order to feed them. This was another reason why ownership alone was regarded as incriminating. In 1450 three members of the Pyper family from Dinthill, Shropshire, were charged with the illegal possession of eight hunting dogs between them. When these

---

36 KB9/287, m 95.
37 Thomas White, yeoman, and John Jurdon, yeoman, both of Reigate hundred in Surrey: *Cal patent rolls Henry VI* v.349.
38 M Freeman, 'Plebs or predators? deer-stealing in Whichwood forest, Oxfordshire, in the eighteenth and nineteenth centuries', *Social History* xxi (1996), 5.
39 FN Robinson (ed), *The works of Geoffrey Chaucer* (1957), 32.
40 HL Savage, 'Hunting in the middle ages', *Speculum* viii (1933), 36.

men took Lord Audley's hares some of their catch was undoubtedly to feed their pack of hounds. And theirs was unlikely to have been a cheerful collection of mongrels but the carefully nurtured strains of specific breeds. Good hunting dogs commanded extraordinary prices, if sold at all. A greyhound bitch and her four pups stolen in Wiltshire in 1440 were valued at £10, which speaks of a society besotted with hunting.[41]

Evidence from Cannock chase in the eighteenth century offers a picture of a tight community of labourers, colliers and farmers around Beaudesert park bound in common defence of the poachers in their midst. A wall of silence faced keepers' enquiries. The plentiful accounts of Victorian poaching also give clear evidence of the sometimes extensive cooperation of village society in poaching activities. These accounts show women ostensibly gathering firewood who collected the night's catch; of villages where, as James Watson recalled in 1891, 'almost everyone from cottage women to postmen, blacksmiths to parish clerks, spent winter evenings mending nets, making wires and breaking in their prized dogs'; and of famous poachers known by their poaching nicknames who acquired even regional reputations.[42]

During the fifteenth century too there must have been a good deal of turning blind eyes and deaf ears to the marketing of illegal fish and game. It is hard otherwise to explain how large catches were disposed of – catches the size of the three bucks and six does caught in September 1448 in Bodiam park by a group of Sussex poachers led by a Salehurst dyer.[43] The Penshurst poachers of 1450 took the precaution of wearing long false beards and smearing their faces with charcoal to hide their identities, but that was likely to have been for the benefit of those who might catch them rather than to hide from their neighbours, as well as being a liberating 'disguise from them-selves'.[44] If their raid had a commercial as well as a political edge to it they must have been known and had their contacts with a market for illicit venison before they attempted to carry off eighty-two deer from the park. Fish, a more perishable commodity than flesh, made even more imperative an efficient network of transporta-tion and sale. Sale may not have been a great difficulty as freshwater fish were valued much more highly than saltwater; pike and eels were most particularly prized and expensive. But the problem of transportation and secrecy remained. The poachers already mentioned as having drained the pond at Littleworth in 1457 carried off a haul estimated to be on the heroic scale of two hundred pike, one thousand tench, two hundred bream, one hundred carp, two thousand eels and ten thousand roach.[45] There would have been, potentially, a good ready market for fish at this season, as it was Lent, but how could vast quantities, even if in reality numbering hundreds rather than thousands, have been carted and sold without the neighbourhood's knowledge of who was involved?

---

[41] KB9/241, m 24 (Beket); KB9/259, m 15 (Tiler); KB9/264, m 5 (Pyper); KB9/233, m 35 (greyhounds).

[42] D Hay, 'Poaching and the game laws on Cannock chase' in D Hay, P Linebaugh, JG Rule, EP Thomp-son and C Winslow (eds), *Albion's fatal tree: crime and society in eighteenth-century England* (1975), 198; DJV Jones, 'The poacher: a study in Victorian crime and protest', *Historical Journal* xxii (1979), 840–2; GE Mingay (ed), *The unquiet countryside* (1989).

[43] KB9/122, m 2.

[44] A Howkins and L Merricks, ' "We be black as hell": ritual, disguise and rebellion', *Rural History* iv (1993), 49.

[45] CC Dyer, 'The consumption of fresh-water fish in medieval England' in M Aston (ed), *Medieval fish, fisheries and fishponds in England* (British Archaeological Reports 1988); KB9/287, m 95.

Both the suggestions offered above, that poaching was a criminal activity which brought together men from different parishes and that it was tolerated and shielded by the surrounding inhabitants, can of course be accepted without seeing in poaching the makings of insurgency. After all, a commercial aspect appears implicit in any large-scale poaching. However, there is evidence that poaching, in the south-east at least, could often be an activity quite self-consciously charged with political and social tension. The inhabitants of the region said as much themselves. According to Knighton's chronicle, among the demands made by the rebel leader Wat Tyler in 1381 was a petition that:

> all warrens, as well in fisheries as in parks and woods, should be common to all; so that throughout the realm, in the waters, ponds, fisheries, woods and forests, poor as well as rich might take the venison and hunt the hare in the fields.[46]

Although to take animals from the wild was not an explicit customary right such as housebote, hedgebote and ploughbote (the rights of taking wood for house repair, fencing and implements) there appears to have been a strong instinctive sense that the issuing of rights of free warren was an infringement upon a natural right: wild creatures should be common to all. In 1381 at St Albans, where the abbey was in dispute with its tenantry, Tyler's broad demands were echoed but narrowed down to a purely local application. That year the insurgent peasants made a solemn procession to destroy enclosures and gates in the woods of the abbey, and at a mass meeting townsmen and peasants swore an oath of fealty to each other and gave one another possession of the warren and common woods and fields by handing around branches. Then members of the crowd took a rabbit which had been caught near the town and fixed it on the town pillory as a sign of the free warren they had won.[47]

The authorities, for their part, said that they saw in poaching the making of insurgency. The preamble to the 1390 statute alleged that hunting by such persons as artisans, labourers, servants and grooms afforded them the opportunity for 'assemblies, conferences and conspiracies for to rise and disobey their allegiance'.[48] These men, it was feared, might stir up riot and sedition against the king. Poaching was not far from rioting. This was what was seen as one of the most dangerous and offensive aspects of the poaching gang.[49] It was an obvious affront to notions of hierarchy, property and allegiance. Writing about poachers in the seventeenth and eighteenth centuries Munsche has observed that the game laws for the English gentry of the time were not so much to do with the preservation of game as with the preservation of the social order – and so it appears to have been with their inception at the end of the fourteenth century.[50]

That poaching continued vigorously through the political turmoil of the wars of the roses should give us no surprise. Evidence for this is to be found in an act of 1485 against unlawful hunting in forests and parks:

---

[46] MH Keen, *The outlaws of medieval legend* (1961, 1987 edn), 166.

[47] R Faith, 'The "great rumour" of 1377 and peasant ideology' in RH Hilton and TH Aston (eds), *The English rising of 1381* (1984), 65–6.

[48] *Statutes of the realm* ii. 65.

[49] EB Fryde and N Fryde, 'Peasant rebellion and peasant discontents' in *The agrarian history of England and Wales* iii *1348–1500*, ed E Miller (1991), 784.

[50] PB Munsche, *Gentlemen and poachers: the English game laws 1671–1831* (1981), 7.

Despite ordinances and statutes made in divers parliaments against inordinate and unlawful hunting in forests, parks, and warrens, divers persons in great number, some with painted faces some with visors and otherwise disguised, riotously and in manner of war arrayed, have often times in late days hunted as well by night as by day, in divers forests, parks and warrens . . . by colour whereof have ensued in times past great and heinous rebellions, insurrections, riots, robberies, murders and other inconveniences.[51]

This statute also made plain that this was a problem afflicting one region of England more than others, stating that these offenders hunted, 'in diverse places of this realm, and in especial in the counties of Kent, Surrey and Sussex'. And indeed in 1486, 1487 and 1491 the poachers bound over for good behaviour came from villages in western Kent in the vicinity of the weald: Otford, Brasted, Westerham, Chipstead, Sundridge, Sevenoaks, Seal, Ightham, Edenbridge, Chiddingstone, Penshurst and Leigh. Those poachers bound over in Sussex came from a great sweep of country in the middle of the county: Ifield, Horsted Keynes, Chailey, Ringmer, Lewes and Glynde.[52]

In 1961 Trevor Aston pointed out a need to know 'much more of the real outlaws, and of crime in general'.[53] Although this present study does not deal with actual outlaws, only peasants and artisans borrowing the names of legendary ones, it does throw a little light on one corner of the now well explored field of medieval crime. It suggests that stalking through the medieval forests and parks were not only outlaws but also much subtler subverters of the law: yeomen and artisans who lived within the protection of the law but who covertly defied it. Here, enmeshing whole communities, were networks of sedition thriving within the bounds of supposedly 'ordinary' life. Mavis Mate has highlighted the economic and social roots of Cade's rebellion.[54] In poaching there is perhaps another facet of the complex social background from which uprising sprang. Not only did poaching enable men better to orchestrate action on an inter-village and even inter-county scale: more importantly its day-to-day presence in villagers' lives may well have eroded their respect for their social superiors. In 1450 the yeomen of the south-east, spurred into action by the rumour that Kent was to be designated a forest in punishment for the duke of Suffolk's murder, called for better government, not just because they could not get justice in their local county courts and because the war with France was being lost, but also because they had long felt the injustice and indignity of being deliberately excluded from access to the animals of the countryside in which they lived.

---

[51] *Statutes of the realm* ii. 505.
[52] *Calendar of the close rolls preserved in the Public Record Office, Henry VII* i (1955), nos 236, 237, 538.
[53] TH Aston, 'Communication: Robin Hood', *Past and Present* 20 (Nov 1961), 9.
[54] M Mate, 'The economic and social roots of medieval popular rebellion: Sussex in 1450–1451', *Economic History Review* 2.xlv (1992).

12

'Laymen's Books':
Medieval Images in Theory and Practice

MARGARET ASTON

In his journal for 23 September 1854 Eugène Delacroix wrote some musings 'on silence and the silent arts'.

> I confess my preference for the silent arts, those mute things which Poussin used to say that he professed. Words are tactless, they interrupt one's peace, demand attention, and provoke discussion. Painting and sculpture seem more serious; you have to seek them out. Books on the other hand are importunate . . . You have to turn the pages, follow the argument and continue to the end.[1]

Delacroix, good writer though (or perhaps because) he was, found words bothersome and time-consuming compared with paint. When it came to works of painting and sculpture, it was the immediacy of apprehension which pleased him. Without having to turn pages and search through fatiguing words, pestered by the unwanted presence of the author, Delacroix, when facing the work of art, felt he was in touch with 'tangible reality'.

> The works of painters and sculptors . . . are all of one piece, like the works of nature. The author does not appear in them, is not in touch with us like the writer or orator. He offers, as it were, a tangible reality, yet one that is full of mystery. He does not need to lure us into giving him our attention, for the good passages in his work can be seen at once . . . Books are different. Their beauties are . . . too much intermingled with passages which cannot be so interesting . . . the [author's] images cannot be so striking as to prevent our forming a picture of our own.

The objections to verbal imaging were proved for Delacroix by 'our dislike for long books'.[2]

Rudolf Arnheim, commenting on this passage, takes Delacroix's painting of *Hamlet and Horatio with the grave-diggers* (Louvre, Paris) and considers what it does and does not do in comparison with the words of the scene in Shakespeare's play. The 'immediacy of . . . symbolization' in the painting, for which there is no counterpart in the medium of language, shows the power of visual art to present a fundamental theme (in this case *memento mori*) through direct sensory experience. This is the

---

1 *The journal of Eugène Delacroix*, ed H Wellington, trans L Norton (1951), 258; *Journal de Eugène Delacroix*, ed P Flat and R Piot (3 vols 1893–5) ii.462–3. I am grateful to those who heard and helped this paper over more years than I like to mention, and apologize for any resulting failure of acknowledgement.
2 *Journal*, ed Wellington 259, ed Flat and Piot ii.464–5.

'eloquence' of painting or sculpture. On the other hand its limitation lies in its inability to formulate mental concepts – a limitation which – as Arnheim remarks, 'does create problems for pictures intended to convey information'.[3]

The fact that Delacroix got stuck reading *Émile* has a direct bearing on the perennial relationship of word and image – something that has been under discussion for as long as people have been talking about human communication. What changes is not the topic, but the medium. Delacroix's words and his painting point us towards a problem that was present from the beginning in the theory and practice of ecclesiastical art in the middle ages: the silent arts could move people with direct dramatic impact; but how effective could they be as sources of learning?

The text which became central for the concept of pictures as lay people's books is in a letter written by Gregory the Great to Serenus, bishop of Marseilles, in the year 600. Serenus was an iconoclast who, having discovered that pictures in his diocese were being worshipped, had had them broken. The pope's reaction was firm. He condemned the image-breaking on the grounds that images had an admonitory value that justified their existence in church, since the illiterate could see in them things they were unable to read in books. Learning from pictures and worshipping pictures were separate activities. He wrote:

> For it is one thing to worship a picture, quite another to learn from the story depicted what should be worshipped. For what writing (*scriptura*) is to those who can read, a painting (*pictura*) presents to the uneducated who look at it, since in it the unlearned see what they ought to follow, and in it those who know no letters can read. Hence painting serves as reading, specially for the people.[4]

This letter, which passed into canon law through its incorporation in Gratian's *Decretum*, became an established authority for the entire middle ages.[5] Gregory's words were repeated, copied, cited and paraphrased in countless places for the better part of a millennium, since it was only in the early years of the sixteenth century that this concept of church imagery was attacked and jettisoned by northern reformers, and the council of Trent's response gave the statement new life. The early fourteenth-century view that 'literate people can have knowledge of God from the scriptures, but ignorant ones ought to be instructed by books for laymen, that is, by pictures', was an accepted commonplace, and the papal text came to be seen as the justification for every kind of religious depiction, from manuscript illumination to roadside

---

3   R Arnheim, 'The images of pictures and words', *Word and Image* ii (1986), 308–10.
4   *Aliud est enim picturam adorare, aliud picturae historiam quid sit adorandum addiscere. Nam quod legentibus scriptura, hoc idiotis praestat pictura cernentibus, quia in ipsa ignorantes vident quod sequi debeant, in ipsa legunt qui litteras nesciunt; unde praecipue gentibus pro lectione pictura est.* In an earlier letter to Serenus, Gregory had written: *Idcirco enim pictura in ecclesiis adhibetur, ut hi qui litteras nesciunt saltem in parietibus videndo legant, quae legere in codicibus non valent. S Gregorii magni registrum epistularum,* ed D Norberg (1982), 768 (register IX, letter 209), 874 (XI.10).
5   *Corpus iuris canonici,* ed E Friedberg (2 vols 1879–81) i.1360, *De consecratione,* dist 3, ch 27, 'Perlatum'. For an exhaustive survey of the Gregorian statement through the centuries, focused on the question of whether images can be 'read', see LG Duggan, 'Was art really the "book of the illiterate"?', *Word and Image* v (1989). The literature on Gregory's statements has grown greatly since I first wrote this paper. For recent work see HL Kessler, *Spiritual seeing: picturing God's invisibility in medieval art* (2000), 120–4, 149, 190, 207, 230–1, 239, 253; CM Chazelle, 'Pictures, books, and the illiterate: Pope Gregory I's letter to Serenus of Marseilles', *Word and Image* vi (1990); M Camille, 'The Gregorian definition revisited: writing and the medieval image' in J Baschet and JC Schmitt (eds), *L'image: fonctions et usages des images dans l'occident médiéval* (1996).

crucifix.[6] The famous twelfth-century St Albans psalter (now at Hildesheim) included the text of the letter in both Latin and French, presumably as vindication of the story of Christ's life being told in full-page pictures without any accompanying text.[7]

Since so much came to be built on Gregory's words, and such a lot of invective was thrown against them in the reformation, it is important to try to see into the pope's original intention. I shall be suggesting that though the pope's statement continued to be seen as the keystone, both theory and practice moved away from him in the course of the medieval centuries. Perhaps we ought also to consider whether our judgement of this question has not been affected (unconsciously or half-consciously) by the reformers' fierce polemic. Have we – at least until lately – adopted their antithetical categories in thinking about words and images, pictorial and linguistic symbols, and the kinds of people who used them?

Protestant evangelicals were certainly most outspoken in their condemnation of Pope Gregory and the theory for which he was held responsible. Papal teaching about imagery came to be seen as a smokescreeen that obscured the essential truth and openness of scripture. Zürich met head-on the defence that 'Pope Gregory directed pictures to be made as books for laymen: thus to have images is not wrong.' 'We should be taught', insisted Zwingli, 'only by the word of God; but the indolent priests, who should have been teaching us without respite, have painted doctrines on the walls, and we, poor, simple ones have been robbed of teaching thereby, and have fallen back upon images and have worshipped them.' Instead of teaching and preaching God's word, priests had deprived believers of knowledge of the faith through the false idea that images could teach. Man 'must be taught from God's word and not from images', Zürich reformers told the bishop of Constance; in Bullinger's words, 'let the bishop teach, and painters paint'.[8]

It is noticeable that image-suspecting reformers, with their scriptural focus, shifted the ground. Gregory's dictum was, quite unjustifiably, attacked for making images into teachers. English reformers such as John Hooper and Thomas Becon ridiculed the idea that 'blind and dumb images' could 'teach, or give any good instructions'. Was it possible to imagine any more 'unmeet . . . vain and unprofitable schoolmasters'? James Calfhill used the example of the crucifix. 'The cross, with a picture of a man upon it, with arms stretched, body pierced, and feet nailed, may peradventure put me in mind of a man so executed: but who it was, for what cause it was, to what wholesome end and effect it was, no picture in the world can tell me.' He was satisfied that 'it is proved that images do not, according to Gregory's mind, teach; but, in all respects,

---

6 *Hanc cognitionem* [of creator and individual soul] *possunt litterati habere ex Scripturis / Rudes autem erudiri debent in libris laicorum, id est in picturis.* However the author made it clear that in making his book *ad eruditionem multorum* he was writing for both clerks and laymen. *Ut autem tam clericis quam laicis possit doctrinam dare, / Satago illum facili quodammodo dictamine elucidare. Speculum humanae salvationis,* ed J Lutz and P Perdrizet (2 vols 1907–9) i.2, prologue, lines 1–12; *The mirour of mans salvacioun: a Middle English translation of Speculum humanae salvationis,* ed A Henry (1986), 18, 35.

7 O Pächt, *The rise of pictorial narrative in twelfth-century England* (1962), 22; O Pächt, CR Dodwell, F Wormald, *The St Albans psalter* (1960), 4, 49–53, 137–8, pls 14–34, 37; Camille, 89–91.

8 C Garside, *Zwingli and the arts* (1966), 135, 147; *Huldreich Zwinglis sämtliche Werke,* ed E Egli and G Finsler *et al* (14 vols 1905–59) ii.698 (1523 Zürich second disputation), 656 (Zwingli's *Brief Christian introduction* of 1523), iii.170 (Zürich's 1524 'Christian answer to Bishop Hugo'); Heinrich Bullinger, *De origine erroris in divorum ac simulachrorum cultu* (1529), sig D8v (*Doceat ergo episcopus, et pingant pictores. Doceat autem verbo non penicello*).

be vain and foolish'. And this dictum came to be entered into England's new orthodoxy with the homilies' endorsement that 'images in the church do not teach men,
according to Gregory's mind, but rather blind them'.[9]

Modern commentators may agree with this premiss: pictures cannot speak, and
they cannot instruct unless their subject-matter is first comprehended. But the idea of
image as primary teacher is not implied by Gregory's text. What those without the
knowledge to read books gained from pictures on church walls was fuller understanding of what they should worship. Image, like book, presented *exempla*. Those
who saw a picture learned more about patterns of the holy. Gregory's central passage
did not use either the word *docere*, to teach, or the word *discere*, to learn, but
addiscere, to learn more – to add to a stock of pre-existing knowledge.[10]

Long before the reformation there were some who believed that the full sufficiency
of the gospel message spoke to all men and women with a directness that made the
medium of art needless – as well as dangerous. It was a sense of priorities that was
already present in the early fifteenth century, as expressed by the Lollard William
Thorpe in his autobiographical account of his trial. He told the archbishop of Canterbury that the holy living and true and busy teaching of priests were sufficient 'books
and calendars' to know God and his saints by, without any image made with man's
hand.[11] God had spoken and been heard. The word was incarnate and preached, not
carved and painted. The parity of *pictura* and *scriptura* was totally rejected. Prominent in this polemic is the assumption that traditional imagery was didactic. Zwingli
and others were affronted by images being regarded (as they saw it) as teachers,
preachers, schoolmasters. The *books for laymen* theory was seen as something that
fobbed off the poor 'simple ones' with second-class alternatives. Those who had not
the means of access (through lack of education and literacy) to read books, *the* book,
for themselves, were given as substitute another kind of book, a picture book, which
was supposed to teach them about the faith. The sense of such deprivation became
acute at times of growing awareness of the divide separating the abilities of the literate
and clerical from the illiterate (or non-Latinate) laity.

If we go back to Gregory's words we can see how misleading these later construc-
tions were. Learning from pictures is not at all the same as being taught by them. Can
a picture ever teach in the sense suggested by these accusers? Gregory's pictures –
pictures of histories[12] – were not primary informants but delineations of already
known stories and events, intended to act as prompters. Those who saw on church
walls depictions of holy persons and happenings were to gain additional understanding of what to worship (*quod sit adorandum addiscere*), and the moral examples
that they should follow (*quid sequi debeant*). Their faith and knowledge would be

---

9 Thomas Becon, *Catechism*, ed J Ayre (1844), 62; James Calfhill, *An answer to John Martiall's treatise
   of the cross*, ed R Gibbings (1846), 47, 350; *Certain sermons or homilies* (1844), 181. On Hooper see
   AJ Nichols, 'Books-for-laymen: the demise of a commonplace', *Church History* lvi (1987).
10 This last point is made by HL Kessler, 'Reading ancient and medieval art', *Word and Image* v (1989),
   1, and has been helpfully developed by Chazelle, 'Pictures, books, and the illiterate'. For the polemical
   shift to images as teachers see Nichols. On the misconception that art can instruct see Duggan, 'Book
   of the illiterate', 242–3; A Henry (ed), *Biblia pauperum* (1987), 17–18.
11 *Two Wycliffite texts*, ed A Hudson (Early English Text Society [hereafter EETS] ccci 1993), 58.
   Thorpe's *bokis and kalenders* conveys the sense of objects for learning and reminder.
12 On the important distinction between narrative pictures (histories) and portrait images (icons) see
   Kessler, *Spiritual seeing*, 1; H Belting, *Likeness and presence: a history of the image before the era of
   art* (1994), 9–10; Chazelle, 141.

strengthened. *Pictura* was not a substitute for *scriptura* but its supporter: it uplifted by making visible words that needed to be lodged in the memory's inner eye. It was not supposed or expected to be silent; it helped to articulate the oral, the essentially spoken word.

'The books of the laity can suggest divine things to the unlearned, and stir up the learned to the love of the scriptures.' So, about 1200, wrote the Cistercian author of the text called *Pictor in carmine* ('The painter in poetry'), who had a clear view of the kind of biblical subjects that might be depicted in places of worship. But he was deeply worried about the licence of contemporary painters, and anxious for reform, having been shocked by some of the 'foolish . . . and meaningless' – if not vain and even profane – paintings he had seen in cathedral and parish churches. All believers were not only to know of Christ's death on the cross; they were also to carry the image of the crucifixion with them in their visual memory. In the late fourteenth century this seemed a central argument to John Mirk, the Augustinian canon whose sermon collection, the *Festial*, proved popular well into the days of printing:

> Images and paintings are lewed [ignorant] men's books, and I say boldly that there are many thousand of people that could not imagine in their heart how Christ was done on the rood, unless they learn it by sight of images and paintings.[13]

Gregory's letter refers to the illiterate – the *idiotae* and *ignorantes* – the body of the people who were unable to use texts and whose scanning of church pictures would bring them closer to the scriptures. However, it is surely tendentious (or plain wrong) to see as the corollary of this that pictures are for the people and books for the learned. The learned, just as much as the unlettered, learnt from the depicted as well as the scripted, witness the words of *Pictor in carmine* just cited. Luther himself, professing his mental image of Christ, exemplified Mirk's statement about the crucifix in the heart. And a prototype for a man of learning who gained something from the image that he had not got from the page is St Gregory of Nyssa, whose example was cited at the second council of Nicaea in 787. As often as he saw the sacrifice of Isaac depicted the story moved him to tears, such was the power of the painted image.[14] Images spoke to believers who had knowledge of the faith – whether that came from the spoken or written word. As St John of Damascus put it, defending the use of images in the eighth century: 'just as words edify the ear, so also the image stimulates the eye. What the book is to the literate, the image is to the illiterate. Just as words speak to the ear, so the image speaks to the sight; it brings us understanding.' People were led through images, as they were by looking at the ark and Aaron's rod, 'to remember the wonders of old and to worship God'.[15] Literate and illiterate alike could benefit from this address through the sense of sight.

Before we leave Pope Gregory another point needs to be made. It concerns the reading of picture and scripture. If this seems familiar enough, we need to remember

---

13 MR James, '*Pictor in carmine*', *Archaeologia* xciv (1951), 141–2; TA Heslop, 'Attitudes to the visual arts: the evidence from written sources' in J Alexander and P Binski (eds), *Age of chivalry* (exhibition catalogue 1987), 29–30; *Mirk's Festial*, ed T Erbe (EETS extra series xcvi 1905), 171. By 'images' Mirk meant sculpture, carvings.

14 *Patrologia graeca*, ed JP Migne (161 vols 1857–96) xlvi.571–2; EJ Martin, *A history of the iconoclastic controversy* (1930), 138. St John of Damascus also quoted the example of St Gregory of Nyssa: *Patrologia graeca* xciv.1361–2; John of Damascus, *On the divine images*, trans D Anderson (1980), 40–1. On Luther see M Aston, *England's iconoclasts* (1988), 437.

15 *Patrologia graeca* xciv.1247–8; John of Damascus, *Divine images*, 25; Kessler, *Spiritual seeing*, 30.

how unlike the scanning of page and wall which he had in mind was from our own, or that which Delacroix wrote about. It belonged to a world in which the dominant medium of discourse was speech and the heard word. The ancient comparison between poetry and painting (later attached to Horace's phrase *ut pictura poesis*, 'as is painting so is poetry') saw both in terms of rhetoric: speaking picture and silent poem. But the Gregorian letter looked on painting and book as alternative forms of reading (*lectio*), a voice speaking aloud, uttering or muttering words. The picture on the wall and the writing on the page were equally valid mediators of the spoken gospel. Though there is an obvious sense in which the word is always a necessary accessory to the image, the symbols of paint and ink were once intimately related to sound, to the spoken voice, to what could be collected (*lectio*, gathering) by this means. Thus, according to John of Salisbury in 1159, 'letters are shapes indicating voices. Hence they represent things which they bring to mind through the windows of the eyes. Frequently they speak voicelessly the utterances of the absent.'[16] Written word and painted story both invoked the sound of the speaking voice.

But *lectio*, as Leclercq made so clear, is a word with layers of meaning. It involves not only the voices that come out of pages, but also the meditative rumination attached to *lectio divina*. A devotional image is 'read' and 'speaks' in its own special way, often to the solitary individual. This use of pictures was specifically addressed in an eighth-century insertion in another of Pope Gregory's letters, sent in 599 to one Secundinus who was leading an enclosed life. Significantly presenting a valuable defence of image-use in the period of Byzantine iconoclasm, the pope in this interpolation is shown responding positively to a correspondent who wanted a painting of Christ to assist his devotion: he sent the recluse depictions of Peter and Paul, as well as Christ and the virgin, with a wholehearted approval of the devotional use of images.

> Your request pleased us greatly, since it shows that you seek single-mindedly with all your heart him whose image you desire to have before your eyes, so that having his bodily appearance daily present in the picture, you are inflamed in your heart with love of him whose image you wish to see. We do no harm in showing the invisible by means of the visible.[17]

Paulinus of Nola (*d.* 431), who built a new church at Nola in honour of St Felix, described how he decorated the porticoes with a series of paintings illustrating the pentateuch, for the benefit of the pilgrims who visited the sanctuary. He sounds apologetic. 'It may be asked how we arrived at this decision, to paint, a rare custom, images of living beings on the holy houses.' Paulinus's justification may seem peculiar. He believed it would distract from gluttony and drunkenness. The crowds of peasants who came from afar to visit St Felix, 'not devoid of religion but not able to read', behaved as if at pagan cults, eating, drinking and carousing day and night. Paulinus's idea was:

16 John of Salisbury, *The metalogicon*, bk 1, ch 13, cited by M Camille, 'Seeing and reading: some visual implications of medieval literacy and illiteracy', *Art History* viii (1985), 31 and 46 n27 in a valuable exposition of the interdependence of speech and writing, hearing and seeing.

17 *S Gregorii magni registrum epistularum*, 698–704 (IX.148), appx 10, 1110–11; Kessler, *Spiritual seeing*, 120–2. On monastic *lectio divina* and the meaning of *lectio* and *meditari* in the middle ages see J Leclercq, *The love of learning and the desire for God: a study of monastic culture*, trans C Misrahi (1961), 16–22, 89–93.

gaily to embellish Felix's houses all over with sacred paintings in order to see whether the spirit of the peasants would not be surprised by this spectacle and undergo the influence of the coloured sketches which are explained by inscriptions over them, so that the script may make clear what the hand has exhibited. Maybe, when they all in turn show and relate to each other what has been painted, their thoughts will turn more slowly to eating, while they saturate themselves with a fast that is pleasing to the eyes.[18]

Paulinus was ambitious. As well as intending art to diminish physical appetite and improve habits of behaviour, he worked on the assumption that these rural viewers, illiterate though they were, would be in a position to discuss together old testament murals of Joshua and Ruth which he presented for their pleasure and edification. One has to suppose that some guide would have been on hand to prompt and assist this group perception. Probably it was bible stories of this kind that Pope Gregory had in mind when he wrote to Bishop Serenus. As well as Paulinus's sense of the need to justify what he had done (those strange and unusual figurative representations on consecrated walls) we should notice the presence of the explanatory texts which seem to vindicate the images. If there was some feeling that it was reprehensible to introduce such imagery into the sanctuary, the accompanying inscriptions (*tituli*) extenuated the offence. Picture was annexed to scripture – an ingrained consciousness that we have seen perhaps operating centuries later in the St Albans psalter – and should help to bring it home.

As time went on and imagery multiplied, spreading into every quarter of religious life, there was a discernible shift in the theory of *laymen's books*. It accommodated itself increasingly with the devotional alongside, or even over, the informative purpose. In its fully developed form in the later middle ages the conventional justification of church images was a triad, claiming the threefold functions of the instructive, memorial and devotional. Aquinas, Bonaventure and Durandus were among those who gave classical expression to this concept in the thirteenth century. As stated by St Thomas Aquinas:

> There was a threefold reason for the institution of images in the church. First for the instruction of the simple who are informed by them as through books; secondly in order that the mystery of the incarnation and the examples of the saints may be more present in memory when they are daily represented to the eyes; thirdly to excite feelings of devotion, which is more effectually roused by things seen than things heard.[19]

According to St Bonaventure those who were unable to read texts (*scripturae*) were to 'read' the sacraments of the faith through the 'more open scriptures' of sculptures and paintings. Second, devotion was increased by having bodily representations before the eyes, since feelings are stirred more through eye than ear. And last, imagery helped the memory of all believers, given the weakness of the memory to retain things only heard.[20]

---

[18] *Paulinus' churches at Nola*, ed and trans RC Goldschmidt (1940), 60–5. I have changed Goldschmidt's translation of *omnes picta vicissim ostendunt releguntque sibi* in this passage from 'reread' to 'relate', since *relegere* here seems more likely to have the sense of 'collect again', 'go over or through again', 'ponder carefully'.

[19] Thomas Aquinas, *Scriptum super libros sententiarum*, ed FP Mandonnet (4 vols 1929–47) iii.312, bk 3, dist 9, q 1, art 2, sol 2 ad 3um (*ad instructionem rudium qui eis quasi quibusdam libris edocentur*).

[20] Bonaventure, *Commentaria in quatuor libris sententiarum*, bk 3, dist 9, art 1, q 2, *conclusio* in *Bonaventurae opera omnia* (10 vols 1882–1902) iii.203. It should be noted that this statement forms part of a discussion of whether *latria* ought to be given to the image of Christ.

The substratum of ancient thought remained intact, but there was a definite change of emphasis. The value of seeing and the seen was given an enhanced role. For the earlier cautious 'we do no harm in showing the invisible by means of the visible' there was now the certainty that we are most moved by what we see. And, coupled with this confidence in the sense of sight (highest of the senses), the devotional image – a statue, an image in the round, as well as a painting – had moved into place beside the historical depiction from which believers learned.

So far had the ecclesiastical arts evolved in the course of six centuries that Gregory's premiss could now be presented as a reason for valuing images above books. For, in the words of William Durandus (*c*1230–96), bishop of Mende:

> it is seen that a painting moves the soul more than what is written. In a painting some action is placed before the eyes; but in writing the action is recalled to the memory as it were through the hearing, which stirs the spirit less. So it is that in church we do not show as much reverence to books as we do to sculptures and paintings.[21]

Ecclesiastical promotion of the visual came to extend far beyond surrogate reading. The objective of stimulating devotion could override all other considerations and dictate the form of a given work of art. Churches could be seen as places that uplifted through sheer beauty and splendour, and what was seen and admired by churchgoers did not necessarily contribute to their devotional understanding.[22] The arts of the church, moving on from Gregorian endorsement, came to do much more than inform and inspire. They attached people to the church, alluring them by curiosity and delight in the spectacular, uplifting even when uncomprehended. Hearing music, watching processions, looking at gilded altars and painted walls, touching and kissing statues, all brought believers closer to God. Or so it was thought. If such externals took people into places of worship for reasons other than spiritual, the church was not the loser. They might otherwise not have been there at all, and sinners had to be present to be converted.

Even museum-like curiosities could be justified on such grounds. 'In some churches', wrote Durandus, 'two eggs of ostriches and other things which cause admiration, and which are rarely seen, are accustomed to be suspended, that by their means the people may be drawn to church, and have their minds the more affected.' Naturally even an ostrich egg could be a religious symbol, but doubtless that was not the first reason that attracted visitors to gaze. The arts ministered to God, and the ability to tell a story was by no means their only function. They served God by serving the congregation: its curiosity, its wonder, and its affections, as well as its religious knowledge. The most famous early defender of images, St John of Damascus, described his own idea of the sanctifying sense of sight, imagining himself entering a church when preoccupied with prickly thoughts: 'and thus afflicted I see before me the brilliance of the icon. I am refreshed by it as if in a verdant meadow, and thus my soul is led to glorify God'.[23]

21 G Durandus, *Rationale divinorum officiorum* (1859), 24 (bk 1, ch 3.4, *non tantam reverentiam exhibemus libris, quantam imaginibus et picturis*), trans JM Neale and B Webb as *The symbolism of churches and church ornaments* (1843), 56 and (on Gregory's dictum) 53.
22 C Gilbert, 'A statement of the aesthetic attitude around 1230', *Hebrew University Studies in Literature and the Arts* xiii (1985); R Berliner, 'The freedom of medieval art', *Gazette des Beaux-Arts* 6.xxviii (1945). On Durandus and image-making see M Camille, *The gothic idol* (1989), 45–6, 204–6.
23 Durandus, *Rationale*, 30 (bk 1, ch 3.42), trans Neale and Webb, 79; John of Damascus, *Divine images*, 39. On ostrich eggs and their symbolism see GG Coulton, *Art and the reformation* (1953), 255, 322; J Hall, *Dictionary of subjects and symbols in art* (1974, rev edn 1979), 110–11.

Plate 1 The visitation, coloured woodcut from *Auslegung des Amts der heiligen Messe* (Nuremberg *c*1482); photo Warburg Institute

So much then for the official theory of religious imagery. What of actual practice? To what extent did it correspond with this theory? Did parishioners learn from and use images in the way that the doctrine of laymen's books suggested? Can we say anything realistic about how people looked at works of art? These are questions that affect an important part of popular religion, and there are obvious limitations in our ability to answer them – the most conspicuous being that everything we can learn about the illiterate comes through the reporting of the literate. However, given that difficulty, it is possible to find some worthwhile examples of how images were seen to be used in the officially recommended way, respectively as informers, as reminders of holy persons, and as devotional objects.

To start with an unusual example of a sermon that told unlettered hearers how to use a specific image, explaining to them how to ponder and meditate on it, we have the words of John Geiler of Kaisersberg, the great fifteenth-century preacher of Strasbourg.

> If you cannot read, then take a picture of paper where Mary and Elizabeth are depicted as they meet each other; you buy it for a penny. Look at it and think how happy they had been, and of good things . . . Thereafter show yourself to them in an outer veneration, kiss the image on the paper, bow in front of the image, kneel before it.[24] (See plate 1)

The image in this case was a private devotional object, and Geiler's advice gives us a rare point of entry into a world which is mostly lost to us – the world of portable domestic imagery. The printing of paper images made it possible for representations of the holy and miraculous to reach humble hands and homes. Cheap single-sheet woodcuts of the kind Geiler had in mind had by this time been on the market for over a century, and were probably sold in thousands at thronged pilgrimage centres – though only a tiny proportion of them have survived. But we can imagine the visitation scene of which Geiler spoke being pinned to the wall over some hearth or bed, where the members of a household could look at it, discuss it, kneel before it – just as we can see a woodcut of St Christopher attached to the mantelpiece behind the virgin in a painting of the annunciation (now in the Musées Royaux des Beaux-Arts, Brussels) attributed to Robert Campin (*d.* 1444), or the more expensive small vellum painting which hangs behind the sitter's head in Petrus Christus's *Portrait of a young man* (*c*1450–60) in the National Gallery in London. Both were pictures with texts: the latter has a prayer to St Veronica beneath the frontal face image of Christ with which the saint was associated; the lines below St Christopher probably described the benefits that came from looking at his image. By the end of the fifteenth century devotion was aided by images within images, or images of images, like Israhel van Meckenem's print of the revered mosaic icon of Christ in the church of Santa Croce in Gerusalemme in Rome (see plate 2).[25]

---

[24] Cited in M Aston, *Lollards and reformers* (1984), 119. I have not traced the original source of this quotation.

[25] D Kunzle, *The early comic strip: narrative strips and picture series in the European broadsheet from c1450 to 1825* (1973), 11. On the Petrus Christus image (which was attached to a panel before being hung on the wall) see J Dunkerton *et al*, *Giotto to Dürer* (1991), 105–7; L Campbell, 'Robert Campin, the master of Flémaille and the master of Mérode', *Burlington Magazine* cxvi (1974), 644 and fig 12. I have benefited here from a National Gallery seminar paper by Catherine Reynolds on 'The head of Christ in the portrait by Petrus Christus'. See Coulton, 304 for an illustration of a St Christopher woodcut with two lines of text comparable to those in the Brussels painting. For an example of a small

Plate 2 Israhel van Meckenem, *Imago pietatis*, engraving, 1490s
Albertina, Vienna

Geiler, we should notice, expected devout use of the cheap paper picture to include physical as well as mental activity; the woodcut was to prompt thoughts about the story as recounted in the first chapter of Luke, and also to move its owner to veneration by kissing it and kneeling in front of it. The sense of touch was important, and must not be left out of account. It was an integral part of such acts of worship, a valued link in the chain of communication between believer and God. Lollards attacked those who placed so much trust in carvings like those of our lady of Walsingham or the rood of grace in Kent, clinging to them, 'stroking and kissing these old stones and stocks'. Reginald Pecock, on the other hand, was one of those who spoke up for the practice of venerating images in physical ways, and of course holy books were also venerated thus.[26]

The privately owned image (however cheap, whatever its quality) made possible an immediacy of contact that was comparable to that of the devout believer retiring to his or her room with a book. If all devotional images had the ability (as Pächt put it) of establishing 'a kind of direct, mystical communication between image and worshipper', such communication was surely specially direct when the image was held in hand, a personal possession. Here is Delacroix's 'tangible reality' at its closest, the image speaking to its owner with physical immediacy. Saints talked with saints in this way. St John Chrysostom (*c*347–407) had an icon of St Paul which he kept in his place of retirement, and while reading St Paul's epistles he would fix his eyes on it 'as if it were alive', and address himself to it 'as though the apostle himself were present and could speak to him through the image'. In the early 1320s Henry Suso took with him to Cologne a devotional image on parchment, which he hung in the window of his cell and used in his meditations.[27]

In England two poets gave literary accounts of the effects of paintings – murals in both cases – in their respective religious houses. John Lydgate (*c*1370–1449/50) recalled in his *Testament* the impact made on him as a child, still less than fifteen, by a crucifixion seen in the cloister at Bury St Edmunds.

> Mid of a cloister, depict upon a wall,
> I saw a crucifix, whose wounds were not small,
> With this word 'vide', writ there beside,
> 'Behold my meekness, O child, and leave thy pride.'

Lydgate places this impression at the end of his long purportedly autobiographical poem, to stand as the ostensible prompt of this whole enterprise of verse meditation and confession, undertaken in 'my last age'. Remembering the image, recalling the

---

parchment drawing with inscription, possibly produced for pilgrims to Bromholm in Norfolk, see MR James, *A descriptive catalogue of the manuscripts in the library of Lambeth Palace* (1930), 749–50; F Wormald, 'The rood of Bromholm', *Journal of the Warburg Institute* i (1937–8). On domestic religious imagery see Dunkerton *et al*, 68. On Petrus Christus and Israhel van Meckenem see *The image of Christ* (exhibition catalogue, National Gallery, London, 2000), 86–9, 150–1 and D Landau and P Parshall, *The renaissance print 1470–1550* (1994), 58–9.

26 *Selections from English Wycliffite writings*, ed A Hudson (1978), 87; Reginald Pecock, *The repressor of over much blaming of the clergy*, ed C Babington (2 vols Rolls Series 1860) i.207, 268–72, including kissing the feet of the image of the crucifix. For the description by a convert of how he had once 'kissed and devoutly licked saints' feet' see G Williams, *The Welsh church from conquest to reformation* (1976), 541.

27 Pächt, *Pictorial narrative*, 30; *Patrologia graeca* xciv.1363–6; John of Damascus, *Divine images*, 45–6; S Ringbom, 'Devotional images and imaginative devotions', *Gazette des Beaux-Arts* 6.lxxiii (1969), 163.

inscription beside it, he started (he said) to write his meditation on the passion. What he had once learnt from the picture, imprinted lifelong in his memory, moved him in his last years to compile his *Testament*. That, at any rate, was how he wished to present it – in the conventional triad of processes attached to the admonitory image. *Vide*, behold, started him off. The looking led to all that followed.[28]

The poet Alexander Barclay, who was born a century after Lydgate and died in the midst of reformation in 1552, used a mural in Ely cathedral to illuminate a passage in his *Eclogues* on how God loves poor pastors. The painting (now vanished) showed the shepherds, their flocks, and the three kings.

> I saw them myself well painted on the wall,
> Late gazing upon our church cathedral,

says one of the characters in the dialogue, describing the painted sheep and lambs, the horsemen on the slope of a hill, and the three kings with their glittering crowns. To which comes the answer

> Lately myself to see that picture was,
> I saw the manger, I saw the ox and ass.
> I well remember the people in my mind,
> Me think yet I see the black faces of Ind:
> Me think yet I see the herds and the kings,
> And in what manner were ordered their offerings.[29]

'I saw . . . I well remember . . . Me think yet I see. . .' Such tranquil recollection of the painting of the epiphany, long studied and remembered day by day through the round of offices in the cathedral, is surely akin to what eighth-century iconodules represented Pope Gregory as expecting of Secundinus. The years Barclay spent as a monk at Ely gave him ample opportunity to imprint firmly on his mind the murals in the abbey church, and his poem showed how visual rumination of this kind could operate as a prompter of the devout memory.

If Geiler's sermon shows how people were supposed to learn from images, and Lydgate and Barclay how they could be helped to remember, another English literary source, the now well known early fifteenth-century book of Margery Kempe, tells us something about the third part of the lay books' triad. Margery Kempe's account illustrates vividly the way in which images could excite feelings of devotion. If Margery's gift of tears sometimes strikes us (as it also struck some contemporaries) as exhibitionist, her devotional pursuits were quite conventional. More than once it was the sight of a particular image which moved her to extremity, so that her feelings became uncontrollable. In Norwich a *pietà* was the trigger. 'And', she recounted, 'through the beholding of that pity her mind was all wholly occupied in the passion of our Lord Jesu Christ, and in the compassion of Our Lady', inducing loud crying and weeping (cf plate 3). At Leicester the same thing happened when Margery saw a crucifix 'piteously devised and lamentable to behold' – and again the seeing provoked the devotional outburst; 'through which beholding', as Margery revealingly puts it, 'the Passion of our Lord entered her mind' and reduced her to tears.[30]

---

[28] *The minor poems of John Lydgate*, ed HN MacCracken (2 vols EETS extra series cvii 1911, original series cxcii 1934) i.356–7, lines 743–6 and following; D Pearsall, *John Lydgate* (1970), 294–6.

[29] *The eclogues of Alexander Barclay*, ed B White (EETS clxxv 1928), 199–200.

[30] *The book of Margery Kempe*, ed SB Meech and HE Allen (EETS ccxii 1940), 111, 148; Aston,

Of course all these literary sources place us at a second remove from the realities of images and their use. They start, in varying degrees, from received expectations, and themselves reflect the conventions (literary and homiletic) attached to the topic – though Margery Kempe's account seems nearer to personal experience than most.

Accounts of the moralizing effects of one of the commonest images, the last judgement, are to be found, though subject to the same limitations. There are for instance the famous lines of François Villon, who in his *Testament* of the early 1460s bequeathed to 'my poor mother' a ballad addressed as her prayer to the virgin.

> I am a woman poor and ancient,
> who knows nothing; can read no letter.
> In my parish church I see
> paradise painted, with harps and lutes,
> and a hell where the damned are boiled;
> One frightens me, the other fills me with joy.
> Bring me to that joy, high goddess,
> To whom all sinners must resort,
> filled with faith, without pretence or sloth:
> In this faith I wish to live and die.[31]

The doom painting – it was in the Celestine church in Paris, and was destroyed at the revolution – reminded the old woman of the pains and pleasure of the afterlife, and moved her prayer to the virgin. Villon resorts to a familiar topos to present what purports to be the literal faith of a simple believer, stirred by one of the commonest and most readily legible of church images.

Another, earlier, account is suggestive of how a preacher might have used such a doom. The thirteenth-century life of St Hugh of Lincoln represented the bishop as giving King John a most outspoken sermon after his accession, using a carving of the last judgement over the church doorway at the abbey of Fontevrault. The bishop conducted John 'to the left side of the Judge where there were kings in full regalia amongst the damned, about to hear the words, "Go ye cursed into everlasting fire" ', and called on the new monarch to dwell on this example and take steps to escape the eternal torments towards which he seemed to be heading. 'He said also', adds the report, 'that such sculptures or pictures were at the entrances to churches for a very good reason', namely to remind those going inside of their need to pray for forgiveness for their sins in view of this last extremity. It was stern stuff. John in response took the bishop by the hand and drew him over to the other side of the portal, where the sculpture showed kings wearing their celestial crowns, being led by angels into paradise. 'My lord bishop', he said, 'you should have shown us these, whom we intend to imitate and whose company we desire to join.' We are to believe that for three days John was a reformed man.[32]

Lollards and reformers, 120–1; the gift of tears – Margery's 'religious capital' – is considered by CW Atkinson, *Mystic and pilgrim: the book and the world of Margery Kempe* (1983), 58–65.

[31] *Le testament Villon*, ed J Rychner and A Henry (1974) i.80, lines 893–902. Cf R Manselli, *La religion populaire au moyen âge: problèmes de méthode et d'histoire* (1975), 116–17; L Gougaud, 'Muta praedicatio', *Revue Bénédictine* xlii (1930), 170. Avril Henry, commenting on these lines by Villon, observes that the doom 'cannot have told her anything she did not already know': *Biblia pauperum*, 18.

[32] *Magna vita sancti Hugonis: the life of St Hugh of Lincoln*, ed and trans DL Douie and H Farmer (2 vols 1961–2) ii.140–2. Bishop Hugh officiated at the funeral of Richard in 1199, and then accompanied John to Fontevrault to visit Richard's widow: WL Warren, *King John* (1961), 49.

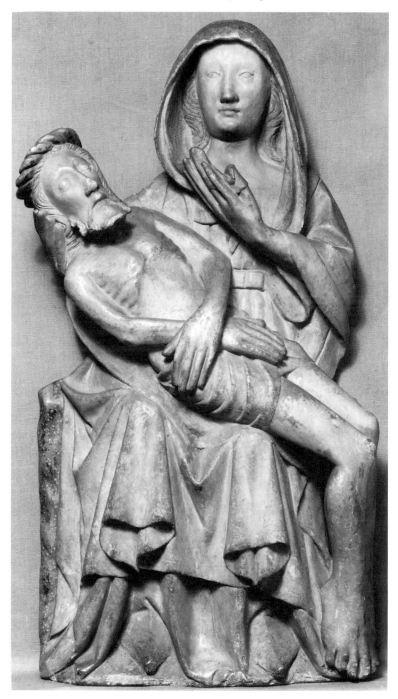

Plate 3 Lamentation over the dead Christ, English alabaster, early fifteenth
century; © the board of trustees of the Victoria and Albert Museum

There were certainly a great many images that were not at all easily understood. If the unlettered learnt without too much difficulty to familiarize themselves with the commonest scenes of the gospels and the redemption (annunciation, nativity, crucifixion and last judgement) there were countless less well known events, persons and symbols that could not possibly be recognized by believers without specific verbal explication. Some of them continued to fox iconographers into modern times. What happened then to the untutored lay people who were supposed to benefit from such representations? Ideally books of imagery, like books of letters, were expounded, interpreted and mediated to lay men and women by the clergy, as John Geiler of Kaisersberg expounded the woodcut visitation. But if the clergy had been in the habit of elucidating imagery or using it for instructive purposes, one might have expected to find more evidence in sermon literature. Such references are in fact rare.[33] The notices that appear in late medieval England may be attributed in large part to the challenge to church images posed by the Lollards. This certainly accounts for John Mirk's defence of church crucifixes in the Corpus Christi day sermon in his *Festial* quoted above. And the unusual iconographical guide that filled ten chapters of the early fifteenth-century *Dives and Pauper* formed part of a defence of the ecclesiastical position against the critic's expressed view that all images amounted to idols and should be burnt. So in answer to the question 'how should I read in the book of painting and of imagery?' we find here a series of directions on how to understand and use these depictions. This starts with the crucifix, and the meaning of its constituent parts; there follow explications of the emblems of various common saints, the significance of depicting the apostles barefoot, and of different items of saints' clothing, and the symbols of the evangelists.[34]

In practice hearsay and invention had to fill many gaps, and we get reports of the misunderstandings that could arise. According to John Mirk there were people who took literally the symbols of the evangelists, so that (he said) 'many lewed men suppose that they were such beasts and not men'. His short St Luke's day sermon aimed to remedy such misconceptions among parishioners by explaining these symbols.[35] The image-makers themselves quite often provided, besides identifying insignia, lettered elucidation in the shape of saints' names, or the inscribed scrolls carried by prophets, or speeches attached to the disciples in manuscript illumination. Pictures could dramatize the impact of verbal communication, but without the assistance of words and readers they could be obscure and misleading. Those who feared the dangers of misused images exploited ambiguities of this kind. In the late eighth century the *Libri Carolini* pointed to the absurdity that identical female figures were venerated and execrated respectively as the virgin and Venus simply on the basis of the descriptive caption.[36]

A satirical example of the problem country bumpkins had with church images comes in the fifteenth-century *Tale of Beryn*. The Chaucerian pilgrims of this poem

---

33 Duggan, 'Book of the illiterate', 250 n137 cites Coulton, *Art and the reformation*, 317, 566 and GR Owst, *Literature and pulpit in medieval England* (1933, repr 1961), 47–55, 136–48 on this lack.

34 AJ Fletcher, 'John Mirk and the Lollards', *Medium Aevum* lvi (1987), 217–24. *Dives and Pauper*, ed PH Barnum (EETS cclxxv, cclxxx 1976–80) i.81–101; this discussion forms part of the exposition of the first commandment and refers (i.82–3, 90) to *De consecratione* in the canon law (see n5 above), attaching the 'reading' of the book of imagery to this base.

35 *Mirk's Festial*, 261.

36 Camille, 'Seeing and reading', 33–4.

are presented arriving at Canterbury to make their offerings. While the knight and his companions made their way to the shrine of St Thomas the other (less well educated) members of the party sat down in the nave and started to argue about the stained glass in the windows high above their heads.

> The pardoner and the miller, and other simple fools,
> Sat themselves in the church, right as silly goats,
> Peered hard, and pored, high upon the glass,
> Counterfeiting gentlemen, to emblazon the arms,
> Unravelling the painting, and immersed in the story,
> And read it just as right as old rams are horned:
> 'He beareth a balk-staff', said the one, 'or else a rake's end.'
> 'You're wrong,' said the miller, 'you're completely mistaken;
> It's a spear, if you can see, with the point before,
> To push down his enemy, and through the shoulder bore.'
> 'Peace,' cried the host of Southwark, 'let be the window glazed!
> Go up and make your offering! You two seem half amazed!'[37]

Perhaps it was something of a literary topos to scoff in this way. Émile Mâle cites a similar passage in a thirteenth-century fabliau in which a villein had his purse stolen while he was busy pointing out the figures of Pepin and Charlemagne on the façade of Notre Dame.[38] Such jibes bear the hallmarks of literate-proud reportage. But we can set this group discussion of the window alongside Paulinus of Nola's hopes for his murals. It was not unreal to expect people to talk about imagery.

Was the imagery in stained glass always something of a special case? How much could churchgoers make out of the depictions in painted windows that were often so far above their heads, physically, let alone iconographically? To what extent were stained glass images used, or intended to be used, to inform believers?

Madeline Caviness approached these questions by examining the glazing programmes of various monastic and cathedral churches of the late twelfth and thirteenth centuries. The impression left by her investigation is that the understanding of lay people, pilgrims included, was very much a secondary consideration. Although pilgrims to the shrine of St Thomas Becket might have been aroused by seeing, as they neared it, dramatic scenes of healing depicted in the glass, at Canterbury, as at St Denis, the typological windows were esoteric, designed more for the meditation and study of resident monks than for the comprehension of visiting lay persons. Moreover even those windows that did contain gospel narratives did not lend themselves to easy reading, given the non-linear arrangement of their scenes which could be hard even for the initiated to follow. Yet it was possible to treat glass icons in ways parallel to carved or painted images – witness the testator of 1511 who left money for a light to burn before a St Christopher image in a window.[39]

Some stained glass depictions carried their own explanatory or instructive texts.

---

37 *The tale of Beryn*, ed FJ Furnivall and WG Stone (EETS extra series cv 1909), 6, cited by HS Bennett, *Chaucer and the fifteenth century* (1947), 17.

38 É Mâle, *Religious art in France: the thirteenth century* (1984), 176.

39 MH Caviness, 'Biblical stories in windows: were they bibles for the poor?' in BS Levy (ed), *The bible in the middle ages: its influence on literature and art* (1992). GMcN Rushforth, *Medieval Christian imagery* (1936), 4–5 suggested that realization of the illegibility of glass placed in high windows of the nave clerestory may have affected the glazing scheme at Great Malvern priory, Worcestershire. R Marks, *Stained glass in England during the middle ages* (1993), 60–1 (1511).

Plate 4 Hans Springinklee, *St Wilgefortis and the fiddler*, woodcut, 1513.
© copyright the British Museum

Such was the case with creed windows (of which there are various late medieval survivals, such as those of Drayton Beauchamp in Buckinghamshire, Fairford in Gloucestershire, or the glass once in the chapel of Hampton Court in Herefordshire) which set clauses of the creed around depictions of the individual apostles to whom they were traditionally credited. Placed in parish churches, in aisle or east window, where their texts were legible, such windows would have aided the credal learning that the church was expected to provide. And perhaps occasionally churches (monastic rather than parochial) contained written explanations of their stained glass. It has been suggested that the Guthlac roll of about 1210, with its roundels (containing inscriptions) of the life of St Guthlac, might have been a guide to a church window, and the same function has been proposed for a fourteenth-century roll recording the inscriptions in the typological windows of the choir aisles at Canterbury.[40] But even if the literate, or partially literate, were offered such advantages, confabulations of the kind lampooned in the *Tale of Beryn* were unlikely to have stopped.

Churchgoers certainly did discuss the meaning of images – and get them wrong. Mistakes could be formative. A new saint might be made of a misread image. The cult of St Wilgefortis (Liberata or Uncumber, an embodiment of a story that goes back to Gregory the Great) seems only to have appeared in Flanders in the fourteenth century, and spread thereafter in northern Europe, to find its place in breviaries and martyrologies (including the Roman martyrology). In the legend the saint's beard grew in answer to her prayers when her father (a pagan king of Portugal) planned to marry her to a pagan Sicilian – as the result of which resistance he had her crucified. The new cult may have sprung from misinterpretation of the *volto santo* of Lucca, a crucifix which showed Christ crowned, with open eyes, long hair and beard, and clothed in a tunic. Unfamiliarity with this form of the crucified Christ possibly gave rise, as pilgrims spread knowledge of it north of the alps, to the story of St Uncumber, an entirely fictitious person, whose sainthood resolved for puzzled northerners the apparent peculiarity of a bearded crucified royal woman (see plate 4).[41]

Images were surely often misread – and misvenerated – and by the sixteenth century reformers were all too ready to exploit such mistakes. Imagery proliferated beyond all bounds, far beyond the ecclesiastical capacity for informing, and literate critics exploited tales about the actions of credulous Christians. Though identifying surnames were added to the statues of Becket's murderers at the south door of Canterbury cathedral, it was no insurance against the misplaced devotions of those who knew no better. Such behaviour had power to shock. Calvin used an early memory of the treatment of images to illustrate his indictment of the confusions that had overtaken relics.

---

[40] Marks, 61, 78–9; MH Caviness, 'Fifteenth century stained glass from the chapel of Hampton Court, Herefordshire: the apostles' creed and other subjects', *Walpole Society* xlii (1968–70); H Wayment, *The stained glass of the church of St Mary, Fairford, Gloucestershire* (1984), 12, 14, 42–50, pls XV–XVIII. On the Guthlac roll see J Alexander and P Binski (eds), *Age of chivalry* (exhibition catalogue 1987), 215–16, no 37.

[41] M Aston, *Faith and fire* (1993), 12, 280–1; DH Farmer, *The Oxford dictionary of saints* (1987), 437–8; J Gessler, *La légende de Sainte Wilgeforte ou Ontcommer, la vierge miraculeusement barbue* (1938); GG Coulton, *Five centuries of religion* (4 vols 1923–50) i.189, 546–51; *Butler's lives of the saints*, ed H Thurston and D Attwater (4 vols 1956) iii.151–2. On the *volto santo* of Lucca see H Belting, *Likeness and presence: a history of the image before the era of art* (1994), 304–5; and K Kamerick, *Popular piety and art in the late middle ages* (2002), 57–8 (which appeared after this paper was written).

I remember seeing as a small child what was done to the images in our parish church. On the feast of St Stephen people decorated with chaplets and ribbons not only the image of the saint himself, but also those of the tyrants (to give them a common name) who stoned him. When the poor women saw the tyrants dressed up like this, they took them for companions of the saint and burned a candle for each one. What is more, the same thing happened to St Michael's devil.[42]

Maybe advancing literacy made virtual commonplaces of such observations.

Iconography has never been an easy subject. Even the learned and well read could mistake images, and it was only when the reformers of the sixteenth century began to attack ecclesiastical imagery on a scale unknown since Byzantine iconoclasm that such misreadings assumed serious proportions. One such unfortunate mistake was made in the 1540s by Stephen Gardiner, bishop of Winchester, who, in rebuking a particularly shocking case of contemporary image-breaking, pointed to the king's great seal as an example of the usefulness of imagery in inculcating respect among the illiterate.

Even a person who cannot read, said Gardiner, when he looks at the great seal, 'can read Saint George on horseback on the one side, and the king sitting in his majesty on the other side', and reading the imagery he will, if an honest man, put off his cap. It proved a most unfortunate choice. Gardiner's remarks were forwarded to Protector Somerset (himself a good iconomach), who penned a long riposte to the bishop in which he did not fail to point out the latter's error. St George on horseback on the king's seal? 'Rude and ignorant people' sometimes called it such, but certainly quite wrongly. The king was depicted on both sides of the seal: on one, mounted as in war, the chief captain and defender of his subjects; on the other enthroned in peace in the seat of justice. There was neither spear nor dragon of St George, and the inscription made the double image quite clear. This mistake, in so well read a man as Gardiner, seemed indicative of the generally misleading nature of images. 'Indeed', wrote Somerset, 'images be great letters, yet as big as they be, we have seen many, which have read them amiss . . . Nor it is not great marvel though in reading of them the lay people are many times deceived when your lordship, as appeareth hath not truly read a most true and a most common image.'[43]

Up to the reformation most people were able to take a tolerant view of such errors. The devotion seemed more important than the misconception. Looked at through the eyes of evangelistic reformers, however, the devotion itself began to seem misconceived. The church taught Christians to visualize and remember holy events and persons as they saw them represented. Believers did so, and their internal images of saints tended to resemble the gilded and richly clothed and decorated figures they saw in churches – something that scripturally conscious critics found abhorrent.

The external images were always closely related to internal mental ones, and lay books succeeded in their stated purpose of stocking believers' minds with holy icons.

---

[42] *The colloquies of Erasmus*, trans CR Thompson (1965), 304. Jean Calvin, *Traité des reliques* (1543), ed FM Higman in *Three French treatises* (1970), 96, cited by THL Parker, *John Calvin: a biography* (1975), 2. I have adapted Parker's translation; Calvin's word for the images is the contemptuous *marmousetz* (marmosets, grotesque figures, little monkeys).

[43] *Letters of Stephen Gardiner*, ed JA Muller (1933), 274; John Foxe, *Actes and monuments* (1563), 730–1; *The acts and monuments of John Foxe*, ed J Pratt (8 vols 1853–70) vi.29 (letter of Somerset to Gardiner datable to 27 May 1547).

Plate 5 Reliquary statue of Saint Foy, Conques,
mid-tenth century with later additions
photo Warburg Institute

There are plenty of examples that show how literate and illiterate alike visualized or
envisioned the saints in the forms made familiar in church art. At moments of ecstatic
revelation the virgin Mary appeared in the shape of celebrated cult statues. When
Guibert de Nogent's mother dreamt of the mother of God, she saw the virgin of
Chartres cathedral. Witbert, a peasant whose blindness was miraculously cured by
St Foy, had a vision of the saint in the guise of the famous and still surviving figure of
Conques, whose staring eyes participated in the healing of his own (see plate 5).
Christ and the saints took shape in people's minds, conscious or dreaming, in the

forms that artists had given them, however historically inappropriate. Often it was with the sheen and glitter of gold and precious stones.[44]

St Ambrose in the fourth century and St Catherine of Siena in the fourteenth, as much as the people of Knock in Ireland in 1879, recognized the authenticity of their visions through the resemblance of these miraculous appearances to the forms of art. St Ambrose knew it was St Paul who had appeared to him one night because the face was the same as that of the saint's icon. St Catherine saw two figures in her visions looking 'just as she had seen them painted in the churches'. The witnesses at Knock saw the virgin in the robed and crowned conventions of artists, and knew the saints who appeared with her from their resemblance to their statues. In the same way St Bernadette of Lourdes (1844–79) rejected the proffered reproductions of Italian art (Botticelli, Raphael, Leonardo da Vinci) as visual descriptions of the lady who kept appearing to her. The identifying likeness that she found nearest was the statue of Notre Dame des Eaux in the neighbouring church at Nevers. By what we might well regard as an essentially circular process, art – through the mental image – informed and authenticated the religious experience.[45]

Huizinga used the famous phrase 'religious thought crystallizing into images' to describe the mental habits of the middle ages. Since visual imagery is part of our thought processes, and our mental models are derived from our perceptions, there is of course a perennial truth in the observation. Malcolm Lambert's description of the visual workings of the mind of St Francis of Assisi may seem not too far removed from our own. 'His thought was always immediate, personal, and concrete. Ideas appeared to him as images. A sequence of thought for him . . . consists in leaping from one picture to the next.' Before he decided to resign from the official leadership of the order, Francis had a dream of a small black hen which, hard as she tried, was unable to cover all her brood with her wings.[46]

There is nothing unique in perceiving or presenting reality through the isolated form of a symbol. But the medieval imagery I have been considering had a content unlike most of the imagery we use nowadays. The 'mystery' and 'tangible reality' that Delacroix found in images was not the same as Margery Kempe's or St Francis of Assisi's. This is best illustrated by thinking about the role of statuary.

When considering the edifice that came to be built on Pope Gregory's words it is important to bear in mind the difference between paintings and sculpture. A painting, particularly a narrative church mural (which might, through a succession of scenes or a compilation of events, tell a story) was something quite different from a three-dimensional bust or figure of a saint. The former is obviously more analogous to a text or a book, and 'reading' it the eye is called upon to move and construe in a way comparable to following the letters on a page. The latter invokes a different kind of looking: looking *in* rather than looking *round*; the viewer may find himself or herself

---

[44] J Sumption, *Pilgrimage: an image of mediaeval religion* (1975), 52; for examples of holy persons and Christ envisioned in gold array see Aston, *Faith and fire*, 221–2.

[45] *Patrologia latina*, ed JP Migne (221 vols 1844–1903) xvii.743, epistola ii.4; Ringbom, 'Devotional images', 161; M Warner, *Alone of all her sex: the myth and cult of the virgin Mary* (1985 edn), 95, 115, 249–50 and (on St Catherine Labouré's 1830 vision) 259; V Cronin, *Mary portrayed* (1968), 156 and pl 88. On the problem of mental images in cognitive psychology see H Barlow, C Blakemore and M Weston-Smith (eds), *Images and understanding* (1990), 358–70.

[46] J Huizinga, *The waning of the middle ages* (1955), ch 12; MD Lambert, *Franciscan poverty: the doctrine of the absolute poverty of Christ and the apostles in the Franciscan order, 1210–1323* (1961), 33, 34.

less invited to work things out than to work, through meditative gazing, towards and into the person represented. This is a more isolated kind of activity, and holy images of this sort more readily allowed believers to invest the holy image with the reality of a real presence.

Carvings of Christ and the saints – specially perhaps those portable wooden images which were sometimes used as actors in liturgical drama – were a special kind of bridge between the visible and the invisible. Believers (and clerical actors) who saw a figure of Christ or the virgin enacting the part of these holy persons were encouraged to make some identification between the representation they beheld and the virgin and Christ they prayed to. There was a 'mystical equation'.[47] Statue-reliquaries which held remains of a venerated person (like the glistening bust of St Foy, or the martyr's crown of Becket at Canterbury) were specially potent images in having a physical link with their prototypes.[48] It was objects such as these, invested with the holy powers and presence of saints, that drew people in such numbers to pilgrim centres and which helped to foster belief in the active potency of the image. Such ambiguous art forms encouraged ambiguous attitudes, and the church seems to have been slow to formulate distinctions between the respective roles of images and relics. The fusion or confusion of relic and representation may have helped to foster what we might call the static veneration of cult imagery, as opposed to active, or inter-active learning from images. When the physical representation of the saint was also the physical repository of his mortal remains it became that much easier to attribute a vital presence to the image – something that always threatened the theology of worship returning to the prototype.

There were plenty of devout believers who found an almost hypnotic effect in the sculpted image at which they gazed with profound expectations. For this was a mutual relationship, given that so many holy images seemed to offer visual responses to their supplicants. Bernard of Angers, visiting Auvergne for the first time early in the eleventh century, and shocked to find gilded busts of saints revered on the altars of churches, used the vivid phrase 'with reverberating eyes' (*oculis reverberantibus*) to describe the power of eye-contact with saints' images. To many peasants who looked into the clear gaze of the image, he wrote, it seemed that through these reflecting eyes their prayers would be answered. Centuries later the same visual contemplation was remarked on by Erasmus, who wrote of the 'intent gaze' of those who prayed before images, and by Thomas More, who described London fishwives staring 'so fixedly' at a statue of the virgin, 'that they imagine it smiles upon them'.[49]

The Gregorian commonplace was pulled in different directions through the long centuries of the church's growing encouragement of the arts. Perhaps looking at the

---

[47] This is the expression of IH Forsyth, 'Magi and majesty: a study of romanesque sculpture and liturgical drama', *Art Bulletin* l (1968), 222, cited in Aston, *England's iconoclasts*, 403, where this question is pursued further.

[48] Belief, not actuality, was of course what counted. On the question of Becket's skull see AJ Mason, *What became of the bones of St Thomas?* (1920), 49–55, 96–107 and J Butler, *The quest for Becket's bones* (1995), 31, 90, 125–6.

[49] Aston, *England's iconoclasts*, 25 n16, 107 n40, 401 n65, 420 n13. In a sermon of 1375 Thomas Brinton spoke of eagles looking at the sun *sine oculorum reverberacione*: did this expression (literally striking back or rebounding gaze) originate in the vocabulary of optics? *The sermons of Thomas Brinton, Bishop of Rochester (1373–1389)*, ed MA Devlin (2 vols Camden 3rd series lxxxv–vi 1954) ii.251.

changing vocabulary in which these matters were discussed may help to clarify some of the alterations that took place in this theory of church imagery. We need to be on the alert to these verbal shifts when trying to unravel the meaning of that problematical term, *laymen's books*.

Pope Gregory, though he mentioned those who could not read *codices*, the *idiotae*, was thinking in terms of *lectio* rather than books, and the images he had in mind were paintings of histories (*picturae historiam . . . depingi historias . . . admisit*) in which people could learn stories (*scientia historiae*). Two centuries later it was still historical paintings (*picturae historiarum*) of Christ and his saints that concerned Walafrid Strabo. He described such painting as 'writing for the unlettered' (*litteratura illitterato*) from which histories of the ancients could be learned, and went on to observe that the 'simple and ignorant' (*simplices et idiotae*), who could hardly be brought to the faith by words, were greatly moved by the picture of Christ's passion, so that forms of this kind could be impressed on their hearts like letters.[50]

When we reach the thirteenth century the images that are to serve non-readers include ornaments as well as pictures, and sculptures may come before paintings. Those who were to benefit from such representations are the ignorant and simple (*rudes simplices* or *simplices*; the *simplicium ruditas* of Aquinas and Bonaventure), for whom these works are the 'readings and scriptures of the lay people' (*sunt laicorum lectiones et scripturae*) in the words of Durandus. 'A token and a book to the lewed people' was the phrase used early in the fifteenth century by the author of *Dives and Pauper*, simultaneously citing Gregory and paraphrasing the extrapolations of the thirteenth century. The first use of the term *libri laicorum* that I have noticed is in the *Pictor in carmine* of about 1200, where it is applied to paintings in churches that can suggest divine things to the unlearned and stir up the learned to the love of the scriptures.[51]

Perhaps we can detect the effect of two concurrent processes at work here, two processes that were already under strain and that were eventually to pull apart: the growth of imagery and the extension of literacy. What had started out as a complementary liaison of *scriptura* and *pictura* had almost turned into an apposition of *scriptura* and *sculptura* – and in some hands it did turn into a physical contest. In the thirteenth century there were increasing numbers and more kinds of both books and images. Sculptures and ornaments were enlisted alongside scriptural paintings as aids to Christian learning and devotion, and devotion and learning did not go hand in hand. Those who defended church imagery were less likely to write about its value for the learned and literate. Meanwhile the extension of vernacular literacy brought its own challenge to the fully *literati*.

---

[50] *S Gregorii magni registrum epistularum*, 874 (XI.10). Walafrid Strabo in *Patrologia latina* cxiv.927–30: *Primum quidem, quia pictura est quaedam litteratura illiterato, adeo ut quidam priorum legatur ex picturis didicisse antiquorum historias . . . Et videmus aliquando simplices et idiotas qui verbis vix ad fidem gestorum possunt perduci, ex pictura passionis dominicae vel aliorum mirabilium ita compungi, ut lacrymis testentur exteriores figuras cordi suo quasi litteris impressas.* Cf Duggan, 'Book of the illiterate', 230.

[51] James, '*Pictor in carmine*', 142 (*picturis delectentur que tanquam libri laicorum simplicibus divina suggerant, et literatos ad amorem excitent scripturarum*); Aquinas, *Scriptum*, ed Mandonnet iii.312; *Bonaventurae opera omnia* iii.203; Durandus, *Rationale*, 24, trans Neale and Webb 56; *Dives and Pauper* i.82–3. Camille, 'Gregorian definition', 92 points to Albert the Great. The phrase that became established in the twelfth century was *litteratura laicorum*: GB Ladner, *Images and ideas in the middle ages* (2 vols 1983) ii.68; Camille, 'Seeing and reading', 32.

It is surely no coincidence that the phrase *libri laicorum*, though it had a long ancestry, came into currency at a time when books were growing in number and importance, and when the clerical estate was increasingly conscious of its standing vis-à-vis the laity. As more lay people became book-conscious and book-capable, lay books proper began to compete with the ancient form of laymen's books. The great variety of texts through which people in all classes approached the faith in the later middle ages included both illustrated books and texts without pictures. In the fourteenth century the illustrated *Speculum humanae salvationis* was presented as a laymen's book to instruct both laymen and clerks, while early in the fifteenth century the imageless vernacular text of Nicholas Love's *Mirror of the blessed life of Jesus Christ* had in mind men and women of 'simple understanding', whose spiritual edification had to be fed on different meat from that of the clergy; 'a simple soul . . . can not think but bodies or bodily things', and needed a special spiritual diet.[52]

Maybe there were miscalculations here. Certainly there were 'simple souls' with a taste for clerical food. The dismissal of the 'dumb schoolmastering' of images took place in a world where lay people found their own revelation by reading scripture. Visual proxies were rejected. Robert Plumpton, twenty years old and studying law in London, wrote home to Yorkshire about 1536 to tell his mother that she must waste no time; she must study the new testament for herself. Never before had divine truth been so directly accessible. 'The teaching of the Gospel . . . is the thing that all we must live by . . . I would desire you for the love of God, that you would read the New Testament, which is the true Gospel of God, spoken by the Holy Ghost . . . Mother, you have much to thank God that it would please him to give you licence to live until this time.'[53] In Robert Plumpton's day images were losing their voices, thanks to the new accessibility and assertiveness of scriptural word and page.

---

[52] Nicholas Love, *The mirrour of the blessed lyf of Jesu Christ*, ed LF Powell (1908), 8–9.
[53] AG Dickens, *Lollards and protestants in the diocese of York* (1959), 134.

13

The Triumph of the Hall in Fifteenth-Century Oxford

JEREMY CATTO

Trevor Aston's fascination with the academic halls of Oxford was an abiding theme in his long involvement with the history of the University of Oxford. It resulted in one important article on John Rous's list of the halls, and in the particular attention to halls which he ensured in the making of the computerized index to Emden's biographical registers of the university. As a result it was possible to make the most of the evidence of particular halls and their known inhabitants in the two earliest volumes of the History of the University of Oxford, and to tabulate the information in two annotated maps which have taken further than before our understanding of their place in both the city and the university. The following observations on these elusive institutions, while they may not have elicited his assent, might perhaps have been accorded his amused indulgence at an apparent paradox. They may at least be a tribute to his memory.

'If one change more than another characterized the passing of the medieval order in the University of Oxford, it was the supersession of the Halls by the Colleges.' In these words, touched with a note of regret, AB Emden opened his extraordinarily original and groundbreaking study of his own society, St Edmund Hall, published in 1927.[1] It was an evident truism that by then, with the exception of St Edmund Hall, colleges stood where once there had been halls, performing the task of undergraduate education which had originally been aularian business. The fact of the matter was beyond contradiction, underlining the exceptionalism of the solitary survivor. From a peak of 123 known halls in 1313 their number had declined to about 70 in 1436, 62 in 1505, 18 by 1513 and only 8 by 1552.[2] But decline in the number of academic halls does not of necessity imply the destitution of the halls, particularly when it is observed that of those 123 halls, the sites of one hundred, or 82 per cent, are still in academic use today. Indeed the contrary case will be argued here, namely that the idea of the hall and its education swamped and extinguished the original concept of the college in the fifteenth and sixteenth century; and that this development exemplified in England a new set of cultural values, which in Italy was expressed and practised by Vittorino da Feltre and Guarino Guarini and which generally prevailed in early modern Europe.

---

[1] AB Emden, *An Oxford hall in medieval times* (1927, repr 1968), 1.
[2] For halls in 1313 see JI Catto and TAR Evans (eds), *The early Oxford schools* (History of the University of Oxford i 1984), map 3 (compiled by J Munby); for the caution list of 1436 see *Registrum cancellarii oxoniensis 1434–1469*, ed HE Salter (2 vols Oxford Historical Society xciii–iv 1932) i.21–2; for the number of halls in 1505, 1513 and 1552 see JK McConica, 'The rise of the undergraduate college' in JK McConica (ed), *The collegiate university* (History of the University of Oxford iii 1986), 52.

The academic halls were the cells of which the body of the medieval university was constituted. While it would not be true to say that every matriculated student lived in a hall, the vast majority probably did by the fourteenth century. Here some definition is required. In essence, the academic hall was simply a house; the name 'hall' is derived from the hall-houses of any thirteenth-century town; a typical shape, among many varieties, might be the L-shape of a narrow street frontage and a long wing behind, two storeys high, of which the central feature was a hall rising through both storeys and open to the roof above a hearth in the middle. Such houses were rented from a variety of owners, most frequently from one of the local religious houses; some, notably Tackley's Inn, may have been built specifically for the academic market. But they could fluctuate between academic and lay domestic use, as one of the chief sources of evidence, the rentals of Oseney Abbey and the hospital of St John, often record.[3] However there was a further distinction: a proper academic hall was ruled by a principal, who exercised some authority over the inmates. Communities of this kind must have achieved a certain regularity by the time the statute *De domibus* was enacted, perhaps about 1290; the statute implies that the academic hall and its principalship were already established institutions.[4] The hall provided an exclusively academic environment for the young scholar; within its framework the university allowed masters of arts or doctors of higher faculties to sustain themselves through the enterprise of educating undergraduates. It accorded them certain privileges if they undertook to be principals, recognized their authority, and regulated their position by recording the caution money they paid year by year for the right to rule a particular hall. It would be reasonable to assume, though before the fifteenth century difficult to prove, that the halls in general were units not only of residence but of education: the principal being also the master and the members of his hall his matriculated pupils, allowing for a kind of tutorial or informal teaching within the walls to supplement the public lectures.[5]

The academic hall, then, must have been adopted as a deliberate stratagem by the university, a sensible elaboration of the control which the system of matriculation afforded it. If every scholar must be registered on a master's roll before enjoying academic privileges, there was an obvious advantage for public tranquillity and order if his form of residence – a matter of concern already in the earliest university privilege of 1214 – could also be controlled. When this official preference crystallized is difficult to determine: before *De domibus*, certainly, and probably before 1280, the date of the earliest Oseney Abbey rental showing a substantial number of university masters renting premises which would later be academic halls. Scholars living in the house of their master seems to be one of the forms of residence recorded in a deposition recording the names and lodgings of the scholars who rioted against the papal

3   The physical character of the hall is analysed on the basis of specific examples by WA Pantin, 'The halls and schools of medieval Oxford: an attempt at reconstruction', *Oxford studies presented to Daniel Callus* (Oxford Historical Society new series xvi 1964). The rentals of Oseney Abbey up to 1498 are printed in *Cartulary of Oseney Abbey*, ed HE Salter (6 vols Oxford Historical Society lxxxix–xci, xcvii–viii, ci 1929–36) iii.102–286. Another is partially transcribed in Oxford, Bodleian Library, Wood MS D.2, p 429. Those of the hospital of St John up to 1487 are in *A cartulary of the hospital of St John the Baptist*, ed HE Salter (3 vols Oxford Historical Society lxvi, lxxvii, lxix 1914–16) iii.32–292.
4   *Statuta antiqua universitatis oxoniensis*, ed S Gibson (1931), 78–81.
5   The fragmentary evidence for this is collected in JI Catto, 'Citizens, scholars and masters' in Catto and Evans, *Early Oxford schools*, 188–9.

legate Otto in 1238: the well known canon lawyer Mr William of Lichfield and his students are there recorded inhabiting a single house together, the future Wilby Hall in the High Street.[6] But it was only one of several forms of residence recorded in this and other contemporary documents. Some scholars lived with their countrymen apparently without a master, notably a group from Killaloe in Ireland; a group of Scottish scholars, according to a fragmentary account of about 1250, lived in a house rented by their richer compatriot William Bernham, an arrangement which would be common in the fourteenth century.[7] In these earliest years of the university the academic hall evidently had yet to emerge as a distinct category. But the privileges accorded by university statute to such halls by the time *De domibus* was enacted show that before long the university authorities would consistently prefer them as student residences; and by 1410 residence in a hall or college had become, at least in theory, compulsory.

By 1313 it is possible to map the halls, by combining the evidence of the rentals of the two greatest landlords and a city rent assessment; some of them will have been omitted, and the 123 halls to which we can put a name are a minimum. These very numerous, rather ephemeral and doubtless utilitarian units of residence appear together only in rentals and rent assessments, perhaps significantly. It is possibly a sign that they had come to mean something more to their inhabitants that by the 1440s one of them, the antiquary John Rous, should have made a list of them with their specializations of subject and locality: the first of a line of Oxford antiquaries, among whom Anthony Wood, Emden and Aston himself would be numbered, to be diverted by their curious charm.[8] The list was drawn up with some care, probably in 1444 or 1445, when its author was the presumably titular principal of Sekyll Hall, an annexe of Hampton Hall in Turl Street (then St Mildred's Street or Lane). Rous's regard for the halls is matched by other fifteenth-century evidence that by then they were real communities, the foci of student rivalries in spoof letters in the mock-heroic style, and the starting point for some lifelong friendships. Cases involving their administration recorded in the chancellor's register, and the issue of the aularian statutes by Chancellor John Russell about 1490, indicate the care with which the conduct of the halls was monitored.

The careful attention paid to academic halls in fifteenth-century Oxford must put the notion of their decline under question. The progressive decay of that institution, and the rise of the college in its place, has seemed obvious since Hastings Rashdall's account of medieval Oxford in 1895; as Emden put it 'the halls had now [in 1559] been engaged for at least a century in a losing battle with the colleges'.[9] The palpable fact that whereas in 1400 most scholars resided in halls and in 1927 they mostly resided in colleges was to all appearances evidence enough. But if Emden subscribed to this interpretation of the demise of the halls on empirical grounds, Rashdall as the first great historian of the European universities of the middle ages as a whole had a larger conception in mind: he wished to sustain the general theory that an original

---

6 *Close rolls of the reign of Henry III preserved in the Public Record Office* (15 vols 1902–75), iv.136–8.
7 NR Ker and WA Pantin, 'Letters of a Scottish student at Paris and Oxford c.1250', *Formularies which bear on the history of Oxford c.1204–1420*, ed HE Salter, WA Pantin and HG Richardson (2 vols Oxford Historical Society new series iv–v 1942) ii.472–91.
8 See JI Catto and TAR Evans (eds), *Late medieval Oxford* (History of the University of Oxford ii 1992), map 2 (compiled by J Munby); TH Aston, 'The date of John Rous's list of the colleges and academical halls of Oxford', *Oxoniensia* xlii (1977).
9 Emden, *Oxford hall*, 263.

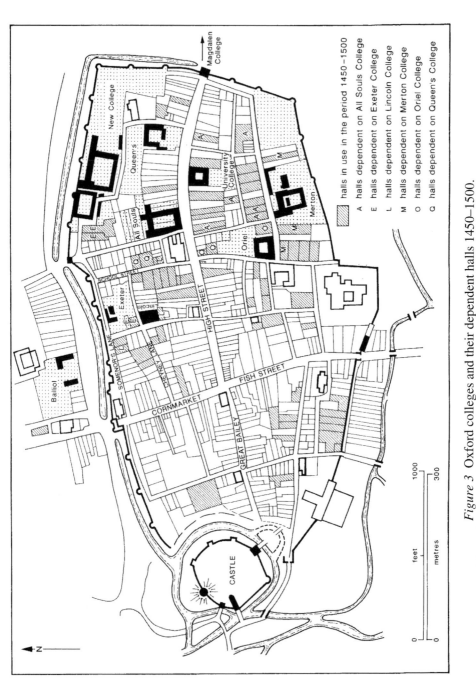

Figure 3 Oxford colleges and their dependent halls 1450–1500.

Adapted version of map 2 in JI Catto and TAR Evans (eds), *Late medieval Oxford*
(History of the University of Oxford ii 1992). Reproduced by kind permission of Oxford University Press

state of student freedom, exemplified in Oxford in the informal societies of the halls, was superseded at the end of the middle ages by a new and restrictive discipline, of which the instruments were the colleges with their rules of conduct and their penalties.[10] His view was fortified by the ancient literary myth or topos of the student reveller, reflected in Chaucer's *Miller's tale*, in the *Tales of Scogan* and countless schoolboy Latin proses, the origin of which can be found in the work of the Anglo-Norman satirists of the twelfth century and in the great drinking songs of the *Carmina burana*. In practice Rashdall took most of his evidence for student freedom from very late sources which were steeped in the student-reveller topos: the reminiscences of the sixteenth-century German wandering scholar Thomas Platter and the Heidelberg dialogues for teaching Latin, the *Manuale scholarium*, written about 1490; both of which, the first more or less factual, the second purely fictional, aimed merely to amuse, or instruct by amusement, within a literary convention.[11] That limitation precludes such sources from throwing any but the most indirect light on the supposedly contemporary imposition of discipline, or any at all on the notional preceding state of student freedom. Nevertheless, Rashdall's general theory has burgeoned in the twentieth century. It has contributed to the far-reaching theme of Philippe Ariès, in his *Centuries of childhood*, that in the middle ages the concepts of childhood and adolescence had not become specific, and that there was therefore no discipline peculiar to the young; the child, before the emergence of the idea of childhood in the early modern era, was treated as an adult and was therefore as free from restraint. The thesis of Ariès has been followed by an impressive effort to analyse fraternities of youth, the *bachelleries*, *jouvenceaux* and 'abbeys of youth', by Natalie Zeman Davis and others, and the theme of folly, the ritual reversal of established authority in processions, carnivals and Christmas plays.[12] Since the evidence for these phenomena, significant as they are, is found only in fifteenth- and sixteenth-century sources, it cannot be used with confidence to posit a residual subculture of student freedom subsisting in the halls, descending from that Atlantis, a golden age of student liberty. It might as well reflect, in its harmless seasonal manifestations, the students' effective domestication as their supposed ancient freedom. Rashdall's identification of this prelapsarian paradise with the regime of the Oxford academic halls in even its earliest phase owes more to literary convention than to historical research.

In contradistinction to these large conceptions, the apparently trivial topographical adjustments and domestic arrangements of actual Oxford halls in the age of transition can provide realistic, albeit dry material on fifteenth-century halls. The evidence comes primarily from a rather unpromising source, the sixteen lists of cautions depos-

---

[10] See H Rashdall, *The universities of Europe in the middle ages* (2 vols 1895, new edn by FM Powicke and AB Emden 3 vols 1936) iii.352–97.

[11] Thomas Platter, *Lebenserinnerungen*, ed R Schudel-Benz (1969); *Manuale scholarium*, ed F Zarncke in *Die deutschen Universitäten im Mittelalter* (1857), 1–48. The *Manuale* was a dialogue for teaching Latin written at Heidelberg shortly before 1500 and based on a slightly earlier tract, Paulus Niavis's *Latinum ydeoma*. See G Streckenbach, 'Paulus Niavis *Latinum ydeoma pro novellis studentibus*: ein Gesprächbuchlein aus dem letzten Viertel des 15 Jahrhunderts', *Mittelatinisches Jahrbuch* vi–vii (1970–2); G Streckenbach, 'Das *Manuale scholarium* und das *Latinum ydeoma pro novellis studentibus* des Paulus Niavis', ibid x (1975), 232–70.

[12] P Ariès, *Centuries of childhood*, trans R Baldick (1962); NZ Davis, 'The reasons of misrule: youth groups and charivari in sixteenth-century France', *Past and Present* 50 (Feb 1971); RC Trexler, 'Ritual in Florence: adolescence and salvation in the Renaissance' in C Trinkaus and HA Oberman (eds), *The pursuit of holiness in late medieval and renaissance religion* (1974).

ited by principals of halls preserved in the surviving chancellor's register of 1436 to 1469, and to a lesser extent in that for the years 1498 to 1506.[13] The intervening register is unfortunately lost. These lists record the names of particular halls with their annexes, and the names of the masters who had offered their pledges to take them as principals for the following year. The names of the principals, thanks to Emden's work, can be given flesh and blood and we can partly see, as the lists accumulate, what they were about.[14] It was a rule that no principal could put down a caution for more than one hall, and also that once a property was rented out for the use of scholars it could only return to lay use if the owner proposed to reside there personally.[15] Both these rules were being strained to breaking point in the fifteenth century as larger, more articulated halls struggled to be born, and the caution lists give glimpses of the underlying reality. For the lists, if tabulated systematically, show that an informal system of undergraduate colleges was already coming into existence, not by superseding the halls but by incorporating them in larger schemes of education: a system which could just as accurately be described as the takeover of the colleges by the business of aularian education as by the victory of the colleges over halls. The caution lists, unlike the rentals, offer evidence directly on the actual use of the halls; their ownership remained fragmented. That is what makes their real character difficult to isolate. Their occupiers seem to have found it perfectly feasible to maintain elaborate institutions with no property and no legal existence for several generations in these conditions. Such informality simplified their own projects, but makes difficulties for the historian.

The more familiar feature which comes to light from examining the caution lists is the informal but often enduring relationship between groups of halls and a particular college, fellows of which occupy the principalship in succession. Sometimes this followed from a college being the landlord of particular halls, such as Oriel of St Mary Hall and Bedel Hall, or Exeter of Hart Hall in New College Lane.[16] But it could just as

---

13 *Registrum cancellarii 1434–1469* i.21–2, 39–41, 123–5, 132–5, 214–16, 247–9, 284–7, 336–9, 403–6, ii.1–4, 48–51, 85–9, 121, 291–3, 321–2; *Registrum cancellarii 1498–1506*, ed WT Mitchell (Oxford Historical Society new series xxvii 1980), 41–2, 55, 184–5, 215–17, 247–9.

14 Emden himself used the material to examine the careers of aularian principals in his 'Oxford academical halls in the later middle ages' in JJG Alexander and MT Gibson (eds), *Medieval learning and literature: essays presented to RW Hunt* (1976).

15 *Statuta antiqua*, ed Gibson, 81, 79.

16 All Oxford properties mentioned below are identified by the reference numbers given in HE Salter, *Survey of Oxford*, ed WA Pantin and WT Mitchell (2 vols Oxford Historical Society new series xiv, xx 1961–9). Oriel's group of halls was compact, contiguous to the college, and stable from at least 1436. St Mary Hall and Bedel Hall (SE 27 and SE 80), both the property of the college (Bedel Hall only after 1455), regularly had its fellows as principals and were amalgamated into one by 1505: see Pantin, 'Halls and schools', 41–6. Martin Hall (SE 79) was also contiguous; its principal was a fellow (or the provost) throughout the period covered by the chancellor's registers, though it was the property of St Frideswide's priory until 1503. The connection of Exeter College with Peter (or Wiger) Hall (NE 66) and Checker Hall (NE 67) in Turl Street was similar. They adjoined the college's site and were probably in use by its fellows early in the fifteenth century, as William Andrew (fellow 1404–22) was successively principal of Checker Hall (1411) and Peter Hall (1417): see AB Emden, *A biographical register of the University of Oxford to A.D. 1500* (3 vols 1957–9; hereafter *BRUO*) i.36. Checker Hall was bought by the college in 1405, Peter Hall in 1470. Black Hall (NE 197) and Hart Hall (NE 198) in New College Lane were further away, but were occupied by fellows of or sojourners in Exeter from 1436 at least, and from 1468 possibly together. Though Nicholas Gosse (principal of Black Hall 1450–2) and John Arundel the younger (principal from 1461 until at least 1469) were not fellows they were south-westerners closely connected with the college: *BRUO* ii.795, i.50–1. The elder John

easily happen through custom or proximity, and without property rights. Fellows of All Souls took over George Hall, opposite the college in the High, about 1450; in the 1460s they extended their dominion over Lion Hall to the south, in Magpie Lane; by 1500 their informal empire reached down as far as St John's (Merton) Street, to Beam Hall.[17] Queen's had a fluctuating but recurrent interest in the three halls opposite Brasenose, in School Street, which have long been levelled to make Radcliffe Square; from 1501 the college transferred its interest to St Edmund Hall, of which it took a lease from Oseney Abbey about 1530.[18] Lincoln, a newcomer to the business, had a natural interest in Hampton Hall next door from the 1440s, and sporadically in Glasen Hall, one of the School Street halls, from the same decade. Later it developed the policy of acquiring property rights in halls and awaiting the chance to colonize them: Hampton Hall in 1463; Staple Hall, the central property of the School Street block, in 1483; and Laurence Hall in Somenor's Lane (now Ship Street), occupied by a succession of Exeter College principals, in 1476. Hampton Hall was evidently incorporated into the college, and Laurence Hall had a Lincoln principal by 1503, while the whole School Street block was taken over from Queen's in 1501.[19] Merton College was content to expand eastwards, over Alban Hall, and westwards over Corner Hall which it owned and Urban Hall, both on the site of Corpus.[20] Only New College and Magdalen stood aside from the scramble for halls, having within their walls accom-

---

Arundel, whose aularian accounts of 1424 survive, seems to have been principal of this hall in 1419, if a reference to 'John Arundel, clerk' as a neighbouring occupier to a house in Cat Street refers to him: Salter, *Survey* i.96 and HE Salter, 'An Oxford hall in 1424' in HWC Davis (ed), *Essays in history presented to RL Poole* (1927).

17   William Potman (fellow of All Souls 1447–59) was the first of a series of fellows to occupy George Hall (SE 32); Robert Byrt combined with it the neighbouring Lion Hall through a nominee in 1467. John Game (fellow 1488–1501 or later) was principal of Beam Hall with St John Hall attached (SE 187–8) in 1501–2, while Thomas Mors (fellow 1495–1501) was principal of William Hall (SE 222) opposite them in Kybald Street. *BRUO* iii.1506–7, ii.335, ii.741, ii.1315–16.

18   John Trope (fellow of Queen's 1436–51 or later) was principal of Staple Hall (NE 101) in 1436 and 1438, and of Little Black Hall (NE 102) from 1452 to 1462 or longer. By 1469 Thomas Hudson (fellow 1466–76) was in his own or nominees' names principal of both these halls and of the adjoining Glasen Hall (NE 99). *BRUO* iii.1909, ii.979. They were still grouped together, with fellows of Queen's as principals, in the next surviving caution list, that drawn up in September 1501, but at the end of October they had passed to Thomas Drax, fellow and future rector of Lincoln: *Registrum cancellarii 1498–1506*, 247; *BRUO* i.593. His predecessor at Staple Hall, Thomas Cawse (fellow of Queen's from 1497 until at least 1503), clearly the actual principal of all three halls, ceded his right to Drax on transferring his and the college's interest to St Edmund Hall in Queen's Lane, a closer and more convenient property; Cawse was the first of a long line of principals who were also fellows of Queen's. *BRUO* i.375–6; Emden, *Oxford hall*, 222. The association of Queen's with Little Black Hall may have been of even longer standing, as John Wyclif, a sojourner in the college in the 1370s, seems to have been under house-arrest there, presumably as its principal, in 1378: JI Catto, 'Wyclif and Wycliffism in Oxford' in Catto and Evans, *Late medieval Oxford*, 207.

19   John Tristrope (fellow of Lincoln from 1445) was principal of Glasen Hall 1444–9; William Layly (fellow 1445–8) was principal of Hampton Hall 1438–47. *BRUO* iii.1908–9, ii.1114. As these examples show, Lincoln was in some ways an association of existing principals of halls. On Lincoln's purchase of Hampton Hall (NE 62), its acquisition of Laurence Hall (NE 27) by the legacy of Richard Bulkeley the grammar-master, and its acquisition of Staple Hall see Salter, *Survey* i.51, 35, 72. See also VHH Green, *The commonwealth of Lincoln College 1427–1977* (1979), 32, 38, 42–3.

20   Alban Hall (SE 199–200), a property of Littlemore Priory which Merton leased in 1496, had fellows of Merton as principals from the earliest surviving caution-list which mentions it (1438): Salter, *Survey* i.250. The succession of fellows as principals of Urban Hall (SE 206) and Corner Hall (SE 208) began in 1457, after which they were effectively united: ibid 251–3; *BRUO* i.290 (Henry Bryan), iii.1606–7 (William Rumsey).

modation for undergraduates. It is clear, therefore, from the accumulation of evidence for a casual but consistent and enduring relation of colleges with particular halls, in which an undergraduate population was taught by some of the fellows, that at least from the 1440s a number of broader college communities were in process of formation. These larger bodies, the majority of whose members were engaged in the process of tutorial learning and teaching, were closer in character to the small academic hall of the fourteenth century than to the collegiate corporation of masters. All the colleges founded before 1379 had been in various forms bodies of masters and bachelors. Their founders did not ignore the duty of education: the portionists of Merton, the poor boys of Queen's, the sophisters of Exeter attest to their variably directed but consistent interest in the formation of younger scholars. But none of these arrangements resulted in more than a handful of young scholars, most of them in a rather lowly position, in institutions whose primary purpose was the encouragement of more advanced studies. The idea of an integrated institution where undergraduates, bachelors, masters and doctors of the higher faculties could study within the same walls in the regular course of events was introduced to Oxford only with the foundation of New College in 1379, though it evidently had a precedent in the King's Hall at Cambridge.[21] But if New College embodied the pedagogical values of its era in an ideal form, it could not be imitated without a princely benefaction. The emergence of informal networks of halls, therefore, may be seen as a practical alternative inspired by the same values. It was a real, if hidden innovation in Oxford, a century or so before the direct incorporation of undergraduates into colleges became common. The phenomenon certainly does not indicate that halls were a decayed appendage of colleges: they were desirable going concerns, whose principals could make a profit from their halls which well exceeded the meagre emoluments of college fellows. Their activities soon absorbed a large proportion of the fellows of fifteenth-century colleges into the business of instruction of the young.

A less familiar aspect of the fifteenth-century halls soon becomes apparent from the perusal of the chancellor's caution lists. As Pantin showed, they themselves had absorbed neighbouring properties in the course of the fourteenth century, and had often consolidated their buildings into larger, more collegiate-looking blocks, or superhalls, as we might call them. By 1500, for instance, St Mary Hall and Bedel Hall, two short frontages with longer wings behind, had become a single three-sided quadrangle. What has not perhaps been observed is a phenomenon which underlines the vigour of the halls: the emergence of independent groups of halls linked apparently by groups of cooperating masters, or by a single effective principal who employed other masters as his assistants, technically being the principals of dependent halls which might in fact now be gardens – among them, apparently, John Rous, the nominal principal of Sekyll Hall. What we might call 'Greater St Edmund Hall' emerged in the mid-fifteenth century: an amalgam of the original hall, St Hugh Hall to the south and White Hall to the south-east under John Thamys, a bachelor of theology and one of the inner group who ran the university at the time. He maintained at least two tutors, Thomas Lee, who eventually succeeded him, and Thomas Hille, who each had the title of principal of a dependent hall. With new buildings put up about 1460, it was

---

21 See AB Cobban, *The King's Hall within the University of Cambridge in the later middle ages* (1969), 43–65; AB Cobban, 'Colleges and halls 1380–1500' in Catto and Evans, *Late medieval Oxford*, 589–93.

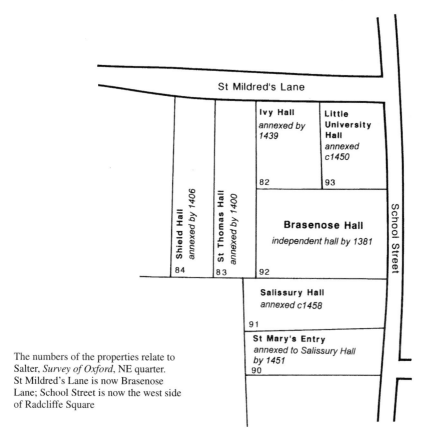

St Mildred's Lane

Ivy Hall
annexed by
1439

82

Little
University
Hall
annexed
c1450

93

Shield Hall
annexed by 1406

St Thomas Hall
annexed by 1400

84

83

Brasenose Hall
independent hall by 1381

92

School Street

Salissury Hall
annexed c1458

91

St Mary's Entry
annexed to Salissury Hall
by 1451

90

The numbers of the properties relate to
Salter, *Survey of Oxford*, NE quarter.
St Mildred's Lane is now Brasenose
Lane; School Street is now the west side
of Radcliffe Square

Figure 4 Site of Brasenose Hall and College 1381–1512

clearly a flourishing institution.[22] Another multicellular organism was emerging in
School Street. Here a group of halls was in the possession of University College, the
original home of which had been on the corner of the street and St Mildred's (now
Brasenose) Lane. When the masters migrated to their High Street site about 1332,
they let their main property, Brasenose Hall, first as schools (lecture rooms) for
university use but by 1381 as a hall, and kept the properties behind, Shield Hall and St
Thomas Hall, as dependent halls.[23] Within twenty years Brasenose Hall, under its

[22] See Emden, *Oxford hall*, 165–73; Pantin, 'Halls and schools', 69–71.
[23] Brasenose Hall (NE 92) was evidently no longer a building with four schools as it had been in 1279
(Salter, *Survey* i.67) since in the rents recorded from 1381 in the University College archives a single
lump sum of £3 6s 8d was paid: Oxford, University College, archives, BU1/F/1 (formerly EE.1.1) and
following. St Thomas Hall (NE 83) had been acquired by the college in 1353, Shield Hall (NE 84)
between 1341 and 1375, perhaps to create a large satellite 'superhall': Salter, *Survey* i.60–1. If so,
plans had changed by 1381, when the latter two halls and Little University Hall (SE 93), the college's
original site, were run as part of the college's domestic operation with repairs appearing on the
accounts: University College, archives, BU1/F/1 (formerly EE.1.1), 1381–2 (St Thomas Hall and
Shield Hall), BU1/F/3 (formerly EE.1.3), 1383–4 (Little University Hall). Brasenose Hall must have
been let on something like a full repairing lease as a separate operation, as repairs are not entered in the

principal Mr John Legh, was on the point of a significant expansion which must have changed its character; a new lease, clearly intended to be permanent, united it with the properties behind to create a 'superhall', a large block of contiguous properties which could house as many inhabitants as many colleges. Though nothing is known of his assistants, he must have employed several if his hall resembled that of Mr John Arundel in 1424. We know nothing of Legh, save that he was a midlander. He may, however, claim to be the true founder of Brasenose. His successors expanded the base of the college: by 1439 they held the garden between St Thomas Hall and Little University Hall that was the site of the former Ivy Hall; they took over Little University Hall, on the corner site, about 1450, and Salissury Hall to the south about 1458; and by 1500 they had established some claim to halls further south and had almost reached the High Street. William Sutton, who was principal from 1467 to 1484, must have been responsible for much of this expansion, and it is clear that the hall commanded the loyalty and affection of its members, among whom in all probability were Sutton's kinsman Sir Richard Sutton and William Smith, later bishop of Lincoln. In 1512 the two putative old Brasenose men completed their purchase of the site, endowed the community and had it incorporated as Brasenose College. In that year it was over one hundred and twenty years old.[24]

The best business prospect for an aspiring principal was probably a hall for canon and civil lawyers. Their students, older and better-heeled, could pay more for their instruction and keep, and it is noticeable that in the caution lists for 1501 and 1503 the surviving small halls, Beke's Inn, Neville's Inn and a few others were all legal halls. Larger legal halls were an even better prospect: there are some signs about 1440 of a large conglomeration forming on the site of Pembroke College; but it would have no continuous existence.[25] The destiny of another legal hall, the White Hall complex in Cheyney Lane (now Market Street) and Somenor's Lane (Ship Street) was more direct. Its core was the so-called White Hall in Cheyney Lane, a property of St Frideswide's priory which had become an academic hall probably between 1313 and 1348. Some time afterwards it absorbed Hawk Hall to the west, and in the early

---

college accounts. In 1400 the plan changed again, with a lease to Mr John Legh for twenty years of both Brasenose and St Thomas halls: ibid E/A2/D4 (formerly A.2.4), renewed in 1418, E/A2/D5 (formerly A.2.5). Thereafter Brasenose and its satellite halls formed a permanent and distinct entity. See *Account rolls of University College, Oxford*, transcribed by ADM Cox, ed RH Darwall-Smith (2 vols Oxford Historical Society new series xxxix–xl 1999–2001) i.2, 1, 24; I am grateful to Dr Darwall-Smith for allowing me to consult his edition in proof.

24 On the absorption of Ivy Hall and Little University Hall see Salter, *Survey* i.60, 69. Salissury Hall was taken by Robert Benet in 1458; as a previous nominal principal of Shield Hall and St Thomas Hall he was an associate of William Church, the principal of Brasenose. *BRUO* i.166, i.421. On Principal William Sutton, Sir Richard Sutton and William Smyth see *BRUO* iii.1826–7 (William Sutton), iii.1721–2 (William Smyth); IS Leadam, 'The early years of the college', *Brasenose College quatercentenary monographs* (2 vols in 3 Oxford Historical Society lii–iv 1909) ii/1.

25 Mr Robert Hall (later a bachelor of canon law) was principal of Broadgates Hall (SW 100) for three days in 1443 and tendered for it in 1444; he was principal of Beef Hall (SW 70) 1444–53 and of Athelstan Hall (SW 69) 1458–69, a property which he evidently owned at his death in 1481. *BRUO* ii.851; Salter, *Survey* ii.61–2. The property was united with its neighbours St Michael Hall, St James Hall, Durham Hall (together SW 103) and Minot Hall (SW 102) in 1501 under the principalship of Mr Thomas Kaye: *Registrum cancellarii 1498–1506*, 248; *BRUO* ii.1027. The amalgamation may well have been effected before 1487 when Mr William Grey was principal of Minot Hall (he was still principal in 1499): *BRUO* ii.825. But it seems to have been separate from its neighbour Broadgates Hall, and by 1550 Beef Hall was leased for the use of townsmen. Broadgates Hall at that time was an annexe of Christ Church, before its eventual transformation into Pembroke College in 1626.

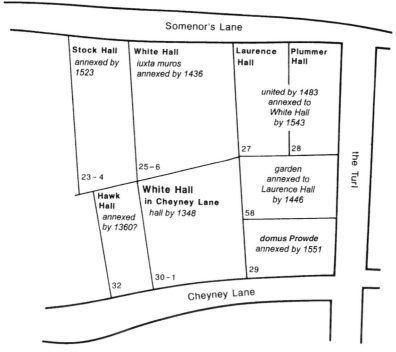

The numbers of the properties relate to
Salter, *Survey of Oxford*, NE quarter.
Somenor's Lane is now Ship Street;
Cheyney Lane is now Market Street

Figure 5 Site of White Hall and Jesus College 1348–1571

fifteenth century the community expanded through the party wall into another White Hall, that in Somenor's Lane, known as *iuxta muros*, by the walls.[26] An arbitration before the chancellor in 1450 shows the real nature of the expanded hall. The principalship was disputed between two civil lawyers, William Ballard and William Godyer; the arbitrators, deciding in favour of Ballard, conceded that Godyer was the nominal principal of the dependent White Hall by the walls. But he was not to exercise on that account any rights of a principal: there was to be no access to his hall except

26 White Hall in Cheyney Lane or Ship Street (NE 30) was not mentioned in the incomplete taxors' list of halls of *c*1313; it was evidently an academic hall by 1348 when it had a manciple. Oxford, Bodleian Library, Twyne MS 23, p 165, from a lost Oxford coroner's inquest of 22 Edward III. Hawk Hall (NE 32) was not certainly an academic hall until 1444 when Mr John Stretton made his pledge for it, nor clearly annexed to this White Hall until 1445 when Stretton succeeded Mr Hugh Gerard there: *Registrum cancellarii 1434–69* i.102, 123; *BRUO* iii.1805 (Stretton). But the connection may well be much earlier. White Hall *iuxta muros* (NE 25) was not certainly academic until 1413, when the canonist Mr William Ulff was principal; its subordinate position to its namesake was made clear in 1450, though the relation of the two halls may again have begun long before. *BRUO* iii.1928; *Oseney cartulary* iii.207; *Registrum cancellarii 1434–69* i.209–10. On the dispute of 1450 see JL Barton, 'The legal faculties of late medieval Oxford' in Catto and Evans, *Late medieval Oxford*, 309–11.

through the main gate in Cheyney Lane, each and every scholar and resident there was to take commons and to attend lectures and corrections in the main hall, and to obey the authority of Principal Ballard. So White Hall had become multicellular – a superhall – already by 1450. It could be argued that by 1529 White Hall was in steep decline, as it was then reported that there were few scholars and no lectures in civil law. But this was a premature obituary: by 1531, students were signing on, and in 1552 there were a respectable twenty in residence.[27] By that time Laurence Hall and its dependencies, and the remaining building between White Hall and the Turl had also been occupied.[28] This was the institution which Dr Hugh Price, a Welsh lawyer who may well have attended it – there is no direct evidence – had incorporated in 1571, acquiring the freehold and calling it Jesus College. Like Brasenose, it was not a new community when it received its charter; like its counterpart in School Street, it was a spontaneous institution of the early fifteenth century, answering therefore to new but real and enduring educational requirements.

So what were these new requirements for the education of undergraduates? They had not only impelled principals of halls to band together and form larger, more regulated bodies for the purpose, but had exercised a magnetic force on the existing endowed societies or colleges, distorting the intentions of their founders and involving the fellows in the tutorial teaching of their juniors. A university statute had laid down about 1411 that all scholars must be members of halls or colleges; it was now accepted that residence within the halls had pedagogic value in itself.[29] The nature of the residence they approved is set out in the so-called aularian statutes, issued by various chancellors of the later fifteenth century and codified by chancellor John Russell in 1490.[30] The most striking feature of the aularian regime is the primacy of corporate activities: the *aulares* – as they were now designated – must appear at mass together, sing antiphons in the hall on numerous occasions, sit down to dinner and supper together, drink in hall as a group (the *biberium*), and all attend on Saturday night the practice of corrections, when an 'impositor', one of the students elected for the week as a kind of prefect, reported any misdemeanours to the principal, who might impose immediate punishment. Even recreation was compulsory: when the scholars went off to the fields to play, no one was to stay behind.[31] We must imagine these activities in a community of perhaps twenty or thirty, with a principal, another master or so and two or three bachelors, all (except sometimes the principal) not much older than the undergraduates; the seniors gave aularian lectures and held disputations, the direct ancestors of the tutorial system: since corrections took place after Saturday night drinks and the singing of a rousing Marian antiphon, they might well qualify, too, as the direct ancestor of the bump supper and the rugby club dinner. Perhaps the university was just trying to make the best of the inevitable. But the compulsory sports hint at something more, a positive spirit of playing up and playing the game; which

---

27 JK McConica, 'The collegiate society' in McConica, *Collegiate university*, 724; McConica, 'The rise of the undergraduate college', 52–3.

28 Mr Robert Otes was principal of both White Hall and Laurence Hall in 1527: Oxford University Archives, register EE, fo 76v. For the other properties on the site (NE 28, 29, 57, 58) see Salter, *Survey* i.35–6, 49. I am very grateful to Dr Brigid Allen, archivist of Jesus College, for help on the history of the properties incorporated into Jesus.

29 *Statuta antiqua*, ed Gibson, 208.

30 On the date see the statute on their publication, ibid 295–6; for the text, ibid 574–88.

31 Ibid 574 (mass), 575 (antiphons), 580–1 (dining), 585 (*biberium*), 585–6 (corrections), 577 (games).

appears to indicate that Chancellor Russell and his predecessors were sensitive to the demands of a moral education as it would be understood by the enlightened pedagogues of the Italian renaissance.

The aularian statutes were framed by university authorities who were steeped in the ideal of a moral education. Dr Russell had cited his predecessor, Dr Gilbert Kymer who had served a second term as chancellor from 1447 to 1453, as one who had issued a part of his consolidated code.[32] But the statutes' underlying principles were most explicitly idealized by the most substantial of the intervening chancellors, Dr Thomas Chaundler, warden of New College from 1453 to 1475 and twice chancellor (1457–61 and 1472–9), in a rather neglected work, his *Collocutiones*.[33] Composed about 1462, and in form a humanist exercise, a dialogue designed to show that William of Wykeham possessed all the Aristotelian virtues, it is a passionately felt, if rather glutinously expressed, exposition of the ideal of humane teaching in a closed, intimate environment. Chaundler's own sentiments are expressed by the character *cancellarius*. Addressed by his interlocutor 'great doctor, warden and chancellor, care for your pupils as they grow up!', he promises that he is ready to minister to them at any hour of the day or night. His programme of study for them prescribed Cicero as a model to peruse and imitate, in addition to Aristotle: the life of Cicero, the model of public responsibility, should inspire their admiration as much as his works should fire their eloquence.[34] The *Collocutiones* were an exercise conceived within the walls of New College, and applied pre-eminently to the education of its large body of scholars, one of whom, from 1447 to 1462, was John Russell. They expressed what must have been in Russell's mind as the ideal of watchful care for an undergraduate community when he put together the aularian statutes, and their precepts were if anything even more applicable in an academic hall of thirty or so than among the seventy scholars of New College.

Taken in isolation, Warden Chaundler's sentimental attachment to the personal touch in the nurturing of undergraduates might be dismissed, with the aularian statutes themselves, as an Oxford eccentricity. A larger perspective, taking in the novelties of college foundations and other pedagogic experiments during the century, shows that it was not. Before the fifteenth century the emphasis had been in the main on the training of young adults for skilled professions: for canon and civil law, for theology, for medicine. The endowments of the early Oxford and Cambridge colleges were primarily for training masters of arts in these useful skills, and had been provided for their public utility typically by bishops in the active service of the crown, or by the crown itself. The latest of such foundations, and the most austerely professional, had been All Souls College, founded in 1437. Even William of Wykeham, the first to make a separate foundation – at Winchester – for the education of boys, had in mind with his two colleges a complete cursus from cradle not exactly to grave, but at least as far as the advocates' door at the court of arches, the gateway to a canonist's professional success. The new departure came about 1440, with Henry VI's founda-

---

[32] On Kymer see *BRUO* ii.1068–9. His contribution to the aularian statutes seems impossible now to identify.

[33] Chaundler's *Collocutiones* are in Oxford, New College, MS 288, fos 5r–31r; there is a transcript in S Bridges, 'Thomas Chaundler' (University of Oxford B Litt thesis 1949), the most extensive study of Chaundler himself. See also R Weiss, *Humanism in England during the fifteenth century* (3rd edn 1967), 133–6; *BRUO* i.398–9.

[34] New College, MS 288, fos 19v, 21v.

tion of Eton; here too there was a double foundation, with King's College in Cambridge, but it is clear that the king and his ministers put their greater effort and ingenuity and the larger endowments into the school.[35] Chaundler's patron Thomas Bekynton, bishop of Bath and Wells, was one of the prime movers. Though the extensive archives of Eton nowhere define what the founder and his ministers intended their new school to achieve, Bekynton's statutes for Wells cathedral school throw light on what they had in mind. The master at Wells was to be a chaste and sober example to boys whose morals, manners and good behaviour were to be at least as much under his eye as their understanding; and their understanding itself was to be nurtured by personal attention and tutorial care. Bekynton distinguished between learning and intelligence: he looked for promise, originality and adaptability, and was not averse to severe correction to get the best out of the boys.[36] It is probable that the young Etonian of the 1440s was to be broken in by similar means. Equipped with civil manners and facile speech, with or without further professional training he was fit for the new social world of the court. In the hands of Bekynton, then, and about 1440, a cultural rather than an intellectual model of education, a model of sociability, established itself in England, alongside the older and still vigorous training of university higher faculties. As the good offices of the bishop procured the simultaneous re-endowment of Winchester and New College, bound with Eton and King's since 1444 in *amicabilis concordia*, it is not difficult to recognize the milieu in which Chaundler's principles of pedagogy were formed.[37] Modified doubtless and simplified, but still with a powerful attraction, Bekynton's notion of the moral formation and socialization of young scholars goes far to explain the viability of the 'superhall' as a framework for education in fifteenth-century Oxford.

It would be possible to trace the model further afield. Bekynton was in touch, through the circle of Humphrey, duke of Gloucester and other channels, with the remarkably similar institutions of northern Italy, the *contubernia* or 'comradely dwelling places' of the educator Guarino Guarini in Verona and Ferrara, boarding schools in effect, or the *casa giocosa* of Vittorino da Feltre at Mantua, where in the best public-school tradition the Gonzaga boys, scions of the ruling house, were made to muck in with the rest.[38] If these exotic parallels seem a long way from the workaday Oxford halls in School Street and the Turl, it is instructive to recall one promising *aularis* of the later fifteenth century. Thomas More was resident, almost certainly in St Mary Hall, about 1493; he must have been subject to the aularian statutes and participated in the life of the hall. But by 1499, improved only by attendance at Lincoln's Inn during the intervening years, he was civilized enough and learned enough to become a close and enduring friend of the most brilliant man in northern Europe, the young Erasmus. His Oxford training under the shadow of Dr Chaundler and his pupils must have had its effect. The inner world of the academic hall remains

35 On the foundation and early years of Eton and King's see KE Selway, 'The role of Eton College and King's College, Cambridge, in the polity of the Lancastrian monarchy' (University of Oxford DPhil thesis 1993).

36 See the statutes for the vicars choral, ed A Watkin in *Dean Cosyn and Wells cathedral miscellanea* (Somerset Record Society lxvi 1941), 139–49.

37 RL Storey, 'The foundation and the medieval college' in J Buxton and P Williams (eds), *New College, Oxford, 1379–1979* (1979), 14; TAR Evans and RJ Faith, 'College estates and university finances 1350–1500' in Catto and Evans, *Late medieval Oxford*, 649, 692.

38 PF Grendler, *Schooling in renaissance Italy* (1989), 126–32.

hidden; but the example of More, as much as the conversion of the original colleges to the aularian way of life, justifies a change of perspective on the fate of the halls which would perhaps have tempted Trevor Aston: a revision which allows these elusive institutions, in place of the terminal decay attributed to them by his predecessors, a substantial future in collegiate disguise.

14

The Defences of a College:
The Law's Demands and Early Record-Keeping
in St John's College, Cambridge

MALCOLM UNDERWOOD

The defence of property with or without recourse to lawsuits is a constant and major feature of corporate history; indeed one of the definitions of a corporation is that it can sue and be sued as a legal person.* The need to produce the evidence conveniently in such circumstances was what prompted medieval monastic houses to draw up cartularies recording, sometimes by verbatim copies, the *cartae* or deeds by which their property had been conveyed to them. The colleges of Oxford and Cambridge in some cases succeeded to their endowments. The deeds of these and later benefactions came to be referred to collectively as 'evidences' because of their primary legal function. Often the strong places where the evidences were stored also held the money and other valuables of the institution.[1] In the case of the colleges the strongrooms or treasuries were sometimes in towers or other buildings inside the college precincts, but from the mid-fifteenth century onward they were normally in a chamber above the main gates.[2] The necessary alliance between the assets of the colleges and the documentation of their property was reflected at different periods in the kindred occupations of the chief college officers and those who acted as registrars and scribes.

St John's College was founded in 1511 in execution of the will of Lady Margaret Beaufort (*d.* 1509), the mother of Henry VII and also the foundress of Christ's College in Cambridge. St John's occupies the site of an earlier foundation, the hospital of St John, dedicated like its successor to St John the evangelist. The hospital was dissolved and replaced by the college which inherited its possessions, and the hospital's cartulary, with a large collection of deeds relating to its lands, remains in the archives of the college. A major part in framing the college's statutes, and in securing greater endowments for it, was played by John Fisher, bishop of Rochester, Lady

---

* Acknowledgement is due to the master, fellows and scholars of St John's College, Cambridge for the use of their archives in this article, and to the Society of Archivists which published an earlier version as its specialist repositories group occasional paper 1 (1983).

[1] St John's kept its money in a great chest in its treasury until a bank account was opened in 1765: H Howard, *Finances of St John's College, Cambridge, 1511–1926* (1935), 80.

[2] At Oxford, Merton (1264), the oldest college in either university, had a purpose-built treasury in a corner of its court; at New College (1379) it was in a tower built against the hall and chapel range; Magdalen, Oxford (1448) had a similar tower room. All Souls at Oxford (1443) and Queens' (1448) and Christ's (1505) colleges at Cambridge had their strongrooms above the gate; this was also the case at Brasenose, Oxford (1509), St John's, Cambridge (1511) and Corpus Christi, Oxford (1517).

Margaret's chaplain and confessor and chancellor of the University of Cambridge until his execution in 1535. A statute about the safekeeping of valuables, including documents, figured in the first complete code of statutes given by Bishop Fisher soon after the college was opened in 1516. It was modelled on a statute of the same name in the code of 1506 for Christ's College.[3] Six kinds of muniments were described in the statute: charters, letters patent, confirmations, evidences, indentures and obligations or bonds. These were all to be placed in the treasury with the chests holding plate and money, but the documents were to be housed separately in *scrinia* – containers dedicated to records. The code of statutes issued in 1524 included a statute dealing specifically with the administration of great and small chests, perhaps suggested by a similar one in the code of statutes drawn up in 1517 for Corpus Christi College, Oxford by Bishop Fox, Fisher's friend and colleague as executor of Lady Margaret Beaufort. Fisher's statute gave details about storage: the great iron-bound chest in the college's tower was to hold three smaller chests. In one were to be kept the licence and charter of foundation, the code of statutes, and the common seal; and in the others funds for emergency borrowing and a reserve for purchases of land and legal expenses. Another chest was to house papal bulls, ordinations (of vicarages), appropriations, episcopal letters, royal charters, 'as well as original records of other important personages (*aliorum dominorum*)'. It was doubtless considered necessary that the key foundation documents should be housed in a strong, locked and fireproof container. In *scrinia* were to rest transcripts of bulls and royal charters, and documents of the college's treasurers, or bursars, namely their rolls of receipt and accounts copied out in the form of indentures. Another series of *scrinia* would hold the documents described in 1516 as evidences: the court rolls of manors, terriers, and title deeds of estates in each county. Smaller boxes called *scriniola* were to be placed within the *scrinia*, to separate the documents relating to each property 'whether manor or benefice'. The third and fullest of Fisher's codes, that of 1530, for the first time treated documents under a separate statute – *De evidentiis, munimentis et scriptis* – from the plate, jewels and money of the college. Little had changed in the text of the statute except that *scrinia* were called *capsae* and *scriniola* termed *capsellae*. This wording, however, reflected that of both Fox's codes of statutes for Corpus, drawn up in 1517 and revised in 1528. Both *scrinium* and *capsa* could also be used of reliquaries. The statute itself and the two preceding it – *De custodia bonorum collegii* and *De cistis et sigillo* – had the same titles as, and were clearly modelled on, Fox's statutes.[4] The prologue to the statute *De*

---

3   See H Rackham, *Early statutes of Christ's College* (1927), 54–7. For the successive codes of statutes of St John's see JEB Mayor (ed), *Early statutes of St John's College, Cambridge* (1859) under the following heads: *De tuta rerum custodia*, 1516 (357), 1524 (274); *De cistis et cistulis, De locis in quibus ista ponenda sunt*, 1524 (276–80); *De evidentiis, munimentis et scriptis*, 1530 (196, 198).

4   Cf the three statutes in a manuscript of the statutes of Corpus Christi College, Oxford, dated 20 June 1517 and preserved in St John's, now bound up with Fisher's code of 1524: St John's College, Cambridge, archives (hereafter SJC) C1.2, fos 104v–7r; the code of 13 February 1528 for Corpus is printed in *Statutes of the colleges of Oxford* (3 vols Royal Commission 1853) ii. 89–94, and the text of Fisher's code of 11 July 1530 in *Early statutes*, 188–97. Cf also the statutes for Cardinal College, Oxford, founded by Wolsey in 1525, printed in *Statutes of the colleges* ii. 111–16. In the manuscript of Fox's code the titles of college officers have regularly been corrected to accord with the practice at St John's. There are variations of detail between all three texts; the exact relationship between Fisher's and Fox's statutes, and that of both to those of Wolsey, on which Fisher may also have relied, is a subject beyond the scope of the present article. The organization of the Corpus treasury is described by Trevor Aston in 'The college archives', *The Pelican* [magazine of Corpus Christi College, Oxford] 1981–2.

evidentiis of both colleges is of interest because it shows why care was taken over the storage of records, and particularly over those described as evidences:

> Moreover, so that the master and fellows may be prepared when the college becomes involved in lawsuits, and shall not go into battle unarmed, we ordain that their weapons – that is their documents of title, charters and other writings – shall be placed in the upper chamber of the tower.

The theme of defence was no mere rhetoric. While the royal and ecclesiastical privileges accorded to the college could be kept in a great chest for posterity, the evidences relating to oft-disputed properties had to be carefully arranged in their boxes within boxes for ease of access. The first code of statutes ordered an inventory of writings to be kept with the original statutes, but there was no reference to this in subsequent versions, and no general inventory survives from the period before 1545. The cartulary of the hospital of St John, which preserved for its successor college a record of the deeds inherited by it, could serve as a rough guide for the ancient title of some properties in Cambridgeshire and adjoining counties. Nevertheless new purchases were made and these sometimes entailed disputes. Fisher and his agents had often acted as feoffees for the college, and subsequently the ground and extent of its title were not always clear. The college early began to register its own leases, inventories of goods, and important letters as directed by the statute *De tuta rerum custodia* of 1524, but it is not until the mastership of Dr John Taylor (1538–47) that we meet with a general survey of the evidences.

Between 1541 and 1547 the earliest surviving portion of a register of documents borrowed shows the kinds of evidences that were most in use.[5] The majority of them were terriers; one example of a dispute in which the college was involved will illustrate their importance. During 1544 Bartholomew Brokesby of Great Bradley, Suffolk, claimed parcels of land in Great and Little Bradley and Little Thurlow, with rents, services, commons and liberties of sheepgates. These, he implied, had become wrongly attached to a sale by his 'ancestors' of the manor of Great Bradley to the college. He backed by appeal to the lord chancellor his claim that the college should sell or exchange land, and the college countered by writing to the chancellor in its turn. On 1 April 1544 the master, John Taylor, withdrew six boxes (here called *pixides*) of evidences of Bradley, with fourteen items (*pecies*) not enclosed in a pyx. His deputy, the president of the college, took certain of the evidences to London and also journeyed to Bradley. On 30 June an agreement was drawn up setting out 'the certeinte of all the lands tenements and hereditaments of the said college in the towns aforesaid'.[6] Brokesby resigned his claim to the lands, but the college agreed to respect his commons rights by pasturing no more than 120 sheep in place of 300.

The terrier produced by this agreement with Brokesby is the last document transcribed in a catalogue of the college's evidences made during Taylor's mastership. The same flourished but disciplined hand which made the terrier is seen at work in other terriers of lands in the fields of Cambridge and its district. The signature of the scribe at the foot of two of them is plain: William Rustat (see plate 6).[7] He was a servant of Taylor's and had been paid since 1540 at piece rate for writing terriers of

---

5   SJC D106.6, fos 71–3v, 75–7v.
6   SJC D50.51. In the bursars' accounts for 1543–4, SJC D106.17, fo 228v, are the entries: 'Item to Mr Brokesby upone agrement, xiii lib vi s viii d. Item to Rusted for writting the same vs.'
7   SJC D30.29.2, D31.5.1. In the bursars' accounts for 1542–3, SJC D106.17, fo 180r, are the entries:

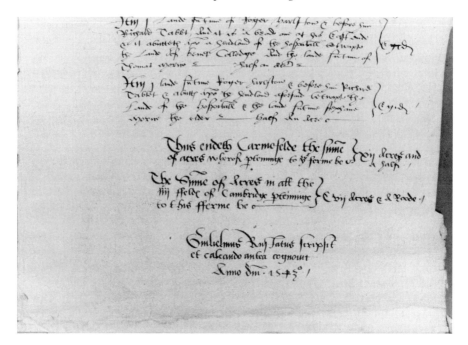

Plate 6 Latin inscription by William Rustat at the foot of a terrier of 1543 in the archives of St John's College, Cambridge ('William Rustat wrote this document, and paced out the land beforehand'); reproduced by kind permission of the master, fellows and scholars of St John's College, Cambridge

land in Nottinghamshire, Kent and elsewhere. In 1541–2 he began to receive a regular stipend 'for writing'. In 1543 he accompanied the master, the presidents of Clare Hall and Corpus Christi College and others on surveys of the college's lands in Cambridge, Grantchester and Newnham. The assemblage of these heads of houses underlined the importance of the occasion: all were owners of lands in the west fields of Cambridge and the adjoining townships anxious to establish the extent of their respective properties. From one terrier it appears that Rustat took part in a physical inspection for it is stated that 'William Rustat wrote this, having made a perambulation beforehand'. At the end of the largest terrier he noted: 'And these be all the lands that belonge to this farm in Cambridge, Newnam and Grauncestre fields that we can as yet find, but by our evidence we should have much more to the knowledge whereof I truste hereafter we shall better come to.' Rustat's hand is also apparent in the college's register of letters and leases. In the valor made for the commissioners of Henry VIII in 1546 Rustat is described as 'scribe of writings concerning lands and other matters of the said college'; his wage is noted as 26*s* 8*d* per annum, a mark less than that of the auditor, but twice as much as that of the keeper of books.[8]

'Expensis in makyng tariars in Cambrigfeelds ut patet xlii s iiii d. In makyng of terers at Grancheseter, Cotton, Chesterton and Mylton, ut patet xli s iid.'

[8] SJC C17.1, fo 5r.

Rustat not only shared the work of preparing new descriptions of college land but also copied out old ones, and this ability fitted him to undertake a catalogue of evidences, in which the master showed a considerable interest. Taylor's borrowing register beginning in 1541, his notes to copies of terriers, and a short list of deeds in his hand, all point to his concern with the contents of the treasury. He drew up an index to deeds of certain lands in Milton and Chesterton, Cambridgeshire, on 3 October 1546, and checked the bounds described in them against the college's terrier.[9] Alongside such particular efforts, the work undertaken by Rustat provided a systematic guide to the college's title to its lands.

The catalogue is now in three separately bound parts. The two smaller parts retain original parchment leaves of old manuscripts as the outer covers, one of them a bifolium from an early version of the first code of the college's statutes. The first and largest part, bound in leather in the eighteenth century, deals with the properties in Cambridge and Cambridgeshire, the nucleus of which was inherited from the hospital of St John. The second concerns Kent, where great holdings had passed to the college from the hospital of Ospringe and the priory of Higham. The third deals with lands in other counties, from Bedfordshire to Wiltshire. None of the parts is signed or dated, but the latest date of any evidence recorded is July 1544.[10] As with the thirteenth-century cartulary of the hospital the purpose of this catalogue is to set forth the origin of title to the properties, adding some details of leasing by the college. It differs from the cartulary, however, in representing a conscious history of properties, and also in giving references to particular *pixides* or other receptacles. The following is an example of an entry:

> St John's College bought from John Watson, clerk, one messuage lying in the parish of St Giles, between the messuage late that of John Moryce, gentleman, on one side . . . *[remaining bounds given]* And various other lands and tenements in the same parish, by a charter dated 14 Henry VIII.
>
> Item one tenement beyond the bridge in the same parish . . . *[bounds given]*
>
> These evidences are housed among others *[in the box]* where is inscribed 'The evidences of the great bearne / the first boxe of the same'.[11]

The directions for finding the documents always end rather than head the description of the title and its records: although this tripartite catalogue was more of an inventory than a cartulary, it was not an inventory of the records in the modern sense.

The catalogue of evidences gives details which show its practical use. Of a charter giving a right of entry through a neighbour's tenement it is noted that it affects the repair of guttering; the terms of former leases and rates of rent are recorded for future renewals and revisions. Because the title of many of the properties was ancient, prac-

---

9 SJC C7.5, fo 176 ('index'), fos 25–30 (terrier).
10 SJC C7.6–8. In the bursars' accounts for 1545–6, SJC D106.17, fo 309r, there is a payment 'to Wyllyam Rusted for wrytyng the extents of owr lands, xx s. Item, to the auditors at the same tyme xx s.' Were it not that 'extent' is normally the specific word used for a list of lands on a manor I would conclude that this rather general commission was in fact the composition of the catalogue. As it is, I am in some doubt.
11 'Collegium Sancti Johannis perquisivit de Johanne Watson clerico unum messuagium scituatum in parochia Sancti Egidii inter messuagium nuper Johannes Moryce generosi ex una parte . . . Et diversa alia terrae et tenementa in eadem parochia per cartam datam anno Henrici octavi 14. Item unum tenementum ultra pontem in eadem parochia . . . Includuntur inter alias evidentias ubi inscribitur "The evidences of the great bearne / the first boxe of the same"'. SJC C7.6, fo 9r.

tical use sometimes required detective work. We find the phrases 'uncertain places in Cambridge whose whereabouts must be investigated' and 'it appears by another charter to be . . .', where the holding mentioned in one grant is more fully described in another. The archival duties of arrangement and reference naturally followed from the need for clear identification. There are traces of such activity in the form of a memorandum to place certain evidences together; and references to the deeds of neighbouring properties being moved into a single box, so that another is now empty. The many small properties of Ospringe hospital, Kent, made it sensible to identify the Ospringe boxes by numbers: a rare expedient, since most – as in the example entry – were called by name. Where boxes within boxes were referred to, the terms generally used were *arcula* and *maior arcula*. Some of these small wooden boxes survive, with titles that agree with the books of evidences. The compilation of the books was nearly contemporary with the physical arrangement, for in 1541–2 we learn from the bursars' account book that 'two hundred tackets [nails]' were bought 'for boxes of evidence'.[12]

Rustat continued his labours for the college until 1546, when his name disappears from the bursars' account rolls to be replaced by that of one Oliver Warner, *scriptor registri*. Taylor ceased to be master in 1547, taking up his residence as dean of Lincoln, of which he became bishop in 1552. He had been put into St John's by the king in 1538, and so presided over the introduction of the royal statutes which replaced Fisher's in 1545. Among some of the fellows he was unpopular, and his servant Rustat shared his unpopularity. In 1544 Rustat had been granted the reversion of a lease of the manor of Ramerick in Hertfordshire, due to come in to the college in 1555. Before this happened the fellows wrote to their erstwhile master to cancel the arrangement:

> Wherre as about ix yeares past, yow beinge then Mr of our college, we dyd grant the reversion of Ramwrik ferme from our honest fermer Godlington to yowr servant W Rusted, wch thinge we dyd manifesdly rather at yowr sute than uprightly of good consiens: for as much as we nowe know it is like to turne to the utter undoing of our honest fermer. We therefore moved in consiens, both of pitie, and for thonestie of the man and his poore familie; and partelye because we persayve that such a man shall be put in to occupie our said ferme as we can not with good wyll aloow, most instantly desire yor goodnes, that as we were easilie entreated at yowr frendly request to give yowr said servant the reversion of Ramwrik frely. Even so now by yowr means yor servant may be persuaded to sell his said leese to Godlynton our said fermer at this our godly request, for a conveniant some of monei. And thus ye shall not onlie do a godlye act in relevyng our fermer wt his poore wyffe and children, wch els shall be utterly undone; but also we all shall thankfully accept this benefit, as done to our owne sellfes . . .[13]

Taylor apparently made no argument and on 28 June 1555 licence was granted to Rustat to sell his reversion to Godlyngton, who took over the lease.

Unpopular though Taylor may have been at a time of fierce partisanship in religious and political affairs, we have seen that his mastership saw a major effort to organize the legal 'defences' of the college. The employment of a *scriptor registri* continued until in 1560 the title became *register* or *register collegii*. By the time we have a named 'register' in the bursars' accounts, in 1575–6, the duty has been assumed

---

[12] Bursars' accounts, SJC D106.17, fo 137r.
[13] From the thick black book, SJC C7.12, p 298.

by a fellow. From the variety of hands at work it seems that the actual scribal work was shared by others, despite an order of 1630 that the register should himself write the admissions book started that year. The later sixteenth century saw the systematic adoption by the college of a system of beneficial leases, which were granted and renewed upon payment of an entry-fine, and of the routine granting of licences to alienate. The office of register became linked with these increasingly profitable practices, and with other financial matters. Successive holders of the office can be found accounting for payments due on sealing leases and licences, making memoranda about the payment of rent, and witnessing the grant of arrears of an exhibition and of a licence for a fellow to travel abroad. The office was really that of an assistant to the senior or estates bursar, and it is not surprising than an energetic bursar would regard it as more of ornament than of use. In 1716 Francis Robins, fellow, wrote to a new bursar, John Bowtell, about matters including the recent history of the register- or registrarship:

> As to the registrar's office it was not filled up for many years after Dr Berry was chosen bursar [in 1694] but as he still executed the office so he received the full profits of it. But at last Dr Gower [master 1679–1711] made two distinct offices and elected Mr Orchard into the register's place and after his death Mr Brome. This I remember Dr Berry complained of as an hardship or injustice done him because no man, he said, could do the business of that office but the bursar, who by virtue of his place was to keep the leases and lease books in order to set fines. And accordingly Dr Berry performed everything that belonged to the office and the two above gentlemen had half the profits.[14]

The link between the bursar's work and the evidences in the college's treasury is illustrated by two papers drawn up in 1639, written in an extremely neat sloping secretary hand. In that year the college was on the track of arrears of rent from some tenements in Cambridge marketplace: a list was made from the rentals of sums paid since 1556, with a note of the first year in which they were withheld.[15] As an appendix the history of the tenements was given, drawn from the grants made to the hospital of St John in the thirteenth century, and giving the names of two lessees in the fifteenth. For such work it was important to have the title to property readily available; the same neat sloping hand produced twenty more leaves of transcripts and abstracts of evidences. The scribe used the work done under Taylor a hundred years before, for the occasional page references to *liber collegii* agree with those in the books of evidences. Important terriers are also noted, for example 'an old terrar of landes called Morrice landes extracted out of their several evidences by John Taylor in the box with the horne over the inscrip[i]on of old deeds of the hospitall landes but not made to the hospitall: the second box'. The transcripts made by this scribe included some of foundation documents of the college and of inquisitions into former monastic property acquired soon after.[16]

As with the books of evidences there is no signature on these transcripts, but the scribe is likely to have been Thomas Dowsing the elder of Cottenham, public notary.

---

[14] SJC D109.431.

[15] SJC C7.10.

[16] SJC C7.9. Intermixed with this hand is another, upright and more formal but also neat and small, which produced a third of the transcripts. While another writer cannot be ruled out, I believe this to be a second hand of the same scribe. A few leaves have been annotated in a much more sprawling hand which bears no resemblance to the other two in discipline or size.

Plate 7 Two leather-covered wooden document boxes from the archives of
St John's College, Cambridge (upper box 7x5 inches, lower box 6 inches
in diameter); reproduced by kind permission of the master, fellows
and scholars of St John's College, Cambridge

The familiar sloping hand is found at various dates between 1620 and 1650 in the audit or 'balance' books and rentals. In 1638–9 there were expenses on commons, candles, paper and entertainment for Dowsing, and payments were recorded for his attendance at audits throughout the 1630s. The college employed him in 1640 as public notary to set his hand to a warrant and in 1646–7 to write accounts.[17] Besides the transcripts there is other evidence of his work in the archives. A wrapper in this hand encloses 'divers rentals and arrearages due to the hospitall'.[18] In the same neat secretary is a copy of the building accounts of the first master of the college, 'being truly copied out Oct 1 1638 [of] the original thereof being decayed with rain'.[19] Sections for repairs and miscellaneous expenditure in the college's rentals in the two previous years show that this work was prefigured by additions to the equipment of the treasury, and by Dowsing's presence during the summer. In 1635–6 money was spent 'in ord'ring the treasury this summer, for boards to mend the old presses and to make two new ones, in each study one, and other charges for new boxes etc'.[20] The next year we meet 'charges for ordering the treasury this summer when Mr Dowsing was here'. According to this description the treasury was partitioned into smaller areas or 'studies' like other college rooms, each holding presses and an increasing number of boxes as well as chests of money and plate (see plate 7). Despite this evidence of work in transcription and housing documents we do not possess a catalogue or calendar from this period on the vast scale undertaken by the antiquary Brian Twyne at Corpus Christi College, Oxford, in 1627. There too, however, it is clear that Twyne's preoccupation was with deeds of title to bolster the college in litigation. He too worked on the ancient 'cartulary' principle, providing accessible transcripts or abstracts of such documents, while those documents not useful for legal purposes were listed more briefly and classed as *reiectanea*.[21]

In the early eighteenth century the bursar kept a list of terriers, alphabetically by estate, and these are cross-referenced to the pages of the fine-books which give details of the letting history and the fines imposed on each property.[22] The list has no means of reference back to the original terriers and they were presumably found by the descriptions on the presses and boxes. Towards the end of the list there is a section on Cambridgeshire terriers and rentals which do have the classification 'box A no. 1'. These terriers are found reclassified in the first complete classed catalogue of 1787. This catalogue allows us to see the kinds of storage used at that time. The documents are described in four classes, evidently representing presses able to hold the boxes and drawers in which all documents except those in chests were placed. Chests were retained to store old statutes, legal papers, papers relating to the foundress of the college, and the account rolls drawn up by past bursars. (These bursars' parchment

---

[17] The Dowsing family leased lands at Cottenham from the college from 1609 to 1753. A counterpart lease of 1623, SJC D72.30, sealed and signed by Thomas the elder, bears an attestation in the familiar sloping hand. The whole of a terrier of the lands, made in 1634, SJC D70.2, is compiled in it. Commons and other payments were entered in the rentals: 1638–9, SJC SB4.5, fos 130v–1r; 1639–40, fo 153r; 1646–7, fo 342r. In 1646 Dowsing also acted as a feoffee for the college during the transfer to it of property in London bought with the benefaction of Susan Hill: D54.77–8.

[18] SJC D2.15.

[19] SJC D6.32.

[20] SJC SB4.5, fos 52v, 81v.

[21] TH Aston, 'Muniment rooms and their fittings in medieval and early modern England', below; CM Woolgar, 'The archives of the college in the seventeenth century', *The Pelican* 1981–2, 65–8.

[22] List of terriers, SJC C23.3.

rolls or *computi* continued to be drawn up alongside the more accessible volumes of annual accounts until the reform of college accounting by the master, William Powell, in 1770 – a witness of the fidelity of the college to the letter of its sixteenth-century statutes.) The catalogue of 1787 was the work of William Craven, bursar 1786–9, master 1789–1815. Craven also began a new fine-book which is arranged alphabetically by counties and estates. In the borrowing register of documents there is no mention of classmarks before 1787; after that year they appear against the entries for withdrawals, and it is fair to deduce that Craven began, or at least refined, the system. It endured, with the addition of metal fireproof boxes in the nineteenth century, until 1891 when the contents of the treasury were transferred to a new fireproof muniment room next to the college's library.

Archives in the treasury were generally used to answer the daily claims made on the college as landowner and manorial lord, except on historic occasions like the day in 1576 when 'an old book of statutes' and other records were withdrawn 'by special commandment of the queen's majesty's commissioners'. The sixteenth-century statutes stressed the need not to reveal documents lightly: no doubt the fear of giving away secrets which would deplete the legal armoury was reinforced by the need to protect the money and plate which were also housed in the treasury tower. Thomas Baker, the fellow and antiquary who undertook his history of the college in 1707, says in his preface that he only gained access to the treasury with difficulty. He criticizes a previous history written in Latin by David Morton, bursar 1667–74, on the grounds that for one with such free access to the treasury he made little use of the materials. Baker was introduced there in 1692 when he witnessed withdrawals by the senior bursar Thomas Broughton, and was later allowed to borrow freely, with another fellow as witness. Most of his sources are given the simple reference *inter archivas*, perhaps because, as we have seen, the only alternative was description of the relevant box. This makes for difficulties when a reader tries to locate from Baker a source outside the main college registers. Perhaps it was frustrations of this kind which persuaded Craven to classify the archives. Forty years after he had done so the master, James Wood, could write with confidence to the warden of Merton College, Oxford, about a disputed plot near St John's:

> The grant itself which describes minutely the boundaries is in our possession; and copies of the leases granted to our tenants in succession, and the sums annually received from them up to the present time, regularly entered in our lease books and bursars' accounts, are lodged in our treasury . . . and I trust you will not think me taking an improper liberty in requesting you to furnish your steward of courts with necessary documents and instructions to meet our solicitor . . . here upon the spot, that the matter may be fairly and amicably considered and the best plan adopted for settling the question without the expense of further proceedings.[23]

As with Bartholomew Brokesby in 1544, so with Merton College in 1825, the legal armour was to be employed not as a spur to litigation, but to save its inordinate expense.

---

[23] Letter-book of James Wood, SJC M1.3, p 509.

15

Muniment Rooms and their Fittings in Medieval and Early Modern England

TREVOR ASTON

Muniments, fortifications for the defence of one's rights, have a very long ancestry, highly coloured with sacral connotations.* In the ancient world the safest and most proper way of preserving the record of a decision or other significant fact was by an inscription in bronze or stone placed in a temple or other holy place. For instance the peace treaty at the end of the Peloponnesian war (422–1 BC) was erected on at least five sacred sites, Olympia, Delphi, Isthmus (sites of religious festivals), on the acropolis at Athens and in the amychaeon at Sparta. Moving on a thousand years to the Ireland of the early laws we meet something rather similar in the ogham stones placed at the head of one's grave and on the very boundary of one's property, stones which served as one of the best titles to an estate, only to be overridden, literally, by horses driven across the boundary next the stone. More or less on a level with these 'immovable stones', as they were called in a late seventh-century law, were the 'divine ancient writings', that is records copied into liturgical and gospel books, such as the book of Kells. In Anglo-Saxon England there is the very language of the landbooks to remind us constantly of the sacral element in the property deed. And there too we will find such things written into gospel books, and in at least one case a document placed in the king's *haligdome*, his reliquary. After the conquest, in the eleventh and twelfth centuries and later, we continue to find copies of deeds and the like in holy books. In at least one case we find something even more remarkable, a combined cartulary and gospel book. This is the mid-twelfth-century missal from the Benedictine abbey of Shaftesbury in Dorset, sumptuously bound with its top board decorated with Limoges enamels and perhaps originally ivories. It was compiled as protection against the kind of challenge to their rights that the monks had then recently suffered at the hands of

* As keeper of the university archives Trevor Aston reported at their annual visitation to the delegates of privileges, the university body formally responsible for the archives. He developed the practice of his predecessors Strickland Gibson and WA Pantin in combining an exhibition of items from the archives with an oration on some aspect of the archives or the history of the university. These were frequently very substantial studies based on extensive original research, only some of which found their way into print. This paper is essentially the oration of 19 May 1973; versions were given to the Furniture History Society on 13 September 1973; to the south-eastern region of the Society of Archivists on 29 March 1980; and to the British Records Association on 9 December 1982, as reported in *Archives* xvi (1983–4), 178. On these occasions the talk was accompanied by numerous slides taken for the purpose, but the text printed here retains its considerable interest even without the benefit of those illustrations. Simon Bailey, university archivist, kindly made available several texts of this paper and provided a full list of Trevor's orations.

Bishop Jocelin of Salisbury. It was an altar book, a missal and a book of privileges, tampering with which could be construed as sacrilege. And there are more than a few echoes of these sacral origins and connotations in medieval archival vocabulary: *pyx* and *scrinium*, common words for small containers for deeds and other records, had powerful and continuing liturgical meanings also.

As we make our way through munimental and more generally archival arrangements in the middle ages and beyond – I shall continue my story up to the seventeenth century – we should not forget these awesome aspects. But, of course, for all their sacral benefits, gospel books and reliquaries early became inadequate in size either for the copies or for the originals of documents. There thus emerged the cartulary in its various manifestations, the earliest extant English examples of which are three of the eleventh century, all from the cathedral priory of Worcester. From the twelfth century about thirty survive. And then in the thirteenth and fourteenth centuries come a large number from all parts of the country, along with inventories and other associated records. I wish I could say a little more here about cartularies and similar documents and their arrangement, since they are very closely related to the whole question of archive storage – some indeed, like Merton College's *liber ruber*, have actual location marks for the originals, and most show clear signs of reflecting archival arrangement. Be that as it may, the proliferation of cartularies in this period emphasizes what of course we can see as a great explosion of documentation, and the complementary development of increasingly sophisticated legal and accounting procedures that required careful storage of the records themselves. And I am disposed to think that the muniment room as a separate end specially designed thing originates in this same period – certainly our earliest extant examples, including our earliest Oxford example, are from this date.

Because the muniment room was a relatively late development, it is not surprising that the room itself was not infrequently a place which originally had some quite different purpose, and this is true of even some of the greatest archives of the middle ages. Most notably, of course, the royal archives. But on a smaller scale, take Canterbury. The priory's archives were stored in a good, very early first-floor room next to St Andrew's chapel; the archbishop's, however, were not on his own premises at all but in an *edes sacra*, which on further investigation turns out to be the priory of St Gregory at Canterbury, a small priory dissolved in 1536 when it did indeed come into the ownership of the archbishop. Or take the secular cathedral chapter at York. Its muniment room in the later middle ages was what Archbishop William Zouche (*d.* 1352) had intended to be his own chantry chapel, off the south ambulatory (though it has been argued that it was probably built as a muniment room about 1500). Or again Westminster Abbey: its muniment room was, as it still is, in a gallery open to the church overlooking the south transept. Early in the sixteenth century, and to take an example from Oxford again, Wolsey, whose plans for Cardinal College were nothing if not grand, was apparently content (to judge from his statutes) to have the muniments kept in the chapter house, an especially interesting case of dual usage in view of the late date.

But long before then there had evolved in Oxford and elsewhere a very clear idea of what a muniment room or combined muniment room and treasury should be. It should be proof against fire, and against burglars or others who had no right to see the archives and secrets of the institution, as well as against vermin and airborne intruders – New College had some trouble with doves in the early sixteenth century – and, of course, against damp. In practice this meant that the room and its approaches should be entirely constructed of stone; it should be on at least the first floor, if not the second or third; it should be well ventilated, yet with windows small enough and grilled to keep out intruders; it should have its windows either shuttered or glazed or both to keep out the weather; it should have a carefully guarded approach; and finally its fittings should be of stout oak timbers, strengthened with iron, with the door or doors iron-plated for extra protection against fire. Such stringent and expensive require-ments – expensive in terms of space no less than of money – were not often all met. The secular cathedral of Salisbury, for instance, had a first-floor muniment room approached from the vestry up a stone newel through three elaborately secured doors. One door was at the foot of the newel with an ingenious locking vertical bar in addi-tion to ordinary locks, then two further doors formed a small lobby for the room itself; all three doors had internal bolts so that anyone who had entered could ensure that no unauthorized person followed. The floor was of encaustic tiles, over a stone vault; and the windows were good. So too were the chests, extensively cross-bound in iron though not totally iron covered. But Salisbury fell down, so to say, with its ceiling: very fine, but of timber.

In medieval Oxford the university itself – which was not only poor but had little property and relatively few title deeds – did not in the thirteenth century have its own muniment room at all. It used the chapter house of St Frideswide's, just as at Cambridge until the early fifteenth century the university used Great St Mary's church. Then early in the fourteenth century we have that momentous thing, the first university building. That building, put up very close to St Mary's church, was paid for by Bishop Cobham and was of two storeys. Its upper storey was to be the university library – the first extant English example of a room specifically built as a library. Its ground-floor room was to be the congregation house and it came also to be used for the university's archives, money and other valuables. This was an improvement on St Frideswide's, but the university was not even so meeting the requirements of best medieval practice for the storage of its archives: they were on the ground floor and in a room which, though stone-vaulted, also served other, more public purposes. It was only rough comment on this failure to meet the proper standards that the university's archives were disastrously burgled for the valuables stored with them in the mid-sixteenth century.

One might be inclined to say that perhaps no one in early fourteenth-century Oxford really knew what a good muniment room looked like were it not for the fact that a full generation earlier a nearly perfect muniment room had been built there. This was Merton's, constructed as one of the first specifically collegiate buildings in 1288–90: stone newel guarded by a good door, first floor over a vaulted ground floor, tiled floor and stone vault above. Doubtless it had good chests though we know nothing of them except that there were two. Its only slight shortcoming was that the door was not iron plated. It was complemented by an inventory of deeds and endow-ments, the *liber ruber*, made about 1288.

Though now part of mob quad, the Merton muniment room was originally a free-standing structure, all to the good for security against fire. This prompts me to jump a hundred years to William of Wykeham. Here we can and should consider New College along with its sister foundation at Winchester. In both cases Wykeham, perhaps the most far-sighted of all collegiate founders and outstandingly revolu-tionary, determined on the most careful keeping of muniments and records and extremely stringent precautions for their preservation. At New College as at Winchester College he followed in the wake of Merton in having a separate, though not a freestanding, building, but he went one better and had it a veritable tower, three storeys at Winchester and four at New College. It is possible that he himself conceived the idea of a muniment tower – he was certainly great enough in mind and concept for that – but it is worth remembering that, especially since the reforms in the royal exchequer and wardrobe under Edward II, the Tower of London had come to be a major royal repository and could readily have given anyone moving in high government service as Wykeham did the idea of a specially designed tower. Be that as it may, the muniment rooms at New College and at Winchester are about as near the ideal as one could get – an ideal which, modern utilities apart, can serve us as well now as it did six hundred years ago. Both have secure approaches – Winchester's from the chapel, New College's from the screens passage in hall. Both of course have stone newels and are indeed entirely constructed of stonework of the highest quality. The actual muniment room doors are iron plated, Winchester's about 3/32 inch and iron-bound, New College's with massive 5/32 inch plate and cross-bound in iron. They have tiled floors of course, stone vaults above and below, and fine chests. New College had two large chests, Winchester also two, somewhat smaller, though it soon added two or three more; taking the original chests only, the two at Winchester are a little better than those at New College in being extensively cross-bound in iron, though the locking arrangements at New College – a thick iron bar as well as locks – are by contrast slightly the more sophisticated. Minor differences such as these are, however, quite incidental: the salient point is that both muniment rooms are of the very highest quality. And the key and lock arrangements were very elaborate: the warden, subwarden and at least four other fellows had to be present to get at New College's common seal which was, as was customary, kept with the main muniments; and three fellows were needed to get into a chest at Winchester College.

Only one other Oxford college ever had a separate muniment tower, and that was Magdalen. Its tower and muniment room, built late in the fifteenth century, are good but not quite as good as New College's or Winchester's: no iron plating on the door and a timber ceiling. Apart from that Magdalen's muniment tower is extremely interesting because of its approach. Like Winchester's, the tower was beside the chapel, and like Winchester's too there was a stone newel up from the chapel. But the founder, William Waynflete, decreed in his statutes that this approach from the chapel was only to be used in case of emergency. The normal approach was to be up the nearby founder's tower and through the president's lodgings of which this latter tower formed a part.

The device of making the approach through the lodgings of the head of the college is a nice illustration of the search for even more security than a multiplicity of locks and keys provided within an overall context of shortage of space and doubtless money. But it was not invented by Waynflete. The first Oxford muniment rooms to embody this particular combination of sophistication and economy were at Lincoln College by 1431 and at Exeter College about 1432 (about a hundred years after its foundation) in Palmer's tower, originally the main entrance gate to the college, giving on to Exeter Lane, which ran along the city wall at this point. Both were very plain and in both the muniment room was on the top floor. Their importance is that, at the cost of some sacrifice in security against fire – for the room beneath could not be vaulted and was in any case in daily use – they set the norm for Oxford for at least the following two centuries. That norm was to make provision for a muniment room in the original college buildings and to place it into the upper room of the gatehouse tower which itself, on the first floor, provided the state room, so to say, for the head of the college, through whose apartments it was usually though not invariably necessary to pass to obtain access to the muniment room newel. Thus All Souls, St Bernard's and Balliol in the fifteenth century (though when St Bernard's became St John's in the next century the president's lodgings were moved to the east range of the front quadrangle, and the Balliol building is not extant); Brasenose and Corpus Christi early in the sixteenth century (though the staircase arrangement at Corpus Christi has been obscured by the demolition of the original newel to the lodgings in the north-east corner of the quadrangle and the opening up of an entrance to the internal newel at ground level); and Wadham early in the seventeenth. Thus too the university itself, for when the schools quadrangle was built between 1610 and 1624 it of course included an entrance tower one of whose upper rooms was, I have no doubt, intended for (as it soon became) the university's new archive room, the lower archive room of today.

At Oxford we may say that the muniment room, which was born at Merton in 1288, came of age in the following centuries, most notably at New College and Magdalen, but also at the other colleges I have mentioned; and their lead was followed by those colleges which, in rebuilding schemes, placed the muniment room in an upper storey of the gatehouse tower, as did Oriel and University College in the seventeenth century. Overall the standard was high, though the achievements of Wykeham at New College and Winchester were never equalled. The inclusion of the muniment room in the gatehouse tower over the head's lodging meant, as I have mentioned, less security against fire; wood tended to replace stone for floors and ceilings, as of course with the university archive room in the tower, and even, as at Corpus Christi, for the newel; and the tendency to combine treasury and muniment room provided a potential danger to the latter from burglars interested only in the former.

But if there was some minor decline here and there from the highest standards of the late thirteenth and the fourteenth centuries in the actual construction, there was advance in the internal fittings, and I now want to turn from the rooms as such to their contents. There is abundant evidence that the normal, proper place for the storage of muniments by the high middle ages was the chest, most often called *cista*. These chests came in all sizes and fall into two main categories, the rectangular and the round-topped: I propose to call the former chests and the latter coffers. Of the two, coffers are the less common, and were unlike chests not only in being round-topped but also in being frequently if not usually made of softwood. Thus Hereford. Thus too Magdalen College. Apart from liability to decay, softwood was, of course, easier to break into. So, though the university's chest of the five keys made in 1412 was of soft-wood, it was entirely encased in iron bands.

Coffers are not usually very large. Chests were far more variable in size, seldom less than about four or five feet in length. They must, therefore, normally have been made up in the muniment room itself. The largest I know of are the late twelfth-century chests in Westminster Abbey: one 12 foot 7 inches long by 2 foot wide by 17 inches high excluding the legs, or stiles as I prefer to call them; the other about twice that size, a colossal 13 foot 6 inches long by no less than 3 foot 9 inches wide by 27 inches high excluding the stiles. Both were somewhat unusual in having fairly high stiles. At the other end there is the small Salisbury chest, a mere 29 by 13 by 14 inches, chained to the wall because it could have been removed down the newel. Unlike private, domestic chests, muniment chests were normally quite plain, though occa-sionally the ironwork might be slightly indulgent, and even (as with the two earliest Westminster chests) the stiles. They were strictly utilitarian, made always of oak of stout dimensions, and usually very good oak, most often of planks though sometimes panelled; more often than not iron-bound and frequently cross-bound. Though no one can have intended to move them about much they not infrequently had iron handles at each end, or iron loops through which one or two carrying poles could be placed – as with two of the chests at Salisbury and one at Hereford.

In large archives it was of course vital to distinguish the various chests and this was done by signa, either letters or symbols of one kind or another as used extensively in the royal archives. With smaller archives a simpler, descriptive terminology would suffice: the great chest, the common chest (as at Winchester College for example) and so forth are often found. By the fifteenth century the University of Oxford had at least four administrative chests. First in order of date is the proctors' chest, which antedates 1347. In that year it was superseded as the main administrative chest by the chest of the four keys, which in its turn was superseded, though not replaced, in 1412 by the chest of the five keys I have already described. In addition there was a *cista rotulorum*, a chest for rolls, from at least 1367.

Although on occasion one finds double, treble or even quadruple chests, chests were not, I think, often subdivided internally – though the smaller of the two great late twelfth-century Westminster chests was divided into six. A more interesting or at least now more intelligible subdivision of chests, this time from the reign of Edward IV, is found at Ely. There we have six chests, the first five of which were divided into a series of subsections, each denoted by letters, while the sixth contained two large boxes. In the first chest for example, arranged into seven subsections, were the royal documents (references A1–5) and episcopal acts (references B1 and 2). Each subsection had a label detailing its contents, and the documents contained therein were duly endorsed with the chest number, the subsection number, a reference and the name of the estate. Quite as important – here as at Durham and later at Corpus Christi College in Oxford – there are cross-references to the documents thus firmly located on the one hand and to the cartulary on the other. One could thus move readily from the cartulary, which would be the normal place of first resort, to the original deeds – a simple sophistication but curiously enough not, I think, all that often found in the surviving evidence. The only internal compartment that is at all often found built into the chest is a small oblong one at the top right- or left-hand corner, and occasionally both, such as is commonly found in domestic chests, though their archival use must have been slight.

In view of the sheer size and depth of the chests – one of Corpus Christi College's two original chests is 3 foot deep, a veritable coffin of a thing that I have often wrestled with – this lack of internal subdivision was a serious deficiency and various expedients were employed to overcome it and to keep the documents in at least some sort of order. One, for which provision is often found in Oxford college statutes, was to have within the main chest a small chest for the seal and for documents of special importance. For the rest one might simply tie up the documents in bundles, a fairly primitive method but found as late as the early sixteenth century in the otherwise quite good archive of the dean and chapter at York. Another device was to use canvas or leather bags, *pucheae*, as for example in the royal archives or in the university's. Another was to have hanapers made of wood, rods or leather, sometimes iron-bound. And then one meets with containers of unknown nature such as the *vasa* at Canterbury. For large documents one could have specially designed containers such as the long boxes in the university archives and elsewhere. These and other receptacles could then be labelled with signa or other identifiers.

But bundles, bags and hanapers, even when carefully labelled, were themselves difficult to keep in order. Wooden boxes were a much better proposition. These seem to have gone under a variety of names, but one of the commonest and the one I intend to use generically is *pixides* (singular *pix* or *pyx*). In their simplest and in my experience commonest form they were small, or smallish, oblong oak boxes, usually not very deep – up to 6 or so inches is quite usual – and having for their top a sliding lid with, in the best examples, as at Winchester College, separate finger holds for opening and for pushing shut. In well organized archives the pixides were either given an identifying symbol or letter or, either instead or in addition, had some brief indication of their contents written on the top (that is on the lid) or the front.

Not surprisingly, time, and archivists, have not been kind to these small and unpretentious objects; and even where they have survived they are not always recognized for what they are – I have discovered previously discarded but excellent examples in two colleges, and one has recently turned up even nearer at hand. But, looking only to Oxford, we can prove their existence, either from surviving pixides or from documentary evidence, in some five colleges as well as in the university archives. To take just one example, Magdalen College still has a splendid collection of pixides which are especially interesting in two respects. First some of them, and these include some of the originals, have their contents very fully described on their lid, that is on top, clearly for storage in chests. Second some of them are subdivided internally for ease in keeping the contents in order. In addition to those Magdalen pixides with their contents indicated on their top lid there are others – and among those that survive these are the majority – which have original labels or writing on the front. Now a moment's reflection will suggest that this is probably a very significant difference for it must indicate that these pixides were meant to be stored in receptacles where their fronts would be readily visible. This could be in chests, of course, if the pixides were stored vertically. But I am very much disposed to think that they point to a quite different place of storage, the cupboard.

In the nature of this as of almost every other case of origins it is impossible to say when the cupboard first emerged as a place for the storage of archives. But let me begin with an early, though not the earliest, extant example. This is the cupboard range, of which only two sections survive, at Winchester College. As I have already emphasized, Winchester had a fine muniment room, with two original chests which were added to in the course of time so that there were five or six in the end. And I do not doubt that Winchester continued to regard chests as the proper place for the storage of muniments, as opposed to the more general category of archives or records that needed preservation. Its fine cupboard was constructed in 1412–13, as recorded in the accounts, at a total cost of several pounds. But the cupboard was not for the muniment room itself; it was for the quite separate exchequer room which is approached from the screens end of the hall, through an excellent door (made in 1399) up a stone newel, and which had a tiled floor though a wooden ceiling. And the cupboard, the *almaria* as it was called (slightly later the *armariolum*, in the vernacular probably 'hutch', which is how it is now known) was said to be for books of accounts and court proceedings: in fact it must have been for rolls, since Winchester did not go over to books for such purposes until the mid-sixteenth century. There are several points worth making. First the architectural separation of exchequer from muniment room: Abingdon Abbey is a nice example near to Oxford. Second the contrast between the cupboard and chests in the matter of security: the cupboard had no locks at all. Third the emergence of a separate storehouse for records in the business office, despite ample space in the muniment room, pointing to a very common and understandable medieval – and modern – situation where the actual office wants its own records ready to hand. We may compare this development at Winchester with the position in another institution that I will mention again in a moment, that of the vicars choral at Wells: there the treasury, in the same tower as the muniment room and only approachable from the latter, had its own archival cupboards in the fifteenth century, probably from about 1420.

Going back a generation or thereabouts we have the beautifully made cupboard at Westminster Abbey, originally painted red and clustered with white stars; though it has recently been dated to the late fifteenth century we know from the accounts that it was in fact built in 1380–1. It was more secure than the Winchester and Wells cupboards since each of its sections had a lock and, with some sacrifice in ease of access, the actual doors were kept to a minimum in width. Moreover it was placed – in fact constructed – in the muniment room itself. Even so I would hazard the guess that it too was intended for rolls and the like rather than for muniments strictly so called, since Westminster had ample chest space for these latter and added to it in the fourteenth century and later.

But if we move on about a century or less we will find the cupboard promoted to hold real muniments in some instances. This may have been the case with the fine cupboard range in the muniment room of York minster, probably of the mid-fifteenth century. In Oxford I am rather inclined to think that Magdalen College may have been first to have a cupboard and to use it for deeds as well as for rolls. The cupboards themselves are in style very like those at Corpus Christi College to which I will come in a moment and which are unquestionably of about 1517. My reason for thinking that the Magdalen cupboards are perhaps a little earlier derives, as I have already indicated, from the surviving pixides. Most of these have their table of contents on the front which implies horizontal storage – as indeed they are used and stored now. If this interpretation of the significance of the front labels on the pixides is correct, it is really distinctly surprising that, like the Winchester cupboard, the Magdalen cupboards had no locks (though it is just possible that the padlocked chain which goes through the drop handles of each compartment door is either original or at least early). Still, though some of the Magdalen archives may thus have been in unlocked cupboards from very early days, Magdalen was very adequately supplied with chests, to which it added in the early sixteenth century, for its most valuable records; and there can be no doubt (as his statutes show) that Waynflete thought of chests as the proper place for the storage of such deeds.

The first absolutely conclusive evidence for munimental as opposed to more generally archival use of cupboards in Oxford comes from the statutes and surviving furniture of my own college, Corpus Christi, founded in 1517. This is the more interesting because the founder, Fox, had been lord privy seal for exactly thirty years when his college came into existence; in other words he knew what he was doing when he gave detailed regulations for the keeping of the college's records. As one would expect, the most important muniments were to be in a chest or chests. But account rolls were to be placed either in a chest or in a cupboard. And then we come in the statutes to some rather enigmatic statements about records, including what we would call muniments relating to college properties, which were to be kept in *capsae* (a term which also appears in Wolsey's statutes for Cardinal College) and others which were to be kept in *capsellae* within *capsae*. Now until I began looking more closely into these matters the nature of the *capsae* was totally obscure, and it was thought that none survived. I believe we can now be clearer about what the *capsae* were. Some were in fact pixides placed in one or other of the two original chests. But the majority seem to have been the individual compartments within the two cupboard ranges that still survive. Unfortunately these cupboards have been dismantled, but some years ago I helped to reassemble them as far as possible. They are very utilitarian, altogether plain – no cornice such as the Westminster Abbey cupboard has – but they are very well made of fine oak upwards of three hundred years old. These cupboards have always and traditionally been thought to have been designed by Brian Twyne, the college's archivist, early in the seventeenth century; but with the help of John Fletcher using tree-ring evidence they have now been conclusively dated to the early sixteenth century. There can be no doubt that these were what Fox referred to in his statutes as *armaria*, and, without going into any of the details of the argument, I believe it can be shown from Twyne's inventory and transcript of the college's deeds in 1628 that they were also the *capsae* of the statutes, the *capsellae* probably being what I have been calling generically pixides, placed inside the compartments of the cupboards as at Magdalen College. Indeed the Corpus Christi cupboards are in most respects strikingly similar to those at Magdalen – a point of some interest, especially since we know that the original lecterns in the Corpus Christi library were copied from those in Magdalen, and that in other respects the connection between the two colleges was very close.

Archival cupboards, of course, had a long future ahead of them. The dean and chapter of Hereford had two excellent and very large cupboard ranges reminiscent of those at Magdalen and Corpus Christi made in the late sixteenth or early seventeenth century (one is slightly later than the other). Each had forty compartments or 'capsules' with labels (now lost) on their doors. But I want rather to go back to some earlier cupboards, those at Durham. Simply as cupboards they are very like those at Westminster, Winchester and Wells. What gives them special importance in my story is what they contained – not the superbly arranged and catalogued documents, but the containers. These containers – not now in the cupboards – were known as *locelli* and date from the fourteenth century. The *locellus* was in fact a developed pix of the kind I have already talked about and particularly of the kind at Magdalen with internal subdivisions. There were two things that were different about the Durham *locelli*. First, each of the separate compartments of which they were composed – they had from two to six such subsections, often of varying size, doubtless to match the size of the folded or rolled contents – had its own sliding lid, and each lid its table of contents. Second, each *locellus* had in addition a table of contents and an iron drop-handle at the front. This and the general design proves that the *locelli* were stored horizontally since, had they been stored vertically the back lids would have opened in the act of lifting them up. More important typologically is the simple point that once one has an oblong box with a device for pulling it out from a pile of such boxes – and the Durham *locelli* must have been in piles – one is very near indeed to the next piece of archival furniture of which I wish to speak, the chest of drawers: for a chest of drawers is nothing other than two or more piles of *locelli* housed in a frame.

As with cupboards so with chests of drawers it is impossible to point to the precise date of origin. But there is an excellent example which I am much disposed to think must be near the beginning of things; it is in and contemporary with the muniment room of the vicars choral at Wells, built in 1420. The bishop at the time was Nicholas Bubwith, a man widely experienced in church and state and an alumnus of the University of Oxford, to which he bequeathed £250 for the celebration of masses in the university by priests, beneficed or unbeneficed, studying there. He was interested in building, and left 1,000 marks to the dean and chapter for, among other things, the building of a new library over the east walk of the cloister. Equally to the point he had a most distinguished career in royal service: probably a chancery clerk as early as 1380; a king's clerk in 1387; king's secretary and keeper of the rolls in 1402; keeper of the privy seal in 1405; and treasurer of England in 1407. Of course we are dealing with the vicars choral at Wells, not with the bishopric as such; but it must be accounted as at least possible if not probable that Bubwith, like Fox a hundred years later, drew on his experience in royal administration to help in some really up-to-date archival storage. Be that as it may, the Wells chest of drawers – each drawer with a table of contents on its front, of which only the beautifully made securing nails now remain – stands for a really important development in archival fittings and storage. In passing I should mention another innovation or at least early development in the same muniment room: that is the use of open shelves, again the first example of which I know. Small though it is, this muniment room and its fittings must be reckoned both extremely interesting and of a high standard.

From about the same date, around 1422–3 (or perhaps later, it has been suggested), comes the earlier of the two chests of drawers at St George's chapel, Windsor. The room for which it was constructed, the *aerarium* or aerary, is on the first floor of the imposing entrance to the dean's cloister erected in 1353–4. It was well placed to be a combined muniment room and treasury, being very difficult of access – it seems one had to go over the roofs to get to the short stone newel which led, via two good doors, to the room itself with its tiled floor. No doubt chests were originally used for the storage of documents here as elsewhere and this is perhaps one of them (it has iron handles). The chest of drawers is a very utilitarian, not particularly well constructed piece of furniture. But typologically it is, of course, important. It has larger drawers at the bottom, perhaps for rolls.

In the next century, at an uncertain date which may on stylistic grounds be said to lie between 1525 and 1575, we find the extremely fine pair of chests of drawers, not perhaps quite simultaneous in date, at Winchester College. As with the other examples I have mentioned these chests of drawers must have been intended to supplement not replace the chests themselves, for Winchester was amply supplied with chests: though there are only five in the muniment room now there were seven there in 1609. These two ranges of chests of drawers, though perhaps inferior in design to some others in that all the drawers were of the same size, are among the most pretentious and expensive from the stylistic point of view, with their fine linen-fold ornamentation.

In Oxford we find the chest of drawers making its appearance in the sixteenth century. First, perhaps, at New College about 1525–30, as a supplement of course to its chests. Then just possibly at St John's, though I am extremely uncertain about the date. The first absolutely firmly dated example is from All Souls, and a very fine double chest it is. As at New College it was to supplement not to replace the chests. It was constructed under, and we may be fairly sure conceived by, Warden Hovenden in 1582. It is remarkable as one of the few pieces of archival furniture I have mentioned that, like the Winchester cupboards, has more than a little pretension towards the beautiful about it, with its nicely moulded two pairs of doors and cornice. And the care with which it was designed is shown in the variation in the depth and width of the drawers.

Moving on a mere twenty years or so from the All Souls chest of drawers we come to that great archivist Brian Twyne, first keeper of the university archives and archivist extraordinary at his college, my own. To speak briefly of him is to risk doing him an injustice, for by any reckoning he was a remarkable man, perhaps the greatest archivist England has ever produced. He saw – as did his anonymous predecessors at Durham – that unless an archive has been utterly upset the vital thing is to work from what is there and not unnecessarily to tamper with things. Unlike so many archivists he did neither too little nor too much. The university and the college are in his everlasting debt.

At Corpus Christi College he inherited, as I have said, from the early sixteenth century at least two chests and the two cupboards I have described. As for the contents, they were deeds, rolls and some registers in bound volumes. He did not undertake, he did not need to undertake, much in the way of binding. What he did do was to concentrate on the deeds and the like which were partly in the chests and partly in the cupboards, probably mostly in smaller containers. His achievement with the deeds was remarkable, and it made full use of the idea of chests of drawers. It was a complex process meticulously carried out, but I must simplify. First, in 1627–8, he compiled, mostly with the help of his colleagues from the president downwards, and also some junior members, a thirty-volume cartulary or transcript of all the documents, each on a separate sheet or sheets. These he sorted into a logical order by place and county. He then in 1628 had constructed small nests of nine drawers, each to fit neatly within some seven or so of the compartments of one of the cupboards. The drawers were of somewhat varying sizes, and all were internally subdivided into smaller compartments. He could now place all the documents into their appropriate places in a logical order by county and place. He gave each drawer a reference on its front, and each compartment within each drawer a detailed list of contents with references pasted to its back for ready legibility on opening the drawer. Within each compartment the deeds were wrapped up in paper bundles, *fasciculi*, each bundle again being given on its front a list of contents, the *evidentia*, with references. The documents were duly endorsed with their full reference which was also entered in the margin of the cartulary which consequently provided a means of very ready access to the originals. We thus have six interlocking entries or pieces of information distributed between the cartulary as a kind of master index, cupboard compartment, drawers, subdivisions of drawers, bundle wrappings and individual documents with endorsements. It was a magnificent achievement which has in effect endured to the present day, though the cupboards, nests of drawers and bundles have been discarded – and I can see no reason why it should ever be altered save in the most minor details.

In the university archives, where he was busy from the very early years of the seventeenth century, Twyne had in fact a more daunting task and he did not live to complete what he had undertaken. The university's archives were not so different from those of his college – a mixture of deeds, rolls, a few bound volumes and also (which was different) a large number of unbound quires. But the location was less than satisfactory, and the arrangement, if any, almost certainly parlous following the disastrous burglary of the old congregation house in 1544. That burglary had not only robbed the university of all its valuables and destroyed its whole three-hundred-year-old system of loan chests; it had also caused havoc to the archives. From the debris only one of the medieval administrative chests was salvaged, the chest of the five keys, ordered to be restored at the end of 1544. But it was removed to University College and I know of no evidence that either it or any other chest was used for the university's archives after the burglary of 1544. What Twyne inherited at the opening of the seventeenth century was therefore something which had lost its main component, the chests. He concentrated his attention during the early decades of the century on two things. First the binding up of the loose quires of the registers of congregation and of the register of letters that was returned to the university in 1605 by the master of University College, George Abbot (later chancellor of the university and archbishop of Canterbury). Second the compilation in 1631 of an inventory of the contents of all the pixides and long boxes in the old congregation house, which most probably he had to put in order; he did not include the registers in this inventory, but otherwise it was complete outside the papers of the chancellor's court.

Fairly early on in Twyne's time, on 27 October 1609, the university decided that, for the better keeping of its archives, there should be constructed 'a convenient *capsula*, in English a Presse, with many pixides', and that this should be placed in the vestry of All Souls chapel. The fact that there is no evidence for any such press ever being put in All Souls has led previous scholars to assume, without further thought, that the press itself was never made. I do not think this is so. I believe it was made, that it was a chest of drawers, and that it is the *abacus* or press with four keys mentioned by Twyne in one of his volumes of collectanea as being in the old congregation house. It does not, of course, survive, though I believe Twyne's 1631 inventory probably relates to its contents and so shows the minimum number of drawers it had.

Then, with the building of the schools quadrangle and tower, the room in the tower we know as the lower archive room became available, as I feel sure was intended in its design, as the university's main archive room. As a muniment room it was not quite ideal, though well up to the standards of early seventeenth-century Oxford: it had an independent stone newel; of its original door we know nothing, but in any case it had a wooden floor and ceiling (that same ceiling the woodwork of which was rediscovered in the 1950s, mistakenly was not replaced, and has since been lost and almost certainly destroyed). Twyne had a press built for it which, despite appallingly bad treatment when the tower was restored in the 1950s, may still be said to survive. It is partly shelves and partly drawers, with a pair of doors originally secured by four locks. Into the drawers were transferred in time all the archives Twyne had listed in his 1631 inventory without any alteration in the arrangement of the documents which, of course, had their appropriate endorsements giving location. Twyne's immediate successors continued his work with the construction of two more presses, again some shelves but mostly drawers, the present north-east and south-east presses. And his work may be said to have been brought to an end with the repertory of the whole archive made by the third keeper, John Wallis, in 1664 – though the indications are that Twyne himself would not have been content with a mere inventory but was already in 1630 looking to a cartulary or series of transcripts as at Corpus Christi College.

There is one final piece of early modern archival furniture that I must mention before I end, because it is a simplified form of the chest of drawers and also because it is something we have become so familiar with. This is the pigeonhole. Twyne was not a pigeonhole man – his standards were too high. But a somewhat younger Oxford scholar, Obadiah Walker (1617–99), fellow and later master of University College, was. William Smith wrote disapprovingly in his *Annals of University College* (1728) that Walker:

> caused a Frame of Wood to be made, and divided like Pigeon-holes, to sever these Writings into, but so, as most of them could not be come at without a Ladder, and having their Fronts open, and nothing to preserve them from the Dust rising daily out of the Street . . .

It was not, by Smith's account, a successful innovation and was soon disposed of so that, of course, nothing of the pigeonholes remains. But Walker was not the only man then using pigeonholes for documents, as is clear from the monument to John Jones, alderman and diocesan registrar, in the south-west corner of Gloucester cathedral, where the consistory court met. Jones is shown with, in addition to two drawers, pigeonholes full of documents on each side of him dated variously from 1581 to 1630, the year of his death.

Pigeonholes, chests of drawers, cupboards, open shelves – these have taken us, as they took the archivists of the time, a very long way from oak chests and even more from that ultra-secure and sacral environment in which archival documentation began and of which I spoke at the beginning of this paper. In its way this story, which has continued on from the seventeenth century with which I have ended, can be seen as part of the secularization of our culture which has been so pronounced a feature over the centuries. And yet I think we must allow that something intangible still remains to link our secular sentiments over archives with the sacral sentiments with which I started. Writing is no longer sacred, no longer a special act. But who can deny the deep feelings which some document of great antiquity and importance can still evoke in even the most detached and sophisticated, not to say scientific, historian. I myself never look at the foundation charter of my own college or its 1528 statutes, each both signed and sealed by our founder, without some sense not only of gratitude but of reverence and awe. So much so that last year I had two boxes, pixides, made of old oak and lined with rich velvet, especially constructed to contain them. You may think this merely romantic, and my collegiate colleagues would probably think it plainly extravagant. But in looking beneath the surface of what I did, I am very ready to admit that I did more than was strictly necessary for physical protection, and very happy to acknowledge the ties that thus link me with my ancestors as archivists of upwards of a thousand, not to say two thousand and more years ago.

Index